HARVARD HISTORICAL STUDIES

Published Under the Direction of the
Department of History

From the Income of
THE HENRY WARREN TORREY FUND
VOLUME LXVI

PATRIOTISM ON PARADE

The Story of

Veterans' and Hereditary Organizations in America

1783-1900

WALLACE EVAN DAVIES

HARVARD UNIVERSITY PRESS

Cambridge, Massachusetts

1955

Library of Congress Catalog Card Number 55-11951
Printed in the United States of America

To the Memory of My Mother

DAISY HITCH DAVIES

Who Exemplified the American Zeal for Joining, Genealogy, and Patriotic Enterprises

Foreword

IN the early 1920's a small bespectacled boy used to wiggle impatiently in the back corners of Rufus King's old mansion in Jamaica, Long Island, quite unaware of any social implications to the group before him, but waiting eagerly for the salted almonds that always followed the business sessions of the Elizabeth Annesley Lewis Chapter, D.A.R. His mother was its registrar and, like many of her colleagues, had so succumbed to the "joining" passion that she also belonged to the Society of Mayflower Descendants and the Daughters of 1812 and only regretted that she could not afford to accept the repeated blandishments of the presumably even more aristocratic Baronial Order of Runnemede, composed of the offspring of the barons who had forced Magna Carta from King John, or the equally esoteric Societé de Guillaume le Conquérant, limited to the progeny of the Norman invaders of 1066.

The boy himself, in addition to the dubious distinction of being the "flagpole" in one of the "living flags" that his mother formed among the neighborhood children for the United States Flag Association, later found himself president of the Eleanor Parke Lewis Society, Children of the American Revolution. He was patted on the head by Miss Margaret Lothrop, the first member of that organization, but at the time chiefly glamorous to him because her mother had written *The Five Little Peppers*. He gave an address of welcome at a state convention which astonished but delighted the delegates by being only three sentences long. Finally, he was appointed to recite the C.A.R. creed at the national convention in Washington. The moment of apotheosis arrived, and he forgot his lines. Curiously, no one else in the audience knew the creed well enough to prompt him. It was a suggestive object lesson as to how seriously most members took the order's ritual.

Thus, despite the blemish of having on the paternal side an immigrant grandfather, which makes his position within the charmed circle a trifle insecure, the author can confidently claim that he is no armchair historian of the hereditary societies at least. These early experiences may not have resulted in a full understanding of their total impact, but they did leave a sympathetic tolerance for individual members. From constant attendance at local D.A.R. meetings and trips to two "Continental Congresses" before he was thirteen he realized that the average Daughter should have been sketched by Helen Hokinson rather than by Grant Wood. This firsthand knowledge suggested that the chief motive for joining the society was social rather than any determination to abet reactionary forces or even a strong abstract interest in patriotism. Except for a harmless, though possibly over-pretentious, absorption in genealogy, which becomes as much a hobby as solving crossword puzzles or collecting postage stamps, affiliation often had no more significance than joining any other women's club. For the author the stereotype of a D.A.R. member will never be anything more sinister or disagreeable than a pleasant, somewhat parochial, gray-haired woman who had emerged from a comfortable middle-class home on a quiet tree-lined residential street in such a respectable, if unexciting, Long Island suburb as Kew Gardens, Hollis, Floral Park, or Hempstead. She did well behind the tea urn, but never could sustain any protracted interest in public affairs such as her critics ascribed to her.

These were the impressions acquired during the writer's age of innocence. But in the early 1930's, as part of the sophistication of college years at a time when the united front was making fellow traveling the favorite pastime of would-be intellectuals, the youth adopted the liberal's customary attitude of scorn toward the D.A.R. and the American Legion. Doubtless the preceding college generation, weaned on the *American Mercury,* had felt a similar antipathy, but it had been more a disdain for the "booboisie's" social pretensions. But the youngsters who read the *New Republic* as assiduously as the *New Yorker,* argued bitterly whether to vote for F.D.R., Thomas, or Browder, organized into the American Student Union, held vociferously belligerent peace demonstrations, and generally carried on a spirited flirtation with Marxism without, of course, ever reading Karl Marx, based their opposition on loftier political and humanitarian grounds; indeed, Mencken's anti-democratic tirades seemed socially anachronistic. They damned patriotic societies for their intransigent resistance to all current progressive panaceas and for their sturdily militaristic and nationalistic outlook, well symbolized in that decade by their support of the teachers' oath movement and defeat of American participation in the World Court.

This conflict between early environment and liberal credo presented an awkward dilemma. The writer had to recognize that there has certainly been a high correlation between membership in patriotic societies and conservative, even reactionary, opinions which he finds distasteful. In later years the D.A.R.'s deplorable entanglements in the racial problem only intensified this repugnance. Yet he has never forgotten that as individuals their members are often warm-hearted and well-intentioned. Somehow a person who has so often relished the fish chowder and chocolate doughnuts of the local regent in a small Maine town, or has had a middle western state regent confide in him her difficulties in getting into her girdle for official receptions, can never really launch into an unqualified denunciation of the society. At a subsequent stage in his academic career the necessity to pick a Ph.D. topic in American history seemed a good opportunity for a detailed investigation of what these societies had actually stood for over the years, what motivated them and what they had actually accomplished. With his particular combination of family and intellectual background the writer hopes he has achieved some balance in this task. The brave aspirations of the days when he listened admiringly to fireside chats and the Blue Eagle spread its wings over the land may make him critical of many doings of patriotic societies, but his early contacts with the rank and file of members make him more tolerant than most commentators on these groups.

At the suggestion of Professor Arthur M. Schlesinger, Sr., the scope of this study was expanded to include not only the hereditary bodies such as the D.A.R. and S.A.R. but also what he termed their "first cousins," the veterans' organizations and their affiliates. This meant shifting attention to a somewhat different and far more important subject, for such groups as the D.A.R., tempting targets as they may often seem, have not really been a major influence and are chiefly significant as examples of certain tendencies in American society rather than as forces in themselves. But the millions of our citizens who at present are racked between the competing claims of the American Legion and the Veterans of Foreign Wars, the Amvets and the A.V.C., not to mention the inhabitants of any city that has played harassed host to a Legion convention, need scarcely be reminded that the organized veterans are as integral a part of the American way of life as the hot dog, the juke box, and T.V. Not a veteran himself, as the recipient of a G.A.R. prize and an American Legion scholarship in his day the author feels an obligation to approach these organizations without prejudice.

With these additions the field became so large that it was essential to call a halt to the story at the year 1900. Even so there have been excluded the nativist and nationalist secret groups which from the time of the Know-Nothings through the A.P.A. and the Ku Klux Klan to the Silver Shirts have represented an important if unpleasant aspect of organized patriotism. The final emphasis falls largely on the activities of the Civil War soldiers, especially as expressed in the Grand Army of the Republic, and on the nationalist feeling of the 1890's which converted the veterans' groups into self-conscious patriotic societies as well as producing the large crop of hereditary associations.

In an ancient and possibly admirable academic tradition, this work does more reporting than evaluating. While amassing a storehouse of factual material does not necessarily guarantee objectivity, the volume is not a venture in debunking but instead aims to present enough data on this particular manifestation of the American spirit in action for the reader to form his own conclusions.

W. E. D.

Acknowledgments

THIS work could not have been possible without the coöperation of the staffs of the Harvard College Library, the Massachusetts
State Library, the Boston Public Library, the Massachusetts Historical Society, the New York Public Library, the Indiana State Library,
the Newberry Library, the Wisconsin State Historical Society, and,
above all, the Library of Congress. The opportunity to visit these
various depositories came through the grant of a Sheldon Travelling
Fellowship by Harvard University. Particularly I wish to express
my deep appreciation for the assistance and sympathetic interest
that Miss Ruth G. Hedden of the Massachusetts State Library
gave me in the early stages of this project. I am grateful to Mr.
W. Neil Franklin, then of the National Archives, for drawing my
attention to important material on the War of 1812 veterans. Miss
Lucy McDannell and Miss Grace Hurd courteously allowed me
to examine records at the headquarters of the Daughters of the
Revolution and the Daughters of Veterans respectively.

I feel under especially strong obligation to Mrs. Charles L.
Dearing (Marie L. Rulkotter). Not only were her own researches
an invaluable aid to my work, but over a period of years she
has been unfailingly coöperative in furnishing me with additional
information and making helpful suggestions. The varied back-
grounds of four good friends, Marshall Dill, Jr., Elizabeth Peterson
McLean, Donald W. McPhail, and Roy F. Nichols, have made
their criticisms of the manuscript most valuable. Finally, it is a
privilege to join the long list of former students who have publicly
expressed their indebtedness and gratitude to Arthur Meier
Schlesinger.

Contents

CONTENTS

PATRIOTISM ON PARADE

I

The Cincinnati Story

AMERICANS have long been "a nation of joiners." Over a century ago from the vantage point of a foreign observer the ever-quoted Tocqueville noted our penchant for voluntary associations of all sorts, and in a more recent period the novels of Sinclair Lewis documented our Rotarian tendencies more acutely than most academic histories. Americans have also long been ardently and aggressively patriotic. Such at least has been the fairly consistent verdict of travelers from other lands, who have found a "spread-eagle" bragging one of our most annoying national characteristics. Being thus both gregarious and nationalistic, Americans have naturally turned to the forming of numerous patriotic societies.[1]

Two varieties of this activity have been especially conspicuous. The first has been the banding together of the veterans of our armed conflicts to commemorate common memories and to advance their interests as a group. For the present generation the American Legion best exemplifies this, though the pattern was really set by the survivors of the Civil War in the Grand Army of the Republic.[2] The second has been the hereditary societies open only to those of requisite pedigree, formed by the descendants of those who performed military service, or perhaps merely lived on this continent at some point sufficiently remote in the past. Here names such as

---

[1] For a brief but incisive survey of "joining," see Arthur M. Schlesinger, "Biography of a Nation of Joiners," *American Historical Review*, L (Oct. 1944), 1–25. Charles W. Ferguson, *Fifty Million Brothers* (New York, 1937), gives a more detailed but also more superficial popular account. The best historical study of American patriotism is Merle Curti, *The Roots of American Loyalty* (New York, 1946).

[2] Dixon Wecter, *When Johnny Comes Marching Home* (Cambridge, Mass., 1944), tells in readable and reliable fashion what happened to the veterans of the Revolutionary, Civil, and First World Wars.

the Daughters of the American Revolution and the Society of May-flower Descendants come readily to mind.

The real story of both types of societies does not begin until after the Civil War. No conflict before that time produced any general organization for all its veterans, and it was not until the 1890's that the American woman discovered the satisfactions of being a D.A.R. or a Colonial Dame. Since then the two categories have attracted thousands of adherents. Their significance has been social in more than one meaning of the word. During the past three-quarters of a century they have filled the same purpose in a country increasingly preoccupied with how to spend its leisure time with other people as have the various fraternal orders. The D.A.R. has been one more women's club, the Grand Army of the Republic was in many respects a counterpart of the Masons or the Elks. This largely explains their attraction for individual members. But though in the broadest sense therefore their story becomes part of the entire history of voluntary associationalism, more specifically it is also a study in organized patriotism that casts considerable light on one phase of our intellectual history. Finally, in their efforts to carry out their self-appointed patriotic mission these organizations quickly found themselves involved in many public issues that all too often also made them examples of pressure groups in action. Any survey of their careers must keep in mind all three aspects: their importance simply as social bodies, their concept of patriotism, and their influence upon public opinion and legislation.

Though large-scale organized activity of this sort was non-existent before 1865, the United States has never been entirely without such groups since the moment it achieved its independence from Great Britain. The prototype for both veterans' and hereditary associations of a later day was the Society of the Cincinnati, an organization of Revolutionary officers whose brief mention in many histories has made its name somewhat more familiar than is warranted by its long-run importance. Ironically, this first American patriotic society so startled the citizens of 1783 that they promptly denounced it as both un-American and unpatriotic. While veterans' and hereditary groups since then have often tried to monopolize the right to apply these epithets, at the time this innovation impressed so many as likely to subvert the fledgling republican experiment that it aroused an outburst of public suspicion and hostility unequaled by any similar order since. Though separated by nearly a century from the main currents of American patriotic societies, the vicissitudes of the Cincinnati anticipated all the major issues posed by groups claiming special privileges because of wartime service and special distinctions because of ancestry.

Although at the close of the American Revolution there were some two hundred thousand men who might have formed the first comprehensive veterans' organization, no such move materialized. The population was over 90 per cent rural, transportation facilities were crude and far too expensive for the ordinary individual to travel any distance to meetings and, with the possible exception of the introduction of Masonry earlier in the century, there were as yet no precedents for societies on a national scale for the type of person represented by the enlisted men. But with the officers it was a different story; their social and economic background enabled them to maintain the many more bonds they had in common. On May 13, 1783, shortly before the Continental Army disbanded, a group gathered at General Steuben's headquarters in a story and a half Dutch-style stone structure known as the Verplanck House, near what is now Beacon, New York. There they formed the Society of the Cincinnati, open to all officers who had served for three years or were in the army at the end of the war. Their choice of name reflected the neo-classic spirit of the infant nation which often compared itself with the ancient Roman republic and presently was to be sending "senators" to deliberate in a "capitol." The officers fancied themselves as eighteenth-century counterparts of Cincinnatus, who had left his plow to defend his country but afterward returned to his farm.

A brief examination of the order's constitution, which rather pretentiously was called the "Institution," at once explains why the public became so excited. In the first place, membership was hereditary, and even then passed only to the eldest male descendant of each original officer. At a time when the American Revolution had not only overturned monarchical rule but also occasioned attacks upon the doctrine of primogeniture in several states, this naturally struck many as the first step instead toward an American nobility. Almost as ominous to some was a provision to admit as honorary members citizens "whose views may be directed to the same laudable objects with those of the Cincinnati," for this meant that the order might not be as limited in influence as its strict criteria for eligibility had first indicated.

A suggestion that each state society send circular letters to all the others concerning not only its own affairs but "the general union of the States" sounded a political note to many who recalled how successfully they themselves had used committees of correspondence to overthrow the established order. When they further learned that each officer was to contribute one month's pay to a permanent charitable fund, they saw in this only a treasury ever full to finance whatever sinister designs the association might develop. Finally, as a sign of membership, which was to hang on a blue and white ribbon, the Institution provided for an elaborate medal in the form of a gold eagle, designed by the same Major L'Enfant who was later to be the architect of the city of Washington. Added to hereditary membership, constant communication on the state of the country and the accumulation of funds, this flaunting of what would soon be a badge of ancestral distinction seemed the final insult to worried democrats.[3]

The name of the first president-general was more reassuring, however, for the founders shrewdly turned to George Washington himself. This in many ways was the first example of the subsequent tendency to choose as official leaders not the persons who instigated or really controlled the organizations but rather individuals of prominence who lent prestige and perhaps even financial support but otherwise were often merely figureheads. Actually, though Washington approved a permanent social organization that would also provide charitable assistance to needy members, he was reluctant to endorse such novelties as insignia, badges, and the other regalia of a hereditary military order. But the pleadings of his subordinates prevailed, and he finally accepted the post which was to fulfill his forebodings and to prove a source of more embarrassment than pleasure to him. In due time societies appeared in all the thirteen original states and even in Paris among the French officers who had

---

[3] The Institution has often been reprinted since 1783; a convenient modern work that includes it is William S. Thomas, *The Society of the Cincinnati 1783–1935* (New York and London, 1935).

served the American cause. Within a few months the Cincinnati enrolled some 2300 members, but only in Massachusetts and France did it have more than three hundred followers in any one state branch, while in New Hampshire and Delaware it commanded barely thirty adherents. Thus the society was launched, but on seas that were to prove rough and stormy before it reached the calm, almost stagnant, waters of a new century.

If the commander-in-chief of the Continental Army viewed the new order with some hesitancy, the public at large proved even more suspicious. Many at once concluded that anything so un-American was obviously the work of foreigners. John Adams, it is said, termed the society a "French blessing," [4] and the connotations of "French" to an eighteenth-century New Englander were far from complimentary. Others suspected the more Teutonic influence of Baron Steuben. But those who ascribed to foreigners the genesis of the Cincinnati seriously underestimated Yankee inventiveness, or at least imitativeness. Soldiers of fortune like Steuben or young romantics like Lafayette, obviously far more experienced than the colonials in such matters, were doubtless willing to supply information on medals, badges, and ceremonies, but they probably not so much instigated the order as suggested it to envious Americans by the mere possession and wearing of European military decorations. The shrewd Franklin perhaps came nearest to the truth when he surmised that the founders "have been too much struck with the ribands and crosses they have seen hanging to the button-holes of foreign officers." [5]

Actually there existed a variety of forces, social, charitable, aristocratic, and even mercenary, strong enough to cause the officers to band together. Ever protesting that the order's "intention is pure and uncorrupted by any sinister design," [6] its early leaders naturally emphasized the social and charitable motives. The social aspect, always so attractive to the members of all patriotic societies, has especially appealed to ex-officers, a relatively small homogeneous

[4] Marquis de Lafayette to John Adams, March 8, 1784, Charles Francis Adams, ed., *The Works of John Adams* (Boston, 1851–1856), VIII, 187.

[5] Benjamin Franklin to Mrs. Sarah Bache, Jan. 26, 1784, John Bigelow, ed., *The Works of Benjamin Franklin* (New York and London, 1904), X, 274.

[6] Henry Knox to Benjamin Lincoln, May 21, 1783, Henry Knox Papers, XII, Massachusetts Historical Society.

group ever fond of convivial reminiscent gatherings about the banquet table. While the prospect of an annual reunion with those who had shared so many experiences would alone have been sufficient reason for most officers to favor such an association, there was also a desire "to erect some lowly shelter for the unfortunates against the storms and tempests of poverty. . . ." [7] Such concern for indigent colleagues and their families has always been conspicuous in all veterans' associations and their auxiliaries, but it was even more understandable in 1783. The former soldiers had not yet learned how successfully they could bring pressure upon the government to protect them from ill fortune, nor did social welfare legislation protect those in need then. In that far more individualistic period people had to rely on private and voluntary assistance, which, however, an association might well implement. As a model for such a fraternity both social and philanthropic, at the same time conducted with considerable ceremonial and secrecy, there already existed the Masonic Order, in which several early leaders of the Cincinnati, including Washington, were active.

Numerous contemporary critics, less convinced of the innocence of the Society of the Cincinnati, stressed aristocratic pretensions and economic self-interest as more compelling reasons for forming the organization. To many self-conscious republicans it looked suspiciously like an effort to start an American hereditary nobility which would introduce "stars, garters, and diadems, crowns, sceptres, and the regalia of kings, in the yet simple bosom of their country." [8] Just how much basis there was for this accusation it is almost impossible to say. Doubtless the officers were quite sincere in their protestations that they were primarily interested in the social and charitable aspects of the society and had no ambitions incompatible with republicanism, but at the same time many may have suspected that an American nobility might develop and that, if so, its logical source might well be a group like the Cincinnati. Such a prospect would not necessarily dampen enthusiasm which had already been aroused for the order on less exceptionable grounds.

Of more immediate concern than such speculations over future

[7] *Ibid.*
[8] Mercy Warren, *History of the Rise, Progress and Termination of the American Revolution* (Boston, 1805), III, 284.

family distinctions was the officers' conviction that Congress was neglecting their financial interests. Indeed, those who prefer an economic interpretation of all historical events will feel that this situation provides sufficient explanation for the society's origin. Just at the close of the Revolution the officers finally won a campaign to receive five years' full pay in the form of government certificates bearing 6 per cent interest in place of half-pay for life which had been granted in 1780. But there still remained the problem of securing full value for these certificates, which as a matter of fact did depreciate rapidly, and, in view of the feeble taxing power under the Articles of Confederation, it was equally uncertain whether even the interest would be fully or regularly paid.

Actually it is not possible to make a precise connection between this unrest and the formation of the Cincinnati. But unquestionably its founders were enough concerned with the problem so that, even if Washington later did try to dismiss the supposition as "ridiculous," [9] doubtless many were peculiarly receptive at that particular moment to any organization which might be able to bring pressure to insure the payment of interest and maintenance of the certificates' value. On the other hand, possibly conservative leaders like Washington welcomed a patriotic society of officers as a method of warding off more dangerous expressions of discontent.

Whatever the motives, which were doubtless an amalgam of all those mentioned above and probably were never present in exactly the same proportions in any two members, the introduction of so great a novelty as a hereditary military order produced sharp repercussions. The real attack began with the publication of a fifteen-page pamphlet called *Considerations on the Society or Order of Cincinnati* in Charleston, South Carolina, in the fall of 1783. Though issued under the determinedly classical pseudonym of "Cassius," it soon was known to be the work of a colorful, eccentric, and highly articulate Irishman named Aedanus Burke. Friends of the society at once charged that his opposition arose not so much from principle as from lack of eligibility and that it had mounted to fever pitch only after he had been refused admission as an honorary member.

[9] George Washington to Thomas Jefferson, May 30, 1787, Worthington Chauncey Ford, ed., *The Writings of George Washington* (New York and London, 1889–1893), XI, 157.

This, of course, is reminiscent of the reaction to William Morgan's charges against the Masons in the early nineteenth century and especially of the "sour grapes" theory of present-day criticism of college fraternities, and certainly must be considered whenever an "out group" attacks an "in group."

Yet in the terms of that day Burke's record was so consistently "liberal" that his sincerity should probably receive the benefit of the doubt. At this time Burke was about forty years of age. He had served in the American army and then as associate justice of the South Carolina state courts had shown strong democratic leanings. Later, like most good democrats, he opposed ratification of the Constitution and thereafter his anti-aristocratic sentiments of course made him an anti-Federalist. Elected to the first Congress under the new government, he attacked undue idolatry of Washington, expressed fears that a monarchy was about to be established (he even favored an amendment prohibiting the reëlection of presidents), and eventually found time to be Aaron Burr's second in a duel at Hoboken, though not at the more celebrated one at Weehawken. Conservatives are often cynical about such continued displays of democratic rectitude, and modern psychiatry might suggest that many unconscious drives and frustrations really underlie such behavior. All that one can say is that Burke's attitude would probably still seem quite justifiable to members of the A.D.A. and be just as incomprehensible and obnoxious to followers of General MacArthur and Fulton Lewis, Jr.

The gist of Burke's argument was that the members of the Society of the Cincinnati were actually showing no desire to imitate Cincinnatus by returning to obscure citizenship. The order, he thought, would soon develop into a hereditary peerage which within a century would monopolize all civil and military offices, reduce the rest of the populace to a mere rabble, and destroy all hopes that republican theories could work in practice. This indictment, as Thomas Jefferson noted, made the society "the subject of general conversation" [10] that commenced six months of widespread and acrimonious debate.

[10] Thomas Jefferson to Meusnier, June 22, 1786, Paul Leicester Ford, ed., *The Works of Thomas Jefferson* (New York, 1904–1905), V, 53.

The intensity of opposition varied, but throughout the thirteen states the progress of Burke's pamphlet northward can be traced by the outbursts of animated newspaper discussions, the appearance of equally spirited rebuttals, and the flurries of agitated correspondence among public figures. New England especially developed strong antagonism to this apparent threat to republican institutions. Contrary to a legend which even a century later so reputable a historian as John Bach McMaster was perpetuating, the Rhode Island legislature does not seem to have disfranchised the society's members, but the Massachusetts General Court did declare the order "dangerous to the peace, liberty and safety of the United States in general, and this Commonwealth in particular." [11]

Some members, especially those with any political ambitions, began to question the expediency of their affiliation. For example, when Washington sent "letter after letter" to the president of the Rhode Island branch, General Nathanael Greene, urging his attendance at the general meeting of the society in May, that cautious gentleman decided that his health would not permit the trip. "The Doctor thinks my life would be endangered by attempting to cross the Water," he informed the president-general, "and my pain in my stomach increased by riding by land." [12] In neighboring Massachusetts the legislative censure so distressed another member, General William Heath, who was also a candidate for the state senate, that when the time came for the annual session of the society, as General Henry Knox sardonically noted, "he left us in the lurch and did not attend the meeting having prudently caught cold." [13] Next Heath started a rumor that he had resigned from the order. Though this was "known by many to be wholly devoid of truth, so industriously was the *Lie* circulated that he had most of the Votes." [14] Shocked at his success, Samuel Adams, who thought the society "as rapid a Stride towards an hereditary Military Nobility as was ever made in

---

[11] *Independent Chronicle* (Boston), March 25, 1784.

[12] Nathanael Greene to Washington, May 6, 1784, Edgar Erskine Hume, ed., *General Washington's Correspondence Concerning the Society of the Cincinnati* (Baltimore, 1941), p. 165.

[13] Knox to Baron Steuben, Feb. 21, 1784, Knox Papers, XVII.

[14] Stephen Higginson to Elbridge Gerry, April 28, 1784, Miscel. MSS Higginson, New York Historical Society.

so short a Time," mourned that "the Citizens are not so vigilant as they used and ought still to be." [15]

This sentiment, it soon developed, was almost universal throughout the country. "I thought it had been confined to New England alone," Greene reported in August 1784, after traveling from Rhode Island to South Carolina (his health apparently had taken a marked turn for the better immediately after the Cincinnati meeting which his physical condition had made it impossible to attend), "but I found afterwards . . . all the inhabitants in general throughout the United States were opposed to the order." [16] Thomas Jefferson declared that he knew only one member of Congress who was not hostile. An explicit indication of this feeling came when the legislators began drawing up an ordinance for western lands. In March 1784, a committee headed by Jefferson struck a deliberate blow at the Cincinnati by proposing that the governments of any new western states "shall be republican, and shall admit no person to be a citizen who holds any title." [17] Congress later eliminated this clause, but, according to Washington, friends of the society were unable to secure this deletion until the results of the order's general meeting, shortly to be held in Philadelphia, could be known.

The turmoil over the Cincinnati even reached across the ocean. As soon as Americans in government service abroad received letters and newspapers from home, they too became outspoken in their criticism. John Jay "went the other day so far as to say that if it did take well in the States he would not care whether the Revolution had succeeded or not," while John Adams stigmatized the order "as the first step taken to deface the beauty of our temple of liberty." [18] Gentlest of the critics was Franklin, who in a letter to his daughter deflated the entire theory of hereditary honors and expressed regret that the society had followed the nation in choosing as its symbol

[15] Samuel Adams to Gerry, April 19, 1784, and April 23, 1784, Henry Alonzo Cushing, ed., *The Writings of Samuel Adams* (New York and London, 1908), IV, 299, 301.

[16] Greene to Washington, Aug. 1784, George Washington Greene, *The Life of Nathanael Greene* (New York, 1867–1871), III, 526.

[17] Gaillard Hunt, ed., *Journals of the Continental Congress 1774–1789* (Washington, 1910–1936), XXVI, 250–251.

[18] Col. Gouvion to Knox, March 1784, Francis S. Drake, *Memorials of the Society of the Cincinnati of Massachusetts* (Boston, 1873), p. 30; Adams to Charles Spencer, March 24, 1784, John Adams, *Works,* IX, 524.

the eagle, "a bird of bad moral character" and a "rank coward," who was no proper emblem for "the brave and honest Cincinnati of America. . . ." [19]

Basically these attacks centered on two points. First, the society established an aristocracy contrary to the spirit of a republic. Secondly, it might become a powerful influence in public affairs and even take over the government for its own selfish purposes. Subsequent criticism of patriotic societies, all of which in some sense trace their ancestry to the Cincinnati, has followed the same lines. Hereditary associations, like the D.A.R. and Colonial Dames, have been attacked from the first viewpoint; veterans' organizations, like the G.A.R. and the American Legion, from the second. At no time, however, has the assault been so extensive or so virulent as in the 1780's, when the complete novelty of such an order tremendously magnified all apprehensions.[20] Also noteworthy is the way in which this criticism was not limited to "liberals." For Thomas Jefferson or Samuel Adams to raise objections was almost predictable, but men like John Adams and John Jay were good stanch conservatives later to become leaders of the Federalist Party. Perhaps in these instances men who had achieved distinction as civilian leaders of the Revolution objected to military service as the basis of distinction, and it is not hard to imagine the Adamses disliking an aristocracy in which they were not to be members.

This furor soon convinced many members of the Cincinnati that they would have to alter their constitution drastically at their first general meeting in May 1784. On the banks of the Potomac, Washington, the president-general, grew increasingly perturbed. He had hesitated to join the order in the first place, and, though he had at last accepted titular leadership, he was in no sense its active director, even having to write Henry Knox asking what the president was supposed to do lest he make some blunder "mortifying to myself." [21] But as he received a steady stream of reports of the growing hostility

---

[19] Franklin to Mrs. Bache, Jan. 26, 1784, Franklin, *Works*, X, 279.

[20] For detailed accounts of the attack upon the Cincinnati, see Edgar Erskine Hume, "Early Opposition to the Cincinnati," *Americana*, XXX (Oct. 1936), 597–638 (strongly sympathetic to the society) and Wallace Evan Davies, "The Society of the Cincinnati in New England 1783–1800," *William and Mary Quarterly*, 3d. Ser., V (Jan. 1948), 3–25.

[21] Washington to Knox, Sept. 23, 1784, Washington, *Writings*, X, 321.

during the winter and spring months of 1784, he could not avoid a feeling of responsibility. A letter from Lafayette tactfully but unmistakably questioning the propriety of the hereditary clause especially impressed him. For further advice he wrote to his fellow Virginian, Jefferson, who, however, was hardly the person to give him any consolation but instead proceeded to denounce every aspect of the society.

Washington finally decided that strong measures were necessary. En route to Philadelphia he stopped to see Jefferson. "It was a little after candle-light," Jefferson later recalled, "and he sat with me till after midnight, conversing almost exclusively, on that subject." [22] Jefferson's version was that Washington wanted to abolish the society outright. Since his account was written forty years later and he may well have wanted, consciously or unconsciously, to identify Washington's viewpoint with his own ideas, this statement is perhaps exaggerated, but it does suggest that Washington was strongly aroused.

Certainly at the meeting, speaking "warmly and in plain language," Washington forced more severe modifications than most of the delegates wanted. The gathering finally abolished hereditary descent, honorary membership, and correspondence among societies. It limited its future meetings to the election of officers and the disposal of charitable funds. State societies were to apply to their legislatures for charters and with their consent lend their capital to the various commonwealths and use only the interest. Unofficially the delegates agreed to wear their badges only at meetings or the funerals of members, except in Europe, where it was felt a friendlier climate of opinion would permit them to display their decorations more freely.[23]

But unfortunately the Cincinnati's Institution, like the Articles of Confederation, lacked an amending clause, with the result that for these changes to go into effect every one of the state societies had to approve them. Such unanimous consent proved just as impossible

[22] Jefferson to Martin Van Buren, June 29, 1824, Jefferson, *Works,* XII, 367.

[23] The brief official account of this meeting is in General Society of the Cincinnati, *Proceedings,* John C. Daves, ed. (Baltimore, 1925–1930, I, 5–17), but the actual details of the discussion are to be found in Winthrop Sargent, "Journal of the General Meeting of the Cincinnati in 1784," *Memoirs of the Historical Society of Pennsylvania,* VI (Philadelphia, 1858), 79–115.

for the Cincinnati as it was to get the thirteen states to alter the Articles. Though ten of the fourteen branches ratified the new constitution, the remaining ones did not, and it therefore never became operative.

This failure to adopt the measures which he had so vigorously championed greatly annoyed Washington, for he was still convinced that such changes were imperative. The refusal to support him placed Washington, always extremely self-conscious about prestige and public opinion, in a position which he irritatedly described as "delicate." Thereafter he would have preferred to have nothing to do with the order at all. The only reason that he even attended the next general meeting of the society in Philadelphia in 1787 after much backing and filling was because it came at the same time and place as the Constitutional Convention, at which he was most anxious to be present. Thus he could find no plausible reason that would keep him from one and still allow him to go to the other. But, although he retained his high office until his death, he never attended another meeting and his connection with the association became purely formal. On the whole the episode of the Cincinnati was not a happy one for the dignified and prudent Virginian.

Meanwhile, the tide of popular suspicion began to ebb. To be sure, men like Jefferson and John Adams remained implacably hostile and there were other signs of lingering dislike. The same Mirabeau who was to play so prominent a role in the early stages of the French Revolution translated Burke's pamphlet, with a few embellishments of his own, giving the society further notoriety, while an equally unfavorable account (based largely on information supplied by Jefferson) appeared in the French *Encyclopédie*. When the outbreak in France sharpened the lines between aristocrat and democrat in this country, General Heath rushed to the fore again with a public renunciation of his membership.

But these were the last echoes of once loud objections. Newspapers widely publicized the revised Institution, but the subsequent failure of ratification escaped their attention and, apparently satisfied that the crisis was past, the press turned to the new nation's commercial difficulties, the government's inability to remedy them, and the fresher sensation of the balloon craze. Even the founding of the Society of St. Tammany during this period does not seem as clear-cut a democratic reaction against the aristocratic Cincinnati as has often been thought. By appearing to yield to the public's clamors, the society deflected its wrath, the general pattern changing from suspicion to indifference and even indulgence. For example, Hugh Henry Brackenridge's rambling novel, *Modern Chivalry,* published in 1792, contained a number of satirical comments on the order, but the author's conclusion that "it is a thing which can do little harm" represented gentle mockery rather than bitter alarm.[24] West of the mountains, in what the followers of Frederick Jackson Turner often regard as the valley of democracy, a more positive and permanent sign of approval came in 1790 with the naming of the city of Cincinnati in honor of the society. When the failure ever to ratify the changes proposed in 1784 finally led the general meeting of 1800 to declare that the original constitution of 1783 was still in force, the announcement occasioned little outcry.

One reason for this was that the society's efforts to carry out its professed purposes of perpetuating wartime friendships, aiding the unfortunate, and preserving "union and national honor" among the states had not proved particularly nefarious or even very energetic. Socially the meetings were quite successful. Everywhere the members enjoyed the convivial attractions of the annual meetings in each state, usually held on the Fourth of July. Preparations for the gathering of the Massachusetts officers at the Bunch of Grapes Tavern in Boston in 1789, for example, certainly belied any stereotype of dour Puritanism. "As we are of the opinion that the best liquors will be most acceptable to the Society," a committee reported, "we have agreed for the best Madeira wine at fourteen shillings lawful money per gallon, and the best claret wine at two shillings per bottle." [25] Usually a symbolic thirteen toasts were drunk to such unexceptionable propositions as "Public honor and private happiness" or "The progress of science and benevolence" until the utmost hilarity prevailed. What produced the hilarity can be surmised from the New York Society's bill at its July 4, 1789 meeting for "72 Madeira, 43

[24] Hugh Henry Brackenridge, *Modern Chivalry,* Claude M. Newlin, ed. (New York, 1937), p. 74.

[25] Report of the subcommittee for the July 4, 1784 meeting, quoted by Drake, *Memorials,* pp. 53–54.

Claret, 24 Porter, 35 punch, 7 glass, a pail Grog, 2 Ga. Porter, 2 do. Brandi & water, 1 pint brandy." [26]

In all fairness to the officers, some gatherings were more sober in every respect. At a typical one in Connecticut, ever known as the land of steady habits, the society marched to the meetinghouse instead of to a tavern. First came a prayer, then the secretary read the Declaration of Independence and Theodore Dwight delivered an oration. After "sundry select pieces of sacred music were performed by the ladies and gentlemen of the City, highly to the credit of the performers, and to the entertainment of the society and audience," another prayer closed the exercises, and only then the members "partook of a very elegant dinner, composed of all the varieties of the season." [27] Whether primarily frivolous or pompous, in either case these sessions scarcely appeared calculated to overturn the republic, and at that they occurred only once a year in each of the original states.

In the period immediately following the Revolution the charitable functions of the Cincinnati were not very important, probably because the officers had above average means. But gradually the demands on the order's funds grew as the Revolutionary survivors became old and incapacitated or died leaving needy widows and orphans. By the early nineteenth century the principal business of meetings was passing upon such cases. The New Jersey Society, for example, for many years contributed to the support of an officer's daughter named, rather unfortunately under the circumstances, Miss Reckless.

Similarly, as long as the members did not sufficiently feel the pinch of poverty or age to require charity, they were also slow to start any agitation for pensions or other forms of government aid. The history of American veterans' societies indicates that about twenty years elapse before any concerted drive of this sort begins. It required the titanic struggle of the Civil War, leaving hundreds of thousands of avid claimants for federal largess, to make this a

---

[26] Society of the Cincinnati photostats in possession of The New-York Historical Society.

[27] Connecticut Society of the Cincinnati, *Records 1783–1804* (Hartford, 1916), no pagination.

vital national problem, but nevertheless the efforts of their Revolutionary predecessors, feeble and sporadic as they were, set precedents that have appealed to the veterans of every subsequent war. At first the members showed more interest in securing grants of land than pensions. Then when Congress in 1790 voted to redeem all its certificates at face value, it turned out that during the previous decade many officers had sold those they had received for their five years' pay, usually at a considerable discount. In the early 1790's, therefore, a movement developed to give the veterans the difference between the original value of the certificates and what speculators had paid. The claimants turned logically to the Cincinnati, the only organized veterans' group, as the best medium for carrying on their agitation, and the provision for intercorrespondence of societies, so suspect among early critics of the order, now proved a convenient method of informing officers of the campaign. Despite a few official endorsements, however, the society was not strong enough to push these efforts through to a successful conclusion.

Defeated on this score, the Revolutionary veterans proved as resourceful as their successors in proposing alternative schemes. In the first quarter of the nineteenth century the Cincinnati backed efforts to revive the idea of half pay for life for the commissioned men, and its secretary-general, William Jackson, as official agent for this drive, developed some of the pressure techniques which later veterans' organizations were to perfect. In 1826 Congress finally granted full pay for life to all officers who had been entitled to half pay under the law of 1780, but it is not clear that the society could claim the credit for this action.

Aside from these not very spectacular attempts for governmental aid, the exact extent of the Cincinnati's political influence is uncertain. Despite the suspicions of some contemporaries, there is no evidence that the members had any desire to establish a monarchy in place of the republic. There is little doubt, however, that during the so-called "Critical Period" of the 1780's the order was a force for conservatism. As holders of depreciated public certificates they opposed the financial heresies of the day. Naturally Shays's Rebellion met with little favor. Though "the officers are still unpaid and extremely depressed in their private circumstances," Henry Knox reported proudly to Washington that "the moment the government

campaign for a new constitution. Certainly the proceedings of various meetings as well as the correspondence among the societies showed a strong concern lest the government fail to do justice to its creditors, and by 1787 the order's support of more vigorous union was clearly apparent. "Not only the wealth but all the military men of our country (associated in the Society of the Cincinnati)," wrote Benjamin Rush in June of that year, "are in favor of a wise and efficient government." [31] His juxtaposition of forces does not seem entirely accidental. Yet quite apart from economic self-interest the officers would probably have felt the same way. Presumably service in the Continental Army produced a certain amount of nationalist feeling, or perhaps more accurately it lessened local prejudices. The officers also probably tended to be better educated and better off economically than most people, hence also less provincial minded.

For whatever reasons, the Cincinnati was certainly well represented in the Constitutional Convention of 1787. Of the fifty-five framers, sixteen belonged to the society, while eleven at one time or another became honorary members. Despite the respectability that the society would seem to have acquired in this period of conservative reaction, some delegates still expressed apprehension over its future influence. But the order's support of their work was so evident that later Washington was taken aback to find some critics charging that "the proposed general government was the wicked and traitorous fabrication of the Cincinnati." [32] Although the society was prudent enough not to take any official stand on ratification, its individual members were quite active, some even presiding over state conventions.

As might have been expected, therefore, the Cincinnati developed close affiliations with the Federalist regime. An anti-administration senator sourly observed of a bill establishing additional federal positions, "It really seems as if we were to go on making offices until all the Cincinnati are provided for." [33] The first president of the United States was at the same time president-general of the order,

[31] Benjamin Rush to Richard Price, June 2, 1787, "The Price Letters," *Proceedings of the Massachusetts Historical Society,* 2d ser., XVII (1903), 367–368.
[32] Washington to William Barton, Sept. 7, 1788, *Washington's Correspondence Concerning the Cincinnati,* p. 338.
[33] Edgar S. Maclay, ed., *Journal of William Maclay* (New York, 1890), p. 320.

was in danger they unanimously pledged themselves for it:
while the few wretched officers who were against the go
were not of the Cincinnati." [28] Actually two members of
did participate in the uprising, but at its next meeting the
setts Society, declaring such activity had made them "p:
odious and obnoxious," ordered the month's pay which
originally subscribed returned to them and then issued a
that "they are not and have never been considered memb
Society." [29] The fact that the man who headed the expedi
dispersed Shays's forces was its president, Benjamin Lir
far more satisfaction to the society. In a sense this foresha
later antipathy of veterans' organizations to labor disturb

In 1789 the Rhode Island branch furnished an even m
example of the Cincinnati's financial conservatism when
Joseph Arnold of Warwick, who

by a late tender of the paper currency for a specie dema
standing the most pressing and repeated admonitions to
has forfeited all claims to those principles of honor and
are the basis of the institution, and thereby rendered hims
deserving the friendship of that class of his fellow-cit
patronage of good men.[30]

Not surprisingly when the so-called "Connecticut Wits
these forms of unrest like Shays's Rebellion and the
paper money laws in their satirical *Anarchiad,* they
the Cincinnati against the "visionary fears" of the "er
and the "gall-dipt quill" of Mirabeau.

These same financial interests also tended to make
port the drive for a stronger central government. Alth
plaints after Hamilton's funding of the debt show
officers had disposed of their securities, Charles A. B
his *Economic Interpretation of the Constitution* that t
able to retain them than were the common soldiers
fore the society's compact organization was a poten

[28] Knox to Washington, March 19, 1787, Drake, *Memorials,* p
[29] *Ibid.,* p. 50.
[30] Rhode Island Society of the Cincinnati to the Connecticut So
Connecticut Society of the Cincinnati, *Papers 1783–1807* (Hartfo
nation.

four of his cabinet were members, while a fifth became an honorary one, and so many state officials of the Cincinnati held elective or appointive posts as Federalists that the opposition regarded the society as one of the "machines" utilized by Hamilton, who was later to succeed Washington as president-general, to achieve his financial schemes. Moreover, one can be quite certain that the orations delivered at its meetings by people like Theodore Dwight were thoroughly conservative and even partisan in their implications.

Yet it is dubious whether the Cincinnati did much to mold the thoughts and actions of its members in any direction which they would not have taken anyway. Regardless of whether or not they belonged to a common organization, the officers as a class probably tended to share the same views on public questions, though naturally their society made it easier for them to discover this harmony of opinion. On the other hand, membership in the order did not prevent a substantial minority from becoming anti-Federalists, the most conspicuous perhaps being George Clinton, long-time governor of New York and later vice-president under both Jefferson and Madison.

In any case, by the early 1800's such factors as popular hostility, the members' own indifference, the westward migration of many officers, and the general difficulties of maintaining any organization on a national scale in an era of poor transportation and communication were combining to disrupt the Cincinnati. By 1832 only six of the original state societies were still functioning, and the French society had vanished during the upheavals of the French Revolution. Furthermore, the order stubbornly opposed any measure that would have broadened its scope and thereby perpetuated its existence. Thus it refused to admit more than one descendant of an original member at a time, and efforts to establish new branches in Kentucky and Ohio among the many Revolutionary officers who had settled there collapsed before an inflexible rule that no society could exist outside the first thirteen states. No matter how far a potential member had wandered from his ancestral commonwealth, he could join only the group there, and the well-known mobility of the American people in the nineteenth century correctly suggested what would happen to any organization clinging to such a principle.

Consequently the general meetings of the order, supposed to be held every three years, became more and more infrequent as well as sparsely attended, and between 1812 and 1825 there were none at all. As the old veterans died during this period of hibernation, the order quietly changed to a hereditary association composed of the sons and grandsons of the heroes of '76. So completely did the Cincinnati disappear from public consciousness that today many persons who are vaguely aware that it existed just after the Revolution are startled to discover that it is still functioning with 1600 members. Since the fears about it obviously never materialized, in retrospect the society seems singularly innocuous. Yet it does not follow that the apprehensions were absurd, for what might have developed in the country's formative period had there not been so instant and extensive an outcry must still remain surmise.

Not only did the Cincinnati barely escape complete disintegration, but the two conflicts between the Revolution and the Civil War failed to produce any important new organizations. The War of 1812 left a residue of two or three local groups which seem to have assembled for occasional parades but otherwise were of no significance. During the Mexican War several American officers, including Robert E. Lee and Zachary Taylor, formed the Aztec Club of 1847, a hereditary society modeled on the Cincinnati. This society does not appear to have done anything except to hold an annual banquet at the president's home in Philadelphia. But no union of rank-and-file veterans arose. Of course, there were only about 28,000 men demobilized from the War of 1812, but the approximately 140,000 in the Mexican War formed a substantial basis for such a group. But neither of these wars had been national movements and indeed the New England area, whose greater compactness and urbanization might have been expected to encourage associational activity, was actually hostile to both of them. Moreover, the rural nature of the country hampered communication, its predominantly agricultural economy made it difficult for farmers to get away for meetings, and only the officers had the cash or leisure for trips to some central city (and at that the Cincinnati met only once a year within the states and every three years nationally). Dixon Wecter has summed up the situation in his comment, "The great American excursion rate was still unknown." [34]

[34] Dixon Wecter, *When Johnny Comes Marching Home*, p. 59.

Nevertheless, the tendency to form associations was increasing in the United States during the early nineteenth century but was taking somewhat different forms. Out of the religious revivalism of the period, for example, stemmed a horde of "benevolent" societies which soon led to numerous reform associations organized on a national scale, of which the temperance and abolitionist movements are the best known. Moreover, after a violent flurry of hostility against secret societies in the anti-Masonic outbreak around 1830, fraternal orders like the Odd Fellows, Druids, and Redmen also began to flourish. But while in some respects it was also a period of mounting nationalist feeling, evidenced in flamboyant Fourth of July orations, the historical writings of George Bancroft, and the creation of national heroes like Nathan Hale and myths like the Parson Weems cherry tree story, it did not lead to organized patriotism in the form of veterans' and hereditary societies. A generation which was busily founding peace societies was not apt to commemorate two wars of which many people were not especially proud, and colonial ancestry was not much of a badge of distinction when most of the population could claim it.

When large-scale Irish and German immigration toward the middle of the century made this less true than it had been, the unpleasant consequence was the growth of secret nativist societies in the 1840's and 1850's. These, of course, purported to be strongly patriotic and in a sense they were even hereditary, since they usually required a couple of generations of American ancestry, but unlike present-day veterans' or hereditary groups they did not specifically require either service in a recent war or descent from participants in an earlier one, and they tended to be as much anti-Catholic as anti-immigrant. Actually the convent burning, pornographic pamphleteering, and inflammatory harangues of the Know Nothings may not have appealed to the kind of people whose dignified offspring half a century later, unnerved by the "New Immigration," turned to forming the S.A.R. and D.A.R.

The nearest to societies really based on ancestry were the New England Societies which in this period developed in a number of cities from New York to San Francisco as a consequence of that extensive nineteenth-century migration of Yankees into other parts of the country. Predominantly social, whether for self-protection or self-admiration in strange climes, like the Cincinnati they also often · established charitable funds for indigent New Englanders far from their native hills or coast. The society in New York City made the old Knickerbocker stock so self-conscious that in reaction there arose a St. Nicholas Society in 1835, to which many scions of Manhattan's pre-Revolutionary settlers still belong; appropriately enough, the literary historian of the Dutch era, Washington Irving, was one of the first members. Whether, properly speaking, the New England Societies should be called patriotic is doubtful, since obviously they glorified a section rather than the nation as a whole, unless one identifies New England with America, which is exactly what much nineteenth-century writing from that area did do. Their nascent pride in ancestry, however, in a sense made them precursors of patriotic organizations like the National Society of New England Women and the Society of Mayflower Descendants which later integrated local attachments into the general pattern of national hereditary orders.

More indicative of future developments were the first attempts at an extensive veterans' organization as well as the formation of the first women's patriotic group, both of which occurred in the 1850's. For some time it has been customary to picture the Civil War as a great gash across the nineteenth century, sharply differentiating the society that followed from the one that preceded it. Roughly speaking, this concept applies to the history of patriotic organizations in the same way that it does to many other American institutions. But recently historians have realized that the war did not constitute as abrupt a break in all fields as was once thought and that the early stages of many major postwar phenomena, like industrialism, political corruption, labor unions and the breakdown of *laissez faire,* may be clearly discerned in the previous decade. Similarly, though the great spurt of veterans' organizations did not come until after the Civil War, or of hereditary societies until the nineties, nevertheless the fifties saw two new groups, the War of 1812 veterans and the Mount Vernon Ladies' Association, which, though small in membership and restricted in scope, did have social, legislative, and historical interests that in microcosm prefigured the subsequent era.

About 1853, some forty years after the conflict in which they had served, there appeared long-belated movements in Boston, New

York, and Philadelphia to organize the veterans of the War of 1812. These movements seem to have arisen simultaneously but independently, as if in obedience to the law of multiple invention. In New York there were several state conventions, and two gatherings in Washington mapped plans for a national organization. Though the movement never achieved either the magnitude or the permanency for which its sponsors hoped, it was the earliest effort to mobilize all the veterans of an American war. In many ways the sessions resembled future G.A.R. encampments. The delegates were the first to receive the reduced railroad rates which later military organizations came to regard as their due for having won the respective wars which they commemorated. With this stimulus to attendance, the eleven hundred persons congregated at Syracuse, New York in June 1854 probably constituted the first mass convention of ex-soldiers. With such numbers the next step was to have a parade, which representatives of the Six Indian Tribes, including a warrior's widow aged 116 years, made even more colorful. Here was the primitive but unmistakable ancestor of the confusion, excitement, and general hoopla of a modern American Legion conclave.

The immediate incentive for these meetings was the doubtless correct assumption that organization alone would secure the governmental favors which the veterans felt they deserved. At various gatherings in the mid-fifties speakers outlined the arguments that in their fully developed form characterized many a G.A.R. resolution and Congressional debate after 1865. First there was the appeal to precedent. Since, aside from the Revolutionary soldiers, there were not many examples to cite in this country as yet, recollection was extended back to the "habit of all nations, whether savage or civilized, to reward in some suitable manner, those who had rendered important service to their country." The contention that the soldiers, having saved the nation, had somehow forever after acquired a lien upon it, also made its debut: "Who but the Soldier and his family should eat the bread from the Soil his own blood has enriched?" In addition, the existence of both needy ex-soldiers and a national surplus quickly produced logical suggestions for alleviating both situations with a single blow. These conventions therefore set up a clamor for all veterans to receive "a liberal annuity to be continued during their natural lives" and they appointed committees to correspond with similar groups throughout the country. They also voiced a desire for land grants, a request which the Revolutionary officers had first expressed and which the G.A.R. was later to echo. They felt that all survivors, "for any service however brief," should receive at least 160 acres.[35]

This generation of veterans also formulated the technique of pension pressure more precisely than had the Cincinnati. "Fellow soldiers, the remedy is in your own hands," one speaker instructed his audience. "When you return to your homes, tell the story of your wrongs to your children and your children's children. Unite with them in telling it to the Congress, to the government of the nation. *Carry* its recollection with you to the Ballot Boxes, and justice will no longer be withheld." [36] Both the method and the emotionally worded language were to become more and more familiar as the century wore on.

The War of 1812 veterans, organizing during a decade of sectional antagonism which culminated in civil strife, considered it their patriotic duty to allay this tension. Alarmed at the growth of "partisan feeling and sectional prejudice," one member in New York thought it "well to recur to the glorious incidents of our Revolutionary struggle" and to "the lofty heroism of our fathers." He hoped that "love for the union may be strengthened by being reminded of the sacrifices made to achieve our independence, and of the spirit of forebearance and kindness by which the union was accomplished." [37] But such sentiments proved pathetically inadequate to halt the more imperative historical forces that were pushing the nation toward the cataclysm.

Equally important was the appearance of the first women's patriotic society, the Mount Vernon Ladies' Association of the Union. With it there arrived on the scene the forerunners of a new type, the large-bosomed, beribboned middle-class clubwoman who, along with the veteran, after the Civil War increasingly dominated the field of organized patriotism. Curiously, at a time when almost the

---

[35] *Proceedings of the Convention of Soldiers of the War of 1812 at Corinthian Hall, Syracuse, June 20th, and 21st, 1854* (Syracuse, 1854), pp. 9, 12–15.

[36] *Ibid.*, p. 16.

[37] *Proceedings of the Convention of the Soldiers of the War of 1812, in the State of New York, Held at Schuylersville, Saratoga co., Oct. 17, 1856* (Albany, 1857), p. 31.

only public feminine activities were the temperance, abolitionist, and suffragist agitations of northern reformers like Elizabeth Cady Stanton, Lucretia Mott, Lucy Stone, and Amelia Bloomer which caused the South especially to recoil from such unwomanly displays, the founder of this group was the daughter of a wealthy South Carolina planter. Ann Pamela Cunningham's original appeal in the *Charleston Mercury* in 1853 to save Mount Vernon was motivated by "patriotism and a sense of national and, above all, Southern honor" (her phrasing reflected the paradox of coexistent nationalism and sectionalism in the South, but her hierarchy of values was ominous) and was therefore directed "To the Ladies of the South." [38] In 1856 came the formation of the Mount Vernon Ladies' Association, which by the eve of the Civil War was truly national, with branches in twenty-nine states in all parts of the country.

The most interesting fact about its meetings was that they were held at all. As a pioneer in the women's patriotic groups that sprang up in the 1890's pointed out, its members were assembling before it was socially acceptable for them to do so for purposes other than "reading, study or benevolence." Years later she still recalled vividly the impression that the first of these gatherings in her home town had upon her during a Southern ante-bellum childhood. Arriving late for dinner one day, her aunt replied to questions, " 'Where have I been?' To the Town Hall! And more, to a meeting of ladies—yes, *ladies!* Making speeches and passing resolutions like men!" The astounded children felt that "surely the world was coming to an end." The little girl long remembered her own "subdued feeling" that she "must be very good in the presence of such a state of things, ladies voting and all that, and my own conservative Aunt Mary entering no protest." [39] Surely these assemblages must have immediately reminded husbands and fathers of such current unorthodox phenomena as the women's rights convention of 1848, the early woman suffrage drive and the sensational bloomer fad, while in Miss Cunningham's native South Carolina public appearances of females must almost have inevitably aroused even more painful recollections of the contributions of the Grimké sisters to the antislavery cause.

[38] Quoted by Grace King, *Mount Vernon on the Potomac* (New York, 1929), p. 19.
[39] Mrs. Roger A. Pryor, "The Mount Vernon Association," *American Historical Register* (Jan. 1895), p. 410.

Fortunately for its success, the Association secured a list of state officers more distinguished for social prominence than for intellectual or political leadership. The names of Miss Mary Morris Hamilton in New York, Mrs. Louisa Greenough, widow of the sculptor, in Massachusetts, Mrs. John Comegys, niece of Secretary of State John M. Clayton and wife of the subsequent chief justice of the state, in Delaware, and Madame Achille Murat, a grandniece of George Washington and wife of a nephew of Napoleon, in Florida, were reassuring guarantees of respectability. Miss Cunningham herself made it clear that she had no sympathy with the movements to enlarge women's sphere. She had signed her original manifesto anonymously, as became a Charleston lady, with the pseudonym, "A Southern Matron," though as a matter of fact she was a thirty-seven-year-old spinster. A press account of her activities early in 1861 caused her "amazement and distress" because of her "horror of publicity for a lady—of her name appearing in the newspaper!" When she saw the story, "I felt as if I should faint. My friends tried to console me by saying . . . that the political excitement would be so absorbing that this item would probably be overlooked. This seemed so reasonable that I took courage." [40]

Besides her instinctive assumption that fainting was a lady's most appropriate response to the indignity of public attention, in other ways she fitted the Victorian stereotype of the sickly, dependent female. A youthful fall from a horse had caused a spinal affliction that made her a semi-invalid in constant discomfort and pain. Indeed, at one point in the Association's early history her exertions so overtaxed her strength that she fell into a series of convulsions, thereby halting an entire chain of legal negotiations until she was calm enough to sign the necessary papers. Her combination of apparent frailty and indomitable energy somewhat recalls a Northern contemporary, Mrs. Mary Baker Glover Patterson, who as Mrs. Eddy was a little later to make even more of a mark for herself.

But whether its founder realized it or not, the Association's efforts throughout the fifties to raise the $200,000 required to buy Mount Vernon from John Augustine Washington anticipated the historical activities of many women's hereditary leagues later in the century and of necessity marked an important step in the progress of

[40] Quoted by King, *Mount Vernon on the Potomac,* p. 120.

women's emancipation. Thus the campaign soon led to the publication of a sixteen-page monthly magazine in Philadelphia, called *The Illustrated Mount Vernon Record,* the first of many such periodicals issued by patriotic organizations. By 1860, with the help of such allies as Edward Everett and the Masonic Order, the women completed the purchase and then began the work of repair and restoration, financed largely by the proceeds of steamship visits to the estate. To this day the mansion remains in their care.

Thus by the time the Civil War disrupted the old order of American society the main outlines for the future development of patriotic societies were already apparent. In the Cincinnati and the Aztec Club were the avowed models for the many officers' groups formed soon after the war. The tentative efforts of the veterans of 1812 for national organization and united pressure anticipated the more skillful and successful drives of the Grand Army of the Republic. The New England and St. Nicholas Societies suggested an embryo interest in common ancestry as a basis for association. Finally, timid and well bred as its pleas were, the Mount Vernon Ladies' Association paved the way for wider and more powerful organizations of women. These scattered but unmistakable precedents formed the prelude to the post-Civil War epidemic of associational activity.

II

The Veterans Organize
—and Their Relatives Too

"THIS is an age of Societies and combinations," observed the commander of the New Jersey G.A.R. in 1872.[1] He was well qualified to speak. He was the spokesman for a group comprising thousands of men which not only had been in existence barely half a dozen years but which also was an unprecedented type of organization, a large-scale association of the enlisted men who had served in war.

The forces that were transforming American society in so many other respects in these years were also encouraging an amazing variety of voluntary associations. Chief among these influences was the urban development that accompanied the industrialization of the nation. In 1885 the most prominent paper for ex-soldiers, the *National Tribune,* observed that "organization into groups is the law of our community today. . . . Our population has become so large, and our social system so complex, that subdivisions into societies, associations, orders, etc. has become imperative." The paper felt that these groups compensated for the decline in "neighborliness" that occurred as the population increased in density.[2] By the end of the nineties an officer of another new organization, the Union Veteran Legion, frankly conceded, "The larger towns and cities are the only places in which successsful encampments can hope to be formed," while one of his predecessors, equally shrewdly, had noted

[1] Department of New Jersey, Grand Army of the Republic, *Proceedings of the Fifth Annual Meeting January, 1872* (Camden, N.J., 1872), p. 10.

[2] *National Tribune* (Washington, D.C.,), Feb. 19, 1885.

the converse: "a majority of the derelict Encampments are away from the general line of travel, situated as they are in small hamlets, and possibly composed of farmers who reside long distances from each other, and therefore are deprived of that feeling of *camaraderie* which is so strongly imparted by the touch of the elbow. . . ." [3]

If urbanism encouraged numerous new associations to arise in various communities, equally striking was the tendency of all groups in the post-Civil War era, whether of businessmen, farmers, workingmen, scholars, reformers, or women, to organize on a national basis. So it was with the veterans. The great technological strides in transportation and communication of modern America to a large extent made this possible. Without the railroad there never could have been the convergence upon convention cities so typical of the new mammoth organizations, and improved communication was essential for the centralized direction that also increasingly marked them. Thus, though the fifties had suggested the forms that organized patriotism was about to take, not until after 1865 did there appear any considerable number of societies, large in following and country-wide in scope, based either upon military service or ancestry. The years 1865–1890 saw the mushrooming of Civil War veterans' groups as well as the first organization of Mexican War soldiers, the eighties witnessed the rise of an amazing nexus of affiliated Civil War societies not only for the veteran's sons but also for "his sisters and his cousins and his aunts," while with the nineties came belated Confederate associations, along with the tremendous vogue for hereditary societies of all types.

The first of the veterans' organizations were no more than might have been expected from past experience. The precedents of earlier conflicts made it almost inevitable that the officers would quickly organize. Almost before the cannon roar ceased in the spring of 1865, two prominent doctors and a publisher in Philadelphia founded the Military Order of the Loyal Legion of the United States. Obviously modeled on the Cincinnati and the Aztec Club of 1847, its membership was open to Civil War officers and their eldest male descendants. It spread rather slowly, however, forming branches

---

[3] Union Veteran Legion of the United States, *Proceedings of the Thirteenth National Encampment 1898* (Lewiston, Maine, n.d.), p. 100, *and Proceedings of the Tenth National Encampment 1895* (Cincinnati, n.d.), p. 29.

in only six states in its first decade and then halting during the subsequent depression years. But the eighties saw a new spurt of activity, and in the course of a dozen years the Loyal Legion appeared in fourteen more states before 1891. One reason for its slow growth was the competition of other groups, for the late nineteenth century's mania for association meant that no longer could any one body monopolize even the commissioned men's allegiance. The vast scope of the Civil War led many to prefer joining an order commemorating the particular Army in which they had served. The late sixties saw a rash of these Army societies, the most prominent and long-lived of which were the Society of the Army of the Tennessee (1865), the Society of the Army of the Cumberland (1868), and the Society of the Army of the Potomac (1869). Some of these admitted enlisted men, it is true, but on the whole their membership consisted almost entirely of officers.

All these developments fell into a predictable pattern. What was extraordinary was the rapid appearance of many organizations of enlisted men for the first time in American history. There were, of course, larger numbers available than after any previous war, for more than two million men had served in the Union forces. Never before had so many had to make the transition from military service to peacetime life. The economic adjustment of large numbers of young men, many of whom had gone into the army before securing any specialized skills, created problems often beyond the power of any one individual to solve. So strong did the feeling become that only organization could advance their interests, as well as preserve the memories of their wartime comradeship, that in the two years following 1865 numerous groups appeared independently of each other throughout the East and Middle West, mostly local but sometimes organized on a state-wide basis.

With the current tendency toward national organizations of all sorts, the next step was to weld these into a country-wide association. For a moment it looked as though a group known as the Soldiers' and Sailors' National Union League might accomplish this. It appeared in Washington as early as June 1865 with its ostensible aim to help the veterans secure government jobs, but actually it quickly became an important adjunct of the Radical Republican machine. A national convention at Pittsburgh in September 1866 proved to be primarily a monster political demonstration, and the organization collapsed after it had performed its partisan function in the fall elections.

As it turned out, most of the small local groups which had sprung up were soon absorbed into the Grand Army of the Republic, which first appeared in Illinois in the spring of 1866 and was destined to become the most powerful veterans' organization the United States had yet seen. As was to prove so often the case with American patriotic societies, controversy shrouds its exact origin. Generally accepted as founder is a Springfield, Illinois druggist and doctor, Benjamin Franklin Stephenson, whose medical services during the war had won him the title of "Old Butch." Some have suggested that credit for the original suggestion should be shared with his wartime tentmate, an army chaplain named William J. Rutledge, but the precise details are irrelevant, for certainly it was the doctor who proceeded to translate the idea into fact.[4]

According to Stephenson, the impetus for this decision was his disillusionment about the treatment of veterans upon his return to Springfield. Not only were men "starving for want of work," but the widows and daughters of the slain were "begging for washing and the lowest kind of labor in order to get food for themselves and children and clothes to cover their nakedness." Especially he resented that those who had stayed home tried "to justify themselves by defaming the soldier, saying 'they were afraid he was not honest,' and when asked to assist a comrade's wife, would charge her with immoral conduct." Stephenson determined to organize the veterans into "a power, able to protect themselves and support the families of our fallen comrades." [5] Few would deny that the next few decades witnessed the achievement of his objective.

But according to Mrs. Mary R. Dearing, who has studied the origins of the G.A.R. with a critical eye for the realities behind the

[4] A useful, though understandably laudatory, sketch of Stephenson's career is Mary Harriet Stephenson, *Dr. B. F. Stephenson, Founder of the Grand Army of the Republic* (Springfield, 1894). Robert B. Beath, *History of the Grand Army of the Republic* (New York, 1889), is an account by one of the early participants in the movement which really comes under the heading of source material.

[5] Stephenson to the Minnesota G.A.R., July 29, 1867, Department of Minnesota, Grand Army of the Republic, *Early History From 1866 to 1879* (Minneapolis, 1896), p. 12.

rhetorical façade, this entire account is little more than a highly romanticized legend. She has convincingly displayed that the real parents of the organization were Governor Richard J. Oglesby of Illinois and his close political associate, General John A. Logan, who were hoping that through gathering the veterans into an ostensibly philanthropic association they might be able to send Logan to the United States Senate in the place of the more conservative Lyman Trumbull.[6]

In any case, early in 1866, with the help of various friends, Stephenson drew up a tentative ritual for a secret veterans' organization. Part of his material he derived from the Soldiers' and Sailors' League of St. Louis, while the title may have come from another Missouri group, the Advance Guard of America or the Grand Army of Progress. On April 6, 1866, Stephenson installed the first post of the Grand Army of the Republic at Decatur, Illinois. Throughout the spring various organizers traveled about Illinois forming additional posts until there were twenty-four by June. With creditable filial pride Stephenson's daughter claimed that the doctor paid the expenses of these agents himself, but there seems ground for the more cynical suspicion that the funds secretly came from the political sources which had already sensed the possibilities of such an organization.

Assuming the title of national commander-in-chief, Stephenson soon was spreading the order into neighboring states. Whenever he and his associates learned that prominent veterans were visiting Springfield, they would "take them into some quiet nook or corner, tell them what we were doing, and if they were well disposed to administer the obligation to them, give them a lot of books, tell them to go home and start in their own state."[7] During the late spring and summer of 1866, the G.A.R. invaded Indiana, Ohio, Michigan, Wisconsin, Minnesota, and Iowa.

So far, however, this had proved merely a regional organization, limited to the Middle West. The previously mentioned convention of Soldiers' and Sailors' Leagues in September 1866 gave it the

---

[6] Mary R. Dearing, *Veterans in Politics* (Baton Rouge, 1952), pp. 82–84.

[7] Statement of John S. Phelps in Department of Minnesota, Grand Army of the Republic, *Journal of Proceedings of the Fifteenth Annual Encampment 1895* (Minneapolis, 1895), pp. 197–198.

opportunity to become national. The Hoosier delegation included representatives of 134 Indiana posts, many of them wearing white ribbons inscribed "Grand Army of the Republic." Moreover, their state adjutant-general, Oliver Wilson, had arrived with a supply of constitutions, rituals, and charters in the hope of interesting veterans from other areas. He succeeded in initiating several Easterners who promptly founded new departments, the term for state organizations. The pioneer post on the Atlantic seaboard came in October at New Bedford, Massachusetts. With this expansion came the first national encampment at Indianapolis in November, attended by delegates from nine states but dominated by the overwhelming numbers from Illinois and Indiana. Throughout 1867 and 1868 departments were organized in more states and by 1872 there were twenty-six.

The Grand Army's growth, however, was not to prove smooth or even. Following this period of rapid expansion in the late sixties, the G.A.R. underwent an equally rapid decline in the early seventies. In many Middle Western states the order disbanded entirely between 1868 and 1875, while others maintained the mere shadow of an organization. Illinois, Indiana, and Ohio had each had more than three hundred posts at the end of 1868, but within a few years the first two had only a single one apiece and Ohio could boast of only three. Exactly nine persons constituted the California state encampment of 1877. The Southern branches disappeared almost completely in this same period.

While there were similar losses along the Atlantic seaboard, two-thirds of Pennsylvania's posts having disbanded by 1872, for example, none of the departments there actually vanished. As a result, the center of Grand Army strength now shifted from the Middle West to the East. In 1877 the order's adjutant-general described the latter region as "furnishing the great bulk of the membership, and paying almost the whole of the expenses of management." [8] Massachusetts, New York, and Pennsylvania, each with more than fifty posts, had now become the most active states.

Unlike the inspector-general of the Maine department, who plaintively submitted that this collapse "cannot be explained on

---

[8] Grand Army of the Republic, *Proceedings of the Eleventh Annual Meeting of the National Encampment 1877* (Philadelphia, n.d.), p. 447.

rational principles," [9] other members were able to discern a number of factors contributing to the debacle. Some were essentially matters of internal organization which particularly antagonized the Middle Western members. First, a new and elaborate three-grade ritual was adopted in May 1869. All members not assuming the new obligations by September were to be dropped. The Easterners favored this pomp and ceremony, but the Westerners had no use for such innovations, especially as the top offices in the order were reserved for the highest class of "Veterans." Two years was all that the experiment lasted, but meanwhile thousands of veterans had deserted the association. At the same time others resented increasing centralized tendencies within the organization. In the beginning the state branches were fairly autonomous, but after 1868 a more rigid supervision developed. Insistence upon regular inspection of posts and the obedience of local units to decisions of the national encampment aroused great uneasiness, perhaps as smacking more of military discipline than the veterans cared to revive. Financial tribute to headquarters also caused suspicion. Posts had to purchase supplies, including the new rituals, from the central body, and members were also urged to buy badges ranging in price from forty cents to twenty-five dollars; to some this smacked of "official robbery."

Sometimes purely local conditions injured the society. The ravages of a grasshopper plague led to disintegration in Minnesota, and, dramatically enough, the tiny Mountain Department in the West lost a high proportion of its membership in Custer's Last Stand. The original members in the South of necessity were largely Carpetbaggers who with the collapse of Reconstruction either abandoned the region or found it advisable not to flaunt their Northern connections. Rumors from Kentucky that a member of one post had been assassinated and the commander of another kidnaped and given sixty lashes because they had openly declared their allegiance to the order seem a bit lurid but nevertheless were discouraging indications of public opinion.

Probably two other influences were more significant in explaining the G.A.R.'s collapse. In many states politicians had notoriously

[9] Department of Maine, Grand Army of the Republic, *Proceedings 1867 to 1877, Inclusive* (Augusta, 1877), p. 31.

used the organization for their own partisan purposes and, once they had achieved their ends or found the device no longer effective, had abandoned the society, while at the same time other veterans, suspecting the order was nothing but a political machine, refused to affiliate. This was especially true in the Middle West. Even more important, one suspects, was that by the early seventies most of the ex-soldiers were preoccupied with establishing themselves economically, getting married and raising families and had not yet reached the stage where they sought opportunities for garrulous reminiscing, or had the means to indulge it. In the industrial East the final blow was the Panic of 1873. Many members there were either manual laborers or factory workers immediately affected by hard times. They dropped out because of inability to pay dues or scattered elsewhere in search of work. In either case, many posts had to disband.

Although the Grand Army suffered these severe reverses, it did not disappear entirely, and the decade of the eighties saw a revival that outstripped any previous successes it had enjoyed. Between 1876 and 1890 the veterans reorganized or formed for the first time departments in twenty-nine states, mostly in the West and South. The most active year, 1883, saw seven new branches ranging from Arkansas to a combined Washington-Alaska. During this period the membership also increased from a low of about 25,000 in 1877 to over 400,000 in 1890. The largest influx came in the years 1882, 1883, and 1884, when 185,000 former soldiers joined the order.

This renewed vigor resulted partly from more energetic methods of recruiting. During 1881, for example, the assistant-adjutant-general of the Massachusetts branch wrote each of the town clerks in the commonwealth for the names of six veterans; direct correspondence then often led to the formation of posts. When the Ohio G.A.R. tried the same stunt with the postmasters in 185 towns, soon there followed posts in 108 towns.[10] Similarly, in California the society distributed 7500 copies of a circular on its objects throughout communities where former soldiers were known to live. Elements with a financial stake in enlarging the order co-

---

[10] Elmer Edward Noyes, "A History of the Grand Army of the Republic in Ohio from 1866 to 1900," Ph.D. dissertation, Ohio State University (1945).

operated in this drive. The influential *National Tribune,* the organ of Washington's largest pension-agent firm, throughout 1881 and 1882 repeatedly urged all survivors of the war to join the G.A.R.

Obviously the veterans had now become more responsive to these appeals. Their renewed interest coincided with the return of prosperity which enabled them to afford such activities. At the same time, as they grew older they had both more leisure and more longing for such associations or felt more keenly the desirability of an organization to aid their less fortunate comrades. The movement of population into the West and to some extent into the South also helped the order's growth in those regions. A great influence was the interest in pensions and the realization that only organization would secure them. The G.A.R.'s most rapid expansion came immediately after the society appointed its first pension committee in 1881 and thus began its aggressive campaign for governmental aid to veterans.[11]

The G.A.R. reached its height in 1890 with its stronghold again in the Middle West. There were then 763 posts in Ohio alone, while New York, Illinois, Pennsylvania, Indiana, Kansas, and Missouri (in that order) had more than 400 apiece. Eight more states had over a hundred posts each, and there were even 87 in Tennessee, 77 in Arkansas, 48 in Texas, and 44 in Virginia. Utah had the least, with only three.[12] By 1893 there were also five posts in Canada, one each in Mexico City and Honolulu, and another being organized in Lima, Peru.

This interest in joining and the vast number of recruits now available meant, however, that, although the Grand Army of the Republic was by all odds the most important organization of Civil War veterans, it was not the only one. Other groups, apparently trying to constitute more or less an aristocracy of enlisted men, also arose. Thus the Union Veteran Legion, founded at Pittsburgh in 1884,

---

[11] One student of pension history attributes the order's sudden popularity to the passage of the Arrears of Pension Act in 1879. John William Oliver, *History of the Civil War Military Pensions, 1861–1885 (Bulletin of the University of Wisconsin, History Series,* IV, Madison, 1917), p. 90. The Grand Army, however, had had little to do with securing the law, and the greatest increase in its membership did not come until a few years later.

[12] Grand Army of the Republic, *Journal of the Twenty-Fifth National Encampment 1891* (Rutland, Vt., 1891), p. 66.

required its members to have volunteered before July 1, 1863, and either to have served for two years or to have been discharged because of wounds, while the Union Veterans' Union, started in Washington in 1886, admitted those with only six months' continuous service, but part of this had to have been at the front. Other groups emphasized particular types of service. Scattered local clubs of wartime sailors combined in 1886 to form a National Association of Naval Veterans, while across the country branches of the Union Ex-Prisoners of War also appeared. None of these groups, though national in scope, ever approached the magnitude of the Grand Army. In addition, numerous companies or regiments held annual reunions and banquets which were almost entirely social and otherwise insignificant.

Accompanying the revival of the G.A.R. and the appearance of other veterans' organizations was the growth of auxiliary societies for various categories of relatives. In the late seventies camps of Sons of Veterans, affiliated with G.A.R. posts, sprang up both in Pennsylvania and New York and by 1881 not one but two rival organizations for such progeny had materialized. The larger one, the Sons of Veterans of the United States of America, spread from Pittsburgh until by the mid-nineties it had branches in thirty states. Competing with it in name and purpose was an order which developed in Pennsylvania, New Jersey, and New York from similar camps around Philadelphia but by the early nineties nearly all its units had been absorbed into the larger group. Eventually the Union Veteran Legion sponsored a Sons of War Veterans and the Union Veterans' Union at one time seems to have had a junior organization known as the Loyal Guard.

More significant of new social trends was the rise of several national associations of women connected with the soldiers' leagues. This reflected the growing feminine interest in club life at this time. The first women's clubs appeared in 1868, the Sorosis in New York and the New England Women's Club in Boston; the first Greek letter sorority came in 1870 and the W.C.T.U. was formed in 1873. Popular fraternal beneficial orders were also forming feminine branches, such as the Daughters of Liberty (1875) for the Order of United American Mechanics. During the war many women had participated in Ladies' Aid societies and "sanitary fairs." In the late sixties and early seventies a number of Ladies' Leagues, Loyal Ladies' Auxiliaries and Relief Corps, beginning with the Ladies' Union Relief Association in New York City in 1865, continued charitable work among needy veterans and the families of deceased soldiers. The first to be affiliated officially with the G.A.R. appeared at Portland, Maine in 1869. It inspired the formation of similar auxiliaries in Massachusetts which, at Grand Army instigation, formed the first state-wide Woman's Relief Corps in 1879. In the early eighties Women's Relief Corps and Ladies' Aid Societies spread throughout the East, while another group in Toledo was the model for a similar movement in the Middle West.

The encouragement of the veterans' paper, the *National Tribune,* and of the G.A.R.'s commander-in-chief, Paul Van Der Voort, led to a national organization, known as the Woman's Relief Corps, Auxiliary to the Grand Army of the Republic, which was formed at the Grand Army's Denver encampment in July 1883. By 1900 it had three thousand corps in thirty-six states. Its principal strength was in the Middle Western areas of Ohio, Michigan, Illinois, Iowa, and Kansas, though Massachusetts, New York, and Pennsylvania were also strongly represented. The original concept of the W.R.C., as it was often called, was that each corps should be affiliated with a specific Grand Army post. But by the nineties, while women's groups were still growing, the veterans were declining in number, and clearly such a ruling would soon inhibit expansion. In 1898, therefore, the national convention voted that a corps might be organized independently wherever there were not enough ex-soldiers to form a post.

The women proved no more able to concentrate on a single organization than were the men. When the W.R.C.'s second national convention in 1884 decided to admit all "loyal women," the New Jersey branch, to which only veterans' relatives were eligible, refused to affiliate. Instead, it became the nucleus of the Ladies of the G.A.R., founded at Chicago in 1886 with the stricter eligibility requirement. By the early nineties it had spread into twenty-three states. Meanwhile, the same issue caused the Woman's State Relief Corps of Maine to remain aloof from the W.R.C., but with Yankee individuality it also declined to join with the Ladies of the G.A.R.

Parallel to the Sons of Veterans, but independent of it, there also arose a Daughters of Veterans. Started by some grammar school girls in Massillon, Ohio in 1885, to help the local G.A.R. post observe Memorial Day, by 1890 it had "tents" in several Middle Western states. Meanwhile the other men's groups developed their own auxiliaries. Associated with the Union Veterans' Union was the Women's Relief Union; the Ladies of the Naval Veteran Association of the United States of America appeared at Providence in 1892 for the female descendants of sailors in past conflicts (in the next few years it managed to spread to only five more Eastern cities); while the Dames of the Loyal Legion was formed in 1899 for the female relatives of Loyal Legion members and of deceased eligible officers. Dating from 1883, a Ladies' Aid, Sons of Veterans, admitted relatives of veterans and the wives of Sons and by the mid-nineties had over two hundred chapters throughout the country. The nearest to an actual female veterans' group came with the founding of the National Association of Nurses of the Civil War at the G.A.R.'s national meeting in Washington in 1892; three years later, at the Louisville encampment, it was reorganized as the Veteran Nurses of the Civil War.

The success of these numerous organizations connected with the Union Army eventually stimulated other veterans. It was rather late for the venerable War of 1812 soldiers to do much. They voiced an occasional demand for pensions, but of necessity remained ineffectual. For example, the average age of the twenty-three who met in New York on Washington's birthday, 1876, was eighty-one. Two years later only fifteen members appeared at a meeting of the New England Association. Their age averaged eighty-five, and four were over ninety. Death and debility forced the group's dissolution the following year. While as late as 1888 a few survivors were still meeting in New York City for a dinner and exchange of reminiscences, their day was over.

But the Mexican War soldiers, who were now in what they doubtless considered "the prime of life," were still energetic enough to see how the possibilities which the Civil War veterans had opened up might also be applied to themselves. Their Moses turned out to be a California printer named Alexander Kenaday, a native of Wheeling, now West Virginia. During Kenaday's varied career he had worked on river steamboats in the South and West, enlisted twice in the Mexican War, joined the California gold rush, and then became active in early labor agitation on the West Coast. In order to raise funds to prevent county hospitals from sending the bodies of old soldiers to medical colleges, Kenaday started an association of Mexican War veterans in San Francisco in 1866. Quickly turning to the government for assistance in a manner reminiscent of the Civil War soldiers, this group sent Kenaday to Washington in 1868 to lobby for the establishment of a soldiers' home on the Pacific seaboard. Though not successful, he remained in the capital and, after making Grant's second inaugural in 1873 the occasion for organizing the veterans in Washington, summoned a national convention to meet there in January 1874. Delegates from thirty-three states formed the National Association of Mexican War Veterans, ostensibly "for the promotion of social intercourse, good fellowship, and all proper assistance," but actually to press for a service pension. Local branches developed in various parts of the country, though their connection with the national association seems to have been rather tenuous. A national convention was held as late as 1893 and branches continued to meet even into the early 1900's, but by the turn of the century they too had almost dwindled away.

Despite the profusion of Union organizations, similar Confederate associations were slow to appear. During the late seventies and throughout the eighties, first local groups on the order of the Confederate Survivors' Association of Augusta, Georgia (1878) and then some state-wide bodies arose, but no national society. The urbanism that facilitated such organizations in the North was conspicuously lacking in the rural South and in any case the poverty of the region made it far more difficult for her ex-soldiers to support any orders. Perhaps equally important, not until the late eighties did the ex-Confederates feel they could unite "without exciting suspicion and distrust on the part of the people of the north." But as the wartime acerbities wore away and the North suffered a literary Appomattox as it willingly surrendered to the sentimental "befo' de wah" school of fiction, representatives of ten groups in Louisiana, Mississippi, and Tennessee formed the United Confederate Veterans at New Orleans in June 1889. In the following decade the order spread throughout the South. At its second convention in 1890, delegates appeared from eighteen groups in Texas, Louisiana, Alabama,

Georgia, Tennessee, Kentucky, and even Illinois. By 1895 it had more than four hundred camps in twenty states and, four years later, over twelve hundred such branches. Texas had the largest number, but South Carolina, Georgia, and Alabama also had over a hundred each. The Confederate veterans did not spawn as many subsidiary organizations as did the Yankees, but about 1897 an Association of Medical Officers of the Army and Navy of the Confederate States arose. It apparently did little except to assemble during the annual reunions of the U.C.V.

Since Southern women were notoriously more belligerent about the "Lost Cause" than were the old soldiers, even in the conservative South, so hostile to most expressions of feminism, a counterpart to the Woman's Relief Corps presently followed the formation of the U.C.V. This united a number of local Daughters of the Confederacy which had appeared in at least seven Southern states between 1890 and 1894 for the purpose of assisting veterans' homes and building monuments to the Confederacy. Correspondence between Mrs. L. H. Raines and Mrs. C. M. Goodlett, heads of the societies in Savannah and Nashville, led to the founding of the United Daughters of the Confederacy in the latter city in September 1894. As was so often the case in these organizations, a debate soon arose as to which lady deserved the credit for inaugurating the order. After a long dispute the 1905 convention finally awarded the title of "Founder" to Mrs. Goodlett, who promptly presented the organization with an oil painting of herself toward which many chapters had contributed.

The first U.D.C. chapter was in Nashville, the second in Savannah. Tennessee became the first state division in 1894; Georgia, Maryland, and Virginia followed in 1895. In the next few years eleven more state organizations developed elsewhere in the South, in the border region, and even in Indiana.

Actually it was not as analogous to the Woman's Relief Corps as might have been expected. In its eligibility requirement it was more like the Ladies of the G.A.R., admitting only relatives of those who had participated in the Southern cause. Moreover, while the W.R.C. was frequently hampered because it was an official auxiliary of the G.A.R., the U.D.C. had no connection with the U.C.V. and in its independent career eventually became far more influential than the Northern body. Finally, with an appropriate respect for the traditional states'-rights philosophy, it allowed its state branches far more autonomy. This perhaps resulted as much from the practice of incorporating already established groups as from principle. Thus when Virginia, which had developed its own state organization of Daughters of the Confederacy, joined the U.D.C., it kept its own constitution and refused to be restricted in any way by the national association or to be required to do anything but local work.

More nearly a Southern replica of the Sons of Veterans, U.S.A., was the parallel society for the offspring of Confederate veterans. Arguing that they would preserve the ideals of the Confederacy after the veterans' deaths, local groups sprang up in the early nineties in various cities in Virginia, South Carolina, Mississippi, Georgia, Alabama, and Tennessee. Finally the R. E. Lee Camp of Confederate Veterans of Richmond issued a call for their federation. During the U.C.V. reunion at Richmond in June 1896, some forty delegates formed the United Sons of Confederate Veterans. Much closer to the U.C.V. than was the U.D.C., its constitution required that its conventions be held at the same time as those of the veterans. Two years later the society had over one hundred camps, the largest number being in South Carolina and Georgia.

As the final stage in this hierarchy the Southerners outdid even the energetic Yankees with the formation of a Children of the Confederacy, probably suggested by the recently organized Children of the American Revolution. Its first chapter appeared in Alexandria, Virginia in 1896 and by 1899 the idea had spread into seven more states. With this the champions of institutionalizing the memory of the Confederacy at last halted.

The ex-soldiers, their sons, their womenfolk, and even their little children having all been organized, it seemed as though nothing was left. But at the close of the century events came full circle as the Spanish-American War produced a new crop of veterans' associations similar to those that followed the Civil War. In February 1899, the Naval and Military Order of the Spanish-American War was formed in New York. Modeled on the Cincinnati, the Aztec Club, and the Loyal Legion, it admitted all officers in the recent hostilities and provided for hereditary succession. As a counterpart of the various Union Army outfits, some seventy-five officers founded the Society of the Army of Santiago de Cuba in

July 1898, before they left the island. It received all members of the expeditionary force to Cuba and the lineal descendants of original members. Branches were established in Chicago in 1899 and in New York City, Detroit, and Worcester in 1900.

A more comprehensive organization similar to the G.A.R., though clearly inescapable, was slower to develop. Proposals to include the new veterans in the Grand Army met with little response. In the years after 1898 a number of groups sprang up in the same way that scattered clubs of Civil War veterans had arisen in 1865 and 1866. In September 1899, fourteen men formed the first post of the American Veterans of Foreign Service in a clothing store in Columbus, Ohio. The society soon spread to several other Ohio cities as well as into Illinois and New Hampshire. Another body, known as the Army of the Philippines, held its first meeting in December 1899, at Denver. In 1913 these two joined as the Veterans of Foreign Wars. A rival organization, the Spanish War Veterans, which first appeared in Washington in September 1899, fused with several subsequent groups in 1904 to form the United Spanish War Veterans. In due time women's auxiliaries also arose.

Such was the development of veterans' societies during the half century after the Civil War. In 1865 there had been only a few ineffectually organized War of 1812 veterans and the genteely quiescent Aztec Club. The new century had its choice of G.A.R., S.V., W.R.C., D.V., U.C.V., U.D.C., U.S.C.V., V.F.W., and U.S.W.V., and all this alphabetical jungle had emerged in the most patriotic manner decades before the New Deal. But it was only the beginning, for the 1890's had also been witnessing an equally impressive onslaught of Sons, Daughters, and Dames.

III

Blue Blood Turns Red, White, and Blue

IN 1895 the staid Philadelphia jewelry firm of Bailey, Banks and Biddle thought it worthwhile to publish a seventy-page handbook of patriotic-hereditary societies which listed forty-seven such organizations. Its motives in so doing were not necessarily patriotic or even disinterested, for already it was doing a thriving business supplying elaborate insignia to the members of these societies, so that the mere fact of publication revealed the gain in popularity of these groups. Five years later at the turn of the century a little journal, which in the spirit of the day proclaimed itself the *Patriotic Review,* named seventy patriotic, hereditary, and historical associations, exactly half of which had been founded during the preceding ten years.[1] In short, the late eighties and the nineties were the period in which nearly all the well-known societies of this type originated.

In the largest sense this development was merely one aspect of the steadily mounting interest in "joining," or associationalism, which had earlier produced the wave of veterans' groups and affiliates. These were exactly the same years of the great growth of Masons, Odd Fellows, and Elks, who numbered two and a half million by the end of the century, while more than three hundred new fraternal beneficial societies were formed during the nineties.[2] According to the president of the newly founded Daughters of the Republic of Texas in 1897, "especially in our age is the combining of forces a favorite device for attaining great ends, not alone in

[1] Eugene Zieber, *Ancestry* (Philadelphia, 1895); "Patriotic, Hereditary & Historical Societies," *Patriotic Review,* I (Oct. 1900), 19.

[2] B. H. Meyer, "Fraternal Beneficial Societies in the United States," *American Journal of Sociology,* VI (March 1901), 650, 655–656; Arthur Meier Schlesinger, *The Rise of the City 1878–1898* (Arthur M. Schlesinger and Dixon Ryan Fox, eds., *A History of American Life,* X, New York, 1933), pp. 288–289.

secular business, but in all the concerns of life." [3] "So pervasive is the fraternal spirit," a speaker before the New Hampshire Sons of the American Revolution testified in corroboration in 1896, "that on every hand men and women associate to commemorate some notable event, the memory of benefactions, or for presumed good in material relations." [4] Once again it is clear that this activity was closely connected with the "rise of the city," for it was there that people had both the leisure and the facilities for such enterprises. At the beginning of the decade a member of the New Jersey S.A.R. commented that "it seems to be the tendency of mankind, as civilization advances, to mass themselves in cities, and to promote in all ways the co-operation and centralization of human energies." [5] Any examination of the new patriotic-hereditary societies quickly reveals that very often they originated either in New York City or Washington and that far more than the previous veterans' organizations they flourished primarily in the urban areas of the Northeast.

But the novel development of the nineties was not the numerous new associations in the cities but the extent to which upon their founding so many labeled themselves "patriotic." A speaker before the Minnesota D.A.R. in 1895 echoed almost exactly the words of the G.A.R. official in 1872 noted earlier, but with the addition of a significant adjective: "This is an era of patriotic societies." [6] Magazines of the day ran articles on the phenomenon, sometimes hailing it as "A Renaissance of Patriotism." [7] The contagion even infected the older Civil War organizations, which now for the first time also emphasized their patriotic mission. The explanation of this fervent sense of patriotism is not as clear as the fact of its existence. But ever

[3] Daughters of the Republic of Texas, *Proceedings of the Sixth Annual Meeting 1897* (Houston, 1897), pp. 15–16.

[4] New Hampshire Society, Sons of the American Revolution, *Proceedings 1889–1897* (Concord, 1898), p. 153.

[5] New Jersey Society, Sons of the American Revolution, *Proceedings 1889 to 1893* (Morristown, N.J., 1893), pp. 118–119.

[6] "Celebrations and Proceedings," *American Historical Register* (May 1895), p. 902.

[7] Marcus Benjamin, "American Patriotic Societies," *Munsey's Magazine,* XIV (Oct. 1895), 74–84; Mrs. James B. Clark, "The Influence of Patriotic Societies," *American Monthly Magazine,* VII (Dec. 1895), 521–526; Edward S. Holden, "Hereditary Patriotic Societies in the United States," *Overland Monthly,* 2d ser., XXXI (April 1898), 368–369; George J. Manson, "A Renaissance of Patriotism," *Independent,* LII (July 5, 1900), 1612–1615.

since the close of the Civil War a spirit of "organic nationalism" had
been growing which by the nineties was to be seen in the expansionist sentiments of Henry Cabot Lodge, Captain Alfred Mahan, and
Theodore Roosevelt. In its most exuberant form it culminated in
the country's declaring war against Spain to the tune "There'll Be
a Hot Time in the Old Town Tonight." [8]

An important aspect of this patriotic self-consciousness was a
pronounced interest in the American past as contributing to the
nation's glory. The first of these new societies were based on the
Revolutionary period and stemmed from the centennial celebrations
of those years, especially in 1876, 1883, and 1889, though these were
the occasions rather than the causes of their founding. It was part
of the same historical pride that gave rise a few years later to the
great popularity of romances like *Hugh Wynne* (1896), *Janice
Meredith* (1897), *Richard Carvel* (1899), *Alice of Old Vincennes*
(1900), and *To Have and To Hold* (1900). Emphasis upon the
common past of all sections also aided many of the founders in
their conscious desire to heal the breach between North and South,
but once again this anxiety for reunion was an expression of nationalist feeling rather than a cause of it.

Though the connection is not clearly established, possibly growing
social and economic tensions fostered the type of patriotism that
emphasized the country's history. "The Great Upheaval," the Haymarket Riot, the campaigns of Henry George, and the writings of
Edward Bellamy crowded the last half of the eighties. The nineties
produced such proofs of unrest as the Populist revolt, the Homestead
Strike with the attempted assassination of Henry Clay Frick, the
Panic of 1893, the Pullman Strike, Coxey's Army, and, finally, the
Bryan campaign of 1896. Throughout all this the conservative and
propertied classes watched apprehensively the black cloud of anarchism, a menace as productive of alarm and hysteria as bolshevism
or communism in later generations. Persons of this stratum of society
had never been much interested in the G.A.R. or Sons of Veterans,
but now they flocked to the standards of the Sons of the Revolution,
the Sons of the American Revolution, the Society of Colonial Wars,

---

[8] Merle Curti, *The Roots of American Loyalty* (New York, 1946), pp. 175–181;
Ralph H. Gabriel, *The Course of American Democratic Thought* (New York,
1940), pp. 339–354; Schlesinger, *Rise of the City*, pp. 409–415.

and the Order of Founders and Patriots, whose names suggested a reassuring devotion to the system of their ancestors. Significantly, this same concern seems to have been responsible for the cult of the Constitution which also developed in these years and which was to become one of the fetishes of the new associations.[9]

But even an upsurge of patriotic feeling and an absorption in the American past fail to explain the hereditary form of these societies. Indeed, a renewed interest in republican institutions and the ideals of democracy usually associated with Americanism would seem off-hand inconsistent with such imitation of Old World aristocracy and position based upon pedigree, especially in adopting a practice of the Cincinnati which had so offended patriotic Americans of the very period many of these orders were ostensibly commemorating. The fact is, however, that at the same time that Americans were becoming nationalistic and jingoistic they were also becoming very much absorbed in family trees. During the nineties a number of newspapers introduced genealogical departments; the Astor Library in New York finally set aside a room "for the convenience of the large numbers of searchers after family history and the attendance there attests the popularity of the fad," [10] and by 1896 the *Library Journal* was telling staffs how to help the public in its ancestor hunting. Particularly it became the pastime of women and even more especially of spinsters who, as has been suggested, with no legitimate interest in offspring concentrated on their forebears. In "Octave Thanet" 's Iowa town of the eighties in *The Man of the Hour,* when the factory owner wanted his lineage traced, his superintendent offered, "Let my little girl do it . . . she's looking up those things all the time—why, she's traced me back to Stephen Hopkins who came over on the Mayflower." [11] And look it up for him Miss Emma Hopkins did, and very competently too. Soon an anecdote of the day was describing how a skillful tramp reduced a hard-faced New England old maid to tears with the pitiful whisper, "You may imagine how dark life has been to me, how few advantages I had in my childhood. Our family had but one ancestor in the Mayflower." [12]

[9] Gabriel, *Course of American Democratic Thought,* pp. 398–399.
[10] "Editorial," *Spirit of '76,* V (Oct. 1898), 28.
[11] Octave Thanet, *The Man of the Hour* (New York, 1905), p. 29.
[12] G. W. Dial, "The Value of Genealogy," *New England Magazine,* XXXIII (Nov. 1905), 287.

This interest stemmed partly from literature current in the late nineteenth century such as Sir Francis Galton's *Hereditary Genius* which stressed the importance of heredity. Probably more important was Sir Francis' cousin, Charles Darwin, whose pervasive influence in this era in its worst form gave rise to the racist ideas of Anglo-Saxon superiority expressed by such popularizers—and distorters—as Josiah Strong. In either case the result was to make Americans seek assurance of their individual superiority or national survival by establishing that they came of fit stock or a fit race.

These notions about the Teutonic heritage would never have had the significance they did had it not been for the impact of the so-called "New Immigration" from southern and eastern Europe which became marked in the mid-eighties. Those of higher economic level became alarmed at the effect upon American institutions ("O Liberty, white Goddess! is it well To leave the gates unguarded?" [13] Thomas Bailey Aldrich thought not), for this generation attributed much of the radicalism that so disturbed it to the influence of foreigners. Hence well-to-do individuals often supplied the leadership of the new hereditary societies devoted to preserving the old traditions. "Not until the state of civilization reached the point where we had a great many foreigners in our land, where we realized the necessity of stirring up a love of country and a spirit of patriotism among our people," a president-general of the Sons of the American Revolution testified, "were our patriotic societies successful." [14]

The same fear of immigrants furnished many recruits from among those less secure economically or socially who feared inundation and clung to ancestry as one badge of distinction much as many of the poorer class Southern whites have clung stubbornly to the doctrine of race. The American novelist Winston Churchill, whose earlier historical novels had so well expressed the romantic nationalism of the period, sensed this in a later story, *The Dwelling Place of Light*. The heroine's father, Edward Bumpus, was a bewildered and embittered survivor of rural New England in polyglot, industrialized Lawrence, Massachusetts, economically unsuccessful and socially uprooted and in his frustration finding his only consolation

[13] Thomas Bailey Aldrich, *The Poems of Thomas Bailey Aldrich* (Boston and New York, 1907), II, 72.
[14] Sons of the American Revolution, *National Year Book 1914* (n.p., n.d.), p. 233.

in the Bumpus genealogy, "a hobby almost amounting to an obses-
sion, not uncommon amongst Americans who have slipped downward in the social scale. . . . This consciousness of his descent from
good American stock that had somehow been deprived of its heritage, while a grievance to him, was also a comfort." [15] Membership
in the newly formed Sons and Daughters was often an economic
luxury but an emotional necessity for these people. "Our founders
realized that with the steady immigration of foreigners to our country something must be done to foster patriotism and love of our
country and our flag and to make Americans of them," an early
D.A.R. leader reminisced, "or there was danger of our being absorbed by the different nationalities among us." [16] This confused
and hostile reaction to a new social condition was probably as significant a basic factor as any for the appearance of so many hereditary
societies all at once. The descendants of the older stock took for
granted, of course, that they were automatically the best qualified to
preserve the American heritage and to interpret it to the newcomers.
"As Americans descended from the early settlers and from the
'Heroes of '76,' " declared the regent of the Massachusetts Daughters
of the Revolution, "to us is intrusted the estate of constitutional
liberty, and the land and properties belonging thereto, to have and
to hold for our heirs, and adopted brothers and sisters, now and
forever. . . . Our fathers died to give us this republic—let us, then,
be faithful stewards." [17]

As has been indicated, in many instances the various anniversaries
of Revolutionary events beginning in 1876 proved the occasion for
the formation of these societies. "These observances exerted a remarkable influence on the public mind in every part of the United
States," wrote a historian of these groups in 1890. "They inspired a
pride in Revolutionary ancestry, a shame that the country had come
to neglect the annual observance of the Fourth of July and Washington's birthday, and a new respect for the principles of popular
government." [18] The Centennial Exposition of 1876 in Philadelphia

[15] Winston Churchill, *The Dwelling Place of Light* (New York, 1917), pp. 4–5.
[16] Daughters of the American Revolution, *Seventh Report 1903–1904* (Washington, 1905), p. 92.
[17] "Patriots' Day," *Magazine of Daughters of the Revolution*, II (July 1894), 6.
[18] Henry Hall, *Year Book of the Societies Composed of Descendants of the Men of the Revolution* (New York, 1890), p. 1.

focused wide public attention on celebrating a century of the Declaration of Independence. There also resulted unconnected efforts for an organization of Revolutionary descendants on both the east and west coasts. In New York City John Austin Stevens, a prominent merchant whose historical consciousness was shown by his election as secretary of The New-York Historical Society in the same year, made an unsuccessful attempt to establish a Sons of the Revolution, while in San Francisco a more durable Sons of Revolutionary Sires arose which held annual Fourth of July exercises in the next few years.

In 1883 the anniversary of the British evacuation of New York enabled Stevens to revive his scheme. December of that year saw the formation of the Sons of the Revolution in historic Fraunces Tavern, where Washington had taken leave of his officers. The new organization long showed little ambition to expand outside of New York City, however. Refusing equality of status to groups that might arise in other states, it insisted that they be merely auxiliaries to the New York Society. Not until 1890, when it was facing the competition of a more aggressive rival, did the only three existing branches, New York, Pennsylvania, and the District of Columbia, form a General Society of the Sons of the Revolution, which by the end of the decade had spread into twenty-six additional states. Ever conservative, its constitution was modeled on that of the Cincinnati. Since the latter in turn had largely followed the Articles of Confederation, this made amendment almost impossible. This feature, which the Founding Fathers whom the Sons so revered had quickly discarded, later was to cause the new organization considerable difficulties whenever changes did seem advisable.

Many of the new groups of the nineties resulted from internal dissension within existing societies, a procedure so common in the history of associations in general that the sociologists have devised a term for it: "schismatic differentiation." The hesitancy of the New York Sons to welcome expansion produced the first example of this phenomenon, the Sons of the American Revolution. Its founder, an energetic but eccentric resident of Newark, New Jersey, named William O. McDowell, was perhaps the most extraordinary figure in the history of American patriotic societies. Born in New Jersey in 1848, he had helped to reorganize a number of defunct railroad companies, engaged in various real estate promotion schemes around New York City, dabbled in railroad and mining securities, and for a while manufactured mining and milling machinery. By the mid-eighties he was living in "a handsome brick house" in Newark and was reputed, probably incorrectly, to be worth a quarter of a million dollars.

Even more varied than his business enterprises were the extra-curricular interests of this audacious, indefatigable, and versatile dreamer and organizer. As early as 1879 the press noticed that he "is evidently happiest when running a public meeting." [19] He advocated cheaper transit from New York to New Jersey and agitated for free public libraries in Newark and for an expansion of technical education throughout the state. He served as treasurer of the American Institute of Christian Philosophy, modeled on the Chautauqua movement and the Concord School of Philosophy, whose meetings at Greenwood Lake also publicized one of his real estate ventures. As a close associate of T. V. Powderly he figured in the great railroad strikes of 1886. He also found time to oppose the Chinese Exclusion Act and to attempt to organize a syndicate for the economic development of China. One newspaper described him in 1886 as "a rather undersized gentleman with a suit of dark hair," while another reported that he "is an exceptionally intelligent man, 38 years old, is rather short in stature and talks in a decided way which carries conviction." [20] Wherever he appeared, controversy followed and sometimes litigation too. By the time McDowell was thirty Abram Hewitt had publicly denounced him as "a common scold and a common libeller" as well as a "blackmailer and common liar." [21]

His great interest in the 1883 centennial celebrations turned his attention to the newly formed Sons of the Revolution. He became a member in 1884 and was soon pressing proposals for an elaborate observance of the one hundredth anniversary of Washington's inauguration. Convinced that the society's leaders "were satisfied with a military parade and ball, I felt it was necessary that something should be done to redeem the celebration from being a thing of the

[19] *Newark Daily Journal*, April 11, 1879.
[20] *Baltimore Sun*, April 22, 1886, and *Washington Press*, April 21, 1886.
[21] *Newark Daily Advertiser*, Oct. 31, 1878; *New York Daily Tribune*, Oct. 31, 1878; *New York World*, Oct. 31, 1878.

day, and to make it an influence world wide, for all time." [22] He had meanwhile also managed to become chairman of the Sons of Veterans' committee on participation in the celebration as well as temporary secretary of a citizens' committee advocating a New York World's Fair to begin on April 30, 1889, a project which eventually opened exactly fifty years late.

McDowell's pushing manner, flamboyant schemes, and general instability merely irritated the genteely conservative leaders of the Sons of the Revolution, who presently eliminated him from their committee on the celebration. But when McDowell learned a branch of the Sons had at last appeared in Pennsylvania in 1888, he determined to start another in New Jersey that would be more responsive to his plans. In March 1889, the New Jersey members of the Sons, led by McDowell and Josiah Pumpelly of Morristown, founded their own society and applied to the New York organization for recognition. Not only did the Sons of the Revolution reject this request but presently the society was publicly denouncing McDowell as one whose "combination of pertinacity, vanity, and effrontery is unparalleled, and whose insensibility to the usages of polite life is manifest in every movement." [23]

Undismayed by this rebuff, during March and April McDowell instead turned to forming other branches throughout the country. With his usual ingenuity he appealed in the press for Revolutionary descendants to correspond with him and asked state governors to summon organizing meetings in their capitols. A number of the executives coöperated and by the end of April several societies were in existence. McDowell, Pumpelly, and William S. Stryker, president of the New Jersey Sons, then asked these groups to send delegates to form a national society in New York immediately after the centennial celebration on April 30; in those states where no action had as yet been taken, the governors were requested to name representatives, and several did so. On April 30 McDowell called the meeting to order in Fraunces Tavern. President Timothy Dwight of

[22] William O. McDowell to Luther Tarbell, June 13, 1889, William O. McDowell Letterbooks, New York Public Library.

[23] *An Explanation of Some of the Differences Between the Society of Sons of the Revolution and the Society of Sons of the American Revolution* (Philadelphia, 1890), p. 6.

Yale gave the invocation, a letter of approval from the aged Hamilton Fish, president-general of the Cincinnati, was read, and the National Society of the Sons of the American Revolution came into being.

McDowell then directed his energies to those states as yet unresponsive to his efforts. Through tireless correspondence he won the support of a remarkable number of well-known persons, including President Gilman of Johns Hopkins University, who declared himself "happy to be one of the coöperators in this excellent work." [24] This he followed up with a series of personal appearances throughout the country. "It is like receiving a lesson in American patriotism to talk with William O. McDowell," declared a Chicago newspaper during his visit there. ". . . He has more of the spirit of '76 in him than could be found in a city full of ordinary business men." [25] As one interviewer commented to him, "A friend of yours says that you talk to a person for fifteen minutes, and he is surprised to find himself organized in some patriotic affair." [26] This fervor led to the organization of twelve more states between January and April 1890. Thereafter the society grew more slowly, but by 1900 had outstripped the Sons of the Revolution by existing in thirty-five states.

But the visionary McDowell did not limit himself to the United States. He favored the establishment of societies in every republic of the world which would exchange addresses annually and eventually send delegates to an international congress. In the summer of 1889 he distributed a circular to the presidents of all the world's republics asking them to sponsor similar organizations of the descendants of the men who had established independence in their respective countries. Here McDowell's efforts proved less successful. Edmond de Lafayette, for example, refused to help organize an S.A.R. in France because the offspring of his ancestor's companions were "unknown, or scattered, or disappeared, or separated by the most opposite political opinions." [27] Nor were the leaders of the S.A.R. at home enthusiastic about spreading the organization over

[24] D. C. Gilman to McDowell, May 10, 1889, William O. McDowell Scrapbooks, VII, New York Public Library.

[25] *Chicago Tribune*, Jan. 5, 1890.

[26] "Kate Field's Washington," Jan. 21, 1891, in McDowell Scrapbooks, XLI.

[27] Edmond de Lafayette to McDowell, Sept. 2, 1889 (translation), McDowell Scrapbooks, LVII.

the entire globe. "The Monroe Doctrine, which is dear to every true American, would seem to limit us to our own country," declared the acting president-general at the first national congress in 1890. "Let us make our own Society strong, and do the work we find immediate at our hands before we seek for larger fields or greener pastures." [28] Though branches were formed in Hawaii in 1896 and in France the following year, they were intended solely for those of American descent.

The appearance of the Sons of the Revolution and especially the spread of the Sons of the American Revolution inaugurated a wave of interest in hereditary leagues of all kinds. One result was to stir new life into already existing organizations which had become almost moribund. In the early nineties the secretary-general of the Cincinnati reported himself receiving almost daily letters of inquiry about admittance to the order; he blamed this somewhat vulgar curiosity on the centennial celebrations.[29] The members steadfastly resisted attempts to admit all male descendants of Revolutionary officers, feeling that the Sons of the Revolution offered a sufficient haven for these *hoi polloi*. But the heightened interest led to the revival of defunct state branches. With its usual conservatism the order admitted them almost reluctantly. Ancestral claims received sharp scrutiny, and not until a provisional organization had functioned for several years did it become a full-fledged member of the General Society. Despite these impediments, by 1902 the Cincinnati was back to its full complement of thirteen branches.

Also in tune with the spirit of the time, the almost disintegrated organizations of War of 1812 veterans gained new life as hereditary bodies. At the time of the anniversary of Washington's inauguration in 1889 only five members of the Society of the War of 1812 were present at the festivities in New York City. A movement to convert the society into a hereditary order won the consent of the twenty-two survivors and in 1892 resulted in the incorporation of the Military Society of the War of 1812. Meanwhile the remaining veterans in Philadelphia had witnessed a similar metamorphosis the previous year and then, in conjunction with similar bodies which now arose in Maryland and Massachusetts, in 1894 formed a General Society

[28] Hall, *Year Book*, p. 31.
[29] General Society of the Cincinnati, *Proceedings*, John C. Daves, ed. (Baltimore, 1925–1930), II, 39.

of the War of 1812. By 1900 it had also developed branches in Ohio, Illinois, the District of Columbia, and New Jersey, while in New York to avoid confusion with the Military Society of the War of 1812 it assumed the cumbersome name of the Society of the Second War With Great Britain.

More typical of the era was the founding of entirely new societies. There were several new organizations for men, more for women, a few for both, and some even for children. Since there was now a surfeit of groups based on the Revolution and subsequent conflicts, organizers of new masculine associations turned to the period before 1776. As early as 1885, representatives of the original Dutch settlers in Manhattan formed the Holland Society and in the following decade similar groups appeared in Chicago and Philadelphia. In August 1892, a small group of men in New York City started the Society of Colonial Wars, which admitted the descendants of soldiers and of civil or legislative officials of the period 1620–1775. During the first part of 1893 other organizations arose in Pennsylvania, Maryland, Massachusetts, and the District of Columbia, and in May their representatives met in the New York City Hall to form the General Society of Colonial Wars. By 1898 branches had appeared in twenty other states.

Subsequent associations tended to make their eligibility more stringent and hence presumably more exclusive. The Order of Founders and Patriots, organized in New York early in 1896, welcomed only those having ancestors in the direct male line or in the mother's male line in the colonies before 1657 whose forebears also served in the American Revolution. Societies in New York, New Jersey, and Connecticut formed a General Court of the order at New York in 1896; before 1900, additional branches developed in Pennsylvania and Massachusetts. Even more exclusive was the somewhat oddly named Colonial Order of the Acorn, founded in 1894 by such aristocratic New Yorkers as a Schieffelin, a Rhinelander, and a Van Rensselaer, which was limited to descendants in the direct male line from American colonial families.

Others labored for leagues that would apply something of the principles of the Cincinnati to all American conflicts. In 1894 a New York clique launched the Military Order of Foreign Wars for the commissioned officers of the Revolutionary, Tripolitan, 1812, Mexican, and Spanish (but not Civil) Wars and their lineal male descendants; by 1900 this had spread to several states. The Society of American Wars, started in Minnesota in 1897, admitted officers of the Civil and Spanish Wars, their lineal male descendants, and the similar offspring of officers in all other conflicts in which the colonies or the United States had engaged. By 1899 it had members in twenty-three states. Since they did not adopt the too limiting device of primogeniture, in a sense both gave a haven for the near-misses who may have pined for the Cincinnati.

Far more characteristic of the decade was the formation of hereditary societies for women. Urbanism and increased leisure now enabled the middle-class woman to turn her attention to activities outside the home as never before, and the rise of groups like the United Daughters of the Confederacy, the Colonial Dames, and the D.A.R. in the 1890's was only one phase of the women's club movement which had culminated in a General Federation of Women's Clubs in 1889. The appearance of the W.R.C., the Ladies of the G.A.R., and the Daughters of Veterans in the eighties had heralded this development, but by the end of the century they were lamenting the competition they faced. In 1898 the national organizer of the W.R.C. complained that one small town, "with less than five thousand inhabitants, boasts forty secret Orders for women, thus largely dividing the time, energies and finances of those interested." [30] By that time the new hereditary societies for women, discovering that there were "an unusual number of earnest women whose general culture and familiarity with the great educational and social problems of the last end of the century has led them into Club life," [31] were reporting the same difficulty. Leaders of the various women's patriotic organizations were quite self-conscious about living in the era of the "new woman," and were fond of declaring that the nineteenth century was "essentially woman's century," was "one of woman's progress," or even was "woman's Paradise." [32]

[30] Woman's Relief Corps, Auxiliary to the Grand Army of the Republic, *Journal of the Sixteenth National Convention 1898* (Boston, 1898), p. 167.

[31] "Annual Reports of State Regents," *American Monthly Magazine,* XIV (May 1899), 1089–1090.

[32] "New Jersey Celebration," *Magazine of Daughters of the Revolution,* III (Feb. 1895), 25; "Celebrations and Proceedings," *American Historical Register* (Sept. 1895), p. 126; Department of New York, Woman's Relief Corps, *Journal of the Tenth Annual Convention 1893* (n.p., n.d.), p. 49.

The new women's societies to a large extent paralleled similar men's groups, though not in the sense of auxiliaries like the Civil War groups; as time went on, several also resulted from splits within established associations. The first of these, the Colonial Dames, appeared among New York City's Knickerbocker aristocracy at the very beginning of the nineties, even before the analogous Society of Colonial Wars for men. Its exact origin is as mysterious as that of many other such groups (not surprisingly, William O. McDowell later sought some of the credit, though with no great success). According to one story, which may even be true, one day in April 1890 Mrs. John King Van Rensselaer and Mrs. John Lyon Gardiner were visiting Mrs. Archibald Gracie King at her home in Weehawken. As they strolled near the historic spot where Aaron Burr had killed Alexander Hamilton, Mrs. Van Rensselaer suggested, "Let us found a patriotic society of women descended from colonial ancestry." Shortly thereafter she and Mrs. Gardiner assembled a selected group of eligible ladies who organized the Colonial Dames of America in May 1890.[33] This New York group also sponsored subordinate chapters in Baltimore, Philadelphia, Washington, and Paris.

Just as the arbitrary tactics of the Sons of the Revolution had produced the S.A.R., the measures of the Colonial Dames soon led to a rival society. While the original body intended to become a national organization and to form branches in the various states, it was also determined to remain the parent with full control over those chapters. A group of Pennsylvania women felt that the New York society's methods were too autocratic, its objects too limited, and its attitude towards prospective members too aristocratic. In June 1891, they formed their own organization which the next year became the basis of the National Society of Colonial Dames of America. Its fame soon exceeded that of the original order, for this became the Colonial Dames best known to the general public. Even in its rival's stronghold of New York, constant bickering over such vexing issues as the eligibility of Mrs. William Rhinelander Stewart and alleged discriminations against such prominent families as the Jays and the Livingstons caused a number to with-

[33] *The Colonial Dames of America 1890–1904* (New York, n.d.), p. 3; *New York Sun*, Oct. 19, 1890; "Celebrations and Proceedings," *American Historical Register* (April 1896), p. 216.

draw to join the offshoot. At first the new society was confined to the thirteen original states, but in the middle of the decade it extended its scope and by 1900 had branches in thirty-five states.

Almost immediately after the formation of the first Colonial Dames came the founding of what was to prove the most important of all the hereditary societies organized during these ten prolific years, the Daughters of the American Revolution. The story of the inception of this society is even more confused than the murky origins of so many other patriotic leagues. No less than six persons—five women and a lone man (McDowell—who else?) claimed the credit, and each recorded a slightly different version. In actuality probably each one was entirely correct in his or her subsequent assertion of having contemplated an organization of Daughters during 1889 and 1890. That several persons had the same idea at approximately the same time is merely one more demonstration of the law of "multiple invention." It was an era of hereditary patriotic societies. It was an era of women's clubs. The mere existence of the Sons of the American Revolution was bound to suggest a parallel organization in the same way that the G.A.R. had produced its auxiliaries and the U.C.V. was soon to have a United Daughters of the Confederacy.

At first, as a matter of fact, several branches of the S.A.R. had admitted women, but its desire for union with the more conservative Sons of the Revolution led the first national congress in April 1890 to exclude them. Meanwhile, as early as June 1889, the irrepressible McDowell had begun agitating for a Daughters of the American Revolution. After the decision of the S.A.R. convention, which also happened to deprive him of most of his influence in that organization, he redoubled his efforts, but still with no success.

The immediate impetus for founding the D.A.R. came from a letter in the *Washington Post* in July 1890, written by Mrs. Mary Smith Lockwood. Since 1876 she had been the hostess of an apartment house in the capital. She had founded the Travel Club of Washington and headed a local temperance society and the Woman's National Press Club. Her writings included magazine articles on the tariff, a textbook on ceramics, and a volume on *The Historic Homes of Washington*. In many ways this tiny, white-haired woman typified the transition from the cloistered Victorian female to the

modern woman, active in professional and club life. One acute
observer noted that "in the deep blue eyes of intellectual sweetness
there is mingled a determination of purpose and firm resolve." [34]
Another summed her up as "above all a womanly woman with
advanced ideas." [35] When in the summer of 1890 Mrs. Lockwood
read an account of a meeting of the Sons in Washington, she was
aroused to pen an account of the part women had played in the
Revolution and especially of the services of a somewhat minor
heroine, Hannah Arnett, which the *Post* published on July 13.

By a coincidence which seems most implausible but which apparently was a genuine accident, Hannah Arnett's great-great-grandson
spotted the letter—and he was none other than McDowell. This was
all the encouragement he needed to publish an appeal in the *Post*
for women of Revolutionary descent to send him their names as the
first step toward forming a Daughters of the American Revolution.
He also distributed copies of Mrs. Lockwood's story among a wide
number of persons, including Mrs. William H. Vanderbilt and the
publisher of the Philadelphia *Ledger,* George W. Childs, who he
hoped might become interested enough to supply funds for organizing expenses. Soon he was receiving letters from several interested
women. Three of his correspondents from Washington were to become the officially designated founders of the D.A.R.: Mary Desha,
Ellen Hardin Walworth, and Eugenia Washington.

Like Mrs. Lockwood, all three were women who were earning
their own living and who had participated in public affairs. Miss
Desha, a native of Lexington, Kentucky, had become a government
clerk in Washington in 1885 following her brother-in-law's election
to Congress. Long employed in the Pension Office, she consciously
represented the new interest in club life. "You know we have been
limited for so long to orphan Asylums and Hospitals," she wrote
to McDowell, "that in this the dawn of our freedom we are 'taking
to' historical research and the study of parliamentary law and to the
founding of scholarships, libraries, art galleries and gymnasiums." [36]

[34] Nellie Holbrook Blinn, "Mrs. Mary S. Lockwood," *American Monthly Magazine,* II (Feb. 1893), 197.
[35] Flora Adams Darling to McDowell, Oct. 7, 1890, McDowell Scrapbooks,
XXXVIII.
[36] Mary Desha to McDowell, July 28, 1890, McDowell Scrapbooks, XXXIV.

She was reputedly "a pronounced woman suffragist." [37] At the time of the emergence of the D.A.R. she was also involved in another new women's organization, the "Wimodaughsis" (formed from the first syllables of "wife, mother, daughter, sister"). Incorporated in June 1890, this society had as its motto, "The Nineteenth Century Dawn of Women's Era." Anna Howard Shaw, prominent woman suffrage leader, was its president, and its stockholders included Susan B. Anthony, Elizabeth Cady Stanton, and Clara Barton. Its constituency therefore somewhat justified the charge that it was actually the headquarters of the Women's Rights Society in Washington, though its ostensible purpose was to build a clubhouse for women.

Mrs. Walworth also typified the emancipation of women. "I have lived mainly—first for my eight children till I was *thirty-eight*," she once wrote, "and for these remaining years, since eighteen sixty-eight, for my country and for the advancement of women; always a Suffragist, though not in their societies." [38] By 1876 she had joined the Association for the Advancement of Science, the American Historical Society, the Association of American Authors, and many other organizations, of which she was often the only woman member. She was president of the Society of Decorative Arts in New York, founder of its branch in her home town of Saratoga Springs, and historian and only woman trustee of the Saratoga Monument Association, as well as the first woman elected to a local board of education in New York State. She also became a government worker and was drawn into the D.A.R. movement through a colleague, Adelaide Johnson, who as vice-president of the Wimodaughsis was closely associated with Miss Desha.

The third "official founder," Miss Washington, was the most Southern of the three and also the least representative of the "new woman." A descendant of George Washington's brother Samuel, after her parents' death she too had become a government employee in Washington. On August 9, 1890, she and Miss Desha met with Mrs. Walworth at her home, discussed a constitution for an order of

---

[37] Flora Adams Darling, "To the Regents of the Daughters of the American Revolution," *Adams' Magazine of General Literature*, I (July 1891), 18.

[38] Quoted by Adelaide Johnson, "Ellen Hardin Walworth, Forerunner of the New Times," *Americana*, XXIX (Oct. 1935), 652.

Daughters which McDowell had submitted, and decided to hold another gathering in the fall when more people would have returned to Washington.

A fateful move occurred when they placed on the tentative board of managers a friend of Miss Washington, Mrs. Flora Adams Darling, who was then summering at Culpeper, Virginia. To her admirers this lady was "a favorite writer, a good talker, a true friend, and always an agreeable companion." [39] Actually she was almost as fantastic an individual as William O. McDowell, whose eventual verdict was succinct: "In organizing the D.A.R. we struck one complete fraud, Mrs. Flora Adams Darling." [40]

Despite her coy assertions that "I do not claim to be a 'strong-minded' woman of the new order" [41] (she was about as weak-minded as the late Queen Elizabeth I or Miss Dorothy Thompson), Mrs. Darling represented the restlessness of the "new woman" even more than did Mrs. Lockwood, Miss Desha, Mrs. Walworth, or Miss Washington. Born in Lancaster, New Hampshire, in 1840, in later years she encouraged the impression that she was closely related to Samuel, John, and John Quincy Adams, though actually the connection was extremely remote. She was probably also responsible for the dubious story that President Franklin Pierce visited her father's home shortly before his election and gave her a handsomely bound volume inscribed, "To the child of my heart," and that while in office he presented her with many other books and corresponded regularly (of course, this may have been true, but one quickly learns to question every statement Mrs. Darling ever made). Later she assumed the title of "A.M.," though there is no evidence of her ever having attended college.

In 1860 Flora married a man some twenty-two years older than herself, Colonel Edward Irving Darling, and went to his home in Louisiana. Impartial in her affinity for presidents, she allegedly developed a friendship with Jefferson Davis so intimate that she later assisted materially in the collection of data for his memoirs, and that his last personal letter was addressed to her. This probably has about

[39] Mrs. De Fontaine, "Biographical Sketch of Mrs. Flora Adams Darling," *Adams' Magazine of General Literature,* I (Oct. 1891), 2.
[40] McDowell to Henry Baldwin, Dec. 28, 1901, McDowell Letterbooks.
[41] Mrs. Darling, "To the Regents," p. 18.

as much truth to it as the Pierce story, though doubtless Mrs. Darling
so much wanted these stories to be true that she convinced herself
of their accuracy; she was not much different from McDowell in this
respect. The Civil War brought an incredible series of vicissitudes:
Mrs. Darling's husband was killed, the Federal authorities jailed her
as a spy in New Orleans, she contracted scarlet fever, and the theft
of her securities and jewelry during her arrest led to a protracted
claims case before Congress that extended over thirty years, without
success.

After an attack of malaria in 1876 destroyed her hearing and im-
paired her sight, she too became a government clerk, in Washington.
About 1889 she also began to write a series of novels, all highly
romantic and semi-autobiographical, such as *The Bourbon Lily, or
Romance and Law, A Winning, Wayward Woman* (which might
be considered partially self-descriptive), and *A Social Diplomat* (a
title without the slightest autobiographical accuracy). With two
other people she founded a magazine in New York, *The Gotham
Monthly,* in January 1890, and by August was its sole editor. It was
at this point that Miss Washington brought her into the D.A.R.
movement.

Mrs. Darling became very much interested in the project, started
elaborate plans for its launching, and soon convinced McDowell and
Mrs. Lockwood that the other women in Washington "look to me
as 'Head Centre.' " [42] She decided that October 11, as the anniversary of Columbus' first sighting America, would be the appropriate
date for the society's organization and accordingly sent out invitations. Miss Washington, Miss Desha, and Mrs. Walworth, who had
also been preparing for a fall meeting, were less convinced that Mrs.
Darling was "Head Centre" and upon receipt of her invitation informed her somewhat tartly that they had already formed the order.
Back came Mrs. Darling's undaunted reply: "Well, then we'll simply
have a larger meeting and begin on a larger scale." [43] Though her
three colleagues were considerably irritated, they allowed her to
proceed for the sake of harmony and because they supposed it was
McDowell's wish.

[42] Mrs. Darling to McDowell, Oct. 8, 1890, McDowell Scrapbooks, XXXVIII.
[43] Eugenia Washington, "Our History," *American Monthly Magazine,* VII (Dec.
1895), 499.

On the afternoon of October 11, 1890, the group assembled at Mrs. Lockwood's apartment in the Strathmore Arms. Mrs. Darling, "seated at the table, in her sombre garb of widowhood," called the meeting to order. McDowell was invited to preside, and the gathering then proceeded to elect officers and adopt a constitution. Miss Washington, "serene and satisfied," headed the list of signers. Mrs. Benjamin Harrison was chosen president-general, and Mrs. Darling was made vice-president-general in charge of organization. This was the official founding of the largest and most influential of the women's hereditary patriotic societies.[44]

Unlike many other groups, the D.A.R. subordinated state branches to the national body. "It is entirely proper to perfect the state organizations and make them as efficient as possible," declared an early president-general, Mrs. John W. Foster, "but the controlling influence and central administration at the capital of the Republic should always be cherished and maintained. Our revolutionary forefathers learned by experience the weakness and folly of the irresponsible confederacy system, and let us profit by their experience."[45] The new order therefore began at the top with a national organization that formed local units, instead of consolidating scattered branches already in existence as had the G.A.R., W.R.C., U.C.V., and U.D.C. Colonel Robert McCormick might have been pleased that the first D.A.R. chapter was formed in Chicago in May 1891. Atlanta and New York City followed suit the next month and by 1897 there were 397 chapters in thirty-eight states, Massachusetts and New York leading.

Some idea of how the organization spread can be gleaned from the experience of Kentucky's first state regent, Miss Lucretia Hart Clay. Determined to be "sensible" and "methodical," she prepared a list of all towns in the state with a population of more than a thousand with their dates of founding. She then concentrated on the older places, assuming that they would have a higher proportion

[44] Ada P. Kimberley to Maud Greenwalt, Oct. 6, 1915, "National Board of Management," *Magazine of Daughters of the American Revolution*, XLVII (Dec. 1915), 434; "Minutes of the Earliest Meetings of the National Board of Management," *American Monthly Magazine*, XIX (Sept. 1901), 224; Mary S. Lockwood and Emily Lee Sherwood, *Story of the Records* (Washington, 1906), p. 23.
[45] "Proceedings of Fifth Continental Congress," *American Monthly Magazine* VIII (April 1896), 447.

of Revolutionary stock who might be interested. But then she realized that in hardly any of them did she know even one person who
could be appointed the local regent. By appealing first to a politician,
then to a "literary man," and finally to the clergy she secured the
names of at least one prominent citizen in all but three places.
These leads were successful opening wedges for forming a network
of chapters.[46]

Despite this emphasis on local branches directly subordinate to
national headquarters, state organizations did develop in the form
of annual conferences of chapters. The first of these were held in
Connecticut, Pennsylvania, and New Jersey in 1894. They, however,
did not choose the state regents, who were elected instead by the
various state delegations at the national convention, or continental
congress, in Washington. At the beginning of 1894 there were only
twenty-six such officials, but by the end of 1897 there was one for
every state except Idaho and Nevada. Before the end of the decade,
chapter regents had also been appointed for Halifax, Geneva, Naples,
and Honolulu and a charter issued for a chapter in the last place.

The society made slow progress in two sections of the country,
the West and the South. In 1897 the states or territories not having
a single D.A.R. chapter were Indian Territory, Montana, New Mexico, North Carolina, North Dakota, Oklahoma, South Dakota, West
Virginia, and Wyoming. Those having only one chapter were Arkansas, Colorado, Florida, Louisiana, Mississippi, Oregon, and Utah.
Leaders in the Western states reported little interest in the new
organization. The story of the D.A.R. in New Mexico illustrates
their difficulties. While riding in a steam launch on Lake Michigan
during the 1893 World's Fair, Miss Desha and the president-general,
Mrs. Adlai E. Stevenson, persuaded Mrs. Bradford Prince, wife of
the territorial governor, to become organizing regent. But Mrs.
Prince found little response to the application blanks she distributed.
Many women paid no attention to them at all, "some of the women
were annoyed, others plainly said that they did not even know their
grandmothers' names, others liked the idea but thought it meant
the beginning of an aristocratic set, and frankly said that the Society
could never be started here." For several years Mrs. Prince had no

[46] "Work of the Chapters," *American Monthly Magazine*, XVIII (Jan. 1901), 31.

success. She finally found one woman who agreed to take some application blanks, to whose husband she tried to hand them on the street one day. Pushing them away so emphatically that he backed off the sidewalk, he declared with honest Western vigor, "Madam, we want nothing of that kind." Mrs. Prince, however, rallied with, "Well, take them home to your wife . . . a woman who can claim descent from the Randolphs of Virginia, and from Benjamin Harrison, the Signer, *ought* to belong to this Society." For some reason this retort silenced him, and she won her first recruit, Mrs. Frances Cross. Thereafter for a year these two, the sole members, proceeded to hold meetings, one making motions and the other seconding them, until Mrs. Cross doubled their rolls by finding two more candidates.[47]

That the West proved such unpromising soil was scarcely surprising, for despite pronouncements of the Census Bureau and the writings of Frederick Jackson Turner, even after 1890 it was so close to frontier conditions as to lack the urban development which was essential for the spread of these organizations. Already the S.A.R. had encountered difficulties in areas like South Dakota and Montana because of the great distances and scattered population, and the D.A.R. faced the same obstacles. "In this broad new West, especially in South Dakota, the work of forming Chapters is slow and difficult," declared an early leader in that state. "The enthusiasm created by the friction of mind with mind, which is supreme in cities or densely inhabited neighborhoods, is lacking in this scattered and shifting population." [48] A large proportion of the inhabitants were of recent immigrant background and hence ineligible, while the remainder, far removed from the large libraries that were starting genealogical departments, found it difficult to trace their pedigrees back through several migrations to their original ancestors. A lot of them did not want to anyway. The lack of any local associations with events of the Revolution lessened interest in any organizations historical in nature and certainly a West, never tradi-

---

[47] "Annual Reports of State Regents," *American Monthly Magazine*, XVIII (June 1901), 1094.

[48] "What We Are Doing and Chapter Work," *American Monthly Magazine*, XV (Aug. 1899), 190.

tional-minded at best, which was undergoing a Populist revolt at this same time, was more engrossed in debates over the future than concern for the past.

On the other hand, while the South certainly valued tradition, it was often of a different sort. Moreover, it too lacked urban centers and was scarcely prosperous in these years of unrest. South Carolina's regent argued that "Our people are, by nature, extremely conservative and slow to grasp a new movement." If true, this might seem another manifestation of the South's rural character, though she interpreted this attitude more conventionally: "From Revolutionary days they have shown an independent spirit and a disposition to direct their own affairs and localize their efforts within State borders." [49] Furthermore, Southern ladies saw no need to make public proclamation of their ancestry. "Do you mean to say, my dear, that I must prove I am a lady?" was their question. The "reserved, proud woman, conscious of her birth and breeding," found this "indelicate," and the D.A.R. often seemed to her "full of clamoring pretentious persons eagerly showing chapter and verse to prove their claims." [50] It so happened that the poor condition of public records, compared with those of New England, often made this proof difficult even if they had overcome their scruples. What actually happened in many cases, however, was that to the Southern woman of the nineties who turned to club life at all, the United Daughters of the Confederacy seemed far more important than the D.A.R., a demonstration that even at this late date sectionalism often had a stronger emotional hold than nationalism.

Despite these handicaps, the society's growth was substantial enough so that it was the only one of the Civil War or hereditary associations to contemplate erecting a permanent headquarters. The task of verifying applications soon led to the establishment of a reference library of over eight hundred volumes as well as a cross-reference catalogue of more than six thousand cards. As early as December 1891, the national board of management voted to set aside all life membership fees as a building fund. Throughout the

---

[49] "Third Continental Congress of the National Society of the Daughters of the American Revolution," *American Monthly Magazine,* IV (June 1894), 612.

[50] Mrs. Annie White Mell, "Obstacles to D.A.R. Work in the South," *American Monthly Magazine,* XI (Oct. 1897), 369.

decade the Daughters were busy raising money for this building, proud that it would be "the first structure of its kind raised by women in this or any other country." It was to be a memorial to the Revolutionary fathers that amidst "the teeming materialization of the present age" would remind the nation of its fundamental moral principles.[51] By 1900 $50,000 had been secured toward their goal. Ground was broken in 1902 and the cornerstone of the present Memorial Continental Hall was laid in 1904.

But, as in the Sons of the Revolution and the Colonial Dames, dissension also quickly rent the D.A.R. Within three weeks of the society's formation McDowell was writing apprehensively to Mrs. Darling, "I have feared . . . that you ladies were all at swords points." [52] The trouble was that Mrs. Darling was a domineering, aggressive woman who handled the organization as if it were her private property. "She had got the 'big head,'" McDowell later testified, "all the other ladies were to be her satellites." [53] In vain he warned her that in writing to newly designated officials it would be better to say "You have been elected" rather than "I have appointed you Vice-President" and that it hit the wrong note to reply to a resignation, "I have accepted it with pleasure." "Before the meeting of organization, you were acting individually," he reminded her, "but now officially, collectively, and the 'I' naturally grates." [54]

In the next few months relations between Mrs. Darling and the society's national board of management grew steadily worse. The board refused to pay the bill for ten thousand application blanks which Mrs. Darling had ordered. She in turn ignored the board's decision to change membership fees and continued to send in the previous sum until the board had to appoint a committee to straighten out the financial confusion. In May 1891, Mrs. Darling turned against McDowell, informing him that she had dropped him from the D.A.R. advisory board and was preferring charges against him to the president of the New Jersey S.A.R. for "conduct un-

[51] Daughters of the American Revolution, *Third Report 1898–1900* (Washington, 1901), p. 60.
[52] McDowell to Mrs. Darling, Oct. 28, 1890, McDowell Letterbooks.
[53] McDowell to Henry Baldwin, March 4, 1902, *ibid.*
[54] McDowell to Mrs. Darling, Oct. 29, 1890, Flora Adams Darling, *Founding and Organization of the Daughters of the American Revolution and the Daughters of the Revolution* (Philadelphia, 1901), pp. 178–179.

becoming a gentleman." The national board promptly denied her right to take such action, in retaliation dropped her private enterprise, the *Adams' Magazine,* as the society's official journal, and finally asked her to cease forming chapters. Mrs. Darling replied that she would no longer recognize the national board, forbade the use of her name, declared the board her appointees subject to her direction, insisted its members were conspiring against her, and even threatened them with legal proceedings. By now she was also accusing McDowell of ambitions to become president of the United States, while at the same time that gentleman was casting aspersions on the validity of her ancestral claims and stating she wanted to be "Czar of all the Russias." [55]

On July 1 the board removed her from the office of Vice-President in Charge of Organization of Chapters, and Mrs. Darling withdrew to form her own organization the following month called the Daughters of the Revolution. Its nucleus was the Darling Chapter, D.A.R., in New York City, which in October seceded to join the new group. Though it did not spread as rapidly or extensively as the D.A.R., by 1895 it had organizations in seventeen states and followers in several more, as well as in Canada, Mexico, the Philippines, France, and Sweden. Actually many persons (including Grant Wood in his celebrated painting) have used the term Daughters of the Revolution when actually they had in mind the D.A.R., not knowing there were two rival societies.

This was not the end of the splitting-off process. In 1896 a bitter controversy over the reëlection of Mrs. Edward Steers as president-general of the Daughters of the Revolution required the presence of four policemen. During the voting the "independents" were kept waiting in an unheated hall in near-zero weather, and when the distinguished social historian, Mrs. Alice Morse Earle, slipped into the ballot room she was forcibly ejected, Mrs. Steers "personally pushing her from behind . . . admidst great disorder and cries of 'shame' and 'outrage.' " [56] When the independents won anyway through complicated technicalities involving proxy votes, the de-

---

[55] Flora Adams Darling, "Official Statement from Mrs. Flora Adams Darling, Director-General," *Adams' Magazine of General Literature,* I (Oct. 1891), 31; Mrs. Darling, "To the Regents," p. 18; *New York World,* Aug. 3, 1891.

[56] "Daughters of the Revolution," *Spirit of '76,* II (Jan. 1896), 116.

feated group, led by Mrs. Steers, seceded to form the short-lived Dames of the Revolution, in New York. Here was the end product of a series of schismatic reactions from the Sons of the Revolution through the S.A.R., D.A.R., and D.R.

Meanwhile, not content with the Daughters of the Revolution, Mrs. Darling had extended her empire with the formation of the United States Daughters of 1812, whose first branch appeared in Ohio in September 1891. It admitted women lineally descended from those who had served in either civil or military capacity in the War of 1812 or even during "the period of causes which led to that war" between 1784 and 1812. After additional organizations had been established in New York, Louisiana, Texas, and Michigan, a meeting in New York in January 1895 formed a General Society and thereafter Mrs. Darling appointed regents for several more states.

When, because of ill health, Mrs. Darling turned the work over to Mrs. William Gerry Slade in January 1897, the new national president discovered that most of these state regents had considered their appointments purely honorary. Mrs. Darling's personal influence had kept the association alive in New York, a small group still survived in Michigan, and another had been formed in Pennsylvania. The Louisiana branch, however, maintained an independent existence in the best Southern states'-rights tradition, while the original one in Ohio had completely disintegrated. Furthermore, divergence in eligibility requirements, Mrs. Darling's arbitrary and erratic assignment of membership numbers, and a general confusion in record-keeping had produced such administrative chaos that additional recruiting was postponed for four years. After Mrs. Slade had achieved some system and uniformity, Maryland, Ohio, and Maine reinforced the four existing societies in 1900.

Meanwhile, somewhat to the annoyance of the original order, there had arisen a Daughters of the Cincinnati in 1894, while the following year saw the birth of a feminine equivalent of the Holland Society in the Daughters of Holland Dames and of the New England Societies in the Society of New England Women. In 1898 Miss Eugenia Washington with two of her associates in the D.A.R. formed the Daughters of Founders and Patriots, which complemented the Order of Founders and Patriots. And of course Texas

women had to have their own organization. Though the Daughters
of the Lone Star Republic, formed at Houston in 1891 and renamed
the Daughters of the Republic of Texas the next year, achieved what
the rest of the country might call only local importance, it was
doubtless quite sufficient for its following.

A conspicuous feature of these years was the lack of coeducational
associations. The best known exception was the Society of Mayflower Descendants. Its founder, Richard Henry Greene, is said to
have derived the idea from his frequent chats with the noted
philanthropist, Mrs. Russell Sage, during her visits to the New York
Genealogical and Biographical Society. When she commented one
day, "Captain, do you know that I am a descendant of one of the
Pilgrims?" Greene replied, "Oh, yes, I know it perfectly well. You
are a descendant of Myles Standish." To her astonished, "How did
you know that?" he gave merely a cryptic, "Never mind. I have
known it all along." This curious exchange presumably gave him
the idea for an association of the Pilgrims' offspring.[57] Organized
in the genealogical society's rooms in December 1894, it welcomed
all descendants of the *Mayflower* passengers. It combined with
similar groups that appeared in Connecticut, Massachusetts, and
Pennsylvania to form the General Society of Mayflower Descendants in January 1897 at, appropriately enough, Plymouth. About the
only other organizations admitting both sexes were the Huguenot
Society, formed in New York as early as 1883 for the scions of the
early French Protestant settlers, and the awkwardly titled Order of
Descendants of Colonial Governors Prior to 1750, founded in 1896
by Miss Mary Cabell Richardson of Covington, Kentucky. Presumably the latter was highly exclusive, for it admitted only those heirs
of colonial officials who also belonged to the Colonial Dames, Society
of Colonial Wars, or the Mayflower Descendants (this became a bit
like working one's way via Hasty Pudding toward a final club at
Harvard). Despite these difficult but apparently not insuperable
barriers, by the turn of the century it had a handful of followers in
Michigan and New York City.

This craze for hereditary societies presently reached rather bizarre
extremes. The Order of the White Crane, organized by Dr. J. G. B.

<hr>

[57] Society of Mayflower Descendants in the State of New York, *Bulletin No. 5*
(New York, 1916), p. 15.

Bullard, the Indian Agency physician at Pima, Arizona, after con-versations with one Henry W. Warren of Minnesota, was named for "White Crane, the Hereditary Chief of the Ancient Tribe of the Ojibway Indians, now called the Chippewas" (Warren was de-scended on the maternal side from a Chippewa chief) and admitted the descendants of Aztec, Indian, or Toltec kings or of colonial set-tlers before 1783. With some confusion of purpose, the members had to be Aryan, except, of course, those entering on the Indian lines; there is no evidence that it ever became especially extensive.

Other suggestions never got beyond the paper stage. With so many orders honoring the patriots of the Revolution, one enthusiastic citizen urged that the members of the D.A.R. and S.A.R. who were also descended from Tories start a Loyalist body. "What better open-ing," she asked, "for overtures of peace between children of bitter foes—for an effort towards exterminating those political animosities between the United States and Canada, animosities which can be traced back in most cases to the Loyalist emigration?" [58] But this ancestral ambivalence was apparently too much to ask even of this generation. The next step was a proposal for a Society of Descendants of Non-Combattants, for the progeny of Quakers and others whose principles had forbidden active participation and whose insignia therefore would be an olive branch. Presumably this was a hoax, but one cannot be sure, for almost none of these people seem to have had any sense of humor.

After Americans had exhausted most of the possibilities of native ancestry, they turned to orders based on noble or royal descent. Searches for a family "tree whose branches boast the charms Of mottoes, crests and coats-of-arms" [59] and for aristocratic antecedents among the European peerage aroused the zeal of citizens ranging from William Waldorf Astor to Mary Baker Eddy.[60] Charles H. Browning's *Americans of Royal Descent* appeared first in 1883 in an edition of only 120 copies but then saw a second and third version in 1891 and 1894 and reached its seventh edition by 1911. The genealogist of the Yankee Delanos, for example, in a volume ap-

---

[58] Jane Marsh Parker, "To Descendants of Patriots and Loyalists A Plea for a New Patriotic-Hereditary Society," *American Historical Register* (March 1895), p. 638.

[59] Arthur Guiterman, *Gaily the Troubadour* (New York, 1936), p. 29.

[60] Dixon Wecter, *The Saga of American Society* (New York, 1937), pp. 390–396.

pearing in 1899, traced that seafaring family to nearly every royal house of Europe and always signed himself Mortimer Delano de Lannoy to emphasize his noble origin, while the historian of the S.A.R. chapter in Portsmouth, New Hampshire, boasted that its president, vice-president, and several members "can trace their ancestry to Pharaoh, King of Egypt, in an unbroken line from Dr. Jean Fernald, who was physician to King Henry II of France. . . ." [61]

In 1892 the Aryan Order of St. George or the Holy Roman Empire in the Colonies of America became available for those descended in direct male line from a noble, knight, or a person decorated by royalty, from civil or military officials in the colonies or from families entitled to coats-of-arms. Five years later, after toying with the idea of an Order of the Crown for the descendants of Charlemagne, Browning, a Philadelphian, organized the Baronial Order of Runnemede for the descendants of the barons who had secured Magna Carta, while in 1898 a Detroit lady, herself resplendently named Miss Henrietta Lynde de Neville Farnsworth, formed the Order of the Crown of America for women of royal descent who also belonged to the Colonial Dames. While in a sense these were obviously on the periphery of American patriotic societies, they nevertheless reflected the same passion for heredity as the basis for association.

This ancestral-conscious decade did not spare even the children. At the D.A.R.'s congress in 1895 the regent of a chapter in Concord, Massachusetts, Mrs. Harriet Lothrop (she had moved into Nathaniel Hawthorne's old home, Wayside, and as "Margaret Sidney" was busy turning out the *Five Little Peppers* series) argued the necessity of interesting impressionable youngsters in American history and thereby making them more patriotic. At her suggestion the convention authorized the formation of the Children of the American Revolution to train youthful Revolutionary descendants in American institutions and principles. Fortified by endorsements from former President Benjamin Harrison and Commissioner of Education William T. Harris, the society was incorporated in Washington in April 1895, and the first chapter formed in Mrs. Lothrop's home town of Concord in May. Despite some hostility on the ground that children "have enough to do now in school without adding more

---

[61] Paul Jones Club of the Sons of the American Revolution at Portsmouth, N.H., *Year Book 1897* (Portsmouth, N.H., n.d.), p. 14.

work for the already overtaxed young minds," [62] by 1897 there were one hundred and two societies in twenty-six states, the largest number being in Connecticut, the District of Columbia, New York, and Massachusetts. Not to be outdone by its rival, the Daughters of the Revolution in 1897 created a Junior Sons and Daughters of the Revolution which soon spread to New York, Massachusetts, and Indiana.

By 1900 no man, woman, or child whose lineage went back a century in this country needed to deny himself the company of his genealogical peers. A few years later Octavus Roy Cohen deftly satirized the American mania for "joining" with his stories of Mr. Florian Slappey and his grandiloquent colleagues in the fraternal order of the Sons and Daughters of I Will Arise. He might just as aptly have described the determined and pretentious champions of hereditary merit as the Sons and Daughters of I Will Descend.

[62] "Young People's Department," *American Monthly Magazine*, XII (March 1898), 324.

IV

Recruits and Brass

HOW many people joined these veterans' and hereditary societies? What sort of persons were attracted to them? How much did it cost them? Just how snobbish or democratic were their criteria of eligibility? Were there any contrasts between the followings of the two categories of organizations? What type of leaders did the associations pick to represent them? Were they at all different from the rank and file of members? Were there any tangible rewards for office holding? Did these groups put up a united front or were there family quarrels and feuds among them? These are some of the questions that inevitably arise concerning the membership and leadership of the patriotic leagues.

By all odds the Grand Army of the Republic was the largest of all these organizations. In 1868 and 1869 it was commonly believed to have at least 240,000 adherents, with more extravagant estimates ranging from 400,000 to 600,000. At this time its stronghold was the Middle West. In 1866 Illinois allegedly had 100,000 members; Wisconsin, 50,000, and Ohio, 30,000. With the decline of interest in the seventies came a sharp drop, with the total number throughout the decade ranging between 25,000 and 30,000. Its strength had now shifted to the East, Massachusetts alone reporting more than 10,000 names, while Pennsylvania and New York were next, fluctuating between 3000 and 5000. But 1879 marked the beginning of a climb which lasted for several years. The peak years of this expansion were 1882, when nearly 60,000 recruits pushed the total to 134,000, and 1883, when more than 70,000 additional veterans raised it to 215,000. Thereafter, though the total number continued to rise steadily for some time, the rate of increase slackened and actually during the hard times in the middle of the eighties the order was suspending

25,000 to 50,000 annually for nonpayment of dues. In the twelve months ending March 1886, the 54,000 dropped for this reason amounted to twice the number it had gained. Nevertheless, not until 1890 did the G.A.R. reach its peak with 409,489 members. By then it centered in the Middle West again. In 1890 Ohio was the largest branch, with more than 46,000 members. Though Pennsylvania and New York ranked second and third, seven out of the ten largest departments lay in the Mississippi Valley. The biggest individual post, however, was in the urban East at Lynn, Massachusetts, with over a thousand members; posts in at least five other cities had more than seven hundred each.

After 1890 the order began a slow decline due largely to natural causes. Having passed the peak of life, the veterans were now beginning to die off. Indicative of this was the first death of a commander-in-chief while in office in 1899. Often the members' infirmities caused them to cease attending meetings or paying dues so that the rolls declined further. In some areas there was a noticeable surrender of post charters. Only in a few Southern and Western states to which the veterans were emigrating did the organization still grow. Even so, in 1900 it retained a substantial following of 276,662. At no time, however, had it captured the allegiance of all the veterans. In 1897 the Pension Bureau estimated that there were 1,285,471 survivors of the conflict; at that date the organization claimed only 319,456 of them. Commanders of the various state branches usually guessed that from one-tenth to a half of those eligible within their jurisdictions had joined.

No other Civil War veterans' society came anywhere near the G.A.R. in size. Thus the Union Veteran Legion, hampered by its more stringent eligibility, reached its high point of 9256 in 1894 and at the end of the decade had less than 7000. Over half of these were in Pennsylvania, with Ohio its only other major stronghold. The Naval Veterans numbered about 5000 in the nineties and the Ex-Prisoners of War some 2000. By the turn of the century the small size of these groups was becoming so pronounced that the Union Veterans' Union decided to conceal its numbers, feeling that publication would make it less effective as a pressure group. The associations designed primarily for officers were equally small. The Loyal Legion managed to climb to 9000 by the late nineties, but that was largely because it was also admitting descendants; New York, Pennsylvania, Massachusetts, Ohio, and the District of Columbia accounted for over half this number. The various army societies seem to have had only between 500 and 1000 members.

The affiliated organizations reached fairly large proportions. From 4000 in 1884 the Sons of Veterans grew to 54,000 in 1891, but by 1900 it had dropped to less than half that number. Between 1889 and 1901 the order recruited 163,000 individuals, but at the end of that period retained only 26,000. At its national meetings the leaders constantly discussed this problem without arriving at any solution. Some suspected that there were too many young boys in the order who quickly lost their enthusiasm, while many felt that it would never attract large numbers unless it introduced more ritualistic work or provided insurance features. What strength it had was concentrated in Massachusetts, Pennsylvania, Ohio, and Illinois.

On the other hand, the steady growth of the Woman's Relief Corps was one more sign of the mounting interest of American women in club life. Its 10,000 members in 1884 had become 118,000 in 1900. Ohio and Massachusetts, the homes of the original corps, continued to lead in membership. Its rivals were less successful. The Ladies of the G.A.R., strongest in Pennsylvania, New Jersey, and Kansas, managed to rise to 25,000 by 1898, but the Ladies' Aid of the Sons of Veterans numbered only about 8000, and the Daughters of Veterans about a mere 1000.

It is next to impossible to estimate with any degree of accuracy the following of either the Mexican War veterans or the various Confederate organizations. In 1879 the National Association of Mexican War Veterans claimed about 5000 active members, but it never kept any careful record except a list of people who had applied for its membership badge, and even that figure was cumulative and did not allow for those who had died or lost interest. In deference to the states'-rights tradition Southern associations were so decentralized that there was no reliable count of their total, but again it was the women who flourished. By 1898 the United Daughters of the Confederacy had acquired more than 11,000 members, chiefly in Virginia, Georgia, and Texas.

In striking contrast to the Civil War organizations was the small size of the hereditary societies. They never made any particular effort to attract a wide following and their growth was almost limited to the Northeast. Once again the figures showed that it was the day of organized women, for the D.A.R. was the only ancestral order to achieve any considerable size, more than 30,000 by 1900. It made its greatest appeal in the Eastern states of Connecticut, New York, and Pennsylvania; the largest individual chapters were in Chicago, New York, and Pittsburgh. Though the S.A.R. also advanced steadily, by the end of the nineties it still had less than 10,000 members; its strongholds were Massachusetts, New York, and Connecticut. It never came near McDowell's hope that it might win 100,000 or even 1,000,000 Revolutionary descendants. Its more conservative rival, the Sons of the Revolution, was even smaller. Indeed, for a long time it deliberately confined itself to the sixty persons who could meet comfortably in the famous Long Room of Fraunces Tavern in New York. By 1900 it had progressed to less than 6000, of whom New York and Pennsylvania accounted for more than half. Of the remaining associations, the Colonial Dames reached 4000 by 1900, the Society of Colonial Wars amounted to about 2300, and the C.A.R. was under 1000. All the other societies, both men's and women's, were 500 or less. A striking feature of nearly all these groups was that their strength was almost entirely confined to the highly urbanized states of Massachusetts, Connecticut, New York, and Pennsylvania. Indeed, many of the smaller organizations had scarcely a member outside of one or two metropolitan areas such as New York or Philadelphia.

This limited membership was deliberate. While the veterans' associations were usually anxious to be as large as possible so as to enhance their influence upon legislators, the hereditary societies had no desire to attract hordes of people, for that would render impossible any pretensions to the exclusiveness which was often their strongest appeal. Thus the St. Nicholas Society set its limit at six hundred and fifty, while the Colonial Order of the Acorn allowed only two hundred in each state, and the Society of American Wars but one hundred. Typical of this viewpoint was the report of a committee of the Connecticut Society of Colonial Wars in 1903 "that a society of moderate size, homogeneous in its make-up, emphasizing the social qualities, earnest in its aims, can better attain the objects for which it exists than one much larger which might prove unwieldy and destructive of sociability."[1] In similar vein the Daughters of the Cincinnati, one gathers, found even the D.A.R. too undiscriminating and vulgar. "While there is a long list of applicants for membership," the secretary reported somewhat smugly in 1898, "it is hardly probable that we will ever become a large organization, but our strength will lie in the future as it has in the past, in an avoidance of notoriety, and an absence of strife."[2]

Not only did the two major types of patriotic groups, the Civil War societies and the hereditary bodies, differ sharply in their size, but they appealed to quite different strata of the population. Not surprisingly, since a large proportion of the Union Army had come from farms and the mechanical trades while the wealthier often bought substitutes, the G.A.R. consisted largely of farmers, laborers, and small businessmen of limited means. The United Confederate Veterans, as might have been expected in the South, had so large a percentage of farmers that its meetings had to be scheduled at the times most convenient for them. Statements of the National Association of Mexican War Veterans, though suspect in their emphasis on the ex-soldiers' need for assistance, indicated that its members came from a low-income group. The Sons of Veterans also represented a comparatively humble economic and social level. The great majority were farmers, skilled laborers, mechanics, clerks, and bookkeepers; ministers, physicians, lawyers, and teachers were few among their ranks.[3]

One result was that these groups were obliged to charge modest dues. The original constitution of the G.A.R. required only a dollar's initiation and dues of $2.60. Thereafter the sums seem to have varied according to individual posts, but in the seventies the usual muster-in (or initiation) fee ranged from $1.50 to $2.50 and the per capita tax (or dues) from $1.50 to $2.00. The Union Veterans' Union had an initiation fee of $1.50 and annual dues of $1, while the Union Veteran Legion's figure for each was $2. The Sons of Veterans and the W.R.C. had similar charges. In 1896 the average

---

[1] Connecticut Society of Colonial Wars, *Papers and Addresses* (n.p., n.d.), p. 4.

[2] Daughters of the Cincinnati, *Year Book 1898* (n.p., 1898), p. 29.

[3] Sons of Veterans, U.S.A., *Proceedings of the Eighth Annual Encampment 1889* (n.p., n.d.), p. 113; *Eleventh Annual Encampment 1892* (Topeka, 1892), p. 100; *Fourteenth Annual Encampment 1895* (Des Moines, 1895), p. 125.

muster-in fee for the Sons was $1.55 and the average dues $1.97. The W.R.C.'s initiation fees in the eighties ranged from $.63 to $.95; later it set $1.50 as its minimum sum for membership. The Society of the Army of the Cumberland felt that its charge of $5 was what had kept many ex-enlisted men from joining and so frequently was the proposal made to lure these prospects by a reduction that one official in annoyance called it "Banquo's ghost." The society retained its high assessment, but also its small size.

Another indication of the background of their members was the disastrous effect that the depression following the Panic of 1893 had upon Civil War societies. The Grand Army, already declining from natural causes and vulnerable because of its large numbers in the lower economic brackets, was hard hit. Between 1894 and 1897 department officials from New England to California repeatedly attributed the reduction in revenues, suspension of members for nonpayment of dues, and disbanding of posts to the hard times. With the death rate remaining relatively constant, between 1892 and 1893 the order lost only 2657 members, but during the next year it lost 27,140 and thereafter between 11,000 and 20,000. With the coming of prosperity at the end of the decade, the number of suspensions declined sharply.

The story was repeated in other veterans' and affiliated organizations. Leaders of the Union Veteran Legion complained that it was difficult to establish new branches and that in the existing ones unemployed members were unable to pay their dues. The Sons of Veterans and the Woman's Relief Corps also blamed suspensions and lack of growth upon the "financial stringency." In the South, the economic difficulties forced the United Confederate Veterans first to postpone and then to abandon its meeting for 1893.

The hereditary societies meanwhile were consciously appealing to a quite different group. "The Society is not simply an association of those who have descended from colonial ancestors of distinction," stated a description of the Connecticut Society of Colonial Wars, "but has an equally prime prerequisite—that of honorable career and high social standing . . . and, naturally, attracts the best material only to its membership." [4] In like manner the registrar-general of

[4] "Celebrations and Proceedings," *American Historical Register* (June 1895), p. 1072.

the S.A.R. boasted that "many men of the very brightest social standing and social reputation belong to our organization in all parts of the country." [5] Analysis of the occupations of the members shows that these groups did attract mostly professional and well-to-do businessmen. The greatest number of the S.A.R.'s following in New York, for example, were merchants and manufacturers, while one-third of the roster of the Society of American Wars were in academic life. [6]

As a result, though not large numerically, these leagues had a remarkably high proportion of people of distinction of one sort or another. The smaller the group, the more often it drew almost exclusively from the Social Register. At one time the Holland Society sparkled with no less than ten Roosevelts, four Stuyvesants, nine Schuylers, and ten Van Rensselaers, while the Sons of the Revolution (with Senator Matt Quay striking a peculiar note on the Pennsylvania list and Julian Hawthorne and Paul Leicester Ford lending a quasi-literary tone to the New York Society) had a galaxy of Livingstons, Biddles, Cadwalladers, Hamiltons, Schuylers, Pennypackers, Astors, and Carrolls. The Sons of the American Revolution was considerably less aristocratic but appealed more to men of civic and business eminence like Elihu Root, Chauncey Depew, Vice-President Levi P. Morton, Henry Cabot Lodge and several other Senators, Justice David Brewer of the Supreme Court, President David Jayne Hill of the University of Rochester, the traction king and Secretary of the Navy William C. Whitney, and John D. Rockefeller. But in relation to its size, perhaps no American association has had a more impressive membership than the Society of American Wars, which somehow managed to corral Theodore Roosevelt and Henry Cabot Lodge from government service; President David Starr Jordan of Stanford, Harvard professor Charles Eliot Norton and Woodrow Wilson from the universities; Edward Everett Hale, Charles Dudley Warner, and George W. Cable from literature; Episcopalian bishops William Lawrence and Henry Codman Potter from the church; James Schouler from history; Herbert Putnam from the Library of Congress; and even young Roscoe Pound from

[5] "Celebrations and Proceedings," *ibid.* (April 1895), p. 804.

[6] "Empire State S.A.R.'s First Thousand Members," *Spirit of '76*, II (Aug. 1896), 312–313; "Among the Societies," *ibid.*, III (April 1897), 514.

the nascent field of sociological jurisprudence. Indeed, the very fact that such a curious array of noted men were willing to affiliate with an organization which had almost no vitality or significance suggests once again how ingrained the practice of joining had become even in the most sophisticated circles.

Especially sensitive to social qualifications were the new women's hereditary groups. Entrance into the charmed circle of the Daughters of the Cincinnati came only upon the unanimous invitation of the Board of Managers, and Livingstons, de Peysters, Van Rensselaers, and Frelinghuysens somehow proved the most acceptable. The two varieties of Colonial Dames were even more careful not to bestow their favors too freely. The original society announced that eligibility alone, without express invitation, did not secure admission and even preferred that the names of its members not be revealed to the public. Its attitude received considerable publicity in 1895 when it rejected a great-great-granddaughter of Benjamin Franklin. Rumors varied as to whether this was because Franklin was not considered a gentleman or because there was no proof of his marriage. After considerable turmoil the lady was finally admitted, but this lowering of the standards obliged one of the founders, Mrs. John King Rensselaer, to resign in protest. As the rival order of Dames began to expand, its recording secretary emphasized "the greater importance of exercising an intelligent and judicial judgment upon the fitness of each applicant irrespective of her eligibility by descent. . . ." [7] Such guarantees of discrimination encouraged the Lees and Washingtons of Virginia, Drexels and Biddles of Pennsylvania, Du Ponts and Canbys of Delaware, Van Rensselaers and Livingstons of New York, and Eliots and Lowells of Massachusetts to flock to its banner. Not much room here for the Bumpus girls in their Lawrence flat, despite their impeccable descent from the original Ebenezer!

They might even have had difficulty getting into the less exacting D.A.R. in its early years. At their preliminary gatherings in the summer of 1890 the founders seem to have been interested primarily in women of high social standing. "The Society is to become large, of course, and no invidious lines should be drawn or aristocratic

[7] Colonial Dames of the State of New York, *Reports of Officers 1898* (n.p., n.d.), p. 10.

distinctions established," its first real head recommended to Mrs. Darling, "but, in the beginning, you must have what our colored brethren, with their natural and distinctive discrimination call 'quality folks,' if the organization is ever to become attractive to that element which secures social success everywhere." She therefore advised that the Daughters "entrench ourselves within the charmed barriers of Revolutionary descent *and* of social consequence." [8] Among the socially prominent women appointed honorary state regents at the beginning were Mrs. Schuyler Hamilton, Mrs. Philip Livington, and Miss Louise Ward McAllister (daughter of the man who coined the phrase "The Four Hundred") in New York and Mrs. Potter Palmer in Chicago. Even in starting a society of the Children of the American Revolution in Norwich, Connecticut, its sponsors, who ordinarily belonged to the parent organization, carefully sent invitations to "sixty-five mothers of the most prominent and influential families." [9] An observer of the D.A.R.'s convention in 1895 concluded that "the Daughters are a fine looking body of women, well dressed and prosperous looking, and most of them of dignified and commanding carriage." [10]

But the D.A.R.'s ambition that caused it to outdo its competitors in size and influence also of necessity made it impossible for the Society to maintain very much exclusiveness. In 1896, for example, the National Board of Management ruled that a San Francisco chapter's requirement that admission be by invitation only was illegal. But if its rolls were not as limited to the elite as the Colonial Dames', it did manage to win such varied celebrities as Mrs. Henry Ward Beecher, Julia Ward Howe, Clara Barton, Mrs. Robert Louis Stevenson, and the youthful president of Mount Holyoke College, Mary E. Woolley. There was also a chapter in Poughkeepsie of thirty-two members, all of whom were Vassar students, and one in New York City made the Infanta Eulalia of Spain an honorary member in recognition of the help her ancestor, Carlos III, had given to the American cause.

[8] M. V. E. Cabell to Flora Adams Darling, Jan. 17, 1891, Flora Adams Darling, *Founding and Organization of the Daughters of the American Revolution and Daughters of the Revolution* (Philadelphia, 1901), p. 175.

[9] "Young People's Department," *American Monthly Magazine,* XII (March 1898), 324.

[10] "Celebrations and Proceedings," *American Historical Register* (March 1895), p. 666.

A logical consequence of their different clientele was that the hereditary societies charged higher sums than did the veterans' groups. While the initiation fees ranged from $2 to $25 and the annual dues from $2 to $10, probably the average figures were a $5 initiation fee and then annual payments of $3 to $6. Only the one trying to make the widest appeal, the D.A.R., made more modest demands of $1 for initiation and $3 a year thereafter. Likewise, it was the only one of these groups whose growth was hampered by the depression after 1893.

As "joining" became such a popular American pastime, disputes over eligibility to both the veterans' and hereditary societies became more and more frequent, sometimes absorbing almost the entire attention of both state and national conventions. The Grand Army of the Republic, anxious to be as powerful as possible, realized that the thinning effects of time would inevitably lessen its effectiveness. At different points sentiment developed to expand the order by admitting three new groups of candidates: involuntary members of the Confederate army who had later joined the Union cause, the sons of the veterans, and the participants in the Spanish-American War. The common purpose of all three proposals was to stave off eventual dissolution.

The plea to receive those who had been conscripted into the Confederate forces and subsequently deserted to the Union side came largely from Southerners, especially in Arkansas and Tennessee, who hoped thereby to build up the order south of the Mason and Dixon line, but its chief effect was merely to produce a flood of emotional oratory from Northerners who sensed a plot to honor their former enemies. "I would not ask a child whose father bled, to decorate the grave of the man who made it an orphan; I would not ask a widow who mourns her husband to go and decorate the grave of the man who killed that husband and tried to destroy the Union," declaimed a delegate to the 1885 national encampment who identified himself as a survivor of Libby Prison. "I would not ask to have brought into this organization any man that ever fought against the old flag, either voluntarily or involuntarily." [11] Though the suggestion kept turning up throughout the eighties and nineties,

[11] Grand Army of the Republic, *Journal of the Nineteenth Annual Session of the National Encampment 1885* (Toledo, 1885), p. 240.

the order consistently rejected it. The same desire to enlarge their branches in the former Confederacy also caused the Southern veterans to refuse to charter Negro posts, but the complete account of the far from edifying efforts of the G.A.R. to draw the color line is best postponed until a discussion of the societies' views on the racial question.

To many, the addition of sons appeared a logical method of preventing the order's dying out. Though this won the support of a number of officials and state sessions, especially after the Panic of 1893 had such a disastrous effect upon the organization, more often it aroused such opposition that the national encampment never took any action. Most veterans seemed to feel that only those who had served in the great conflict could really understand their unique bond and that any undermining of it was "un-American." The same proposal also suffered defeat in the Union Veteran Legion, the Society of the Army of the Cumberland, and the National Association of Mexican War Veterans; only the Union Veterans' Union finally made the concession in the late nineties. At various times Alexander Kenaday urged that the Mexican War Veterans add not only sons but grandsons, brothers, other near male relatives, widows, and even the descendants of all those who migrated in the decade after 1846 into the area acquired by the Treaty of Guadalupe Hidalgo, but never with any success.

When the first conflict since the Civil War produced a new crop of veterans at the close of the century, there was at once sentiment to incorporate them into the G.A.R. Though a few states approved the idea, the fact that it would have allowed some ex-Confederates to join turned most Northerners against it. The Union Veterans' Union rejected a similar proposal. These decisions to welcome neither descendants nor the survivors of subsequent wars doomed the Civil War organizations to slow but certain extinction.

The Sons of Veterans' greatest dilemma was what to do about bastards. The issue became acute with the application of a man said to be the illegitimate son of General Robert Anderson of Fort Sumter fame and a Charleston colored woman. Some contended that he was not responsible for the moral lapses of his father, but in true Victorian fashion Commander-in-Chief Bartow Weeks barred him on the ground that "loyalty to the memories of our deceased ancestors imposes upon us an obligation to preserve their good name from the insidious attacks of those who would elevate themselves upon the ruins of their reputation. . . ." [12] After much debate the national convention decided that in the future illegitimate offspring would not be eligible but that those already in the order might remain.

Within the hereditary societies the greatest disputes over eligibility were over whether to insist upon direct lineal descent or to admit collaterals. This led to the great "mother of a patriot" controversy in the D.A.R. As early as July 1890, Miss Mary Desha asked McDowell whether "descent must be lineal. I have several friends who had distinguished uncles." [13] At one of the first meetings of the society's executive board, attended by only six persons, Miss Desha secured an amendment that lineage should be traced from a Revolutionary patriot "or the mother of a patriot." With the comment, "And a little child shall lead them," she later declared that this idea had originated with McDowell's small daughter. According to her colleague, Mrs. Ellen Hardin Walworth, the founders felt that the clause "would throw the new society into the progressive spirit of the nineteenth, the woman's century, by giving tangible form to the part women had taken in the cause of independence, by granting her the special privilege of giving to the society the descendants of childless heroes." [14] The most obvious "childless hero," of course, was George Washington, and Flora Adams Darling later charged that the chief purpose of the measure was to allow Miss Eugenia Washington to enter the society on the most illustrious line possible.

The admission of collateral members soon raised embarrassing problems. Though apparently there never were more than sixty-seven such women in the society, awkward cases arose such as that of a Virginia applicant who descended from the mother of one patriot and several Tories, her direct ancestor having been one of the latter. Subsequently Mrs. Darling claimed that this was the cause of her leaving the D.A.R. and founding the Daughters of the Revolution, a story that is still commonly believed among members of both societies. Although it is true that Mrs. Darling insisted on strict

[12] Sons of Veterans, U.S.A., *Journal of Proceedings of the Eleventh Annual Encampment 1892* (Topeka, 1892), p. 21.

[13] Mary Desha to William O. McDowell, July 28, 1890, William O. McDowell Scrapbooks, XXXIV, New York Public Library.

[14] "Eligibility," *American Monthly Magazine*, I (Nov. 1892), 494.

lineal descent when she formed the seceding body, the controversy on this matter within the D.A.R. did not develop until several months after she had left it and at the time she had not objected to Miss Desha's amendment.

The real champion of a rigorous lineal requirement was Mrs. N. B. Hogg, the state regent for Pennsylvania, who raised the subject unsuccessfully at the society's first national congress in 1892. Thereafter it was debated extensively within the pages of the *American Monthly Magazine* (the D.A.R.'s official organ), at meetings of the national board of management, of which Mrs. Hogg was a member, and at the annual conventions, or Continental Congresses. Opponents of the clause, of course, charged that it was ridiculous to admit the descendants of those who had opposed the American Revolution. Its defenders argued that it honored the heirless patriots and by allowing a larger membership made the society more powerful. Mrs. Hogg eventually converted a majority of the national board, including the grandniece of America's most famous non-father, Miss Washington herself, but faced a determined opponent in Mrs. H. V. Boynton, who had succeeded Mrs. Darling as vice-president-general in charge of organization. A statement that Mrs. Boynton sent out to all chapter regents attacking the proposed change caused a great stir, provoking what became known as the "war of circulars," and finally led to the board's removing Mrs. Boynton from office, whereupon, after an ardent campaign in her defense, many of her followers resigned. By the time the 1894 congress opened, the issue had produced so much bitter debate and so impeded the society's progress that many delegates agreed heartily with Mary Desha when she exclaimed, "I hope I will never hear the word collateral again as long as I live." [15] The meeting settled the question in favor of Mrs. Hogg by eliminating the disputed clause.

If questions of birth and eligibility proved vexing, the selection of leaders also produced many a tempest in an afternoon teapot. One of the most striking features was the refusal to award the highest offices to the founders. In part this was because the most energetic pioneers in patriotic enterprises like Benjamin F. Stephenson of the G.A.R., Alexander Kenaday of the Mexican War Veterans, William

[15] "Third Continental Congress of the National Society of the Daughters of the American Revolution," *ibid.*, IV (June 1894), 626.

O. McDowell of the S.A.R., and Flora Adams Darling of the D.A.R., Daughters of the Revolution, and Daughters of 1812 were so fanatical and eccentric that their leadership often proved impractical or embarrassing. As the veterans' groups became embroiled in partisan affairs either as machines for particular parties or candidates or as pressure groups for certain legislation, it was natural to turn to men prominent in political life, while the hereditary bodies often preferred the prestige of those eminent in public or social affairs. In time the competition for these positions produced bitter campaigning and intense rivalries.

To Stephenson's great disappointment, the first G.A.R. state convention in Illinois in July 1866 did not elect him commander but instead chose Major General John M. Palmer, a political aspirant in whose regiment Stephenson had served, on the ground that a popular soldier should head the new society. Though Stephenson presided over the first national encampment at Indianapolis the following November, again the members distressed him by naming as commander-in-chief another Republican politician, General Stephen Hurlbut of Illinois. The druggist-doctor accepted the office of adjutant-general, but never overcame his sense of injury. The choice of Hurlbut set a pattern for Grand Army commanders-in-chief that was followed throughout the rest of the century. Nearly every one of them was active in the Republican party. The best known were John A. Logan of Illinois, Blaine's running mate in 1884; Ambrose Burnside of Rhode Island, better remembered for the facial adornment that bears his name; Charles Devens, commemorated by an army fort in his home state of Massachusetts; Lucius Fairchild, governor of Wisconsin and minister to Spain; William Warner, Representative and United States Senator from Missouri; and Russell Alger, governor of Michigan, Secretary of War under McKinley, and United States Senator. One of the few times that the order went outside the political arena to fill its highest post was in 1879, when it honored William Earnshaw, chaplain in a soldiers' home.

While the rank and file of the Grand Army were former enlisted men who had become farmers and wage-earners, the officials tended to be ex-officers who had become successful business and professional men of the upper middle class. Consequently, many members felt that the more prosperous leaders did not look after the interests of

their humbler comrades wholeheartedly and especially were willing
to compromise on such issues as a service pension for all veterans.
This suspicion probably accounted for the recurrent "House of
Lords" agitation in which some elements of the organization, backed
by the *Grand Army Record* of Boston, bitterly attacked the right of
past officers to sit and vote in encampments.

For their size the Loyal Legion and the army societies had a higher
proportion of distinguished names among their leaders. The Loyal
Legion's commanders-in-chief included General Winfield Hancock,
General Philip Sheridan, President Rutherford B. Hayes, Lucius
Fairchild, and Admiral Bancroft Gherardi, while U. S. Grant, Lew
Wallace, Admiral David Farragut, Walter Q. Gresham, and Senator
Joseph R. Hawley filled other national and state offices. The Society
of the Army of the Potomac secured George B. McClellan as its first
president, and a president and vice-president of the Society of the
Army of the Cumberland were the "Rock of Chickamauga," Gen-
eral George M. Thomas, and Sheridan.

The auxiliary bodies could not claim as many notables. Certainly
the heads of the Sons of Veterans were not men of great prominence.
Leland J. Webb, for example, was a lawyer from Topeka who had
risen to be justice of the peace there. Similarly the names of such
Woman's Relief Corps presidents as Sue Sanders, Sarah Mink, Agnes
Hitt, Flo Miller, and Harriet Bodge were not those of women who
achieved distinction in other fields. Two of the W.R.C.'s leaders,
however, did express the growing participation of women in public
affairs. Its second head, Mrs. Kate Sherwood, had continued the
publication of her husband's newspaper in Ohio while he served in
the Civil War, later contributed to Cleveland and Toledo newspapers, for many years edited the woman's department of the
National Tribune, and finally became Washington correspondent
for a newspaper syndicate. She was the author of two volumes of
verse and several patriotic playlets. Later active in the D.A.R.
as well as the W.R.C., she was also a pioneer worker in Toledo for
both women's clubs and woman suffrage. In 1889 Mrs. Annie Wittenmyer of Pennsylvania became national president. While working
for the United States Christian Commission during the war, she
first attracted attention by introducing diet kitchens into the army.
She later inaugurated the movement for a soldiers' home in Iowa,

was a founder and first corresponding secretary of the Home Missionary Society of the Methodist Episcopal Church, published two religious papers in Philadelphia, *The Christian Woman* and *The Christian Child,* and also found time to become the first president of the W.C.T.U. and publisher of its monthly organ, *Woman's Temperance Union.*[16]

Like Stephenson in the G.A.R., the founder of the Mexican War Veterans, Alexander Kenaday, never became its official head. For their president the members turned to General James Denver. Though he had once attracted considerable notoriety by killing a California editor in a duel, he was better known as a Democratic politician whom President Buchanan had appointed territorial governor of Kansas and for whom the Colorado city was named. Apparently he possessed important material and cultural qualifications for the post. Reports declared that he "is rich, and his father-in-law is richer." He was known as "one of the best book buyers in the country" and the owner of "a splendid library. His mind runs to history and belles lettres." [17] He headed the Mexican War Veterans for eighteen years until his death in 1892, when General Mahlon D. Manson of Indiana succeeded him. But though never titular head, Kenaday was more successful than Stephenson in retaining control of the organization he had sired. In his position of secretary he actually remained its dominating force. Some members questioned the propriety of his leading the association's drive for pensions at the same time that he operated an office in Washington as a claims agent, and others winced at his strongly partisan political views and amazingly left-wing social and economic opinions, but their criticism had little effect.

The Confederate societies usually followed the pattern of the Union organizations. The veterans selected as their first chief the popular General John B. Gordon, former United States senator, governor of Georgia, and member of the Bourbon political triumvirate of Colquitt, Brown and Gordon. J. E. B. Stuart, son of the famous cavalry leader, became the first commander-in-chief of the United Sons of Confederate Veterans. The early heads of the

[16] W. H. Daniels, *The Temperance Reform and Its Great Reformers* (New York, 1879), pp. 314–320.

[17] Quoted from *National Republican,* March 30, in *Vedette* (Washington, D.C.), April 15, 1883.

U.D.C. were no better known nationally than those of the W.R.C., but the interests of the first president, Mrs. Caroline Goodlett, though largely eleemosynary in nature, showed that the tendencies of the age were affecting even the conservative South. She was the first vice-president of the Humane Society of Nashville, a member of the Board of Associated Charities of Tennessee and of the Board of Managers of the Protestant Orphan Asylum and Home, active in the National Conference of Charities, and president of the Masonic Widows' and Orphans' Home.

While the duties of heads of veterans' societies were almost entirely ceremonial, they nevertheless could constitute practically a full-time job. A Grand Army commander-in-chief was expected to go about the country visiting as many departments as possible, and a state commander similarly inspected the posts within his territory. As the organization grew larger, these demands became quite taxing. In 1881 Commander-in-Chief Louis Wagner reported that he had traveled 11,800 miles, in nineteen states. He had attended "the meetings of twenty Posts, ten Department Encampments, five Reunions, two Encampments under canvas, two Hall Dedications, one unveiling of a Monument, four Memorial Services, fourteen Camp-fires and thirty other gatherings of soldiers." [18] Impressive as was this list, two years later Paul Van Der Voort announced he had gone 40,402 miles in thirty-eight states. He had been absent from home 265 days in the preceding year and given 143 addresses. Though a decade later Thomas Clarkson covered only 36,000 miles, he appeared at meetings in every state and territory except Florida and Arizona. Even the head of a smaller organization, the Union Veteran Legion, traversed 7772 miles during his term. Though as yet the heads of women's auxiliaries were reluctant to travel as extensively, one W.R.C. president attended sixteen state conventions from Maine to Washington, three corps meetings in Montana, and organized a department in Idaho.

The burdens of a state commander were hardly less onerous. While commander of the Wisconsin department, Lucius Fairchild described to his brother the number of "campfires" he had visited. "I have a lot more on my list to attend," he added, "*That* is one of

---

[18] Grand Army of the Republic, *Journal of the Fifteenth Annual Session of the National Encampment 1881* (Philadelphia, 1881), p. 746.

the chief duties of the Commander if he can talk at all & I am determined to discharge *every* duty pertaining to the office that the boys will be glad they elected me." [19] In Massachusetts Commander John Hersey claimed to have traveled 8000 miles during his year of office and to have met 17,000 members.

The financial burden of these tours became so great that it soon seemed that only millionaires would be able to afford office. The alternative was to reimburse the chiefs. Van Der Voort received $1500 traveling expenses for the year 1882–1883, and by 1886 the commander-in-chief was voted $2000 for this purpose. Even so, the new head, Lucius Fairchild, found the sum insufficient. "Do what I can to pinch like the devil in some directions," he complained, "I cannot more than make both ends meet while I am in this semi-public life." [20] Other officers whose duties involved considerable clerical work also received salaries. During 1882–1883 the adjutant-general's income was $1500 and the quartermaster-general's, $800.

State departments began to make similar grants, varying with their size. Commanders secured traveling expenses, ranging from $75 in Arkansas to $1000 in New York, while assistant adjutants-general garnered sums from $300 to $2000 and assistant quarter-masters-general from $150 to $1000. As the decline in membership reduced revenues in the nineties, there tended to be a cutting of salaries.

Other organizations, such as the Union Veteran Legion and the Sons of Veterans, also paid their adjutants-general and quarter-masters-general, but less generously than the more prosperous Grand Army. In 1887 the Woman's Relief Corps was forced to vote $600 for the national secretary and $300 for the national treasurer, though in 1890 it refused to appropriate more than $200 for Mrs. Wittenmyer's wanderings through seventeen states lest it become a precedent for future heads to run up vast bills at the society's expense. As additional compensation, the Grand Army, Union Veteran Legion, and Sons of Veterans usually presented retiring commanders with a gold or diamond studded badge or a gold watch and chain or "a very magnificent gold headed cane."

[19] Lucius Fairchild to Charles Fairchild, April 4, 1886, Lucius Fairchild Papers, State Historical Society of Wisconsin.
[20] Lucius Fairchild to Charles Fairchild, Dec. 27, 1886, *ibid.*

Despite these remunerations, those in charge of funds occasionally absconded with all the not inconsiderable assets at their disposal. In the G.A.R., local rather than state or national leaders were usually responsible for such difficulties, though one of New York's commanders was accused of misappropriating $1250. In Pennsylvania over 90 per cent of the courts-martial of members in the early nineties arose from this problem. The issue was even more acute in the Sons of Veterans. Offenses ranged from withholding the proceeds of tickets sold for the society's benefit to stealing a cornet belonging to a G.A.R. post and selling it for five dollars. Leaders of the order attributed these episodes to the youth, inexperience, and poverty of the Sons and reported a dropping off of courts-martial in the late nineties as the members grew more mature—and economic conditions less bleak. But the Sons was the only association which had to expel a former commander-in-chief for failing to account for $1600.

Officers of hereditary societies received no salaries, partly because their duties were less demanding but also because they came from a social level able to afford the expenses without succumbing to embezzlement, one more indication of the class cleavage between the two groups. The men's orders usually preferred to honor dignified gentlemen of wealth and aristocratic lineage who often were also eminent for their civic service. For many years the venerable Hamilton Fish continued as president-general of the Society of the Cincinnati even after he became too feeble to attend meetings. His successor was William Wayne, a great-grandson of Anthony Wayne, who was a gentleman farmer on his ancestral estate at the end of Philadelphia's Main Line. The first president of the Huguenot Society was John Jay, a grandson of the first Chief Justice and himself a former minister to Austria, a vice-president of the State Civil Service Commission, a founder and early president of the Union League Club, and a president of the American Historical Association. Among its vice-presidents were Robert C. Winthrop, Thomas F. Bayard, Richard Olney, and Chauncey Depew. The first president-general of the Sons of the Revolution, John Lee Carroll, was a descendant of Charles Carroll of Carrollton and a former governor of Maryland; another of its early officers was Joseph W. Drexel, wealthy banking associate of J. P. Morgan who was active in many philanthropic and public enterprises such as the Metropolitan Art Museum, the Philharmonic Society of New York, and the New York Cancer Hospital; and so it went.

As in the case of the G.A.R. and the Mexican War Veterans, the Sons of the American Revolution did not bestow the presidency upon its founder. After considering Hamilton Fish and Rutherford B. Hayes, the society finally turned to Lucius Deming, a New Haven lawyer and judge. McDowell did become a vice-president at large, while the vice-presidents for the different states included Fish, Hayes, President Benjamin Harrison, and the governors of New Jersey, Missouri, and Kentucky. President Timothy Dwight of Yale was the first chaplain.

Deming was merely a temporary choice until someone of greater prominence and wealth could be secured. "The organization needed money and the president did not have it, and the members could not or would not advance it," he later recalled, "and the only way to get it was to find some person who for the honor of being president would pay the bills." [21] Within a few months the society found an "angel" in the person of W. Seward Webb, the son of James Watson Webb, temperamental publisher of the New York *Courier and Enquirer*. Webb had practiced medicine in New York for a while but after his marriage to the daughter of William H. Vanderbilt he became president of the Wagner Palace Car Company and achieved Ward McAllister's original list of "The Four Hundred." Surrounded by such relatives and intimates as Cornelius Vanderbilt, Frederick W. Vanderbilt, President Alexander Webb of City College, W. D. Sloane, and Chauncey Depew, Webb received official notice of his election as president-general at his Fifth Avenue home early in December 1889. His successor was a former secretary to President Grant and vice-president of the Pullman Company, General Horace Porter, who resigned his S.A.R. post when President McKinley rewarded his success in raising money in Wall Street for the 1896 campaign with the ambassadorship to France. There he spent most of his time hunting for the body of John Paul Jones. Subsequent presidents-general in the nineties were the secretary of the Massachusetts State Board of Trade, Edwin S. Barrett, and a New Jersey varnish manufacturer, Franklin Murphy, who later

[21] Lucius Deming to William O. McDowell, Jan. 24, 1902, William O. McDowell Letterbooks, New York Public Library.

became governor of New Jersey and chairman of the Republican national committee.

In their selections the Sons consistently ignored the trio of founders from New Jersey. Of the three, William Stryker had been merely a figurehead and never achieved any further prominence. Josiah Pumpelly, of whom McDowell wrote, "In his weakness in his relations with men, he has made a colossal fool of himself. . . . He is a well-meaning man, easily self-deceived," [22] was ready to resign from the society by 1901. He canceled his subscription to the *Spirit of '76*, a magazine devoted largely to S.A.R. affairs, "for it would only remind me of many things about so-called patriotic societies I would prefer to forget." [23] Later in that year McDowell observed, "He has no standing now in the S.A.R." [24]

McDowell himself had fared no better. As in the case of his former associates in the Sons of the Revolution, conservatives like Horace Porter and Chauncey Depew who had now taken over the S.A.R. had little sympathy with this erstwhile supporter of T. V. Powderly and Henry George who seemed to envelop in notoriety every project he touched, and after the 1890 congress he had no influence in the body. By the end of the decade he was known as the man "who appears to cause discord whenever mentioned to the Sons of the American Revolution." [25]

With unbounded energy McDowell now progressed into increasingly curious movements. With his two strongest friends still remaining in the Sons he organized an Order of the American Eagle to spread republican principles throughout the world. This order never consisted of more than these three. He thereafter agitated for the erection of a Liberty Flag Pole on the Jersey coast, for a Pan Republic Congress at the 1893 World's Fair, for an International Human Freedom League, and for sending a Columbian Liberty Bell about the country as a patriotic symbol. He also found time to support the international peace movement, to work for the relief of political prisoners in Siberia, and was even invited to meetings of the "Peace, Purity and Plenty" movement in Philadelphia, whose

---

[22] McDowell to Henry Baldwin, Dec. 28, 1901, *ibid.*
[23] "Correspondence," *Spirit of '76*, VII (April 1901), 149.
[24] McDowell to Baldwin, Dec. 28, 1901, McDowell Letterbooks.
[25] *Spirit of '76*, IV (Aug. 1898), 358.

motto was "Ripe Fruit and Pure Food." Toward the end of the decade he became an advocate of Cuban independence, worked for the establishment of a National University, was on the fringe of one of the minor but vigorous nativist movements of the day, and became involved in highly peculiar financial speculations trying to beat the stock market. In the early twentieth century he became a lecturer on such subjects as "The Expansion of the Democratic Spirit, or Liberty Enlightening the World," "Cuba and Her Future Relations to the United States," "The Coming Political Union of the English-Speaking World," and "What the Irish Have Accomplished for Liberty."

McDowell dropped out of sight in later years, except for a brief moment of honor when the D.A.R. congress of 1916 invited him to sit on the platform along with President and Mrs. Wilson. He lived on until 1927, generally forgotten by the groups he had started in such an atmosphere of excitement and controversy. A few years ago staff members of the New York Public Library still recalled how the old man haunted the building, apparently having long since crossed the indefinable line between the merely eccentric and the unbalanced mind. Fantastic as he was, filled with incredible energy for promoting impractical schemes, yet he helped to found two of the most permanent and important hereditary patriotic societies whose success set the pace for nearly all subsequent ones. While there was in his personality undoubtedly some driving desire for personal fame, perhaps as compensation for his short stature, and even at times an element of financial chicanery, there was also a solid basis of idealism that members of patriotic societies might do well to recall and critics of such groups to understand.

Like the S.A.R., the D.A.R.'s desire for conservative leadership caused it to shunt aside the more controversial persons who had founded it. At the first meeting the Daughters made Miss Desha a vice-president-general, Mrs. Walworth secretary-general, and Miss Washington registrar-general, and, together with Mrs. Lockwood, they were active in the society as long as they lived, but they all reflected too strongly the new tendencies stirring among American women ever to become president-general. Instead, the organization thought it wiser to select more conventional women known to the public through their husbands' accomplishments, not their own.

In the choice of its first president-general it achieved a tremendous coup. The objective was a woman whose name would attract favorable attention to the new society throughout the entire country, and the spouses of an admiral and an associate justice of the Supreme Court were considered for a while. But the day before the group's formal inauguration the wife of the President of the United States, Mrs. Benjamin Harrison, agreed to accept the post.

In the words of Mrs. Lockwood, the then First Lady was "a conservative woman, standing on the threshold of a new era, still holding fast to the old ideals, even while stretching forth a timid hand towards some things new." [26] So timid was her stretching that it recalled the curious mixture of activity and retirement shown by Miss Cunningham of the Mount Vernon Ladies' Association nearly half a century earlier. Though willing to take the presidency of a national patriotic organization of women, she refused to attend the opening meeting and instead waited to be notified. She announced that she would withdraw her name if a single dissenting vote were cast. Finally, on the ground of lack of experience, she insisted that someone else assume the actual duties of the position (here one would almost suspect that Mrs. Harrison had brushed up on George Washington's experiences with the Cincinnati, about the only comparable precedent available to her). This attitude, soon intensified by her fatal illness, kept her from ever being more than a figurehead in the organization, but meanwhile the prestige of her name attracted thousands of members. In memory of her connection with the society, in 1894 the D.A.R. presented the portrait of Mrs. Harrison that now hangs in the White House.

The actual presiding officer of the D.A.R., at whose home most of the early meetings were held, was Mrs. William D. Cabell. A native of Virginia, "At twelve years of age she had thoroughly read Gibbon; at fifteen she had accomplished a most remarkable course of reading and was in fluent command of the French and German languages." [27] Not surprisingly, after her marriage such talents led her and her husband to establish a girls' school in Washington. Despite some sentiment to recognize the clubwoman type, the choice

---

[26] Mary S. Lockwood and Emily Lee Sherwood, *Story of the Records* (Washington, 1906), p. 94.

[27] "Mrs. William D. Cabell," *American Monthly Magazine,* I (Aug. 1892), 114.

of Mrs. Harrison established a precedent of seeking officers among the wives of prominent men. After Mrs. Harrison's death, Mrs. Cabell and Mrs. Adlai E. Stevenson, wife of the Vice-President of the United States under Harrison's successor, Grover Cleveland, and grandmother of the 1952 Democratic presidential candidate, were nominated for her post in 1893. Though Mrs. Cabell had been the *de facto* head of the society and Mrs. Stevenson, "a delicate little woman, with an oval Madonna face and a complexion like the inside of a pink shell," [28] had been a member for only a week, Mrs. Cabell withdrew from the contest and Mrs. Stevenson was elected unanimously.

When she retired temporarily in 1895 because of the illness and then the death of a member of her family, again a conflict arose between a candidate who represented official Washington life and one who had risen within the organization. Pennsylvania's state regent, Mrs. Nathaniel Hogg, who had gained prominence through her fight for the lineal descent amendment, contested the office with Mrs. John W. Foster, whose husband had been minister to Mexico, Russia, and Spain and later secretary of state under Harrison. Mrs. Foster (perhaps now better remembered as the mother-in-law of Woodrow Wilson's secretary of state, Robert Lansing, and as the grandmother of John Foster Dulles) had further advantages in having been an early member of the society and a close friend of Mrs. Harrison and consequently won by a large majority. At the end of an unobtrusive year as president-general, she retired in favor of Mrs. Stevenson, who now served two more terms.

In 1898 a struggle developed between Mrs. Daniel Manning, whose husband had been Cleveland's secretary of the treasury, and Mrs. Donald McLean, who had been regent of a large chapter in New York City. Mrs. Manning, daughter of a wealthy Albany merchant and descended from the Livingston, de Peyster, Van Cortlandt, and Schuyler families, had entertained lavishly during her husband's term in the cabinet and then became active in the Daughters, serving as regent of a chapter in Albany and as vice-president-general. Her opponent, described as "the most eloquent woman associated with any organization in the country" as well as "a woman of wonderful magnetism, and a physique and carriage that belongs to

[28] *San Francisco Examiner*, July 23, 1893.

the queenliest type of American womanhood," [29] had won a wide and devoted following because of her wit and presence of mind, but again the candidate with an official background won handily. Since Mrs. McLean was inactive in 1899 because of her mother's death, Mrs. Manning was reëlected without opposition and after the expiration of her term served as president of the Board of Lady Managers at the St. Louis Fair of 1904.

In 1901 the Daughters started a new century in the old tradition by preferring Mrs. Charles W. Fairbanks, wife of the United States senator who later became Theodore Roosevelt's vice-president, over Mrs. McLean. The election was a bitter one, and Mrs. Fairbanks' opponents attributed her success to President McKinley's backing. After the decision Mrs. McLean's remarks on calumnies allegedly circulated against her produced a great amount of cheers and hisses among the delegates. Yet Mrs. Fairbanks also represented the new type of clubwoman. She had been president of the first literary club in Indiana, belonged to several art and musical societies, was the first woman appointed to the Indiana State Board of Charities, and the previous year had been made a director of the General Federation of Women's Clubs. Her term marked a transition in the concept of the office. Mrs. Harrison, Mrs. Stevenson, Mrs. Foster, and Mrs. Manning had all been rather passive occupants of the president-general's chair, but not until the regimes of Mrs. McLean (who triumphed at last in 1905), Mrs. Stevenson's sister, Mrs. Matthew Scott, and Mrs. William Cummings Story, women who really devoted their lives to club work, did the organization have active and aggressive leadership.

Wives of public men also served as vice-presidents-general. Among those elected at various times were Mrs. Manning, Mrs. Fairbanks, Mrs. Russell Alger, Mrs. Mark Hanna, Mrs. Levi P. Morton, and Mrs. Harrison's daughter, Mrs. Mary Harrison McKee. But gradually the members turned to women who were themselves distinguished in the professions or, more frequently, prominent in club activities. The first surgeon-general was Clara Barton; one of her successors was Dr. Anita Newcomb McGee, daughter of the scientist Simon Newcomb and herself the first female Assistant-Surgeon in

[29] "Celebrations and Proceedings," *American Historical Register* (Nov. 1895), p. 376.

the United States Army, who also held three other national offices in the D.A.R., while Julia Ward Howe and the historian Alice Morse Earle headed chapters in Boston and Brooklyn. More typical of the modern clubwoman was Mrs. Washington A. Roebling, who served as vice-president-general and was exceedingly ambitious to head the society. To be sure, Mrs. Roebling had prominence enough derived from her male relatives (not so much as sister of the defender of Little Round Top in the Battle of Gettysburg, General Gouverneur Warren, but as daughter-in-law and wife of the builders of Brooklyn Bridge), but she had also won distinction in her own right. To help her invalid husband while he directed the work on the bridge through a pair of field glasses from his Brooklyn window, she studied mathematics and learned the technicalities of bridge construction. She was the only woman in the first party to cross the bridge when there were only wooden planks and became the first woman to speak before the American Society of Civil Engineers.[30] Mrs. Roebling moved on to become active in such varied organizations as the Auxiliary Board of the New York Woman's Hospital, the Prison Aid Society, the New Jersey Historical Society, the Woman's Legal Alumnae Association, the International Press Union, Sorosis, and the New York State Federation of Women's Clubs, not to mention other hereditary groups like the Daughters of Holland Dames, the Colonial Dames, the Huguenot Society, and the Mount Vernon Ladies' Association. (Was her absorption in her own colonial ancestry enhanced by any chance by having to bear her husband's immigrant surname?) To turn to the local scene, in Oshkosh, Wisconsin the organizer of the first D.A.R. chapter, Mrs. Edgar R. Sawyer, was well known as the daughter-in-law of Wisconsin's millionaire Senator Philetus Sawyer. But in addition to her activities in various philanthropies, she headed the Oshkosh Florists' Club and was the first president of the Oshkosh Women's Club.[31] This shift in D.A.R. leadership from the wives of famous men to those who had made their own mark in numerous organizations was itself indicative of important changes in the status of American women.

When Flora Adams Darling flounced off to found the Daughters

---

[30] D. B. Steinman, *The Builders of the Bridge* (New York, 1945), pp. 369, 399, 404.
[31] Richard Nelson Current, *Pine Logs and Politics* (Madison, Wis., 1950), p. 279.

of the Revolution, she was careful to see that its constitution gave her the life title of founder and director general. Because of her deafness, however, she made no attempt to head the society after its formation. She appeared at conventions and made brief speeches, and in turn the order showed its respect by presenting her with badges or baskets of flowers, but her influence soon became so slight that the gatherings did not hesitate to reject her suggestions or to refuse to elect her relatives to office. On the other hand, for several years she presided over and controlled the United States Daughters of 1812 far more than she had the D.A.R. or D.R. When she finally retired in 1898, leaving the order's affairs in almost complete confusion, she retained an active vote in her role of founder and director general. But more than a decade later, during which she had occasionally appeared at meetings and had presented the Michigan branch with a life-size oil painting of herself, she ended up supporting a group that sued the national organization on the ground that it had violated its Congressional charter. Early in January 1910, just as she was about to take a cab from her brother's home in New York to return to Washington, she suddenly dropped dead, a dramatic close to a strange career. In a glowing resolution of sympathy the Daughters of the Revolution were so carried away as to term her "a cheerful and pleasant companion, officially and socially," [32] but a proposal to implement these sentiments by establishing a scholarship in her memory at William and Mary College aroused strong opposition. With a reserve perhaps born of greater experience, the Daughters of 1812 merely characterized her as "a woman of unusual talents, devoted to patriotic causes, a greatly beloved mother, wife and sister," [33] leaving to silence how those not related had viewed her.

There remains the question of how much the members and leaders of these different groups made common cause and how much they regarded each other jealously as competitors. In general, the Civil War societies constituted one distinct block of organizations and the hereditary bodies another, with comparatively little overlapping. Within each group, however, despite certain rivalries, there

---

[32] Daughters of the Revolution, *Proceedings of the Nineteenth Annual Meeting 1910* (Englewood, N.J., 1910), p. 12.

[33] United States Daughters of 1812, *Bulletin*, IV (Feb. 1910), 1.

were many ties, and so extensive was the habit of joining in the higher echelons that the same individuals often turned up as officers in different organizations. As examples of these interlocking direc- torates, two commanders-in-chief of the Grand Army of the Republic also headed the Society of the Army of the Potomac, while at various times others presided over the Society of the Army of the James, the Society of the Burnside Expedition, the Union Soldiers' Alliance, and the Association of Survivors of Rebel Prisons. The founder of the Union Veterans' Union, M. A. Dillon, had been three times commander of a G.A.R. post, the organizer and commander of a Sons of Veterans division, and founder of a local branch of the W.R.C.

On the other hand, the G.A.R. sometimes disliked the existence of other Civil War organizations as undermining its strength and was inclined to emphasize that, unlike the Loyal Legion's snobbish exclusion of the enlisted man, it was a democratic group where "the general and private, the merchant prince and the clerk, the million- aire and the laborer sit side by side as comrades. . . ." [34] In turn, associations like the Union Veterans' Union viewed the G.A.R. a little superciliously because its members had not all seen front-line service. "Into our ranks no man can come who has not heard the zip, zip of the mines or dodged the screaming shell; he must be baptized by fire before he can pass our sacred precincts," boasted one of its commanders-in-chief, who then asked whether such veterans could possibly care to share their honors "with those who never felt the smoke of battle or saw an enemy except under guard?" [35]

As long as the Sons of Veterans remained divided into two groups and insisted on conferring military titles upon members who had never seen the army, the G.A.R. looked rather critically upon it. With the removal of both these objections by the nineties, relations became increasingly cordial, joint meetings were more common, and by 1895 there were over 750 Grand Army members who also be- longed to the Sons. The Woman's Relief Corps, the Ladies of the G.A.R., the Daughters of Veterans, and the Ladies' Aid, Sons of Veterans, in many respects competed for the same patronage and

[34] Grand Army of the Republic, *Journal of the Twenty-third Annual Session of the National Encampment 1889* (St. Louis, 1889), p. 34.
[35] M. A. Dillon, "Union Veterans' Union," *Grand Army Record*, II (April 1887), 6.

were not on very good terms with each other. At one time there was a strong movement within the W.R.C. to declare members of the Ladies of the G.A.R. ineligible for admission; this suggests that many had been joining both. The position of the G.A.R., officially committed to the W.R.C. but besieged by other groups, especially their relatives in the Ladies of the G.A.R., for similar recognition, was quite embarrassing. Many agreed with the Maine commander who observed that the Grand Army was "a sort of Society Mormon, wedded to two beautiful damsels, both attractive and lovely, but the domestic peace would indeed be consummated, if instead of two, one charming woman presided." [36] Since whatever stand the harried veterans took aroused antagonism, they usually took refuge in evasive recommendations that the rivals combine.

Even more than among the veterans' groups and their affiliates there was a tremendous amount of duplication in the membership and leadership of the numerous hereditary societies. Of the founders of the S.A.R., McDowell also served on the executive committee of the General Society of the War of 1812, Josiah Pumpelly was active in the Huguenot Society, and William S. Stryker was president of the New Jersey Cincinnati, while the second president-general, W. Seward Webb, also headed the Vermont Society of Colonial Wars. The Cincinnati and the Sons of the Revolution maintained especially close connections.

The women's organizations reflected still better the mania for joining. The D.A.R.'s founders were as gregarious as the S.A.R.'s. It has already been noted that Mrs. Darling also proceeded to form the Daughters of the Revolution and the Daughters of 1812 and that Miss Washington helped start the Daughters of Founders and Patriots, but it should be added that Miss Desha later joined the Huguenot Society and also served as secretary of the Pocahontas Memorial Association, as president of a U.D.C. chapter in Washington, and as first vice-commandant of the District of Columbia camp of the Dames of 1846. Two other examples of this tendency will suffice. Mrs. Sara Kinney, state regent for the Connecticut D.A.R., was also active in the Colonial Dames, the United States Daughters of 1812, the Order of Descendants of Governors, the Daughters of

[36] Department of Maine, Grand Army of the Republic, *Proceedings at the Eighteenth Annual Encampment 1885* (Augusta, 1885), p. 87.

Founders and Patriots, the Daughters and Sons of Pilgrims, and the Society of Mayflower Descendants, while Mrs. William Gerry Slade was president of both the Society of New England Women and the United States Daughters of 1812. She later founded the Order of Americans of Armorial Descent and was a member of the D.A.R. and the Colonial Daughters of the 17th Century. The large number of husbands and wives who belonged to the S.A.R. and D.A.R. produced cordial feeling between these two groups.

But relations between the S.A.R. and the S.R., the D.A.R. and the D.R., the two branches of Colonial Dames, and the Cincinnati and the Daughters of the Cincinnati were usually extremely unpleasant, and in Philadelphia the Sons of the Revolution and the D.A.R. battled for control of part of Independence Hall until the conservative Sons withdrew to avoid further unfavorable publicity. The D.A.R., broader in its membership and more extensive in its activities, often regarded the Colonial Dames as too snobbish and far less constructive. "No, I don't belong to the Colonial Dames—though I *could*," was one of the comments exchanged at a card party of middle-class women in a small Iowa city in "Octave Thanet" 's *Man of the Hour*. The reply was, "I don't think much of the society, myself; nothing but social function and snippy ways—I belong to the Daughters. There is some sense to them—and real patriotism. They've put up another tablet over the river." [37] Throughout the decade there were efforts to merge the two orders of Sons as well as to unite the warring Daughters, but each group always clung to its particular name, insignia, colors, and form of organization with a stubborn devotion worthy of the Bourbons that made compromise impossible.

There was little crossing the line between the veterans' and hereditary societies, though the Loyal Legion, which had characteristics of both groups, shared several members with the men's hereditary associations and considered itself the "child of the Cincinnati," to some extent winning recognition of this claim. Needless to say, one exception to the general rule was McDowell, who was sufficiently active in the Sons of Veterans to aspire to become its commander-in-chief and who after being rejected by the New York commandery of the Loyal Legion with some difficulty managed to get into the

[37] Octave Thanet, *The Man of the Hour* (New York, 1905), p. 415.

District of Columbia branch. The cleavage between the two categories was even more marked in the case of the women's organizations.

Though the two sets of associations appealed to different followings, they usually regarded each other favorably. The veterans
boasted that the example of the Grand Army's success had stimulated
the formation of equally commendable patriotic organizations like
the D.A.R. and S.A.R., while the Daughters shared this view and
expressed their desire to coöperate with the Civil War societies.[38]
Below the Mason and Dixon line the situation was different. The
societies based on the war of 1861–1865 looked jealously upon the
hereditary leagues, chiefly because they competed for the same
clientele to a degree that was never true in the North. The *Confederate Veteran* warned the womenfolk that the D.A.R. should be subordinated to the memory of the Lost Cause. "Are you closer kin to
your great grandfather than to your husbands and brothers?" it
demanded. "Remember that men of the Revolution were successful,
while your crippled kin of later generations made sacrifices equally
as great without succeeding." [39] As time went on, many Southern
women resolved the conflict by joining both the U.D.C. and the
D.A.R., far more than Northern ones did in the case of the D.A.R.
and W.R.C. Yet divided as the two main groups of societies were socially and economically and different as their interests were on many
matters, especially pensions, on less partisan questions of proper
patriotic behavior they were increasingly to combine their influence.

[38] On the other hand, the Sons of Veterans felt that it resembled fraternal organizations such as the Knights of Pythias much more than it did the S.A.R.
[39] "The Veteran Among Southerners," *Confederate Veteran*, III (Oct. 1895), 304.

V

The Patriotic Press

A striking sign of the growing popularity of veterans' and hereditary patriotic societies was the appearance of nearly seventy newspapers and magazines specifically catering to the new audiences opened up by these groups. From another viewpoint this was merely one phase of the great number of specialized periodicals, representing nearly every category from religion and women through science and agriculture to the arts and sports, which arose in the late nineteenth century, but the story of these particular publications is almost unknown, neglected even by the nearly encyclopedic historian of such enterprises.[1]

Concomitant with the rash of veterans' societies at the close of the Civil War there emerged over forty publications directed toward the ex-soldiers and carrying news of the activities of their organizations. At Stephenson's suggestion the first national encampment of the G.A.R. adopted as its official organ *The Great Republic,* a strongly Radical journal published in Washington during 1866 and 1867. Another prominent paper was *The Soldier's Friend* of New York, endorsed by the Grand Army encampment of 1868. Marked by a strongly religious flavor, it featured moral anecdotes like "Treat Kindly the Drunkard's Child" and, in an effort to aid mutilated veterans, contests for the best specimens of left-handed writing. After its collapse in 1870, the G.A.R.'s adjutant-general, William T. Collins, started *The Grand Army Journal* in Washington. This received the official approval of a number of state encampments.

---

[1] Mott devotes two sentences to veterans' magazines, mentioning only three of them, sandwiched next to the barbers and the launderers in the chapter on "Journals for Printing and Other Crafts." Frank Luther Mott, *A History of American Magazines* (Cambridge, Mass., 1930–1938), III, 132.

But the real wave of these journals came when the revival of the Grand Army in the late seventies and early eighties made prospects for their success seem more likely. The most permanent and influential of all the veterans' papers, one that is still being published, was the *National Tribune,* founded by George E. Lemon, the most notorious pension claims agent in Washington. When the *National Tribune* first appeared in October 1877, the Grand Army had sunk to a low ebb and consequently the paper's first issues did not mention the organization. But as the society acquired new vigor, the paper saw the possible advantages of an alliance and developed a corresponding interest. In the early eighties it began to emphasize G.A.R. news, to press all veterans to affiliate, and to furnish applications for post charters. During the period of this encouragement, when the G.A.R. was growing at its most rapid pace, the commander-in-chief of the order was Paul Van Der Voort, a close associate and subsequent employee of Lemon.

The journal also worked for a strengthening of related organizations, such as union of the two branches of the Sons of Veterans and of the various women's groups. After the formation of the Woman's Relief Corps Lemon offered it financial assistance, and in return the new society urged its members to subscribe to the *National Tribune.* The periodical also suggested that ex-prisoners form local and county associations and then support the paper as the best way to secure favorable Congressional legislation.

By appealing to these different groups and by absorbing smaller competitors the paper built up a large circulation. In 1887 it claimed to have 130,000 subscribers and 650,000 readers. On special occasions, for example, during the campaign of 1884, Lemon distributed as many as 500,000 copies of certain issues. The paper appeared weekly in either eight or ten pages and cost a dollar a year. Its contents reflected its ambition to attract a wide variety of readers. While its chief emphasis was a constant drive for further pension legislation for Civil War veterans, it also included accounts of various campaigns and leaders of the war, articles by prominent military figures, including a serialization of General Sherman's *Memoirs,* and items about various state and local branches of the G.A.R., W.R.C., and Sons of Veterans. It attempted to become the reading staple of the entire family, especially in the rural areas where so many veterans lived, and contained reports of Congressional activities, foreign news, special features on such oddities as mummies, the life of New Zealand natives, and elephant hunting, a page of "Rural Topics" which ranged from how to plant fruit trees to a description of ostrich farming, a "Household Department" for the wives and daughters of veterans, a "Young Folk's Department" for their children, "Health Hints for Young and Old," and a religious section, "Sunday Meditation." Its literary fare ran the gamut from E. P. Roe's *The Gray and the Blue* to translations of Ivan Turgenev. Also enlivening the columns was a diverse collection of advertisements: Lemon's patent attorney firm, cures for catarrh, cholera, and the morphine habit, G.A.R. uniforms, *The Adventures of Huckleberry Finn,* and "Dr. Cheever's Electric Belt for Men Only."

After the death of Lemon in December 1896 (he lies buried in Rock Creek Cemetery not far from the grave of Henry Adams), the firm of McElroy, Shoppell and Andrews acquired the paper. R. W. Shoppell was a publisher and Byron Andrews had been the journal's business manager in New York for fifteen years. The most prominent of the trio was John L. McElroy, who after ten years as managing editor of the *Toledo Blade* had assumed the same position with the *National Tribune* in 1884 and had also served as president of the National Association of Ex-Prisoners of War. The chief changes under the new management, which by the close of the century was emphasizing that "it has not the slightest connection of any kind with any pension attorney or firm of attorneys," [2] were that the paper now serialized several of McElroy's own novels and made hesitant bids to the members of the recently arisen hereditary societies with occasional news of the D.A.R. and S.A.R. Its circulation in 1899 was 112,000.[3]

Other veterans' papers were less national in scope, appealing to one particular region, state, or even city. One of the most successful was the *American Tribune* of Indianapolis which by 1890 was an eight-page weekly, also costing a dollar a year. It carried news of the G.A.R., W.R.C., Sons of Veterans, and the progress of pension legislation in Congress, as well as a number of war stories and reminiscences. It claimed that its circulation of 100,000 was larger

[2] *National Tribune* (Washington, D.C.), Nov. 9, 1899.
[3] *American Newspaper Annual* (Philadelphia, 1899), p. 95.

than that of any weekly newspaper in Indiana and exceeded that of all other veterans' journals combined except one—that probably being the *National Tribune*. Despite expressions of good will the Indiana G.A.R. never made the *American Tribune* its official organ, but the Ladies of the G.A.R. did declare it to be its spokesman.

The paper also followed the *National Tribune*'s course of trying to widen its appeal as much as possible. In April 1894, it assumed the subtitle, "A Modern Family Weekly Paper," added Farm, Household, and Family Circle Departments, and began publishing serials like *Alithorp, or the Newsboy's Ward, Rube the Ranchman, or the Fire Patrol Veteran's Last Shot,* and *Little Grace Garland; or the Waif of the Lost Oregon, A Story of the High Lights and Shadows of Life*. This "family paper" also carried a number of advertisements for the cure of piles and fits and, under the heading of "The Triumph of Life a Happy Fruitful Marriage," such tasteful items as "Complete Manhood and How to Attain It" and "Sexual Power Restored in 2 to 10 Days." When George J. Langsdale took over the editorship in December 1896, he declared that the paper would continue to be "a soldiers' paper so conducted that it will be a welcome visitor to every family, whether it was represented in the war or not." [4] Added to the contents were general literature for the entire family, recipes for the housekeeper, market reports for the farmer, new developments for the mechanic, and current news of military and naval affairs. Like many of the smaller veterans' papers, it ran into financial difficulties. In its efforts to secure more patrons it offered such inducements as a free trip to the G.A.R.'s national encampment at Washington in 1892, copies of either the *Peerless Atlas* or *With Dewey at Manila,* a ladies' fur-lined cloak, a 120-piece tea set, or a double-barreled shotgun. Whether or not because of these devices, its circulation in 1899 was 35,000 [5] and it was one of the few papers to survive into the new century.

In New England the outstanding veterans' journal was the *Grand Army Record,* which began a turbulent career in Boston in 1885. An eight-page monthly costing a dollar a year, it published news of the activities not only of the G.A.R. but also of the Loyal Legion, Sons of Veterans, and W.R.C. throughout the region, as well as the usual

---

[4] *American Tribune* (Indianapolis), Dec. 10, 1896.
[5] *American Newspaper Annual* (1899), p. 203.

amount of wartime anecdotes and reminiscences. Both the G.A.R. and W.R.C. of Massachusetts urged their members to support the paper. Early in 1891 it acquired a cantankerous new editor, a patent lawyer named John M. Perkins, and at once embarked on an aggressive campaign for a service pension, opening a department that would answer all questions about claims without charge. Its ambition to become the champion of the veterans' pension interests led it to launch a series of bitter attacks on its chief competitor, the *National Tribune,* in which it denied that the old soldiers needed the aid of a paper or attorney in the capital and accused the other journal of having corrupted the pension office, thereby creating prejudice against the entire system of grants. When the service pension campaign produced no results, it next tried a vigorous assault on school histories.

In later years the editor became carried away by personal animosities. His private difficulties in a patent-infringement case led to a number of bitter and unbalanced criticisms of certain federal judges which could have done the paper little good. Even more fatal to the success it desired were his charges that the leadership of the Massachusetts G.A.R. constituted an aristocratic "House of Lords." This combination of hostility to the courts and to the Grand Army's chiefs caused the department head to assail the paper for containing statements "utterly devoid of the truth." [6] The *Record* retorted that the commander had refused to attend the dedication of a new G.A.R. hall in Arlington and had instead gone to a whist party and won a silk umbrella. As this controversy increased, the journal began to contain less and less actual news of the G.A.R., W.R.C., and Sons of Veterans and, finally, after the commander condemned it as "long on ambition, perverse in abuse of others, and short on patriotism and self-respect," the state encampment formally withdrew its endorsement.[7]

In December 1898 came the announcement that Perkins would return to the practice of patent law. Heterodoxy had not paid dividends. "While the columns will be open for the discussion of any and all questions relating to the welfare of the Grand Army, making

[6] Department of Massachusetts, Grand Army of the Republic, *Journal of the Twenty-Eighth Annual Encampment 1895* (Boston, 1895), p. 243.

[7] Department of Massachusetts, Grand Army of the Republic, *Journal of the Thirty-First Annual Encampment 1897* (Boston, 1897), pp. 57, 171–172.

each writer responsible for his own writings," ran a statement of new policy, "the editor will take no part in any matter about which the Department of Massachusetts is divided in opinion." [8] The conversion to respectability came too late, and, though its circulation had risen from 3000 in 1887 to 20,000 in 1899,[9] in March 1899 the paper suspended publication. It attempted a revival in the summer of 1900, with much more news of the G.A.R., W.R.C., Ladies of the G.A.R., Sons of Veterans, and Daughters of Veterans throughout New England and a much less controversial tone. Though it was under different management, Perkins apparently was still the owner. The resurrected version lasted only a year.

In New York City the monthly *Grand Army Review*, begun in 1885, emphasized the campaign for veterans' preference in government jobs rather than pensions. Like the *Grand Army Record*, it criticized its rival in Washington because its championing of pensions was scarcely disinterested. It contended that "a great soldiers' paper like the *National Tribune*, to be effective, should, like Caesar's wife, be above suspicion." [10] Having built up a circulation of 10,000 by 1887,[11] it was later absorbed by *Home and Country*, another New York City magazine catering to the ex-soldiers' organizations. This magazine had also started in 1885 and was also mainly concerned with the veterans' rights drive, of which its founder, Joseph W. Kay, was the chief advocate within the G.A.R. It continued the smaller papers' dislike of the *National Tribune*. By 1889 this combined journal claimed a circulation of 150,000. The most popular veterans' paper in the West was the *Western Veteran*, published first in Topeka and later in Kansas City.

These enterprises were only a few of the numerous journals devoted to the veterans' interests which sprang up in all parts of the country in these years. Nearly all of them were local ventures, though often they won the endorsement of the G.A.R. in their immediate neighborhood, and proved short-lived. Some of the smaller veterans' organizations had their own periodicals. The *Patriot* of New York and the *Union Veteran* of Akron, Ohio both catered to

[8] "The Grand Army Record Incorporated," *Grand Army Record*, XIII (Dec. 1898), 89.
[9] *American Newspaper Annual* (Philadelphia, 1887), p. 35; *ibid.* (1899), p. 343.
[10] "Let Us Have Peace," *Grand Army Review*, II (July 1886), 231.
[11] *American Newspaper Annual* (1887), p. 85.

the Union Veterans' Union. *The National Shipmate,* which appeared at Dayton, Ohio in February 1890, aimed at the naval veterans, but its publisher turned out to be "an unprincipled adventurer who was deficient not only in the sense to carry it on, but also in the requisite intelligence for its proper management." His paper collapsed after a few issues, but not before he had succeeded in defrauding several prominent members of the Naval Veterans.[12] There also seem to have been at least ten journals for the Sons of Veterans, which toward the close of the nineties voted *The Banner* of Dustin, Illinois its official organ. The Woman's Relief Corps usually utilized the veterans' papers, though there were a couple that endeavored to subsist on its support alone. For a while the Ladies of the G.A.R. published its own magazine, *The Picket Guard,* but this soon failed from lack of support.

Two years after the *National Tribune* had begun demonstrating the mutually beneficial relations that could exist between a pension claims agency, a veterans' organization, and a paper devoted to the interests of both, Alexander Kenaday began publishing the *Vedette* in Washington to keep Mexican War veterans informed of the progress of pension legislation. By the beginning of 1880 he was sending it to 10,000 persons, including all known veterans of the war, members of Congress, heads of government departments, and leading journalists. Only a fifth of this number, however, were actual subscribers. Kenaday estimated that from 50,000 to 100,000 read each issue. California, Illinois, and Texas were the states receiving the most copies. As a financial venture the *Vedette* was not at all successful in itself, but to the extent that it increased Kenaday's business as a claims agent he found it a good investment.

Though primarily concerned with pensions, for a period in 1882 and 1883 the paper emphasized the labor problem and even received the official endorsement of the Brotherhood of Carpenters and Joiners in Washington. By 1884, however, it had dropped this issue and returned to the affairs of the Mexican War veterans. After the passage of the service pension bill for them in 1887 it agitated for various extensions and minor amendments of the act and also devoted more space to incidents and personal recollections of the war.

---

[12] William Simons, *History of the National Association of Naval Veterans* (Philadelphia, 1895), pp. 52–53.

After Congress adjourned in March 1889, making any legislative favors impossible for the time being, the paper revealed it would suspend until the following December. By that time, however, a Republican administration has come into power and, as it might be expected to be hostile to an organization which included so many ex-Confederates and Democrats, the *Vedette* was not revived as scheduled. With the prospect of a Democratic victory in the fall of 1892, the paper reappeared in February of that year, but had to announce a second suspension in August. Congress had again adjourned without increasing the size of pensions and subscriptions had not paid anywhere near the cost of printing. With the lawmakers' return to Washington, the *Vedette* resumed in December 1892, but finally went down for the third and last time with the end of the session in March 1893.

In contrast to the Northern ventures, journals for the Confederate groups were slow to appear and few in number. In 1883 a *Confederate Annals* started publication in St. Louis, but it was too early for such an enterprise, and the paper soon found it expedient to change its name to *Union and Confederate Annals* so as to include news of the Grand Army and allied organizations. When the U.C.V., U.D.C., and U.S.C.V. began to flourish in the nineties, even then their members seemed able to support only one periodical, the *Confederate Veteran,* which made its debut at Nashville in February 1893, under the editorship of Sumner A. Cunningham. A monthly magazine of between thirty-two and fifty pages, costing the standard dollar a year, it contained the usual reminiscences of ex-soldiers, only from the Southern side this time, as well as news of U.C.V., U.D.C., and U.S.C.V. activities. Within two years it won the endorsement of all three societies. By 1899 the paper claimed a circulation of over 20,000, almost entirely in the South and largely in Texas and Tennessee. But like most magazines devoted to patriotic societies, the *Veteran* constantly bewailed its precarious financial situation. Nevertheless it survived Cunningham's death in 1913. He left the enterprise to a board of officials representing all three major Confederate associations which continued its publication until it succumbed during the depression in 1932.[13]

[13] Mary B. Poppenheim and Others, *History of the United Daughters of the Confederacy* (Richmond, 1938), pp. 174–176.

With the rise of hereditary societies in the nineties there also came several magazines for their members. Compared to the enterprises for the veterans they were not as numerous, no more than about half a dozen in fact. Although their clientele was presumably better able to afford them, it was also far more limited in size. The contents of these journals followed approximately the same pattern: news concerning one or more societies, depending on whether it was the official spokesman of one in particular or was trying to appeal to the following of as many as possible, genealogical information about prominent members, articles about events of the Revolution or historic sites, and sometimes the publication of old documents.

Even before the D.A.R.'s formal organization Mrs. Darling began arranging to convert her project in New York, the *Gotham,* into an organ for the new society. In January 1891, it emerged under the unwieldy name of *Adams' Magazine of General History and Authorized Exponent of the Daughters of the American Revolution.* While the first part of it still contained articles of general interest such as "The Race Question," "A Trip to Westminster Abbey," and "The True Christmas Spirit," its second half now consisted of a "Department of Daughters of the American Revolution." After Mrs. Darling's split with the D.A.R., it adjusted its subtitle to "Official Exponent of Daughters of the Revolution" in October 1891, and became entirely concerned with historical and genealogical matters and the affairs of the new society. When Mrs. Darling withdrew to devote herself to the Daughters of 1812, it bobbed its name to *Magazine of the Daughters of the Revolution.* Though edited by the president-general, Mrs. Edward Steers, as an official journal, the society paid no part of its expenses, which apparently Mrs. Steers bore herself. The stormy exodus of Mrs. Steers to found the Dames of the Revolution meant the end of the enterprise in November 1896.

Meanwhile, Mrs. Darling's control of the *Adams' Magazine* had left the D.A.R. without a periodical of its own. In May 1892, the national board of management voted to establish a magazine to carry reports of the meetings of the board, the Continental Congresses, and local chapters. Under the editorship of Mrs. Walworth it made its first appearance in July 1892 as the *American Monthly Magazine.* The editor envisaged the journal as having an important role in the new era of expanding activities of women. "The difficulty is not in having too many publications for women," she announced, "but it is in projecting such as keep pace with the spirit of the time, and this the AMERICAN MONTHLY will do." [14] It carried accounts of the annual convention, national board and chapter doings, genealogical data on outstanding Daughters, and historical sketches on the order of "Heroic Women of Virginia," "Connecticut in the Revolution," and "Dolly Madison's Flight to Virginia." With the formation of the C.A.R. in 1895 it added a "Children's Department." When Mrs. Lockwood succeeded Mrs. Walworth as editor, she put in a page of comments on current affairs that to a degree anticipated the women columnists of a later day. The magazine was never self-supporting, relying upon subsidies from the national society, and thereby has continued to the present day, though with changes of title first to *Daughters of the American Revolution Magazine* and then to the *National Historical Magazine*. In 1899 it was reaching 32,000 persons.[15]

These two magazines were each limited to a particular organization, but the formation of so many other hereditary societies in the nineties led to the founding of periodicals designed for all members of such groups. Two of them appeared simultaneously in September 1894. The aptly titled *Spirit of '76* was edited in New York by William H. Brearley and put out by a "Spirit of '76" Publishing Company whose treasurer was Henry Hall, one of McDowell's associates in founding the S.A.R. who had long been interested in such a project and who had raised most of the necessary funds. Its first issue announced that the new patriotic societies had been unable to get sufficient space in the newspapers and that it hoped to give accounts of their doings "with less of the hurry and compression incident to reports in the great dailies." [16]

In the summer of 1897 it acquired a new editor and publisher combined in the person of Louis H. Cornish, who until then had been running a journal called *Suburbs* concerned with real estate activities around New York City. The new management promptly won the endorsements of McDowell and Mrs. Darling, support which by this

---

[14] Ellen Hardin Walworth, "The Magazine," *American Monthly Magazine,* II (June 1893), 609–610.

[15] *American Newspaper Annual* (1899), p. 94.

[16] "The Spirit of '76," *Spirit of '76,* I (Sept. 1894), 10.

time would have given pause to cautious souls. McDowell "came to us with various schemes of making the world better," Cornish later recalled ruefully, "and we entered into them and have since paid for it." The editor's conclusion was that the ebullient professional patriot had offered nothing but enthusiasm and impractical ideas.[17] Of more practical aid was the action of a number of organizations, including the Order of Founders and Patriots, the Society of American Wars, the Military Order of Foreign Wars, and the United States Daughters of 1812, in making it their spokesman, but the most important backing came when the S.A.R. named it its official journal. The D.A.R. also took an active interest in the venture, individual chapters often placing copies of it as well as of the *American Monthly* in their local libraries, and indeed at one point the society even considered merging the two periodicals. Though the magazine was never prosperous financially, its circulation being only 3000 in 1899,[18] it survived a series of vicissitudes until 1906.

At exactly the same time in Philadelphia, meanwhile, another newcomer, the *American Historical Register,* subtitled "A Monthly Gazette of the Patriotic-Hereditary Societies of the United States of America," began its even less successful endeavors to tap the same audience, which it estimated at approximately 30,000. The president of the Historical Register Publishing Company, Edgar Linton Lee, was himself a joiner of no mean attainments who belonged to the Society of Colonial Wars, the Society of the War of 1812, the Sons of the Revolution, the Mayflower Descendants, the New England Society, and the Huguenot Society. Editor-in-chief was Charles H. Browning, author of *Americans of Royal Descent* who was soon to found the Baronial Order of Runnemede. Prominent members of different organizations (including Alice Morse Earle and Mrs. Roger A. Pryor) served as associate editors for each of the major societies.

As with similar journals, the magazine was in constant financial straits. Lee appealed to members of patriotic-hereditary associations not only to subscribe to the journal but to purchase stock in the Historical Register Company so as to support the project until advertising and subscriptions should make it self-sustaining. Even though an occasional D.A.R. chapter responded by assessing its

[17] "Editorial," *ibid.,* IV (Aug. 1898), 358.
[18] *American Newspaper Annual* (1899), p. 586.

membership, the venture never got the same official backing as did the *Spirit of '76.* Browning's editorship ceased when a Boston firm took over the publication in 1896. The new backer was an elderly Bostonian named John Collamore who had been active in the Society of the War of 1812, the Society of Colonial Wars, and the Sons of the Revolution but who died in a few months from injuries suffered in leaving a trolley car. The removal to New England did not improve matters noticeably, and several times the magazine had to skip a monthly issue. In the summer of 1897 James Grant Wilson, president of both the American Authors Guild and the New York Genealogical and Biographical Society, became editor-in-chief, but these combined distinctions did not save the magazine from extinction the following fall.

An even less successful enterprise was the *Colonial Magazine,* launched in New York in August 1895 with the slogan, "Directed to the Interests of the Patriotic Organizations of America." Though considerably more attractive in format than most such ventures, it lasted for only three numbers. In September 1900, there appeared *The Patriotic Review,* "published in an artistic apartment house in the fashionable Back Bay District of Boston, Mass." and intended to be "impartially and exclusively devoted to the interests of the various patriotic and historical organizations of the United States." [19] Its editor-in-chief, Marion Howard Brazier, had been the society, short story, and patriotic editor of the *Boston Post* who had introduced a "Red, White and Blue Department" into it on Sundays and had founded a D.A.R. chapter in Boston. Despite a pleasing appearance and the patronage of Mrs. Potter Palmer, William Randolph Hearst, and Mary Baker Eddy, it suffered the usual ups and downs until it finally collapsed in 1904.

Of a different type was the *Mayflower Descendant,* started in January 1899. Edited for many years by George Ernest Bowman and published in Boston by the Massachusetts Society of Mayflower Descendants, it made no effort to win wide appeal as a popular historical magazine or even to carry much news of the organization it represented. Dull and sedate in its gray cover, it confined itself with distinction to its announced intention of being "A Quarterly Maga-

[19] "Trinity Court," *Patriotic Review,* III (Sept. 1902), 5; "Editorial," *ibid.,* I (Sept. 1900), 5.

zine of Pilgrim Genealogy and History." As such, it proved one of the most valuable and reliable sources for the lineage of the old Plymouth families. It particularly excelled in printing the wills and vital records of towns in the Cape Cod area. Because of its official backing it stayed in existence until 1940 without the usual appeals for financial aid or the odd devices of the unsubsidized journals.

The fact that few papers or magazines endeavored to reach the members of both Civil War and hereditary societies was one more demonstration of the cleavage between them. Toward the end of the nineties the *National Tribune* began to print occasional news of the D.A.R., S.A.R., and Colonial Dames, as well as a series of articles by Mrs. Lockwood, but never made any serious efforts in that direction. Conversely, the *American Historical Register* carried some items about the G.A.R., but obviously never developed much following among the veterans and their families. For a few months in 1890 the short-lived *Republic Magazine* of New York, with which Henry Hall of the S.A.R. was connected, featured departments for the Grand Army, the Loyal Legion, and the Sons of Veterans and also devoted considerable attention to the Sons of the Revolution and the S.A.R. Though it had the support of the McDowell element in the last-named society, it too failed to attract many adherents during its brief existence.

The only magazine to combine the two appeals with even a modicum of success was *Home and Country,* the G.A.R. publication in New York which had emphasized the veterans' preference movement. Until September 1891, its editors were George B. Loud, a former junior vice-commander in the Grand Army, and Mrs. Annie Wittenmyer, recently national president of the W.R.C., but at that time it announced the advent of William O. McDowell as editor-in-chief and acquired the subtitle, "Devoted to Popular Government, Universal Liberty and American Institutions." Its financial backer was still Joseph W. Kay, a Brooklyn manufacturer long active in the Grand Army. Not only did the journal carry news of the G.A.R., W.R.C. (Mrs. Wittenmyer's special concern), and the D.A.R., but it also gave McDowell a medium through which to publicize his schemes for a Pan Republic Congress and a Human Freedom League. But he was no person to be trusted with the practical management of any venture, and in the spring of 1892 Kay had to intervene, even though for a while McDowell continued as nominal editor. In the next few months it changed into a magazine of general appeal with fiction, poetry, and articles. By 1893 it had ceased to pay attention to the G.A.R. and Mrs. Wittenmyer contributed only brief items on the W.R.C., though it still ran stories about McDowell's Pan Republic Congress and his subsequent project, the Columbian Liberty Bell, and in 1895 his series of "Historical Events Which Have Told for Freedom." The journal finally suspended in May 1897.

In retrospect, nearly all these journals seriously overestimated the demand for so specialized a type of publication, usually ran into financial difficulties, and soon died, often in a few months and at best after a few years, unless they were subsidized as the official organ of one particular society, were written off as an expense incidental to some more important enterprise as a claims agency, or made determined efforts to transform themselves into periodicals of general interest. They were, of course, invaluable reporters of what the associations were doing. As sources of opinion they must be used cautiously, for often their attitudes showed an unrepresentative extremism that reflected only the editor's idiosyncrasies or a desire to catch attention. Yet at the same time in their desperate search for patronage they certainly emphasized points which they thought would attract rather than antagonize the average member of patriotic societies. Moreover, the very fact that there were so many attempts to reach a public consisting only of the participants in veterans' or hereditary associations was a significant indication of how large a part of the nation's population had acquired the joining habit and was applying it in this particular direction.

VI

From Pink Teas to a Hot Time
in the Old Town

ALTHOUGH critics have suspected other motives, most members of patriotic societies have joined because of the social attractions. This was true as early as the days of the Cincinnati and for the rank and file it has remained about the same ever since, however much their more articulate leaders may have involved the groups in actions or statements calculated to raise the blood pressure of equally determined liberals, democrats, or internationalists. But the average member was merely a gregarious soul with no particular objection to his good times being sanctified by a patriotic halo.

Thus the nostalgic value of reminiscing with his former comrades, the opportunity for an escape from humdrum existence by an excursion to a large convention city, and the hope of one more good time at an age more suitable for harvesting than sowing oats of any description were what induced the ex-soldier to become a joiner. Quickly recognizing that these were the most important elements in building up the order, leaders of the G.A.R. urged local posts to "satisfy that craving for social intercourse of which everybody has more or less, but the soldiers most of all." [1] They particularly recommended such attractions as camp-fires, lecture courses, rifle clubs, literary entertainments "of an innocent character," and open meetings "where we can cultivate the social side of our

---

[1] Department of Illinois, Grand Army of the Republic, *Proceedings of the Seventh, Eighth, Ninth, Tenth and Eleventh Annual Encampments 1873–1877* (Aurora, Ill., 1880), p. 6.

natures, rather than the regular order of business, which at times become monotonous to the most enthusiastic Comrade." [2] When the commander of the Union Veteran Legion reported, "In the country encampments I have known comrades to travel many miles from their homes to the encampments, in many cases unable to get home until long after midnight," [3] desire for companionship to compensate for rural loneliness seems almost certainly the explanation for such devotion to the organization. The real significance of the G.A.R. is seen in the observation of Commander-in-Chief Lucius Fairchild that "In very many places nearly all of the social life and amusements are under the leadership of the local post." [4] Similarly one leader of the Woman's Relief Corps revealed that she had received "hundreds of testimonials" that the society "had brightened the life of many a women, whose only recreation it is from household cares; it has brought into their lives one oasis." [5]

The Grand Army met these social needs in a variety of ways. Early in the eighties a Pennsylvania commander reported that a number of posts "have their club-rooms, wherein to spend a social hour or two. Many have well-stocked libraries, largely patronized by members; and instead of the Post room being used only for business, it is fast assuming the pleasant character of the social circle." [6] After the close of business some turned their meetings into debating clubs, while others tried amateur theatricals. Typical was the Massachusetts post whose minstrel show "entertained the company present with songs, jokes, &c., concluding with a walk round by the entire company." [7] This apparently became so common in the early years that Vermont's commander felt obliged to warn,

[2] Grand Army of the Republic, *Journal of the Twenty-third Annual Session of the National Encampment 1889* (St. Louis, 1889), p. 44; Department of New Hampshire, Grand Army of the Republic, *Proceedings of the Fifteenth Annual Encampment 1882* (Lake Village, N.H., 1882), p. 156.

[3] Union Veteran Legion, *Proceedings of the Thirteenth National Encampment 1898* (Lewiston, Me., n.d.), p. 93.

[4] Society of the Army of the Tennessee, *Reports of the Proceedings 1881–1883* (Cincinnati, 1885), p. 518.

[5] Department of Michigan, Grand Army of the Republic, *Journal of the Sixteenth Annual Encampment 1894* (Ionia, Mich., 1894), p. 113.

[6] Department of Pennsylvania, Grand Army of the Republic, *Proceedings of the 30th and 31st Encampments 1881–1882* (n.p., n.d.), p. 79.

[7] *Grand Army Journal* (Washington, D.C.), April 6, 1872.

"Posts should avoid giving the impression that producing theatricals is their chief business."[8]

Especially popular was the device known as the camp-fire, which ordinarily was an evening social meeting conducted by the local post. At such an occasion in Lewiston, Maine, "speaking, singing and side-splitting stories filled the time till 'the wee sma' hours ayant the twal,' so full, that few could be seduced by any thought of bed to leave a company where Comrade Howard had given unlimited license to all to be as funny as they pleased, and the fire of jokes ran along the line until the pipes went out and taps were sounded at half-past one. . . ."[9] While one commander-in-chief grew alarmed at some camp-fires "where the song, the story or the personal conduct of some present overstepped the bounds of propriety,"[10] none other than General William T. Sherman testified to the way in which they tended "to irradiate the gloom of ordinary humdrum existence."[11]

In their early years, when the veterans were still young men, many posts felt that feminine companionship would be a sure-fire attraction. In Yonkers, New York, in 1872, the local post held a costume ball. A high point, presumably, was the entrance of a group of masked women, "led by a beautifully-formed and graceful lady attired as 'Columbia.'" Accompanying her were Gypsy Girls, Harlequins, Columbines, a Spanish Lady and Don, an Applewoman, Monks, Negresses, and a Dutch Girl. The veterans danced the quadrille until midnight, when at the general unmasking "it was amusing to witness the disconcerted faces of the comrades who had been mistaken in their judgment, and did not know their partners." The entire affair, we are told, "was pleasant, agreeable, and select." Since no liquor was served, "there were no heads aching in the morning."[12]

[8] Department of Vermont, Grand Army of the Republic, *Proceedings of the Sixth Annual Encampment* (Rutland, Vt., 1873), p. 9.

[9] Department of Maine, Grand Army of the Republic, *Proceedings of the Eleventh, Twelfth, Thirteenth, Fourteenth, Fifteenth and Sixteenth Annual Encampments 1878–1883* (Lewiston, 1884), p. 15.

[10] Grand Army of the Republic, *Journal of the Fifteenth Annual Session of the National Encampment 1881* (Philadelphia, 1881), p. 752.

[11] W. T. Sherman, "Camp Fires of the G.A.R.," *North American Review*, CXLVII (Nov. 1888), 502.

[12] *Grand Army Journal*, Feb. 24, 1872.

The growth of the Woman's Relief Corps as auxiliaries to posts gave opportunities for more and more associations with the opposite sex, though probably of a rather sedate nature. One commander-in-chief was confident that "the Post which has the most efficient Relief Corps can give the best entertainments and have the largest attendance at its regular meetings." [13] The corps were also thought to have a beneficial moral influence on the former soldiers. A New Jersey G.A.R. official praised those gatherings where the women "furnished the repast for the occasion, with liquids no stronger than water or coffee. . . ." In such instances the members went home "at seasonable hours, with clear heads, and prepared to go to the ordinary advocations of life on the following day, and no headache." This happy picture he contrasted with other assemblies from which the veterans did not depart until "two or three o'clock in the morning, with so much of the enthusiasm of the night in them to be too full for utterance. After a short rest, get up with headache, not able for the business of the day, consequently a loss of time, and in many cases by Comrades whose families cannot afford to have him lose time." [14] There were instances in which posts fell into the hands of a "drinking crowd" with saloon keepers as commanders and in one instance in Ohio even as chaplain. Much to the dismay of Rutherford B. Hayes, whose W.C.T.U. wife was popularly known as "Lemonade Lucy," such a development occurred in the branch in Fremont, Ohio to which he belonged, but he decided not to accompany many of the teetotallers in their withdrawal. [15]

Indeed, in many respects the G.A.R. and its affiliated organizations can best be studied not as patriotic societies but as one aspect of the general American interest in secret fraternal orders. The founding of the Grand Army came at a time when the press was describing the citizenry's delight "in meeting in guarded rooms, and wearing spangled dresses, and calling themselves sachems, and brothers and comrades, soldiers of Gideon, and sons of Rechab." [16] Following the interest of the fifties in secret nativist orders had come the forma-

---

[13] G.A.R. *Journal 1889*, p. 44.

[14] Department of New Jersey, Grand Army of the Republic, *Proceedings of the Seventeenth Annual Encampment 1884* (New York, 1884), pp. 24–25.

[15] Elmer Edward Noyes, "A History of the Grand Army of the Republic in Ohio from 1866 to 1900," Ph.D. dissertation, Ohio State University (1945), pp. 42–43.

[16] *New York Daily Tribune*, July 2, 1867.

tion of the Elks and the Knights of Pythias in the sixties and the Shriners in the early seventies. The Patrons of Husbandry, better known as the Grange (1867), and the Knights of Labor (1869) both originally were secret and ritualistic, and even the success of the Ku Klux Klan in the South was partly a manifestation of this spirit. In forming the Grand Army of the Republic Stephenson deliberately catered to this instinct by drawing upon his Masonic experiences for a detailed scheme of grips, passwords, and ceremonial. Initiates were required to kneel blindfolded before an empty coffin decorated with a flag, skull, crossbones, and crossed sword. With their left hands on the Bibles and swords and their right hands raised, they then swore to keep the order's secrets, to extend charity to veterans, and to help them obtain employment. Having been told that the penalty for violation of this oath would be the one inflicted on spies and traitors, they were unbandaged, only to "see before them, as they kneel, the open coffin, with spade, shovel, and the usual implements used in Military executions; and the Guard drawn up in front, representing a firing party." [17]

In its first years the Grand Army spent a good deal of its time discussing and altering this ritual. The Eastern members argued that such paraphernalia were essential for successful recruiting, and in 1869 the national encampment inaugurated three grades of membership, Recruit, Soldier, and Veteran, symbolizing the virtues of Fraternity, Charity, and Loyalty. These more elaborate ceremonies caused considerable dissension until the 1871 convention revised them and returned to a one-grade system. As the veterans grew more mature, they lost interest in such trappings. In 1881, for example, the society abolished the requirement of blindfolding during initiation and by the nineties, though other groups of ex-soldiers like the Union Veterans' Union still abounded in signs and passwords, the ritualistic element in the G.A.R. had become fairly unimportant.

Two survivals of the earlier fraternal and ceremonial aspects, however, were the members' practice of always addressing each other as "Comrade" (the word had more innocent connotations at that time) and the tendency of many posts and departments to adopt uniforms which until a few years ago it would not have been neces-

[17] Oliver M. Wilson, *The Grand Army of the Republic Under Its First Constitution and Ritual* (Kansas City, Mo., 1905), pp. 230–231.

sary to describe to any American who had ever seen a Memorial Day parade. The Kansas department, for example, endorsed an outfit consisting of a short, single-breasted blue flannel sack coat with G.A.R. buttons, pants either black or the same material as the coat, white or blue single-breasted vests with Grand Army buttons, a fatigue cap with the letters "G.A.R." and the number of the post on it, white gloves, black tie, and the order's badge on the left breast. Even after such a costume was adopted, the wearing of it seems to have remained optional, but nearly all members were very proud of their official G.A.R. badges.

But as the Grand Army abandoned its affinity with the fraternal orders, the Sons of Veterans continued the passion for grips and ciphers. By the nineties this had produced ill-feeling that took on the proportions of a high church–low church controversy. Many members said that the society could never compete with fraternal organizations such as the Knights of Pythias, the Masons, and the Odd Fellows, which they obviously regarded as parallel bodies, unless it possessed a more elaborate system of degrees and ceremonies. Consequently in 1892 the order voted to award a three-hundred-dollar prize for the best three-degree ritual and in 1894 it proceeded to put one into effect. But the debate did not cease, Eastern members opposing the innovation and Westerners defending it. In 1898 the national convention defeated efforts to abolish all traces of ritual, but did return to the simpler one-degree system.

The other stronghold of ritualistic work was the women's Civil War associations. After considerable discussion the first convention of the Woman's Relief Corps adopted a secret ritual. So zealous was it in preserving these mysteries that it allowed only members to print the forms. But since the number of female printers who happened also to belong to the W.R.C. was obviously limited, the resulting inconvenience forced the national president, though reassuring her followers that she believed in guarding their rites "almost as I would the privacy of our secret devotions," to recommend that G.A.R. men be permitted to do the work.[18] Sessions continued to be secret and much of the time of the 1892 national convention was consumed in debating whether Clara Barton might be admitted to welcome them

[18] Woman's Relief Corps, Auxiliary to the Grand Army of the Republic, *Proceedings of the Fourth National Convention 1886* (Boston, 1886), pp. 25–26.

to Washington without knowing the password. At another meeting the presence of a seven-year-old boy in the gallery produced a minor crisis. The delegates asserted that no child over three should be admitted at any gathering lest he disclose their secrets to his play-mates; in an excess of caution the assembly finally barred all children over two. Some G.A.R. members were inclined to ridicule these pretensions which they themselves had outgrown and once General Sherman had to apologize for laughing too loudly while watching the women go through their ceremonies, but with a considerable display of dignity the ladies replied that their practices refuted "the old slander that a woman cannot keep a secret." [19] While the W.R.C., Ladies of the G.A.R., and Ladies' Aid of the Sons spent much time debating and altering their rites, they never contem-plated their complete abandonment.

Even more beguiling than the local social attractions of these orders were the opportunities to attend state and national conven-tions. The ever mobile Americans responded with enthusiasm to the idea of a trip to the big city and fun away from home. State meet-ings lasted for two or three days and national ones for the better part of a week. They soon became mammoth affairs. The actual number of delegates to a G.A.R. national encampment was a little under a thousand, but by the late eighties and the nineties thousands of other veterans and relatives were congregating with them. In 1891 Detroit welcomed some 50,000 former soldiers and 150,000 additional visitors, and a similar total of 200,000, it was estimated, thronged Pittsburgh in 1894. Even at state conclaves so many assembled that once the Maine veterans asked the Woman's Relief Corps to meet at a differ-ent time or place because the two sessions so crowded the convention towns. Reunions of the lesser groups were less populous, of course. Yet the practice of joint meetings sometimes swelled them, as when the Society of the Army of the Cumberland, the Union Veteran Legion, and the Ladies of the Union Veteran Legion all advanced on Columbus in 1897. Such assemblages were only possible because of the development of the nation's railroad network, and as time went on the companies encouraged them by granting special fares to both state and national conventions. So important were these re-

[19] Grand Army of the Republic, *Journal of the Twenty-Second Annual Session of the National Encampment 1888* (Minneapolis, 1888), p. 172.

ductions that the societies sometimes threatened to alter their meeting place if the local lines did not make this concession; on the other hand, the railroads were indignant if they did not receive what they considered their just share of this passenger traffic.

Since the mercantile elements soon recognized the economic value of these gatherings, a prominent feature of conventions was a spirited debate over the next meeting place in which representatives of different cities offered various inducements. Local committees often pledged large sums of money for the veterans' entertainment. The businessmen of St. Louis contributed $100,000 for the 1887 session; for the Washington reunion of 1892 Congress appropriated $90,000 and the community raised $50,000 more; at Pittsburgh two years later the sum was $125,000, secured from local authorities, the citizens, and the sale of concessions. For this last gathering the city offered schoolhouses and halls for the free accommodation of 10,000 veterans and forced hotels not to raise their rates for the rest of the visitors. Meanwhile, Western cities and territories eager to win immigrants utilized these assemblies to exhibit their products and thus attract settlers. In a similar outburst of "booster" exuberance one hundred and fifty converts to Florida's charms and resources startled the 1891 national encampment by arriving "bedecked in hats, not only of curious construction, but made of natural seaweed" on a special train which included one car devoted exclusively to the state's products, from banana trees in blossom to a live alligator ten feet long.[20]

These influxes quite disrupted the ordinary life of cities. Before the 1888 encampment at Columbus, Mrs. J. B. Foraker, wife of the governor, issued an ultimatum to the local gentry: "Every person who had a house was expected to take guests to the limit of capacity. Not only every house and every room would be in demand, but there would be tents on lawns, the occupants to be fed by the owners of the lawns; committees would inform householders of their obligations on this score." The Forakers moved into one of the finest residences in the city, its owner having decided to remain out of town until the upheaval was past. Among their guests were six governors, Colonel and Mrs. Frederick Dent Grant, and Mrs. John A. Logan and her son. "There wasn't an inch of space unutilized in

[20] New York Tribune, Aug. 4, 1891.

that old mansion by the time the soldiers came," Mrs. Foraker later recalled. "We turned public rooms into bedrooms, . . . canvassed all the porches and filled them with cots. The library, very small, and the dining-room were the only rooms that did not have beds in them." Governors A. P. Hovey of Indiana and J. D. Rusk of Wisconsin slept in the front parlor. Rusk had never before seen a folding bed. "He was fascinated by it—and a little suspicious," Mrs. Foraker remembered. ". . . We spent some time opening and shutting the thing before the Governor concluded that it was no more dangerous than the shellings he had been through in the Civil War, and decided to chance it." [21] What educational effects these meetings may have had on even less sophisticated members can only be left to conjecture.

The official proceedings consisted of greetings from local dignatories and representatives of kindred organizations, the reports of officers, passing resolutions (usually on desired legislation), selection of the next meeting place, and spirited elections for new leaders. The most attractive features of the meetings, however, lay outside these formal sessions. When the Minnesota encampment gathered at the Stillwater Opera House in January 1877, after the officers had been installed according to the ritual, a quartette supplied vocal music and a brass band played such tunes as "Tenting on the Old Camp Ground" and "The Battle Cry of Freedom." "The audience joined in the chorus of the latter, and the effect was inspiring beyond description." The Stillwater Amateur Dramatic Club then presented a farce entitled *A Pretty Piece of Business* "in a manner which called forth the highest praise of critics and the rapturous enthusiasm of the audience." Dancing followed until three A.M.[22] The Pennsylvania Grand Army, assembled at Oil City in 1898, enjoyed a barbecue at the local race track. "In one hour, the committee had served 1,400 pounds of beef, 2,000 loaves of bread, two wagon loads of watercress, 200 pounds of butter, 500 gallons of burgoo soup, and then sent down town and had 50 cooked hams delivered at the grounds, which were also distributed in the form

[21] Julia B. Foraker, *I Would Live It Again* (New York and London, 1932), pp. 114–115.
[22] Department of Minnesota, Grand Army of the Republic, *Early History From 1866 to 1879 Inclusive* (Minneapolis, 1896), pp. 146–147.

of sandwiches, 100 additional loaves of bread being necessary." [23]
At one point the Oregon veterans turned to more exotic diversion
by visiting an insane asylum.

In the seventies, when the veterans were still fairly young, state
branches of the G.A.R. also held semiannual encampments in the
summer which proved to be pleasant outings. After the Minnesota
veterans had finished a picnic lunch at White Bear Lake in July
1872, "the floor of the pavilion was cleared and while some lost
themselves in the mazy dance, others amused themselves by sailing,
rowing, etc." [24] The gathering of the Pennsylvania comrades at
Wilkes-Barre in July 1870 included an excursion to Harvey's Lake,
where they enjoyed lunch, boating on the lake, and a swimming
match among one-legged members. New York's summer session of
1880 featured a boat trip to Glen Island, where the delegates enjoyed
a clambake and perhaps other refreshments, for, sailing home at
night, they sang and cheered everything in sight, especially a canal
boat named "Little Buttercup." Such attractions help to explain why
hundreds of young couples attended these meetings on their honey-
moons! [25]

The two high points of gatherings of veterans were the parade
and the banquet. At Philadelphia in 1876 the national encampment
held its first parade, which soon became a customary part of state
and national assemblies. Because of extreme heat the initial attempt
was not very successful, but at Providence the next year the "streets
were filled with people, and great attention was paid to the parade.
The line was finely arranged and made an attractive appearance." [26]
By 1888 it took five hours for nearly 75,000 veterans to pass the
reviewing stand. Both convention crowds and the general public
found this event a favorite feature of the festivities. By mid-morning
it was usually impossible to move about the downtown area, every
vantage point had been taken, bidding was high for places at windows along the way, numerous bands and drum corps added to the

[23] Department of Pennsylvania, Grand Army of the Republic, *Proceedings of the
32nd Annual Encampment 1898* (n.p., 1898), p. 254.

[24] Minn. G.A.R., *Early History*, p. 142.

[25] Alice Katharine Fallows, *Everybody's Bishop, Being the Life and Times of the
Right Reverend Samuel Fallows, D.D.* (New York, 1927), p. 287.

[26] Grand Army of the Republic, *Proceedings of the Eleventh Annual Meeting of
the National Encampment 1877* (Philadelphia, n.d.), p. 493.

hubbub and on one occasion "1,200 school girls, clad in white and waving banners, welcomed the veterans with patriotic songs." [27]

Some observers worried whether these processions displayed the proper solemnity. "One Illinois Post went by under red, white and blue umbrellas, intended to represent the Star-Spangled Banner, though they had not even troubled themselves to get the number of the stars of the States right," a carping critic recorded in 1891, "others led along with them negroes in particoloured dresses, to serve them with water; women and girls in fancy costumes were also to be seen in the ranks . . . the Minnesota men for example wore wheat-ears, the Kansas men sunflowers, the Texas men a great pair of horns, with the ridiculous inscription, *We never draw in our horns: they are too long.*" [28] On the other hand, a Southern sympathizer, accustomed to the "spontaneous yell of untrammeled enthusiasm" usually given to the Confederate survivors, was "astounded at the apathy, the woodenness of the onlookers." All he heard, and that at long intervals, was "the studied, modulated 'Hip! Hip! Hurrah!' The interstice was filled with the silent waving of a handkerchief here and there." [29] But in explanation of such apparent indifference Grand Army leaders insisted that "there is an enthusiasm of absolute silence." [30] As the veterans became older, the feeling grew that there should no longer be such lengthy parades and the 1895 national encampment voted that future routes should be chosen so as to avoid excessive fatigue. Many members now insisted on assurances that the processions be along shaded streets and that ice water be frequently available along the way. [31]

The climax of these sessions was usually the banquet, much of whose conviviality doubtless resulted from the amount of liquor consumed. Declaring that "we must as far as possible provide our banquets with all that would make them acceptable to the greatest

[27] *Portland* (Maine) *Daily Press,* June 24, 1885, quoted in Grand Army of the Republic, *Journal of the Nineteenth Annual Session of the National Encampment 1885* (Toledo, 1885), p. 305.

[28] "The Grand Army of the Republic," *Macmillan's Magazine,* LXV (Dec. 1891), 133.

[29] Albert Sidney Morton, "Two Great Reunions," *Confederate Veteran,* IV (Oct. 1896), 333.

[30] Grand Army of the Republic, *Journal of the Twenty-Sixth National Encampment 1892* (Albany, 1892), p. 218.

[31] Noyes, "History of the Grand Army of the Republic in Ohio," p. 176.

number," the Society of the Army of the Tennessee indignantly rejected a motion to bar liquors and wines from future dinners.[32] The Wisconsin Loyal Legion's greatest outlay was for wines. "This is unavoidable," an official explained, "as our Companions scold me vigorously if I don't get the best." [33] "The drinks were abundant and very mixed," a member recalled of the Society of the Army of the Cumberland's meeting in 1891. "We had every thing from 'Soda Pop' to 'Duffy's Malt Whiskey.' I recollect being allured by a most enticing beverage, called 'Roman Punch,' and with the assistance of a few glasses of lager, a gin-cocktail or two, and *'sich,'* my speech was destroyed." [34] As the presiding officer finally adjourned this particular meeting, he observed that the members left "feeling that we are better for having been here, even if we feel worse tomorrow." [35]

Teetotallers seem to have been almost as scarce at G.A.R. sessions. At New York's banquet in 1880 "the popping of a hundred champagne corks indicated that the boys were having a good time." [36] Even when the order held its national encampment in the very bailiwick of Neal Dow and the prohibition movement, a delegate observed that "if there are any laws in force in the State of Maine to which the citizens of other parts of the country are unaccustomed, we were not allowed to know their existence, nor to leave the beautiful city of Portland, and its fair daughters, with dry and parched throats." [37]

An appropriation of five thousand dollars for wine at the dinner in Detroit in 1891 caused considerable controversy, not so much on the ground of temperance as because the official delegates who benefited were only a fraction of the veterans present in the city.

---

[32] Society of the Army of the Tennessee, *Report of the Proceedings 1866–1871* (Cincinnati, 1877), p. 481.

[33] J. R. Saville to Lucius Fairchild, March 19, 1885, Lucius Fairchild Papers, Wisconsin State Historical Society.

[34] Society of the Army of the Cumberland, *Twenty-Third Reunion 1892* (Cincinnati, 1892), p. 131.

[35] Society of the Army of the Cumberland, *Twenty-Second Reunion 1891* (Cincinnati, 1892), p. 109.

[36] Department of New York, Grand Army of the Republic, *Proceedings of the Semi-Annual and Annual Encampment July, 1880, and Jan., 1881* (Nyack, N.Y., 1881), p. 51.

[37] Department of the Potomac, Grand Army of the Republic, *Proceedings of the Eighteenth Annual Encampment 1886* (Washington, 1886), p. 20.

Actually this particular banquet seems to have been slim on the food side. One delegate reported that "first they brought on the tiniest amount of some kind of soup. Then what they called 'Frog's Legs'—stringy things which were so tough that he could not bite them—then a little beef steak which was good enough—but there was hardly a mouthful. . . ." He finally became so hungry that he left early to get something to eat.[38] But beverages were apparently more abundant, for one official conceded, "If the boys did not get on a regular drunk, they got pretty tight." [39] The confusion became so great, according to the press, that General Russell Alger had to have a bugle blown to get any attention for the speakers. The commander of the New York department was so distressed at observing that "too many Comrades are debauched by the wines and liquors that flow so freely" that he urged no more liquor be served at banquets.[40] At the same convention California's wine producers gave that state's delegation such a generous supply of their wares that for a week it was able to hold open house for all comers. "The result was that we gathered about us the most glorious army of bummers it has ever been my misfortune to review," the state commander later reported. "It was as painful as ludicrous to see the line formed at our front door before it was opened in the morning to the public." [41]

The Sons of Veterans sometimes took a patronizing attitude toward this infirmity, arguing that their fathers' "bad habits were contracted under trying circumstances" and that they should not be blamed but "should rather be treated like overgrown children. . . ." [42] But the offspring became quite insulted when the Montana G.A.R. announced, "While there may be some reasonable degree of doubt

[38] "Detroit," *Grand Army Record*, VI (Aug. 1891), 5.

[39] *American Tribune* (Indianapolis), Aug. 21, 1891.

[40] Department of New York, Grand Army of the Republic, *Proceedings of the Twenty-sixth Annual Encampment 1892* (Albany, 1892), p. 151. On the other hand, one of the Montana delegates later asserted that the newspapers had greatly exaggerated this "superb affair" and put the blame on waiters and employees who had appropriated much of the wine and become "noisy and disorderly." Department of Montana, Grand Army of the Republic, *Journal of the Annual Encampments 1891–1894* (n.p., n.d.), p. 42.

[41] Department of California, Grand Army of the Republic, *Proceedings of the Twenty-Fifth Annual Encampment 1892* (San Francisco, 1892), p. 31.

[42] Quoted by Dixon Wecter, *When Johnny Comes Marching Home* (Cambridge, Mass., 1944), p. 250.

as to the ill effects on the old Soldiers of the custom of serving wine at our encampments, there can be no possible doubt as to its effects on the young men who are the future hope of the country." It therefore decided not to invite any of the second generation to banquets at which wine was served. The Sons indignantly considered this practically a public statement that they could not hold their liquor and refused to attend any Grand Army functions unless the ban were withdrawn, but the veterans remained adamant.[43]

These various distractions during encampments became so numerous and attractive that many felt the delegates were neglecting their proper business, the transaction of the order's affairs, and that the meetings had become nothing but pleasant social affairs. But that apparently was just what the old soldiers wanted, for efforts to refuse invitations or to restrict the informal features did not get very far.

The sessions of the United Confederate Veterans resembled those of the Grand Army, except that the poignant memory of a Lost Cause charged their gatherings with a far greater emotional content. When the commander-in-chief, General John Gordon, appeared at the reunion in Richmond in 1896, "Almost every one raised from his or her seat, cheered wildly, waved hats, handkerchiefs and umbrellas, the band played Dixie, and the old Confederate yell could be heard many squares away." [44] When the following year at Nashville Gordon attempted to submit his resignation, "With one accord the entire gathering rose to its feet and exclaimed, 'No, no, no. Never, never, never!' " Once again banners, hats, and handkerchiefs went into motion, "others shed tears at the idea of such an action," the band started the inevitable "Dixie" and "quietude and order entirely departed from the convention hall." According to the official report of the meeting, "Such a scene has seldom, if ever been witnessed in any country or in any age." [45]

The appearance of various members of the Jefferson Davis family on the platform usually set off similar emotional orgies, especially if Winnie Davis, the somewhat mature "Child of the Confederacy,"

[43] Montana G.A.R., *Journal 1891–1894,* pp. 14–15, 21–22.

[44] United Confederate Veterans, *Minutes of the Sixth Annual Meeting 1896* (New Orleans, 1897), p. 6.

[45] United Confederate Veterans, *Minutes of the Seventh Annual Meeting 1897* (New Orleans, 1898), p. 85.

was on hand. The last reunion at which she appeared was at Atlanta in July 1898. General Gordon led her forward "and the crowd went wild with joy. The cheering lasted some time, and Miss Davis gracefully bowed her acknowledgments with her eyes filled with tears. . . . There were few dry eyes in the whole house, and hundreds of old veterans broke down completely and cried like babies." [46]

As at the G.A.R. encampments, many others besides veterans flocked to the reunions and some criticism developed that the meetings had become chiefly the occasion for elaborate entertainments for various "maids of honor" and "sponsors" whom the organization had designated. Gatherings of the United Daughters of the Confederacy had equally attractive social diversions. The convention at Richmond in 1899, for example, featured receptions by the Richmond Chapter to meet Mrs. Davis, by the governor and his wife at the gubernatorial mansion, and by the local D.A.R., in addition to a luncheon given by the U.C.V. camp at the Soldiers' Home.

Many of the new hereditary societies limited their activities in these years almost entirely to banquets and similar social gatherings. In contrast to the large assemblages of veterans, their sessions tended to be small. Most of the men's groups were satisfied with a dinner at Delmonico's or Sherry's; they then went home and thought little about the organization until the next repast. The women obviously took even more delight in social functions. The Colonial Dames usually gathered for luncheons at fashionable restaurants or teas at the residences of the Van Rensselaers, Drexels or De Peysters. When the meeting was at a private home, the hostess showed her ancestral relics or read old family letters. In March 1897, for example, the Dames assembled as guests of Mrs. Cornelius Vanderbilt, who displayed her old silver together with some lent by Mrs. William Rhinelander and Mrs. Hilborne Roosevelt.

Even within the Daughters of the American Revolution, which had by far the widest range of activities of all the hereditary societies, the same attractions probably formed the chief inducement for affiliation. One of the first acts of the national board of management was to hold "a grand reception as the best way to give the new Society that social prestige, so necessary to anything emanating from

---

[46] United Confederate Veterans, *Minutes of the Eighth Annual Meeting 1898* (New Orleans, 1899), p. 86.

the city of Washington." On February 22, 1891, Mrs. Harrison received the members at Mrs. Cabell's residence. A leader in the organization reported that no previous social event in the capital "had surpassed this one—in its personnel or the beauty of its appointments." The story of the reception spread through the country and did much to assure the association's success.[47]

As chapters developed throughout the nation, they too emphasized the social aspects. "The social element has always been prominent in all the meetings," declared the society's first report.[48] The proceedings when twenty-four women gathered for a meeting in Huntington, Indiana, in November 1899 will serve as an example of what went on at the average session. After the singing of "America," the regent gave a talk on the British occupation of New York during the Revolution, and a colonial romance was described by a descendant of the couple involved. Then three other members contributed various instrumental and vocal selections. Next the ladies advanced to the dining room for a three-course lunch during which they all received pink and white carnations as souvenirs. Finally they played a game. Each member had to wear on her back a card giving the name of some celebrity and attempt to guess who it was from the questions asked her. Solicitude about poor health turned out to refer to Mrs. McKinley, requests for a song were clues to the wearer's representing Patti, while inquiries as whether she was about to leave her husband were the giveaway to the one representing the Princess of Wales. In many a small American town middle-class ladies reveled in similar harmless pastimes with little thought of any further connotation to the term "patriotic society."

While the hereditary societies never developed annual conventions of the size of the G.A.R.'s national encampments, the D.A.R.'s Continental Congresses had much of the same appeal. Miss Lucretia Hart Clay found this a valuable asset when organizing chapters in Kentucky. "I appealed to the social element, inherent in human nature," she revealed, "and told of the pleasures to be derived from attending the national congress, in our Nation's capital, and of the

---

[47] Mary S. Lockwood and Emily Lee Sherwood, *Story of the Records* (Washington, 1906), p. 26.

[48] Daughters of the American Revolution, *Report 1890–1897* (Washington, 1899), p. 53.

social features connected with the congress." [49] The meeting originally came the week of Washington's birthday, but as this was an inclement season for travel, the date was later changed to the week of April 19, the equally patriotic anniversary of Lexington and Concord.

One of the most popular attractions of the assemblies was a reception given the delegates at the White House. Mrs. Harrison initiated the custom at the first congress in 1892, and her husband and daughter, Mrs. McKee, continued it after her death. In subsequent years Mrs. Cleveland and then President McKinley also received the Daughters. So much did the delegates enjoy these festivities that the less fortunate members who had to stay at home became discontented. One D.A.R. complained that the various dues and initiation fees financed excursions for the officers but all that the average members got were reports "telling us what perfectly lovely times our officers had in Chicago and Albany and at all the big hotels, 'representing' us! And what they wore at the receptions to the Infanta and the Duke, and how Mr. McDowell suggested a lot more nice things to do next year, that would make it necessary for our officers to visit San Francisco or Europe or China. . . ." [50]

But the congresses did not consist solely of "pink teas" or receptions. The business sessions were often so stormy that some members quipped that D.A.R. stood for "Darn Annual Row." The delegates argued violently over such matters as the "mother of a patriot" clause or whether regents of chapters still in the process of organization might vote. The 1894 session proved a particularly acrimonious one. It began with several wrangles over parliamentary procedure and especially over whether the District of Columbia's representatives had been duly elected and were eligible to cast ballots. But the major dispute rose from the quarrel between Mrs. Boynton and the national board of management. In defense of the former, Mrs. Cabell made a personal attack upon Mrs. Walworth which produced hisses, cries of "Shame," and general disorder.

Elections for the national offices produced equal bad feeling. In the novel *The Lion's Share* "Octave Thanet" caught the spirit of

[49] "Work of the Chapters," *American Monthly Magazine*, XVIII (Jan. 1901), 31.
[50] *New York Sun*, quoted in "Notes and Information," *Magazine of Daughters of the Revolution*, I (July 1893), 52–53.

such occasions: "I assure you the other candidates (there were two) tried the very *lowest* political methods . . .," ran the tirade of a defeated aspirant. "There were at least three luncheons given against me. It wasn't the congress, it was the lobby defeated me. And their methods! I would not believe that gentlewomen could stoop to such infamy of misrepresentation. . . . I learned more in those two days of the petty jealousy, the pitiless malevolence of *some* women than I had known all my life before. . . ."[51] Such episodes gave a confused public the impression that the Daughters of the American Revolution were chiefly engaged in fighting the war all over again. These controversies soon had the Daughters lost in such a maze of motions, amendments, and precedents that in desperation many of them found it essential to learn a good deal more about parliamentary procedure than they had ever known before. The editor of their magazine urged that chapters add this study to their work, and many did so.

While the hereditary societies never showed the Civil War associations' interest in ritual and uniforms that marked their close kinship with fraternal bodies (though one wonders if at the time of his addresses to the Sons of the American Revolution Senator McCarthy knew that its members called each other "Comrade"), they did take a great delight in a variety of medals and badges. As in the case of the Cincinnati a century earlier, critics suggested that the right to wear them was a prominent motive for joining these leagues. S.A.R. members wore a rosette with the order's colors in the upper left-hand buttonhole. On ceremonial occasions they wore a silver cross, with a gold medallion in the center, surmounted by a gold or silver eagle, the entire decoration being suspended from a gold ring by a blue ribbon.

The other societies had equally elaborate decorations.[52] "The colored badges of the various classes of members and committeewomen brightened up the assembly," commented an observer of a D.A.R. convention, "and the members of the national board, who were distinguished by their jeweled badges and pins, had adopted a

---

[51] Octave Thanet, *The Lion's Share* (Indianapolis, 1907), pp. 55–56.

[52] For the insignia of a dozen of these organizations, including the D.A.R., Daughters of the Revolution, Colonial Dames, and the Society of Colonial Wars, see Marcus Benjamin, "American Patriotic Societies," *Munsey's Magazine,* XIV (Oct. 1895), 74–78.

new fashion of wearing these decorations pendant from a blue and white ribbon around the neck." [53] A real joiner could make quite a resplendent effect. When Mrs. Washington Roebling spoke to D.A.R. chapters, she "presented quite an official appearance, through the array of badges and honorary decorations which she wore." [54] It was in the nineties that there emerged the prototype of the buxom patriotic lady swathed in ribbons and bands and perpetually descending upon Washington, later immortalized in Katharine Dayton and George S. Kaufman's *First Lady* as Mrs. Louella May Creevy, president of the Women's Peace, Purity and Patriotism League. The badges of each society were in different color combinations: white, buff, and blue for the S.A.R., blue and buff for the S.R., blue edged with white for the D.A.R., pink and white for the Mayflower Descendants, and red, white, black, and blue for the Order of Founders and Patriots.[55] These colors usually had symbolic associations. Thus the Daughters of the Revolution used "the buff of Washington's knee-breeches, and the blue of the coat of Royal blue." [56]

Many groups also boasted mottoes. The D.A.R. began with "Amor Patriae" but soon changed to "Home and Country." Considerable time was spent deciding on the order's seal. McDowell had proposed a cradle containing Baby McKee, Mrs. Harrison's grandson who was the "Buzzie" Dall of his day. Miss Desha, however, felt that the suggestion was "the very quintessence of absurdity" that "will make us ridiculous throughout the entire country. I really wish these men would leave us alone." She had no objections to the face, say, of Abigail Adams, "but the Lord deliver us from Baby McKee." [57] The women finally settled on "the figure of a dame of the Revolutionary time sitting at her spinning wheel." [58]

[53] "Celebrations and Proceedings," *American Historical Register* (March 1895), p. 666.

[54] "What We Are Doing and Chapter Work," *American Monthly Magazine,* XVI (June 1900), 1237.

[55] For a fairly complete list, see William S. Thomas, *The Society of the Cincinnati 1783–1935* (New York and London, 1935), pp. 182–183.

[56] Mrs. Henry T. Kent, Mrs. D. Phoenix Ingram and Others, *History of the Organization and Work of the National Society Daughters of the Revolution* (Concord, N.H., 1930), p. 15.

[57] Mary Desha to Flora Adams Darling, Oct. 24, 1890, Flora Adams Darling, *Founding and Organization of the Daughters of the American Revolution and the Daughters of the Revolution* (Philadelphia, 1901), p. 172.

[58] *Ibid.,* p. 47.

Some of the smaller organizations also catered to the vanity of members through the impressive titles of officers. Thus the Baronial Order of Runnemede had a Marshal, a Justiciar, a Chancellor, a Keeper of the Purse, a Keeper of the Signet, and a Keeper of the Rolls. Not to be outdone, the Order of the White Crane had four Consuls, four Tribunes, a Grand Chamberlain, a Patriarch, a High Priest, a Bard, a Praetor General, a High Steward, a Bearer of the Shield, a Grand Sachem, and an Archdruid. Though this would seem to have provided for almost its entire membership, any additional male members ranked as Equestors and all women as Equestriennes. But the more important hereditary bodies did not go to such bizarre extremes in this particular respect.

But whether tea parties for the ladies or three nights away from home in the wicked city for the boys, these attractions were certainly the major ones for the typical member of both veterans' and hereditary societies. But for the ex-soldiers, additional more practical incentives also soon emerged.

VII

The Veterans Discover the Welfare State

DESPITE their strong preoccupation with social festivities, the Civil War associations did not forget their avowed objective of caring for their less fortunate comrades or their dependents, though increasingly they transferred this responsibility to the government and extended its protection to all their followers.

The G.A.R.'s early appeals for members emphasized the need of "relieving the wants of the disabled soldiers, widow and orphan who may seek aid at our hands," [1] and posts frequently utilized suppers, concerts, amateur theatricals, fairs, and lotteries to raise money for their charitable funds. In its early years the order sponsored so many lectures for this purpose that in 1869 it was described as "resolving itself into a vast lyceum organization." [2] Among those who appeared before the veterans were Horace Greeley, Clara Barton, and E. P. Roe, later the author of the best-seller, *Barriers Burned Away*. Topics ranged from "Six Months in Rebel Prisons" through "The Catacombs of Paris" to Miss Olive Logan's directly titled "Girls," which advocated equal rights and woman suffrage. These talks became less popular by the eighties, when posts found that the appearance of war figures like Lew Wallace and Horace Porter was no longer a great drawing card.

By this time, however, the Grand Army had a larger treasury as a result of its per capita tax levied on each member, the sale of supplies to posts, and charter fees for new branches. The sums expended for charity rose steadily. In the year ending in May 1872, for example, the order distributed $74,675.75 among 673 members and 2161 nonmembers. By 1885 it reported that in the preceding year it had spent

[1] *Soldier's Record* (Madison, Wis.), Dec. 24, 1869.
[2] *Soldier's Friend* (New York), Jan. 23, 1869.

$170,092.77 for the assistance of 15,000 persons, of whom 11,000 were not members, while in 1896 the amount was $247,669.66. The Eastern states led in this work, over half this sum usually being spent in New York, Massachusetts, and Pennsylvania. Massachusetts and New York were usually the most generous of the state organizations, with annual appropriations of over $40,000, but Pennsylvania, Ohio, Illinois, New Jersey, and Connecticut each allotted between $10,000 and $25,000 a year for this purpose.

This prodigality quickly lent itself to abuses, especially during depressions, which naturally increased the demands. As early as February 1868, there was a report of a Western comrade who had succeeded in "bumming" his way across the country from post to post.[3] But this did not become acute until the tramp problem made its first real appearance in the United States as a result of the Panic of 1873. Warning that "we shall often find among the poor tramps of our country many a comrade," the Illinois commander urged, "Finding him worthy of your friendship, stand by him, though all the world assail."[4] Unfortunately, this generous attitude encouraged many vagrants to pretend they were veterans, and soon the order came to alert posts against frauds. The hard times in the mid-eighties necessitated another series of vivid warnings. These itinerant mendicants had various stories of distress. One claimed to be deaf and dumb and the member of a post in Ohio, while a Pennsylvania tramp "is a small man, light complexion, sandy moustache and whiskers; and tells of the death of his mother and unkind treatment by a brother."[5] Another "can have a fit or broken arm whenever it is for his interest to do so; he is not only a beat but a scoundrel, and has been dishonorably discharged from the order."[6]

During the depression after 1893, matters became so serious that the Massachusetts G.A.R. had a Committee on Mendicants which, in coöperation with the W.R.C., provided transportation, meals, and

[3] Dixon Wecter, *When Johnny Comes Marching Home* (Cambridge, Mass., 1944), p. 189.

[4] Department of Illinois, Grand Army of the Republic, *Proceedings of the Seventh, Eighth, Ninth, Tenth and Eleventh Annual Encampments 1873–1877* (Aurora, Ill., 1880), p. 36.

[5] Department of Pennsylvania, Grand Army of the Republic, *Proceedings of the 40th and 41st Encampments July, 1886, and Feb., 1887* (Philadelphia, 1887), p. 17.

[6] Department of Massachusetts, Grand Army of the Republic, *Journals of the Encampment Proceedings from 1881 to 1887 Inclusive* (Boston, 1902), p. 420.

lodging for needy veterans. But also, more than ever before, the official circulars of national and state leaders constantly described dead-beats and imposters. Typical of these unworthy applicants was Ambrose King, who "won't work and curses everybody when refused aid without it." [7] Another was Garrett Joyce, who claimed to be a Grand Army member. "He walks on crutches and drags left foot when sober," according to one of the order's commanders-in-chief. "When drunk, he walks without crutches." [8] By the nineties the Sons of Veterans faced the same difficulties with characters such as Frank McKenna, who roamed New England in 1894 pretending to be a post captain from New York and "has a peculiar habit of nervously moving his head," [9] and George Willson, who had considerable knowledge of the order's secret work and traveled about Eastern states, stating he had lost his overcoat and pocketbook and asking for his carfare home. Needless to say, the mere existence of this situation is a striking clue to the economic and social background of the membership of veterans' organizations.

The very name of the Woman's Relief Corps indicated a strong concern for charity from its inception. One department president described this as "our main work, from which all others branch." [10] As in the case of the G.A.R., the depression in the nineties increased the demand upon its funds. By that decade, therefore, the order was usually spending about $60,000 annually; Massachusetts, Ohio, and California accounted for nearly half this sum. In an effort to secure more money for this work, a number of the society's leaders endorsed Dobbins' Electric Soap and appealed to W.R.C., G.A.R., and Sons of Veterans members to buy it. The organization received five dollars for every thousand wrappers it collected and forwarded to the company.

In addition to this solicitude for distressed veterans, the W.R.C. also took an interest in former army nurses who were not receiving

[7] Department of California, Grand Army of the Republic, *Proceedings of the Twenty-Ninth Annual Encampment 1896* (San Francisco, 1896), p. 145.

[8] Grand Army of the Republic, *Journal of the Twenty-ninth Annual Encampment 1895* (Rockford, Ill., n.d.), p. 382.

[9] Sons of Veterans, U.S.A., *Journal of Proceedings of the Fourteenth Annual Encampment 1895* (Des Moines, 1895), p. 68.

[10] Department of Minnesota, Woman's Relief Corps, *Journal of the Thirteenth Annual Convention 1897* (St. Paul, n.d.), p. 24.

pensions. After the Spanish-American War the women also asked the G.A.R.'s permission to extend their work to the survivors of this latest conflict. Since the society viewed itself as "essentially a charitable association," [11] it soon found itself involved in the organized charity movement which was developing at this time. By 1893, officials in Massachusetts were attending the New England Conference of Charities and in 1894 the national convention voted to send delegates to the National Conference of Charities. At first, the latter body was unwilling to recognize the W.R.C. as a charitable organization under its definition, but finally admitted its representatives.

The United Daughters of the Confederacy took an equal interest in caring for Southern veterans. It particularly felt this responsibility because Confederate soldiers, unlike the Union ones, were not receiving federal pensions. But the hereditary societies paid little attention to charitable work. The Cincinnati continued to assist a few needy descendants of Revolutionary officers, but even this was on a small and declining scale. The New Jersey Society granted sums of twenty or twenty-five dollars annually to a small number of spinsters (as late as 1879 it still had on its list Miss Reckless, who had first received its bounty in 1848), but in 1880 it had only nine pensioners and by 1889 but two. Otherwise relief work was a monopoly of the Civil War organizations. Indeed, the D.A.R. urged its members to concentrate on historical enterprises and to leave charitable activities to other groups.

The G.A.R.'s penchant for beneficial and insurance schemes as another method of helping its members in times of distress is further evidence of the essential similarity between veterans' and fraternal orders. The years between the Civil War and the close of the century saw the founding of six hundred fraternal beneficial societies, mostly modeled on the Ancient Order of United Workmen (1868) and adding to the usual attractions of lodges, elaborate ritual, and secrecy the idea of sickness, disability, and death benefits.[12] Many Grand Army posts also established benefit funds which paid three or four dollars a week in case of sickness. In

[11] Woman's Relief Corps, Auxiliary to the Grand Army of the Republic, *Proceedings of the Fourth National Convention 1886* (Boston, 1886), p. 123.

[12] B. H. Meyer, "Fraternal Beneficial Societies in the United States," *American Journal of Sociology*, VI (March 1901), 647, 649–650, 655.

1886, out of the 4916 posts in existence, 900 reported similar arrangements. Over a third of these were in New York. Opinions varied as to the desirability of this feature. A Massachusetts official thought that it was "an incentive to those who are not members of our organization to become such." [13] On the other hand, a Pennsylvania leader contended that "non-beneficial Posts are generally, and with but few exceptions, in a more prosperous condition, both financially and in membership, than those paying weekly benefits under the beneficial plan." [14] At the close of the eighties the inspector-general reported that the number of posts paying benefits was on the decline.

The Sons of Veterans also adopted this practice sometimes. In 1896, out of 1184 camps reporting, 176 had death benefits and 190 had sick benefits. New York contained the largest number of branches with these features. The highest death rate, an average of $275, was in New Jersey; Maryland had the lowest average sum for sickness, $1.98. Although such projects were contrary to the rules of the W.R.C., which aimed to help the G.A.R. and not itself, colored corps in Kentucky had benefit funds because "the women will not pay their money into anything without the chance of getting something out of it." [15]

In the first years of the Grand Army, when many important insurance companies were appearing in the United States, a number of members hoped that the G.A.R. would inaugurate a large-scale life insurance scheme. While some departments seriously considered such ventures, by the nineties the general opinion was that the veterans had reached an age that made the idea impractical.[16] By that time many of the Sons felt that a comprehensive insurance enterprise would strengthen their society. Worried by the decline in membership, they argued that only then could the Sons compete

[13] Department of Massachusetts, Grand Army of the Republic, *Early History From 1866 to 1880 Inclusive* (Boston, 1895), p. 375.

[14] Department of Pennsylvania, Grand Army of the Republic, *Proceedings of the 26th and 27th Encampments July, 1879, and Jan., 1880* (Philadelphia, 1880), p. 97.

[15] Woman's Relief Corps, Auxiliary to the Grand Army of the Republic, *Journal of the Fifteenth National Convention 1897* (Boston, 1897), pp. 320–321.

[16] Independently of the veterans' organizations, insurance companies such as the National and Provident Union for Civil War survivors and an American Mutual Benefit Association of Mexican War Veterans were organized in the eighties.

with fraternal orders like the Knights of Pythias, the Odd Fellows, and the Royal Arcanum, to which many members already belonged. The center of this agitation was Kansas and the Dakotas, where farmers suffering from hard times found the rates of established insurance companies prohibitive and hoped to start within the Sons a cheaper organization. National conventions debated schemes, but finally concluded that the society was a patriotic and not a fraternal body, a decision which showed how the self-conscious patriotism of the nineties was affecting the Civil War associations.

In a period lacking modern social security or group health insurance benefits, there was a good deal to be said for such private efforts to alleviate the hazards of life. Actually, however, these groups soon learned to depend not on self-aid but on the public treasury. Even though rugged individualism and opposition to governmental intervention have been the battle cries of many patriotic organizations in recent years, veterans' associations were almost as quick as those other traditional champions of individualism, the farmers, to discover the advantages of legislative largess on both the federal and state level. Because of an undue focussing of attention on the national scene, too often this interest has been thought to have been confined to the quest for pensions, but actually that was only one of the many forms of help that the Civil War associations expected from the lawmakers. Eventually nearly all departments of the Grand Army had standing committees on legislation which watched every proposal affecting the veterans and lobbied for the measures they desired. Soon many of them could have echoed the frank boast of Colorado's commander in 1888: "That the influence and numerical strength of our order is a recognized factor in this department, was well established by the prompt passage of every bill asked by us from the General Assembly of Colorado." [17]

In the period immediately after 1865 the veterans were greatly concerned with securing the establishment of homes for the children of their dead comrades. In several states the G.A.R. pressed legislation to found such institutions or sought control of those already in existence. Once they were in operation the departments kept a careful

[17] Department of Colorado, Grand Army of the Republic, *Journal of the Ninth Annual Session of the Department Encampment 1888* (Denver, 1888), p. 13.

eye on them. A customary feature of many state encampments was an annual report on their condition. In Indiana, for example, the order conducted a long and eventually successful drive to have the orphans' home separated from the asylum for idiot children, while the Pennsylvania branch secured the continuance of the shelter there beyond its scheduled closing in 1883.

By the 1870's the veterans also began to seek homes for their incapacitated comrades. Though occasionally they endeavored to raise funds privately, usually they asked the various states to erect these shelters. Whenever they did build institutions themselves, they invariably expected the government to acquire title and maintain them. These efforts to have nearly every state legislature establish such a home usually succeeded, though sometimes only after several years of determined campaigning. Triumph in any one state at once encouraged similar drives in neighboring commonwealths, as is indicated by the message that an Illinois leader sent to the department's delegation at the 1885 national encampment: "Soldiers' Home bill passed to-day. Tell the boys to ask every State to do the same." [18] Some departments also agitated to have Congress erect National Soldiers' Homes within their respective borders. This was particularly popular in the South, where local authorities were not too sympathetic to the care of Union soldiers, and in the West, whose lack of wealth caused it to turn to Washington. In 1883 the national encampment appointed a committee to work for such an institution beyond the Mississippi River and also for the admission of all disabled veterans, instead of only those injured in the war. Following a week's conference with Congressmen in Washington, the committee subsequently reported, "the mails and wires were used freely in keeping the Soldiers' Home west of the Mississippi fresh in the minds of our law-makers,—believing in the efficacy of persistent and pressing importunity." The bill finally became law in the summer of 1884, just before a national election. [19]

After the opening of these homes the Grand Army watched them carefully. Nearly all departments had committees which visited

---

[18] Grand Army of the Republic, *Journal of the Nineteenth Annual Session of the National Encampment 1885* (Toledo, 1885), p. 112.

[19] Grand Army of the Republic, *Journal of the Eighteenth Annual Session of the National Encampment 1884* (Philadelphia, 1884), pp. 102–103.

them and then reported to the annual encampments on the conditions discovered, especially as to the quality of food and the validity
of charges of intemperance among the old warriors. The meetings
usually pleaded for further legislative appropriations to enlarge the
facilities, for the admission of wives, for restoration of the right of
the franchise to the inmates, and, finally, for increased G.A.R.
representation on the administrating bodies. Again the methods of
the Colorado department afford an example. In 1893 its legislative
committee asked the lawmakers to allot $100,000 for the home.
When they voted only $10,000, the committee promptly instructed
all posts to bring pressure. "Many of the Posts responded quickly to
the call with ringing resolutions," it later revealed, "and some of
them by addressing communications to their immediate representatives, while others sent delegates to personally interview members
of the legislature." As a result, the order finally secured $40,000.[20]
So well known was the society's vigilance that in 1894 the National
Dairy Union tried, without success, to have the Illinois department
condemn the soldiers' home at Quincy for serving oleomargarine.
The Woman's Relief Corps and the Ladies of the G.A.R. took a
similar interest in these homes, contributing money, fruit, jellies,
cushions, books, and newspapers. In some cases they furnished certain rooms and also agitated for the admission of women to the
institutions or to their boards of control. In the South, the United
Daughters of the Confederacy felt the same concern for institutions
for ex-Confederates, showering shoes, organs, coffee pots, table
cloths and like items on the defenseless inmates.

Sometimes the women's groups started their own projects. In
1890 the W.R.C. acquired two houses in Madison, Ohio as the nucleus of a National Relief Corps Home and then secured $25,000
from the state legislature. For its support the society set aside one-
half of its per capita tax, which by 1898 had furnished more than
$43,000. The institution admitted army nurses and the wives and
mothers of soldiers, but never had more than sixty-six inmates and
by 1899 was down to fifty-three. Various branches of the order,
notably in Maine, New York, Pennsylvania, and Missouri, also
secured the establishment of such homes and then usually persuaded

---

[20] Department of Colorado and Wyoming, Grand Army of the Republic, *Journal
of the Fourteenth Annual Encampment 1893* (Denver, n.d.), pp. 44–50.

the states to assume their support. Not to be outdone, the Ladies of the G.A.R. in the Keystone state also founded a refuge for the mothers, wives, widows, sisters, and daughters of veterans. Though it sheltered only nine women, the G.A.R. abetted its efforts to have the state share the financial burden.

But soon the Grand Army turned to measures that would benefit all its followers, not merely its more unfortunate ones. Its first national encampment in 1866 asked Congress to equalize the bounties that had been paid to Union soldiers and sailors, a proposal that was the rough equivalent of the modern cash bonus. The sum most frequently suggested was eight and a third dollars for each month of service. A number of national and state conventions repeated this plea during the next few years. Congress proved amenable but a veto from President Grant in 1875 discouraged further agitation for the moment. The *National Tribune* revived the issue upon its founding in 1877 and was still giving it plaintive mention as late as 1890. In the early eighties several Grand Army encampments again endorsed the idea, but with no results. In the middle of that decade there emerged the variation that the government give the veterans the difference between the greenback value of their war pay and the gold value, but the leaders of the G.A.R. usually secured the defeat of any such indirect reflection of the greenback heresy of the day. During the Populist upheaval of the nineties many Western veterans renewed this request, protesting that the bondholders were receiving their interest in gold while the soldiers had been paid in depreciated currency, and somehow they tied this in with the alleged opposition of the Eastern "money power" to pensions.

In the order's early years the possibility of grants of homesteads seemed more attractive than pensions. As was to prove the case in pension agitation, the original impulse came from an interested outside source. As part of its colonization program for its Western land grants the Northern Pacific Railroad hired as its agent Major George B. Hibbard, who induced the Society of the Army of the Cumberland and a number of G.A.R. posts, particularly in New England, to petition Congress for certain modifications in the homestead laws in favor of veterans. Congress yielded to the joint pressure of a powerful corporation and organized soldiery. In 1870 it allowed veterans to take their full one hundred and sixty acres rather than the usual eighty acres allowed other homesteaders within the limits of the more desirable railroad grants and two years later permitted them to include the length of army service as part of the period of residence necessary to acquire title.[21]

Encouraged by these concessions, in the early seventies the Grand Army started agitation for an outright grant of land, usually one hundred and sixty acres, to all veterans in such a way that they could acquire title through the action of an agent or attorney without actually settling on the tracts themselves. The hard times of the eighties revived this drive. The fact that the participants of every previous war had received such gifts seemed to constitute a similar obligation to reward the Civil War veterans. "The deeding of 160 acres of land is no act of charity," according to this theory, " 'tis part of a contract, if not written, often implied." [22] There was a feeling that to the winners of a war belonged territory as spoils. "If we had been a monarchy," Commander-in-Chief Paul Van Der Voort asserted, "we would have confiscated the soil we conquered and given it to the victors." It would now be "the highest ingratitude" to deny land to the men who had saved the nation.[23] Appeals to antimonopoly and nativist sentiment also appeared. At a time when the railroads were receiving such lavish grants, many argued that the soil should go to deserving veterans rather than to grasping corporations, which so often had foreign stockholders to boot. "Unless landwarrants are given soon the public domain will largely fall into the hands of foreign syndicates, alien to our soil and leave the Union soldier homeless and landless," Van Der Voort warned. *"America for Americans* will meet a response in every soldier's heart." [24]

More responsible Grand Army leaders strongly opposed these proposals. They denied that the government had ever made any contract to bestow land upon its soldiers. In any case they insisted that

---

[21] James B. Hedges, "The Colonization Work of the Northern Pacific Railroad," *Mississippi Valley Historical Review*, XIII (Dec. 1926), 319; Benjamin Horace Hibbard, *A History of the Public Land Policies* (New York, 1924), p. 130; Grand Army of the Republic, *Proceedings of the Sixth Annual Meeting of the National Encampment 1872* (New York, 1872), p. 9; Society of the Army of the Cumberland, *Fifth Re-Union 1871* (Cincinnati, 1872), p. 37.

[22] Department of Iowa, Grand Army of the Republic, *Journal of the Tenth Annual Session 1884* (Des Moines, 1884), p. 23.

[23] G.A.R., *Journal 1884*, pp. 111–112.

[24] *Ibid.*, p. 111.

there was no longer sufficient desirable land left for a distribution of some two million land warrants. Critics claimed that it would require about twenty-seven years to survey so much property and that by that time many of the beneficiaries would be dead. They contended further that the experience of the past indicated that the veterans would quickly sell their land warrants and that only speculators would benefit from such a law. The *National Tribune,* disturbed at the prospect of any diversion from other legislation in which it had more of a vested interest, added its opposition. These considerations caused a number of state encampments either specifically to reject such schemes or to fail to take any action favoring them.

But land-hungry G.A.R. members also had answers to these objections. To those who said that there was not enough public land left to take care of all the war's survivors, one Iowa veteran replied that he favored making the grants "if it takes every acre, Rocky Mountains and all, and if there isn't enough there let us go on with the strong arm of conquest, and capture some from Mexico and Canada." [25] To those who estimated that there would be at least two million claimants, another comrade from the same state merely answered, "Thank God if there are that number of survivors." [26] As for the argument that it would take years to map the territory, he would double the number of surveyors and even let the soldiers measure off their own lands. To the contention that the act would only benefit land syndicates, Van Der Voort scornfully retorted, "This would create the idea that the veteran of the war is unable to attend to his own affairs, and would at once fall into the hands of public cormorants." [27] Convinced by these arguments, a few G.A.R. encampments urged Congress to grant the desired one hundred and sixty acres. The issue produced a lengthy debate at the 1884 national encampment. Commander-in-Chief Van Der Voort led the fight in its behalf despite the pension committee's hostility, but after a lengthy discussion the meeting condemned any land-warrant bill. Though traces of this agitation lingered on into the nineties, especially in the Far West, this was the end of the order's

[25] *Ibid.,* p. 119.
[26] *Ibid.,* p. 121.
[27] *Ibid.,* p. 111.

serious consideration of the matter. It had never really had a chance because of the general conviction that genuine homesteaders could get land anyway under the existing law and that the veterans had already received sufficient rewards in the form of the cash bounties when they enlisted.[28]

Other veterans, less interested in having the government help them to become Western pioneers, whether actual or vicarious, anticipated the modern desire for bureaucratic security by pressing for a preferred claim upon government jobs.[29] Their suspicion that they were not receiving a due share of the local, state, and federal offices available was a prominent reason for the appearance of so many soldiers' clubs immediately after the war. Soon in both its department and national gatherings the Grand Army was protesting that veterans were being slighted in the patronage and especially asked that soldiers' homes, navy yards, and government bureaus hire disabled survivors.

But not until the eighties, when the passage of civil service legislation in the Pendleton Act of 1883 and the possibility of the first Democratic administration since the Civil War threatened the veterans, did the G.A.R. launch an aggressive campaign. This began with demands for strict enforcement of an existing measure, Section 1754, dating from 1865, which granted preference to disabled veterans if they possessed the capacity for the positions, but left the determination of that capacity to the appointing officials and provided no penalties for nonobservance. The society also protested, with some success, the dismissal of any former soldiers, especially after the change of administration in 1885 endangered so many Republican officeholders. Fortunately, for this purpose Congress had ruled in the appropriation bill for 1876 that in any reductions veterans should be retained if they were equally qualified. The District of Columbia G.A.R. was particularly concerned because nearly all its members were government workers. It secured the reinstatement of approximately 75 per cent of those discharged by the Public Printing Office and thereafter for a number of years maintained an active employment committee which constantly badgered public officials. The Re-

[28] Wecter, *When Johnny Comes Marching Home,* p. 205.
[29] Paul Josephs Woods, "The G.A.R. and Civil Service," Ph.D. Dissertation, University of Illinois (1941), studies this agitation, though only on the federal level.

publicans' return to power led to equally strong appeals both for the restoration of veterans who had been ousted four years earlier and for new appointments. The local committee got some five hundred ex-soldiers placed in 1889 and throughout the Harrison administration found the Interior Department and the Printing Office especially responsive to their pleas.[30]

Actually in the eighties the veterans' most active champion in this regard was not the Grand Army but an independent pressure group called the Veterans' Rights Union, founded in New York City in October 1882 by Joseph W. Kay. Originally representing one hundred and fifty posts and consisting almost entirely of Grand Army members, it agitated for the enforcement of Section 1754 and the 1876 appropriation bill and for the extension of preference to all veterans whether disabled or not.[31] It proved quite successful in preventing removals and securing the reinstatement of veterans, its chief advantage being that it could engage in political activity more openly than the G.A.R.'s official nonpartisan rule permitted. Though not sharing responsibility for its acts, the G.A.R. nevertheless lent it considerable support and it was sometimes known as the G.A.R. Veterans' Rights Union. In its home state the New York department gave it a formal endorsement, for a while backed it financially, and usually passed whatever resolutions it had drawn up. Though strongest there, it soon developed branches in other areas.

The upheavals that accompanied the arrival of Cleveland in the White House made the Grand Army even more aware of the value of the Veterans' Rights Union, especially as Kay himself had the asset of being a Democrat. Despite the misgivings of some leaders, the national encampments of 1885 and 1886 at last officially commended its work, urged its extension into additional states, and appointed a committee which went to Washington to confer with Cleveland. Within the next two years branches won the approval of half a dozen scattered G.A.R. departments. In Massachusetts, where the group operated chiefly as an employment bureau and helped to make out pension applications, the order even induced the state to pay its expenses.

A few years later the almost simultaneous advent of the second

---

[30] *Ibid.*, pp. 6–7, 20, 32–33, 46–47, 63–64.
[31] *Ibid.*, pp. 34–38, 45–46.

Cleveland administration and the Panic of 1893 intensified the veterans' concern to gain and keep government jobs. Once again the dismissal of many Republican ex-soldiers filled the Grand Army with indignation, but in vain it fulminated against their ouster and endeavored to obtain their reinstatement. Repeated efforts to secure a penalty for the violation of Section 1754 also proved unsuccessful.

The inauguration of McKinley, a good Republican comrade, filled the veterans with joyous anticipation. "Four years of depression and gloom were to be succeeded by an era of prosperity and gladness, and the heart of every comrade was buoyant with happiness and joy," reported the employment committee of the District of Columbia G.A.R. "The year of jubilee had come." [32] Insisting that the new President include the veterans in his patronage, the *American Tribune* asked with a frank logic, "if not, where is the gain, as far as the soldiers are concerned?" [33] Though within the next year nearly nine hundred veterans were appointed and five hundred more promoted, continued pleas for the enforcement of Section 1754 showed that the Grand Army was still far from satisfied and sometimes it was only with difficulty that resolutions censuring McKinley's performance were defeated. The basic obstacle was that the veterans were now growing old and the new administration preferred younger politicians for many places.

During these years the G.A.R. also pressed Congress to amend Section 1754 so as to include all former soldiers, not just the disabled. The argument, of course, was that "the man who went to the front should be preferred for public service to those who remained at home to advance their personal interests while the soldiers were undergoing the hardships of war." [34] Though both national encampments and numerous state meetings from New Hampshire to California throughout the eighties and nineties endorsed Congressional bills to this effect (one of which even passed the Senate once), and the Union Veteran Legion, Sons of Veterans, W.R.C., and Ladies of the G.A.R. added their support, they never achieved this goal. The difficulty seems to have been that, despite Kay's active lobbying in Washington as chairman of the G.A.R.'s veterans' pref-

[32] Department of the Potomac, Grand Army of the Republic, *Journal of the Thirtieth Annual Encampment 1898* (Washington, 1898), p. 37.

[33] *American Tribune* (Indianapolis), March 4, 1897.

[34] "Union Veterans' Union," *Grand Army Record*, II (March 1887), 3.

erence committee, the Grand Army itself always subordinated the movement to the more important pension drive and therefore never exerted its full pressure to combat the equally strong opposition of civil service reformers and the hostility of politicians to any interference with their distribution of the patronage. In January 1902, an executive order of President Theodore Roosevelt at last called for preference to all Union veterans in appointment and retention but apparently was not followed very carefully in practice.[35]

In addition to its drive for special privilege in federal positions, the G.A.R. was active in different states urging the enforcement and strengthening of preference laws, financing suits to establish their constitutionality, demanding the passage of legislation where none existed, and threatening recalcitrant lawmakers with retaliation at the polls.[36] The *National Tribune* insisted that its readers in New York make such a measure the chief issue in the 1885 campaign there and after its passage urged the residents of other states to demand similar acts. Whenever successful, as they often were, the veterans next sought effective penalties for violations. Sometimes this solicitude for veterans backfired upon the G.A.R. In New Jersey the organization secured a law that former soldiers could not be dismissed except for cause and then was chagrined to discover that this applied equally to young men who had just resigned from the regular army.

At the close of the century the Massachusetts Grand Army protested the inclusion of Spanish-American War veterans under the soldiers' preference provision on the curious ground that they hadn't aged enough. "The veterans of the War of the Rebellion waited over twenty years for absolute preference in public employment in this State, and over thirty years before the present law was enacted," declared the 1899 encampment. "The time has not yet come for those who served in so short a war as the one between the United States and Spain to be placed on the same footing as those who fought for years for the preservation of the national existence." [37]

---

[35] Woods, "G.A.R. and Civil Service," pp. 4, 72–76, 91, 97–98, 130.

[36] The defeat of at least one member of Congress was attributed to his having ignored a Grand Army request to support the amendment of Section 1754. "It Is Over," *Grand Army Review,* II (Dec. 1886), 336.

[37] Department of Massachusetts, Grand Army of the Republic, *Journal of the Thirty-Third Annual Encampment 1899* (Boston, 1899), p. 178.

The order's efforts did block legislation to give the newer veterans equal treatment.

Though, next to the pension drive, veterans' preference was one of the Grand Army's major concerns, it by no means exhausted the association's ingenuity for discovering ways in which the government might improve the ex-soldiers' lot. In the late eighties came a movement for states to appropriate special relief funds for indigent veterans. The model for such laws was the one in New York, which provided that these grants should be distributed by G.A.R. posts. The success of campaigns in New York and Ohio caused a number of other departments to make the same demand, which usually was fulfilled. Thereafter the order agitated for increased amounts. Occasionally, however, a branch refused to ask for this assistance, though not always from the loftiest civic motives. The New Jersey commander opposed such a bill on the ground that it "would destroy all hope of getting a pension for the next 20 years, or until the Grand Army has become dead and buried." [38]

The veterans were even less favorable to the idea that states should exempt their property from taxation up to a certain sum, usually a thousand dollars. Though during the depression years in the nineties some departments in the West endorsed it, those in the East opposed it as class legislation. The hard times also accelerated a movement to excuse the veterans from the payments for peddlers' licenses; the New York and Iowa branches backed this, but New Jersey discountenanced it also as being special legislation. The very suggestion, however, was another revelation of the veterans' social and economic status. Other exemptions proposed were to free the ex-soldiers from poll taxes or from jury and militia service, but again departments hesitated to push these.

As the Grand Army's membership began to decline and its revenues to fall off, the organization turned to the government for financial assistance. Again following an example set by New York in the late eighties, various branches secured free headquarters more and more often, usually in the state capitol; they induced the states to print their annual proceedings as public documents; and sometimes even asked that G.A.R. halls and property be exempt from taxes.

[38] Department of New Jersey, Grand Army of the Republic, *Proceedings of the Twenty-Second Annual Encampment 1889* (Camden, 1889), p. 114.

Once again this trend did not receive the approval of all members. The *Grand Army Record* argued that it was unconstitutional and, after a past state commander had declared it would make Illinois "a pauper department," one encampment actually tabled such a resolution.[39]

Finally, the veterans claimed special rights even after death. By the mid-eighties many felt that the states should provide funds for the burial of indigent veterans. A large number of the G.A.R.'s branches succeeded in this agitation and then, as usual, began to clamor for larger sums. The Woman's Relief Corps wanted these benefits extended to wives and widows, but the G.A.R.'s chivalry did not seem to stretch that far.

In short, during the eighties and nineties the Grand Army of the Republic discovered a wide variety of demands that it could make upon both state and nation. Its triumphs were usually greater in the state legislatures than in Congress. A concession merely encouraged it to increase its pleas or to develop new ones, while success in one state stimulated other departments to seek similar favors. But all these efforts faded into insignificance compared with the Grand Army's persistent pressure for more liberal pensions.

[39] Department of Illinois, Grand Army of the Republic, *Proceedings of the Thirty-second Annual Encampment 1898* (Chicago, n.d.), pp. 176–177.

VIII

"The Only National Debt We Can Never Pay"

AN axiom of American history is that sooner or later the participants in all its wars have expected the government to grant them generous pensions. The surprising element is how often the desire has been later rather than sooner, but that it is only because old age increases the need at the same time that it casts a hazy but glorious patina over past services. The ex-soldiers quickly discovered that their associations were the best means for expressing this desire and for securing its achievement. In joining these leagues, already attractive from the social angle, the veterans were often anticipating bread as well as circuses.[1]

In 1871 the increasingly decrepit War of 1812 survivors obtained their long-hoped-for service pension. Though they were too old and disorganized to demand many further favors (only one was left on the rolls in 1900), this grant stimulated the veterans of later wars to seek similar recognition in a shorter lapse of time. The first national convention of the Mexican War Veterans in 1874 beseeched Congress to bestow eight dollars a month on all who had served sixty days and each of their sessions thereafter repeated the request. The association even hesitated to meet in Washington, for fear that only the younger and healthier veterans would be apt to attend and thereby cause the legislators to be less impressed with their pleas for assistance. Local branches and the order's journal, the *Vedette,* echoed these appeals. To some extent they also won G.A.R. support, but more often the Grand Army feared that such a measure would benefit many former Confederates. This consideration long pre-

---

[1] The standard work on soldiers' pensions, which emphasizes the legislation for the Civil War's survivors and the influence of the G.A.R., is William H. Glasson's pedestrian but invaluable *Federal Military Pensions in the United States* (New York, 1918).

vented Republican majorities from passing a bill, but under a Democratic administration in January 1887, an act granted the desired amount to disabled survivors as well as to all those over sixty-two, with certain disqualifications for former Confederates.[2]

For a moment it looked as if the *Vedette*'s editor, Alexander Kenaday, who had never concealed his expectations that such legislation would bring him large fees as a claims agent, had at last come into his own. "He is literally 'reaping the harvest' of a long term of altruistic service," ran one account of how hundreds of applications were pouring into his office, "and every true man should rejoice at his prosperity in his old age."[3] Kenaday filled the *Vedette* with directions for pension applications and assured his readers that he had "secured the services of skilled and faithful clerks and will give the matter our personal attention."[4] But though the number of pensioners promptly jumped from 7500 to 16,000 and the annual expenditures for pensions for the Mexican War from $53,000 to $1,800,000,[5] to his chagrin Kenaday failed to monopolize this new business. He indignantly attacked other agents trying to secure their share as "pension sharks" and complained even more bitterly that Congressmen and the Pension Office sent blank forms directly to the old soldiers so that they did not require the services of an agent. As a result of this undermining of private enterprise he handled only one-fifth of the first 15,000 claims filed. If he maintained the same ratio among the 8500 actually allowed, the usual fee of $10 per case would have meant that his office did about $17,000 of business, perhaps a more modest reward than he had anticipated, but nevertheless consoling.

Though the paper wistfully revealed, "We confess ourselves at a loss to know exactly where to level the guns of THE VEDETTE,"[6] it realized that its editor's prosperity depended upon continued agitation and it therefore stirred up demands for various amendments. The *Vedette* soon sponsored a movement to raise the monthly sti-

---

[2] *Vedette* (Washington, D.C.), Jan. 1887; Glasson, *Federal Military Pensions,* p. 117.

[3] *Origin and Progress of the National Association of Veterans of the Mexican War* (Washington, 1887), p. 8.

[4] *Vedette,* Feb. 1887.

[5] Glasson, *Federal Military Pensions,* p. 119.

[6] *Vedette,* Aug. 1887.

pend to twelve dollars. In its desperate attempts to unearth new issues, no matter how trivial, so as to hold the veterans' support, the journal even demanded extension of the time for filing claims for compensation for horses lost during the war. With the Democratic triumph at the polls in 1892, Kenaday renewed the *Vedette*'s drive for a twelve-dollar rate. In January 1893, Congress bestowed it upon pensioners who were both destitute and totally disabled for manual labor; not until 1903 was it extended to all survivors.

Immediately after the Civil War its survivors showed little interest in general pension legislation. In the seventies the Grand Army made no mention at all of the universal service pension for which it was later to plead so vigorously. Its concern in these years was not so much to add new names to the rolls as it was to increase the amount already granted for various injuries. The original impetus for the Civil War pension drive came not from the veterans' associations but from the pension attorneys. Their business was suffering in the mid-seventies, when that naïve generation thought the peak of pension expenditures had been reached. To correct this melancholy situation George Lemon started the *National Tribune* in 1877, at first emphasizing the needs of the War of 1812 and Mexican War veterans, but despite a more liberal law for the former in 1878 these two groups constituted too limited a field. The paper soon turned to the potential claims of the far greater number of Civil War survivors and began to advocate the equalization of bounties and especially an arrears of pensions bill.

This last measure called for the payment of pensions to the disabled from the date of discharge from the army instead of from the time of establishing the last evidence for a claim. The Grand Army also took up the idea, but the passage of such an act in January 1879 did not so much display the influence of the G.A.R., just emerging from the doldrums, as it did that of the agents. Though an amendment soon required that any claims under this law be filed by July 1, 1880, there was still great incentive for new claimants to establish disabilities. The years 1879 and 1880 proved boom years for the agents. Whereas there had been not quite 26,000 applications in 1878, there were over 47,000 in 1879 and 138,000 in 1880. In the latter year Lemon represented some 30,000 claims and was entitled to $10 for each one that was accepted. Until 1879 the sum paid out for pensions each year had never been more than $30,000,000, but in 1880 it leaped to $56,000,000.[7]

But now the Grand Army realized the possibilities of the situation and after 1880 it increasingly devoted its energies to pension agitation, a move which contributed substantially to its sensational growth. First there was a demand to extend beyond 1880 the time limit for filing applications under the Arrears of Pensions Act. "Common honesty, common decency demands that the United States stop swindling its pensioners," fumed the *National Tribune*. "The arrears are due to every pensioner who has not received them." The provision for a limitation appeared merely a dishonest pretext of the government "to prevent its creditors collecting what is justly due to them."[8] A number of Grand Army encampments and at least one commander-in-chief supported the paper's efforts to have the restriction removed, and in 1884 the New York branch even sent a delegation to Washington to present its plea directly to various Congressmen. Several times bills were introduced, but since the effect would have been a constant encouragement of claims of the most dubious nature, none succeeded.

As for the question of additional pensions, until 1881 the Grand Army's attitude "was one of purely quiescent expectancy that exact justice would be done the soldier by a grateful people."[9] A growing impatience at the slowness of the Pension Bureau's handling of applications caused it to assume a more aggressive role. At its 1881 national encampment the order appointed its first pension committee, which on a three-day visit to Washington in February 1882 informed the lawmakers of the Grand Army's demand that "Congress should take such steps, regardless of the question of dollars and cents, as would result in the speediest possible settlement of the claims of those men whose great deeds and heroic sufferings had made it possible for Congress to exist."[10] At its suggestion, 1210 additional employees were engaged for pension work, at an annual cost of $1,742,430.

[7] Glasson, *Federal Military Pensions*, pp. 166, 273.

[8] *National Tribune* (Washington, D.C.), Dec. 8, 1887.

[9] Grand Army of the Republic, *Journal of the Seventeenth Annual Session of the National Encampment 1883* (Omaha, 1883), p. 52.

[10] Grand Army of the Republic, *Journal of the Sixteenth Annual Session of the National Encampment 1882* (Lawrence, Mass., 1882), p. 873.

Understandably elated by this initial encounter with the legislative power, the national encampment of 1882 voted to establish a permanent pension committee of five to continue the work. Thereafter this group traveled to Washington each year and then gave a report on its success to the national meeting. Various G.A.R. departments had expressed their desire for an increase in the amount given to disabled veterans already on the rolls. The pension committee therefore endorsed a bill granting forty dollars a month for the loss of a leg, an arm, a foot, or a hand. Local branches and the *National Tribune* rallied to its support. During the Congressional session hardly a day passed when petitions did not arrive from twelve to fifty G.A.R. posts. The bill finally passed in amended form in March 1883.

Having tasted blood, during the next session of Congress the committee again visited Washington. Discovering over one hundred bills relating to pensions, it proceeded to consider their merits. In its deliberations it had "the advice and cordial co-operation of the Commissioner of Pensions." Finally it presented its recommendations to a hearing of the House and Senate pension committees. It opposed land warrants, payment of the difference between the greenback and gold values of the soldiers' pay, and a service pension to all veterans and instead concentrated on increases for specific types of disability.[11]

Since with this decision the G.A.R. definitely committed itself as a pension-seeking organization, it soon built up a structure of arguments to justify its demands. Though at this time they applied primarily to a disability bill, with modifications they became standard pleas for years to come.

A basic contention was that a pension for the disabled was in no sense a gratuity but was merely the fulfillment of a contract which the government made with its soldiers when they enlisted. In the words of one G.A.R. leader, the veterans now wished its redemption "as a just claim, as though I had a note against any responsible house or person in the land and ask him to take it up." [12] In 1862 Congress

---

[11] Grand Army of the Republic, *Journal of the Eighteenth Annual Session of the National Encampment 1884* (Philadelphia, 1884), pp. 105–107.

[12] Department of Wisconsin, Grand Army of the Republic, *Proceedings of the Twenty-first Annual Encampment 1887* (Baraboo, 1887), p. 97.

had pledged pensions for those injured in service, but the veterans proceeded to give the term "disability" the widest possible interpretation until it included nearly everyone. A frequent corollary of this concept was the theory that by winning the war the veterans really owned the entire country, or at the very least had acquired a first mortgage upon it, and for that reason were entitled to ask anything of it they wished. In Kansas a speaker told the G.A.R. that "because you saved the nation, you have a mortgage written in blood on every man, woman and child and on every acre of land in these United States." [13] Similarly a commander of the Vermont department pointed out that "In mercantile law, in a rescue from the perils of the sea, the salvor, or rescuer has a lien on the goods or vessel until recompense is made." It seemed clear that the Union soldiers had made such a rescue. "Had they not on many a stricken field saved from spoil and destruction Washington, Philadelphia and New York," he reminded his audience, "the hoarded wealth of those cities would have gone into the coffers of the enemy, and to-day they would have been groaning under a load of taxation . . . to pay the enormous Confederate debt. . . ." [14] The national encampment applauded the logical conclusion of one survivor: "The Grand Army of the Republic owns this country by the rights of a conqueror." [15] Under such doctrine any request of the veterans was a slight one compared to what they might rightfully demand.

Part of the pension argument involved a striking appeal to class feeling that again revealed the make-up of the G.A.R. Pension defenders contrasted the government's treatment of its bondholders and its soldiers. The *National Tribune* repeatedly proclaimed that the total amount paid out in interest on bonds since the beginning of the war was far greater than that expended on pensions. "We say let the bondholders wait for their interest if any class of the Government's creditors must be put off—," it suggested, "the moneys due pensioners . . . ought to take precedence." [16] One Grand Army

---

[13] Department of Kansas, Grand Army of the Republic, *Proceedings of the Sixth Annual Encampment 1887* (Topeka, 1887), p. 4.

[14] Department of Vermont, Grand Army of the Republic, *Proceedings of the Annual and Semi-Annual Encampments 1882–1883* (Bennington, 1883), pp. 17–18.

[15] Grand Army of the Republic, *Journal of the Nineteenth Annual Session of the National Encampment 1885* (Toledo, 1885), p. 193.

[16] *National Tribune,* Nov. 26, 1881.

member, commenting on the outcome of the wartime partnership of Wall Street's money and the veterans' services, concluded bitterly that "one party has the money and the other has the experience." [17] Other class-conscious veterans also suspected that, while the soldiers had been fighting, those who stayed at home had greatly profited. "The foundations of the colossal fortunes which have been built up by the Croesuses of our time were laid in the war, or in the years immediately after it," another member pointed out, "and we did not have an opportunity to share in that prosperity." [18] Encouraging this economic division, the *National Tribune* contended that opposition to pensions came from the upper classes—bondholders, bankers, and moneylenders—who aped English manners, belonged to clubs, wished the lower classes treated as in Britain, and selfishly fought high prices for their liquor, cigars, and kid gloves, the taxes on which were the chief source of pension revenue. It further argued that a high pension rate would benefit workingmen in the same manner as the exclusion of cheap Chinese labor, for a low one would depress the wage level and the standard of living. This type of argument seemed limited to the eighties; by the nineties it perhaps sounded too radical for veterans' groups becoming more concerned about labor disturbances and self-conscious about their patriotic mission.

Another economic argument asserted that the distribution of pensions greatly benefited business conditions. "The money disbursed to pensioners is an actual blessing to the country," Commander-in-Chief Paul Van Der Voort announced. "It goes into the channels of trade. It makes money easy, and, in my judgment the amount scattered throughout the country by the action of the arrears of pensions bill was an actual benefit and prevented a financial crash." [19] If in good times this was advanced as a way to avert panics, during depressions it was proposed as the way back to prosperity. It was denied that pensions involved any extra expense. The necessary funds came from taxes on beer, whisky, tobacco, and oleomargarine, and from customs duties, all of which would be levied in

---

[17] Department of Dakota, Grand Army of the Republic, *Journal of the Fourth Annual Session of the Territorial Encampment 1887* (Fargo, 1887), p. 53.

[18] Wis. G.A.R., *Proceedings 1887*, p. 95.

[19] G.A.R., *Journal 1883*, pp. 9–10.

any case and therefore imposed no additional strain on the taxpayer. The presence of a surplus in the national treasury in those faraway days particularly provoked suggestions that generous pensions constituted the most logical solution to that abnormal situation. "There would then be no question in regard to erecting additional buildings to take care of our surplus treasure," observed one comrade. "The boys would take care of it." [20]

By the nineties there had developed a final contention, which had the least connection with the actual merits of the case but had the strongest emotional appeal. Anyone who opposed pensions was, at the very least, "unpatriotic and un-American" and probably a former rebel or Copperhead. Thus the commander of the District of Columbia branch complained how "these envious non-combatants and their offspring, who were conceived in disloyalty, brought forth in iniquity, and educated in envy, after a silence of thirty years, raise their ignoble heads and give full vent to the spleen and spite which characterized them during the years of the war." [21]

A few voices within the G.A.R. protested this diversion of the organization's energies to pension hunting. They felt that the "Government of the United States has dealt more honorably and more liberally with the civilian soldiers than any nation on earth." [22] To their minds the veterans who were trying to extract all they could from the government "are certainly not the kind of soldiers with whom self-respecting soldiers desire to be associated." [23] According to one unusually self-reliant member, "Every healthy soldier in this country, every man who has his two hands and his brains and his heart, has a country, praise God, in which he can earn a living, and he need not knock at the door of the Government for help." [24] In Pennsylvania a state encampment even declared "that we view with distrust any and all further legislation having for its purpose the

[20] Grand Army of the Republic, *Journal of the Twenty-First Annual Session of the National Encampment 1887* (Milwaukee, 1887), p. 220.

[21] Department of the Potomac, Grand Army of the Republic, *Journal of the Thirtieth Annual Encampment 1898* (Washington, 1898), p. 15.

[22] Department of Pennsylvania, Grand Army of the Republic, *Proceedings of the 26th and 27th Encampments July, 1879, and Jan., 1880* (Philadelphia, 1880), p. 134.

[23] Department of New Jersey, Grand Army of the Republic, *Proceedings of the Sixteenth Annual Encampment 1883* (Trenton, 1883), p. 20.

[24] Grand Army of the Republic, *Journal of the Twentieth Annual Session of the National Encampment 1886* (Washington, 1886), p. 229.

increase of pay for services performed and already paid for. . . ." [25]
But patriotic veterans' societies ordinarily disliked such statements
of economic individualism as subversive of the entire system they
had devised.

Behind the unrest of these critics, moreover, was a suspicion that
these developments had not been entirely spontaneous but represented the behind-the-scenes influence of pension attorneys who were
using the organization for their own selfish purposes. On the floor
of Congress Representative E. S. Bragg, a Wisconsin Democrat,
charged that "at every Grand Army post and every Grand Army
encampment that meets you will see from one to five hundred men
poking through the crowd to get men to make affidavits such as are
needed to procure a pension." [26] Representative A. J. Warner of Ohio
claimed that the Washington agents dominated the organization,
even dictating the choice of its leaders. In particular he singled out
George Lemon as a "lemon squeezer and bloodsucker of soldiers,"
while Bragg said that veterans' papers like Lemon's *National Tribune* "are the friends of the soldiers as vultures are the friends of dead
bodies—because they feed and fatten on them." [27]

Certainly Lemon had become a power in Washington in these
years. As head of the largest pension attorney firm in the capital,
by 1885 he was handling some 135,000 claims. The extent of his
influence became apparent in 1884 when he induced Congress to
increase the fee for agents from ten to twenty-five dollars and to require all applicants whose cases had already been accepted also to
pay the additional sum. That he realized the advantages to himself
of a powerful veterans' organization seems obvious, and certainly he
and his paper had much to do with building up the order's strength
in the early eighties. Commander-in-Chief Van Der Voort appointed
Lemon as one of his aids in December 1882, in recognition for these
services, and later he became one of Lemon's employees on the
National Tribune. The first action of the G.A.R. pension committee,
its complaints about the operation of the Pension Bureau, coincided
with a virulent campaign which the paper was conducting against
the commissioner for the same reasons, and the arguments for pen-

[25] Penn. G.A.R., *Proceedings for July, 1879, and Jan., 1880,* p. 134.
[26] *Congressional Record,* 49 Cong., 2 sess., part 3, 2215.
[27] *Ibid.,* pp. 2218, 2213.

sions advanced by the G.A.R. in nearly every case merely reflected those first disseminated by the *National Tribune* in the late seventies. Rumors even circulated that the pension committee held its meetings in Lemon's office behind closed doors. In modern terminology, it looked as though the G.A.R. was a "front" organization for Lemon's personal enterprises which pretty consistently followed the *National Tribune* party line.

While some elements in the Grand Army attacked the exactions of the Washington agents, "those godless, soulless robbers" and "pension buzzards," their recommendations that veterans instead patronize honest local attorneys suggested no particular aversion to the system as such. At the 1883 national encampment the commander of the District of Columbia department, asserting that "robbery, bold and blank against our comrades is continually perpetrated through the . . . pension agencies, largely at the city of Washington," asked the order to investigate their activities, but the convention upheld the pension committee's contention that no such inquiry was necessary.[28] This action scarcely allayed the suspicion that the members of the committee were "Lemon's satellites," and by the time of the 1887 gathering one of the group, the popular James Tanner, felt impelled to make a formal refutation of these reports. At the same time that he denied Lemon's control, however, he also came to his defense, insisting that "those who know him, know him for an honest man, and I send every friend of mine, who wants any information about the presentation of a claim to him." [29]

But while some veterans had qualms about the ethics of pensions and the influence of agents like Lemon, as a Massachusetts commander reluctantly conceded, "this class is now in a hopeless minority." [30] More typical was the commander-in-chief who admitted that the nation had been "great in her generous justice" but then quickly insisted that this consideration should "in no wise turn us aside from pursuing our further just and temperate demands." [31] That he more accurately sensed the mood of his following is seen in the order's efforts for a disability bill not based on wartime injuries alone. In

[28] G.A.R., *Journal 1883*, p. 140.
[29] G.A.R., *Journal 1887*, p. 43.
[30] Department of Massachusetts, Grand Army of the Republic, *Journals of the Encampment Proceedings from 1881 to 1887 Inclusive* (Boston, 1902), p. 269.
[31] G.A.R., *Journal 1886*, p. 47.

1884 the Republican Senate amended a Mexican War Pension Bill so as to include all Civil War veterans who had served three months and become disabled. The question was whether the Democratic House would take the same action. The *National Tribune,* of course, warmly advocated the bill's passage and distributed between 15,000 and 20,000 petitions in its behalf among its readers. Between November 1884 and February 1885, it claimed to have received over 290,000 signatures in return, chiefly from the midwestern states of Ohio, Indiana, Illinois, Iowa, and Kansas which were now swelling the Gand Army's ranks. Several state encampments of the G.A.R. also endorsed the measure. Commander-in-Chief John Kountz suggested that each post divide its jurisdiction into easily canvassed districts so as to accumulate a million names for the House; the actual result was five hundred thousand. Nevertheless, the bill failed because of the presence of many ex-Confederates in Congress, the desire of the Democrats to present an economy record in the approaching national campaign, and the lack of complete unanimity as yet within the Grand Army, evidenced by the efforts of many posts for a wide variety of proposals.[32]

Undiscouraged, the G.A.R. at once renewed the assault. Announcing that the Senate had again passed a satisfactory measure, the order's adjutant-general, in May 1886, asked every post to petition the House for its passage. Despite thousands of responses to this request, the Representatives reported a somewhat less liberal Dependent Pension Bill, which granted twelve dollars a month to all ninety-day veterans sufficiently disabled to be unable to support themselves by daily labor. Even so, the Grand Army pension committee decided to support this substitute because it established the principle of a pension without proof that the disability resulted from service. In January 1887, the bill passed Congress. Then, to the fury of the veterans, on February 11 President Cleveland, who had just approved the Mexican War Pension Bill, vetoed it.

Three days later Commander-in-Chief Lucius Fairchild asked all posts to let Congress know their reactions. Almost unanimously they demanded re-passage. Only scattered voices supported the President,

[32] John William Oliver, *History of the Civil War Military Pensions, 1861–1885* (*Bulletin of the University of Wisconsin, History Series,* IV, Madison, Wis., 1917), pp. 95–96.

or, like Pennsylvania's discreet commander, who argued that "there was an honest diversity of opinion among my comrades on this subject" and that he "was lacking in the art of saying something that would be satisfactory to every one," said nothing about what he "believed to be the conscientious official act of the President." [33] But when a message from a New Jersey post condemning the bill was read in Congress, a Representative promptly announced, "For every one like that which you can furnish we will show you a hundred on the other side." [34] Department after department passed resolutions denouncing the veto and imploring the lawmakers to override it. To the Kansas veterans, Cleveland's act represented "a new phase of treason which is calculated if not intended to make patriotism odious and heroism contemptible." [35] James Tanner predicted that the bill's failure would mean that henceforth youths would hesitate to fight for their country. Declaring "my patriotism is at a very low ebb," he threatened that in a future war he would urge his sons to go abroad.[36] Some legislators were much impressed as petition after petition from posts with hundreds of members rolled in. Though a majority of the House challenged the veto, the lack of a two-thirds vote doomed the bill.[37]

Still the G.A.R. did not give up the fight. "We are like Oliver Twist," a member of the national pension committee once declared, "we are always asking for more, and we will keep on asking until we get it." [38] The *National Tribune* prodded the veterans to force all political conventions in the North and West to express approval of the bill and to condemn the veto and thus prepare for the next session of Congress. Commander-in-Chief Fairchild insisted that all who had served thirty days, were dependent on their own daily labor, and were now incapacitated for it should receive a pension. "For the future of our country my comrades, I want every old

[33] Department of Pennsylvania, Grand Army of the Republic, *Proceedings of the 42d and 43d Encampments July, 1887, and Feb., 1888* (Philadelphia, n.d.), p. 78.

[34] *Congressional Record*, 49 Cong., 1 sess., part 2, 2218.

[35] Kan. G.A.R., *Proceedings 1887*, p. 45.

[36] Department of New York, Grand Army of the Republic, *Proceedings of the Twenty-first Annual Encampment 1887* (Albany, 1887), p. 97.

[37] *Congressional Record*, 49 Cong., 1 sess., part 2, 2223; Glasson, *Federal Military Pensions*, p. 217.

[38] Grand Army of the Republic, *Journal of the Twenty-Second Annual Session of the National Encampment 1888* (Minneapolis, 1888), p. 131.

soldier kept out of the common pauper house," he proclaimed amidst "cheers and cries of 'that is right' " from the Kansas veterans, "for the sake of common decency I want them to have bread, and I want them to have butter on it to [*sic*]." [39]

The national pension committee promptly drew up a new bill differing from the vetoed measure in being a disability rather than a dependent bill, which therefore did not require proof of virtual pauperism. In June 1887, Fairchild sought the order's reaction. Over 100,000 members expressed approval, while only 3600 dissented. At its national convention in August the Sons of Veterans also endorsed the bill and promised "that we will do all we can to impress the people, the congressman and the executive with the earnest desire to have such a bill upon the statute books." [40]

State encampments, abetted by the *National Tribune,* pressed the passage of the disability bill. The veterans' paper went so far as to print cartoons of babies and small children pleading for its enactment so that they could have more skimmed milk. The Nebraska Grand Army threatened, "it is time we were speaking in thundering tones and sentiments demanding our well-earned rights from the nation we saved, and let it be understood that we are coming three hundred and fifty thousand G.A.R. strong to oppose enemies in high places as we did in the field." [41] Duly responsive, the Senate passed a disability bill in March 1888, but included a so-called "pauper clause" that altered it back to a dependent bill. The House then reported a much amended measure that greatly displeased the Grand Army. The G.A.R. pension committee called it "a mongrel, narrow, picayunish affair" and the *National Tribune* termed it "a sham, a pretense and a mockery." [42] The failure of the Democratic House to take any further action seemed "wholly inexplicable and indefensible" to the commander-in-chief. "I cannot fitly comment upon this subject," he added. "My emotions will not permit it." [43]

The canvass of 1888 saw the triumph of the Republicans, notori-

[39] Kan. G.A.R., *Proceedings 1887,* p. 61.

[40] Sons of Veterans, U.S.A., *Proceedings of the Sixth National Encampment 1887* (n.p., n.d.), p. 56.

[41] Department of Nebraska, Grand Army of the Republic, *Journal of the Eleventh Annual Encampment 1888* (Schuyler, Neb., 1888), p. 92.

[42] G.A.R., *Journal 1888,* p. 21; *National Tribune,* April 26, 1888.

[43] G.A.R., *Journal 1888,* p. 35.

ously more spendthrift with federal funds than the economy-minded Democrats, and the new president-elect, Benjamin Harrison, was himself a former comrade. Soon after the election the pension committee visited him in Indianapolis, "receiving from him the most cordial assurances of his warm interest in the great question of pensions and his greatest desire for generous legislation in behalf of the defenders of the Union." [44] Thus braced, the committee descended upon Washington. It prepared a bill to grant twelve dollars a month to all disabled veterans, who would not need to prove that the disability resulted from service or that their financial situation verged on pauperism, but the lame-duck Congress took no action.

The veterans eagerly awaited Harrison's inauguration. "Some have indulged in the most extravagant expectations from the new administration," warned the *Grand Army Record*. "Let them go slowly and not embarrass it by asking too much. Let all cranks and extremists be kept in the rear rank while level-headed men act as spokesmen for the veterans." [45] Most members, however, could see little virtue in such restraint at the hour of victory. Remembering the hostile attitude of the Cleveland regime, they particularly prayed that the new president would make satisfactory appointments to those offices affecting pensions. The outcome was most gratifying. General John W. Noble, a popular Grand Army member, became Secretary of the Interior. Even more promising was the choice of the legless Corporal James Tanner for Commissioner of Pensions. A former head of the New York department whose oratory could make "Strong-hearted men weep in his presence who have not shed tears before in years," [46] he had been an active member of the national pension committee, was a close personal friend of George Lemon, and had literally stumped the country for Harrison in the campaign. [47] The *National Tribune* was delighted and in a series of open letters to the President, Noble, Assistant Secretary of the Interior Cyrus Bussey, and the new Commissioner proclaimed the veterans' expectation that they would speedily settle pending claims (meaning

---

[44] Grand Army of the Republic, *Journal of the Twenty-third Annual Session of the National Encampment 1889* (St. Louis, 1889), p. 121.

[45] "Our Soldier President," *Grand Army Record*, IV (March 1889), 4.

[46] Mass. G.A.R., *Journals 1881–1887*, p. 316.

[47] Donald L. McMurry, "The Bureau of Pensions During the Administration of President Harrison," *Mississippi Valley Historical Review*, XIII (Dec. 1926), 344–345.

not to examine them too closely) and thus "make the policy of the Pension Bureau rise to the level of the spirit and intent of the legislation enacted by Congress." [48]

Tanner, who at this point won a minor fame in textbooks with his classic phrase, "God help the surplus," did his best to fulfill all these hopes. He not only pensioned many new claimants as rapidly as possible, but he also busily raised the rates of those already on the rolls, making them retroactive so that he could distribute substantial checks throughout the country.[49] Though his conduct soon aroused considerable criticism, the *National Tribune* found him to be "a conscientious administrator of the laws that he finds upon the statute books" who was "only carrying out the clear intent and purpose of the law." [50] Quite accurately it observed, "It is not necessary to tell comrades how truly the heart of Commissioner Tanner beats with them." [51] The paper also hailed Assistant Secretary Bussey's decision that a dishonorable discharge was no bar to a pension as "clear, cold logic, without a flaw." [52] All in all, it concluded happily, "An entirely different spirit has been infused into the pension system, and the good effects are felt everywhere." [53]

Unfortunately for the veterans, Tanner's liberality soon proved too much even for the sympathetic Harrison administration. Far-sighted Grand Army officials became apprehensive about his conduct. Past Commander-in-Chief George Merrill warned that "he was talking too much" and tried to prevent his attending the national encampment at Milwaukee in August 1889. Merrill wrote him "one of the strongest letters I ever wrote to any man, in which I told him it would be madness for him to go where he would be sure to do or say something to break down the already overloaded bridge." [54] Nevertheless, the Commissioner turned up at the meeting, which publicly thanked Harrison for appointing him. At Tanner's own request a declaration condemning "in unmeasured terms the wicked

[48] *National Tribune,* March 28, April 11, April 18, April 25, and May 2, 1889.
[49] McMurry, "Bureau of Pensions," p. 347.
[50] *National Tribune,* June 13 and July 18, 1889.
[51] *Ibid.,* Aug. 8, 1889.
[52] *Ibid.,* Sept. 12, 1889.
[53] *Ibid.,* Aug. 8, 1889.
[54] Interview in the *Commercial Advertiser* (Buffalo), Sept. 10, 1889, quoted in "The Pension Bureau," *Public Opinion,* VII (Sept. 21, 1889), 486.

and malignant criticism of our distinguished comrade" was softened to a statement of "our confidence in his integrity and our approval of his avowed purpose to do all that is possible to be done, under the laws of the land, for the veterans of the war." It also called for an investigation into his conduct so as to vindicate him.[55]

By this time the rumor was current that Harrison and Noble "would like to get rid of him at the earliest moment. Nothing but the Grand Army stands between him and expulsion." [56] But even Tanner's associates in the soldiers' organizations now watched his progress with dismay. "What could have been more indiscreet," asked Merrill in despair, "than the style in which he mounted the housetops and summoned the people of the United States to watch him while he made the wheels go round, or while he pulled a string and dangled the Secretary of the Interior on the other end?" [57] Noble first protested Tanner's actions and finally in September 1889 dismissed him for insubordination.[58]

The veterans' papers rallied to the Commissioner's defense. The *Grand Army Record* admitted that he had some faults, but also recalled "that for the first time in the history of the Pension Office a veteran could get a hearing without excessive humiliation." [59] *Home and Country* portrayed him as "the victim of adverse circumstances and of constant misrepresentation," [60] while the *National Tribune* hastened to assure its readers that there would be no changes in the government's liberal policy: *"This can be relied upon."* [61] Two past commanders-in-chief, Merrill and William Warner, were seriously considered as Tanner's successor, but both refused, and the office went to Green B. Raum, who soon also developed close ties with Lemon. The new commissioner was assumed to be acceptable to the Grand Army, and the Democratic press announced that Raum "may not make Tanner's absurd mistakes, but his aim will

[55] G.A.R., *Journal 1889*, pp. 163–165.

[56] "Grand Army of the Republic, Pensions and the Commissioner of Pensions," *Public Opinion*, VII (Sept. 7, 1889), 448.

[57] "Pension Bureau," p. 486.

[58] McMurry, "Bureau of Pensions," pp. 352–355; Glasson, *Federal Military Pensions*, p. 229.

[59] "Tanner's Legacy," *Grand Army Record*, IV (Sept. 1889), 4.

[60] "A Ghost That Will Not Down," *Home and Country*, V (Nov. 1889), 188–189.

[61] *National Tribune*, Sept. 19, 1889.

be to please the G.A.R. Altogether, the appointment is unmitigatedly bad." [62]

During this furor over the administration of the Pension Office the veterans had not forgotten their desire for a disability pension bill and their gatherings continued to urge its passage. In August 1889, the pension committee reported to the national encampment that "from interviews with leading Members of both Houses, and the liberal views of the Secretary of the Interior and the Commissioner of Pensions," prospects for its enactment seemed at last favorable.[63] Their optimism was justified, for by the end of June 1890, Congress had passed and Harrison had signed a bill granting from six to twelve dollars a month to all veterans who had served ninety days and were so permanently disabled as to be unable to support themselves by manual labor, the rate depending upon the degree of physical handicap. The significant features of the law were that the disability did not need to be the result of service and the interpretation of what incapacitated a person for manual work was so liberal that well-to-do professional and businessmen were just as eligible as the truly crippled and poverty-stricken. In the next two decades the law was to take one billion dollars out of the national treasury.[64]

Having achieved this major objective, which the *Vedette* in a pique of professional jealousy denounced as "a put-up job to corral the soldier vote in order to continue the Congressional attorneys and henchmen of millionaires and corporation managers in possession of all the powers of the general Government," [65] the Grand Army scarcely paused in its voracious quest. "Conceding all that is claimed for this bill as a measure of relief to needy comrades," declared Indiana's commander, "it is still far short of justice." [66] After noting that it "will reach without question the cases which are most

---

[62] *Constitution* (Atlanta), Oct. 21, 1889, quoted in "The Pension Bureau," *Public Opinion,* VIII (Oct. 26, 1889), 54.

[63] G.A.R., *Journal 1889,* p. 122.

[64] Grand Army of the Republic, *Journal of the Twenty-fourth Annual Session of the National Encampment 1890* (Detroit, 1890), pp. 9–10; Glasson, *Federal Military Pensions,* pp. 233–237.

[65] *Vedette,* April 1892.

[66] Department of Indiana, Grand Army of the Republic, *Journal of Twelfth Annual Session 1891* (Indianapolis, 1891), p. 89.

pressing for assistance," the *Grand Army Record* proclaimed, "It now remains for the veterans to present a united front to secure such additional legislation as shall be needed." [67]

The new goal was a service pension for all veterans of the Civil War based upon the mere fact of participation. Even before 1890 the clamor for this had risen to an extent that had seriously weakened the Grand Army's efforts for a disability pension bill. Its advocates had on hand a ready stock of arguments. They saw that everything that had been said for a limited grant could just as logically be used to justify even greater generosity. Thus they turned to good account all the familiar concepts: the idea of an implicit contract, the right of a first mortgage, the encouragement to business prosperity, the existence of a surplus, and the available revenue from existing taxes. Their discontent with the Disability Pension Act of 1890 arose from its implication of charity, for the Grand Army expected pensions as its due. "Comrades, we do not bow the knee in suppliance for our rights. We are not beggars, like blind Belizarius, standing at the door of the treasury you have filled, asking for a penny," General James Baker told the Minnesota encampment amidst applause. "With head erect, with eyes to the front, with the proud consciousness of the immeasurable character of the work you have performed, you *demand* your legal and constitutional rights." [68] The fact that veterans of previous wars had all received service pensions made their plea seem all the more justifiable. Such a grant to Mexican War soldiers in 1887, which involved benefiting a number of former Confederates, seemed good precedent for rewarding all the survivors of a far greater conflict which had saved the Union.

Another argument for pensioning all the participants in the war was that "no man who saw so much as a month of active service can possibly be so well as he would have been had he stayed at home and taken care of himself." [69] This was allied to the contention that the years of service had handicapped the veterans economically because their contemporaries at home had secured a head start in their

[67] "The Pension Outlook," *Grand Army Record*, V (July 5, 1890), 4.
[68] Department of Minnesota, Grand Army of the Republic, *Journal of Proceedings of the Fourteenth Annual Encampment 1894* (Minneapolis, 1894), p. 258.
[69] *National Tribune*, Aug. 6, 1891.

occupations. In any case, the veterans were growing older, were less able to earn a living, and were convinced that they were suffering the effects of army life, even though proof was difficult. A service pension also seemed to have the advantage that it would greatly simplify administration. Each claim would no longer have to be examined carefully when the mere presentation of a discharge certificate constituted all the necessary evidence.

Among the advocates of a service pension there was considerable dispute as to the exact form it should take. Some thought it should start when the ex-soldier was sixty-two; others, when he was sixty. Many favored a flat rate of eight or twelve dollars a month for all who had served ninety days, but others contended that the amount should be proportionate to the length of time in the army and therefore they wanted a per diem bill. This usually involved a monthly stipend of a cent for each day of service. The Union Veteran Legion and the Union Veterans' Union, composed of men with longer records, naturally pressed this version.

For a long time the leaders of the Grand Army opposed so extreme a measure. At state and national encampments they deplored such agitation as revealing a lack of unity within the organization and thereby lessening the chances for a disability bill. They felt that a service pension should not be sought until all the ill and needy veterans had been aided, and sent James Tanner out to convert the midwestern encampments. In 1884 the national pension committee, pleading the cause of the disabled, declared that it seemed "a degree of selfishness closely allied to cruelty to push these claims aside that the attention of the national legislators may be occupied and the funds of the Nation diverted to the affluent and able-bodied survivors of the War." [70] Two years later it announced that it would work for "the aged, the poor and needy, and that until this is accomplished, the rich and well can afford to wait before demanding pensions for themselves." [71] Leaders of the order estimated that the cost of such an act would be so great that Congress would never pass it. Others criticized the morality of such demands. Commander-in-Chief Samuel Burdett feared it would "give just cause to our fellow-citizens to hail the Grand Army not as the Legionaries, but as Mercenaries of

[70] G.A.R., *Journal 1884*, p. 110.
[71] G.A.R., *Journal 1886*, p. 204.

the Republic." [72] He deplored the organization's "seeking to set a money value on its services." [73]

At first some of the veterans' papers also opposed the movement. For a long period the *National Tribune* declared its support of the national pension committee and insisted that it was impossible to secure a service pension as yet and that such pressure would only endanger the disability bill. Though not actually condemning a grant to everyone, the *Grand Army Record* also preferred to work for the disabled. Finally, a number of state encampments refused to endorse resolutions for a service pension, though sometimes only after lengthy debates. Persistent efforts to win the national encampment's approval were long unsuccessful. From 1883 through 1887 the meetings voted down such proposals by large majorities.

But the agitation would not down. Its backers denied it would injure the disabled, but instead argued it would help secure their relief. "Comrades, if a dozen pension bills should come before Congress in one year," asked one delegate at the 1887 convention, "would not members of Congress say: 'Must not we do something at once?'" [74] An ex-soldier in Montana thought that, since Congress appeared willing to grant pensions only grudgingly, it was "desirable to demand of it everything that is just, hoping thereby to extract from it at least, the pittance pensioning the needy, deserving, and disabled and aged soldiers." If a strong pension movement developed, "doubtless in the apprehension that such legislation might pass, the enemies of pensions would strive to weaken that public sentiment by selecting the needy and disabled, as a concession to that public sentiment." [75] As for the cost, the veterans were growing old and the expense would be great for only a few more years. Others maintained that the country should reward its heroes cheerfully no matter what the sum. The magnitude and the significance of the war in themselves justified large expenditures.

Certainly this scheme became increasingly the desire of the rank and file of G.A.R. membership. The leader of the campaign for an eight dollars a month bill was the John A. Dix Post of Boston, which

[72] *Ibid.*, p. 232.
[73] G.A.R., *Journal 1887*, p. 229.
[74] *Ibid.*, p. 219.
[75] Department of Montana, Grand Army of the Republic, *Proceedings of the First, Second, Third and Fourth Encampments 1885–1888* (Helena, 1888), p. 36.

secured endorsements from seventy-eight branches within the department and presented their petitions to the invalid claims committee of the House of Representatives. This last group was sufficiently impressed to suggest that the post ascertain the opinion of all other Grand Army units throughout the country. As a result, by 1886 it obtained the approval of more than 1900 of these local branches as well as of 300,000 other citizens who did not belong to the G.A.R. Such activity, directly contrary to the policy of the pension committee, led the national encampment to vote that all petitions on pensions from individual posts must henceforth be sent through national headquarters.

As the eighties wore on, not only many leaders swung over but also numerous Grand Army encampments, many of which had previously opposed the idea, yielded before the pressure, and instructed delegates to the national meeting to support a service pension. Whereas in 1885 the Massachusetts convention voted 254 to 213 in opposition, the following year it endorsed the proposal by 344 to 148. A poll of 246 Illinois posts in 1888 revealed 6233 in favor as against only 610 dissenters. At the height of the excitement over Cleveland's veto of the disability bill in 1887, the national encampment was told that nine out of ten veterans in the Wabash Valley of Indiana already preferred the more sweeping measure.[76]

In the late eighties such veterans' papers as the *Grand Army Review,* the *Grand Army Record, Home and Country,* and the *American Tribune,* commercial ventures which of necessity were sensitive to public opinion, ceased their support of the Grand Army's national administration and took up the proposal which was proving so popular with their readers. Despite its long alliance with headquarters, in April 1888, even the *National Tribune* promised to support a service pension as soon as the disability bill passed. On the ground that the latter measure was certain to become law soon, almost immediately thereafter it sought the favor of the mass of veterans with a *National Tribune* Pension Bill, a per diem grant for ninety-day veterans with the provision that no one was to receive less than eight dollars a month. In subsequent issues it urged the ex-soldiers to unite on this measure and to secure endorsements in local,

[76] Mass. G.A.R., *Journals 1881–1887*, pp. 297–302, 387–393; G.A.R., *Journal 1887*, p. 231.

state, and national G.A.R. meetings and political conventions.

As the Grand Army's membership developed this craving for a service pension, it became increasingly dissatisfied with the conservatism of the pension committee, which was thought to consist of rich men unsympathetic to the needs of poor veterans and interested only in manipulating the veterans for their own political advantage. Intense indignation also resulted whenever delegates to the national encampment ignored instructions to support a service pension resolution. After James Tanner defiantly told the New York department, which he had once headed, that he would oppose such a motion even should it "pile your instructions to Alpine heights," [77] the meeting asked the national encampment to deprive past state commanders of their lifetime voting privileges. Service pension advocates also made determined bids for both state and national offices in the order and judged candidates for posts on this basis.

The national encampment was the final citadel to be won. In 1888 the pension committee recommended not only the disability bill but also a measure, essentially the same as the *National Tribune*'s proposal, which granted eight dollars a month for all ninety-day veterans and one cent a day for each day's service above eight hundred. Despite the warning of former Commander-in-Chief Wagner that "by asking for too much, we shall receive nothing," [78] the convention accepted this dual report by an overwhelming majority. So far did the official attitude shift that the following year Commander-in-Chief William Warner confidently predicted, "The day is not far distant when an honorable discharge from the Union Army or Navy shall be all the evidence required to secure a pension to its holder." [79]

Despite this apparent triumph, suspicion continued that the national committee was not sincerely interested in the service pension and was sacrificing it while pushing the disability bill. At the Massachusetts convention in 1889 the leaders had great difficulty defeating a resolution that "the rights of veterans have been trifled with and their interests ignored" and that the commander-in-chief should alter the committee's composition.[80] The following year the Indiana

---

[77] N.Y. G.A.R., *Proceedings 1887*, pp. 68–69.
[78] G.A.R., *Journal 1888*, pp. 190–191.
[79] G.A.R., *Journal 1889*, p. 47.
[80] Department of Massachusetts, Grand Army of the Republic, *Proceedings of the Twenty-second Annual Encampment 1889* (Boston, 1889), pp. 8–9, 16–17.

branch elected as commander the president of the Indiana Service Pension Association and demanded the substitution of a committee genuinely sympathetic to more lavish legislation. In the early months of 1890 Commander-in-Chief Russell Alger found it necessary to appear before a number of state encampments in order to defend the committee. He explained that it had emphasized the disability bill because there seemed some chance of its success, while a service pension seemed impossible of immediate attainment.

The passage of the Disability Pension Bill in June 1890 cleared the way for unanimity on the more generous measure. A few encampments still refused to endorse it, but these rare instances of self-denial occurred on the whole just after winning the Disability Bill had momentarily satisfied the appetites of the less ravenous. "What more can we ask than this law affords?" queried the commander of the New Jersey department. To him "the time has come when the Grand Army should no longer knock at the doors of Congress for further pension legislation. . . ." [81] "We have the most liberal pension laws ever enacted in the history of the world," declared Iowa's head in similar vein. ". . . my idea is that the time has come when the Grand Army, as a body, should no longer pass resolutions making sweeping demands in this direction, and charging that Congress and the people are neglecting us." [82] The encampment accepted his views and merely asked for "such further legislation . . . as experience shall show to be practicable and necessary for the correction of defects of administration." [83]

But these expressions were scarcely typical. The only persistent criticism of pensions came from a few individual members who thereby quickly incurred the wrath of the organization. To be sure, General Henry Slocum, once a candidate for commander-in-chief, wrote an article for *Forum* early in 1892 entitled "Pensions: Time to Call a Halt." He argued that further demands would soon create a reaction against all pensions. But he was eccentric anyway, being a Democrat, and hardly a representative G.A.R. spokesman. The outstanding instance of revolt came from the Farnham Post of New

---

[81] Department of New Jersey, Grand Army of the Republic, *Proceedings of the 25th Annual Encampment 1892* (Newark, 1892), appendix, p. 12.

[82] Department of Iowa, Grand Army of the Republic, *Journal of Proceedings of the Seventeenth Annual Encampment 1891* (Cedar Rapids, 1891), pp. 16–17.

[83] *Ibid.*, p. 69.

York City. Distressed by the prevalent suspicion that the G.A.R. existed primarily to raid the treasury, it voted in March 1893 that the only veterans justly entitled to pensions were those who had been injured in the war; it then asked other posts to adopt similar resolutions. Allen R. Foote, a prominent opponent of further pension legislation who a couple of years earlier had tried to organize a Society of Loyal Volunteers with these very principles, promptly gave this action national publicity in an article in *Forum* in which he added his appeal that other G.A.R. posts support this protest.

The plea fell on barren ground. Declaring that the post had violated rules by sending out such a statement, the New York department demanded that it be rescinded. The local commander, John J. Finn, replied that "it is the opinion of this Post that if it is the desire of the Grand Army of the Republic to pay pensions to people who have not incurred their disabilities in the service of the country and to those who do not need them, then this Post does not desire to remain in the Grand Army of the Republic." [84] During the resultant conflict between the local and state organizations, Finn proposed that a questionnaire be sent to all other posts to discover if they really approved such a policy, but this was not accepted. Finally, its charter having been annulled, the post re-formed as the Noah Farnham Independent Veterans No. 1. Grand Army sentiment seems to have upheld the expulsion and there is no evidence that a No. 2 group of critics ever followed.

Instead, again and again throughout the decade of the nineties Grand Army commanders and department encampments in at least twenty-seven states, supported by the Union Veterans' Union, the Union Veteran Legion, and the veterans' newspapers, expressed their longing for a service pension. They all echoed the cheers of New York's session in 1891 when one delegate delivered his ultimatum: "I say, by all means, to-day is the day to pass a service pension bill. We are entitled to it to-day, and do not want to wait until we are all dead, when it will do us no good. Give us the bill if it costs 200,000,000. Let us demand it and keep on demanding it until we get it." [85] The issue produced a lengthy debate at the 1890 national

[84] John J. Finn, "Complete History of the Farnham Post Revolt," *Forum*, XVI (July 1893), 534.

[85] Department of New York, Grand Army of the Republic, *Proceedings of the Twenty-fifth Annual Encampment 1891* (Albany, 1891), p. 260.

conclave. Though a majority of the resolutions committee still opposed such a measure, the meeting finally adopted the favorable minority report by the close vote of 174–160. Thereafter the national organization made some efforts to secure its passage, but never pushed it as vigorously as it had the disability bill. Unlike the enthusiastic state meetings, the more conservative and experienced national leadership probably realized that the generous act of 1890, the return of the Democrats to power in 1893, the hard times that soon followed, and the mounting criticism of all expenditures made any further enactments unlikely in the near future. Not until the eve of the election of 1904 did the G.A.R. gain this objective through an executive order of the opportunistic Theodore Roosevelt, to which Congress at last gave a legal basis in 1907.

Though the Grand Army naturally focused its attention on fairly comprehensive legislation that included as many people as possible, it did not neglect certain special groups. Throughout these years many state encampments, the Sons of Veterans, and the *National Tribune* endorsed the pleas of the ex-prisoners' association that its members deserved special consideration, usually to an amount proportionate to the length of incarceration. The order also supported a movement to increase the rates for widows, though the veterans' magnanimity did not include a proposal that widows' pensions be for life regardless of remarriage.

Though lacking the potent weapon of the vote, the Woman's Relief Corps made a bill to pension the former army nurses its particular concern. When it began this agitation in the mid-eighties, it quickly ran into the hostility of the G.A.R. pension committee, which felt that the auxiliary should not act independently and that it should not start another campaign while the disability bill was pending. Not until after the veto of that measure in 1887 did the women win the order's approval of a bill to grant the nurses twelve dollars a month, and a number of Grand Army posts then added their pleas to the petitions of W.R.C. members. The women now turned to the same lobbying practices as the men. But though the chairman of their pension committee, Mrs. Florence Barker, went to Washington and had the help of such distinguished aides as Mrs. John A. Logan and Clara Barton, they were able to get the bill through the Senate only but not through the House.

Finally the aggressive Annie Wittenmyer spent five months in the early nineties in Washington, "quartered in the back room of the third storey of a hotel, where she worked almost day and night, writing to those who had influence with members of the House." As the campaign reached its climax she summoned to the capital the secretary of the order's pension committee, Mrs. Harriette Reed, who later described how "day after day we haunted the Capital, interviewing the members of Congress and imploring their aid." Her return home after six weeks did not end her efforts: "Letters innumerable were written to influential men and women all over our land by the various members of our Committee, and by word and pen our friends were importuned to aid us." In June 1892, the measure passed the House, but the result in the upper chamber remained dubious. "We all redoubled our efforts to secure a favorable report from the Senate," the women testified, "and letters and telegrams from prominent men and women of the country again went pouring in." Mrs. Reed returned to Washington and she and Miss Barton planned their strategy in conferences with friendly Senators. The end of July at last saw success.[86]

During the next few years the W.R.C. employed Mrs. Wittenmyer to help the nurses take advantage of this law. Of the first 425 claims granted, she had aided 226. In the last half of the nineties she labored for the act's extension to regimental nurses. At one weary moment she sat down on a rickety chair in the House corridor and was pitched onto the marble floor. Though she predicted gloomily that the injury would cripple her for life, she carried on her unsuccessful campaign propped up in bed.

All in all, the veterans and their affiliates made their greatest gains during the administration of Benjamin Harrison. Thanks primarily to the act of 1890, the number of pensioners nearly doubled to approximately 900,000, the amount spent for pensions each year rose from about $80,000,000 to almost $140,000,000, and the problem of the surplus in the national treasury was not nearly as vexing as it once had been.[87] After March 4, 1893, the Grand Army did not really expect any additional pension legislation for the following four years.

---

[86] Woman's Relief Corps, Auxiliary to the Grand Army of the Republic, *Journal of the Tenth Annual Convention 1892* (Boston, 1892), pp. 38, 184–185.

[87] Glasson, *Federal Military Pensions*, p. 273.

Those who recalled with distaste the first Cleveland administration wondered whether they would even hold their own during his second term. The press discussed rumors that the new executive might reduce pension expenditures drastically, and the *National Tribune* warned Cleveland that the veterans would fight any attack on the pension system every inch of the way. The G.A.R.'s energies turned therefore not so much to demands for larger sums for more people as to pleas for a generous interpretation of the existing laws.

The Democratic regime promptly fulfilled the veterans' fears. The 1890 law gave considerable discretion to the Pension Bureau in its rating of disabilities. Its attitude had been extremely liberal under Harrison. The new commissioner of pensions, William Lochren, began to suspend numerous allowances until the cases could be reexamined and cleared of any suspicion of fraud. At the national encampment in September 1893, Commander-in-Chief A. G. Weissert replied that the statutes "should receive a broad and generous construction so as to carry on the humane intentions of the law makers." He attempted to becloud the issue by bemoaning that persons of dubious loyalty were depriving the nation's defenders of their just rewards.[88] The convention condemned the suspensions, demanded the restoration to the rolls of those who had been dropped, and voted, if this was not done, to test the constitutionality of the reductions. The encampment assumed that a pension was a property right of which a veteran could not be deprived without due process of law. When one delegate questioned this view, another arose indignantly to inquire, "If a pension isn't property, in the name of God, what is it?"[89]

The new commander-in-chief distributed the pension committee's criticisms to all posts so as to arouse the entire membership. Next the order instigated litigation to test the suspensions' legality, but the Supreme Court eventually dismissed the case. Subsequent national encampments protested the hostile attitude of the Pension Bureau and urged restrictions on its powers. Meanwhile, in twenty-five states and territories from Maine to Oregon, numerous department officials and encampments had joined in assailing the govern-

[88] Grand Army of the Republic, *Proceedings of the Twenty-Seventh National Encampment 1893* (Milwaukee, 1893), p. 55.

[89] *Ibid.*, p. 235.

ment's stand, reiterating that a pension was a vested right and therefore property. "We demand that in the future those who shall occupy high official station in connection with the pension department of our government, shall be men at least in sympathy with the pensioners," ran the typical statement of the Tennessee department, "and not by those who by prejudice and education shall be unfavorable to their rights." [90] "Instead of seeking for excuses to hold up the pension owned by a soldier, as the highwayman holds up the belated traveller, thus destroying vested rights," the Indiana veterans similarly complained, "United States officials ought rather to seek for reasons to place upon the pension rolls the many whose names are not yet there." [91]

Above all, the veterans bristled at the assumption behind these suspensions that the rolls were honeycombed with frauds. One writer, for example, claimed that, if the pensioners were reëxamined, one-third would fall into this category.[92] Grand Army encampments and soldiers' journals rang with pained denials. Some veterans argued that the large number of deserving pensioners more than compensated for the few instances of deceit. "Because some dishonest soldier gets that to which he is not entitled," queried a member of the 1893 Minnesota encampment, "should every old soldier be deprived of that to which he is rightfully entitled?" Cries of "No" answered his question. "Certainly not," he continued. "Why, my Comrades, I would rather ten thousand times have ten unworthy men get that which did not belong to them than that one deserving soldier or soldier's widow should be deprived of that which they honestly deserve." The delegates hailed this pronouncement with great applause and shouts of "That's right." [93] More often the G.A.R. hastened to avow its opposition to any frauds and to declare that the pension list should form a "roll of honor" and that members should report deceptions. The *National Tribune* repeatedly de-

[90] Department of Tennessee, Grand Army of the Republic, *Eleventh Encampment 1894* (Knoxville, n.d.), p. 94.

[91] Department of Indiana, Grand Army of the Republic, *Journal of Fifteenth Annual Session 1894* (Indianapolis, 1894), p. 170.

[92] John H. Girdner, "To Purge the Pension List," *North American Review*, CLXVI (March 1898), 374–375.

[93] Department of Minnesota, Grand Army of the Republic, *Journal of Proceedings of the Thirteenth Annual Encampment 1893* (St. Paul, 1893), pp. 196–197.

manded that the commissioner of pensions publish full reports on one or two thousand consecutive cases, confident that this would prove their probity. The Grand Army, however, did not welcome the proposal that the entire list be published in order to expose the unworthy.

The veterans were particularly stung by a public comment of President Charles W. Eliot of Harvard in the spring of 1896 that the Grand Army of the Republic was chiefly interested in getting money out of the public treasury. Several state encampments at once denounced his "outrageous, false, unpatriotic and utterly un-American statements." [94] At the New York convention James Tanner, first describing Harvard's tribute to the Civil War dead, Memorial Hall, then turned his attention to Eliot and suggested "that on bended knee he crawl into that sacred presence, and lift his eyes and gaze upon the tribute that Harvard paid to the loyal dead of the country. Then I would still advise, that without rising, he turn and crawl out, and seeking for the nearest pigpen, crawl into that and apologize to the swine for his presence among them." [95]

Many delegates at the national assembly in September 1896 favored a vote of censure, but the committee on resolutions, after declaring its disapproval of Eliot's views, refused to "dignify them by any formal resolutions of condemnation" and graciously added that it did not associate his statements with the institution he headed.[96] Several months later, in February 1897, the issue still provoked a violent discussion at the Massachusetts encampment. A number of condemnatory resolutions were presented. One declared that Eliot's attitude "is an insult to the veterans of the late war and should receive the condemnation of all true lovers of American liberty." Another assailed his views "as being not only unpatriotic, but disloyal to the city and college which he represents, and treasonable to the highest degree." Though declaring that "No leniency can find excuse for such unpatriotic and unqualified language, whether spoken by a cultured scholar or unlettered boor," the committee on

---

[94] Department of Wisconsin, Grand Army of the Republic, *Proceedings of the Thirtieth Annual Encampment 1896* (Milwaukee, 1896), p. 142.

[95] Department of New York, Grand Army of the Republic, *Proceedings of the Thirtieth Annual Encampment 1896* (Albany and New York, 1896), p. 100.

[96] Grand Army of the Republic, *Journal of the Thirtieth National Encampment 1896* (Indianapolis, 1896), p. 223.

resolutions finally decided that it "merits only silent contempt." Though a post commander pointed out that it was too late to give Eliot silent contempt after he had been under discussion for half an hour, the encampment endorsed the committee's statement. "I suppose that this treating with 'silent contempt' don't prevent us 'cussing' him privately," was one member's last taunt.[97]

The veterans also resented repeated assaults on the allowances for widows because so many women had married elderly comrades merely to secure pensions. "What patriot will object to an old soldier marrying a young wife?" asked the commander of the Maine department. "I would advise him to, if he married at all, marry a young woman, and if young women will marry old soldiers and take care of them in their old age for their pension after they are gone, so much the better for the old soldier."[98]

On one point the Grand Army and its critics occasionally agreed. The opponents of excessive expenditures often put the blame on the claims attorneys. Many leaders within the G.A.R. also attributed to their influence whatever frauds existed. By the nineties the only ardent defense of this group came from the veterans' papers, which often had close connections with these firms. "The most of the disreputable pension attorneys have been weeded out of the practice," insisted the *American Tribune* toward the close of the century, "and there is probably no more reputable class of men in any profession than those engaged in this one."[99] But more frequently the order took comfort in assurances that all these unpleasant accusations represented merely the efforts of former rebels, Mugwumps, or the Eastern money power to attack the entire system and to deprive the deserving worthy along with the few undeserving.

After the Democratic debacle in the 1896 election the veterans expected the McKinley administration to restore their fortunes. "I am thankful that the people have put a soldier lover in the White House, and a comrade in spirit and in truth, and at the head of the Pension Department another comrade well worthy of our faith and trust," declared the commander of the West Virginia department in

[97] Department of Massachusetts, Grand Army of the Republic, *Journal of the Thirty-first Annual Encampment 1897* (Boston, 1897), p. 185.

[98] Department of Maine, Grand Army of the Republic, *Proceedings of the Thirty-first Annual Encampment 1898* (Augusta, 1898), p. 60.

[99] *American Tribune* (Indianapolis), April 7, 1898.

May 1897. "I honestly believe our cause is in safe hands and that the pension laws will now be administered in the broad liberal spirit intended by the framers of such laws and the Grand Army of the Republic." [100] At the 1897 national encampment the pension committee greeted "the dawn of a new era in the history of the Pension Department of the National Government." It hailed McKinley's choice for pension commissioner, H. Clay Evans of Tennessee, and predicted that "the comrades may safely look forward, under his administration of the Pension Office, to a just and, at the same time, liberal interpretation of the pension laws, so far as such interpretation lies in his power." "Within the last few months," gloated the commander-in-chief, "the latch-strings have been loosened and many justly entitled pensioners have had their cases acted upon; others, stopped without cause, have been restored to the rolls, and the machinery of that great department of the government seems to have been oiled with the oil of human kindness and honest obligation, and to be running much more smoothly and with less friction than before." [101] Evans' remarks to the Society of the Army of the Cumberland and the Union Veteran Legion seemed to confirm this happy picture: "I shall endeavor to do my duty towards the soldiers of the Union who saved the nation. I shall do it within the limits of the law, but from a liberal standpoint." [102]

But this harmony proved short-lived. In May 1897, the Grand Army pension committee met in Washington and confidently gave the new commissioner a long memorandum asking a return to the practices of Commissioner Raum in the Harrison administration. The bureau, however, proved hesitant to adopt all these suggestions. Soon state encampments were angrily demanding speedier settlement of claims and objecting to the idea that a disability should really have to incapacitate a claimant for manual labor. Typical of these sentiments was the resolution of the Massachusetts convention: "The Congress of the United States having passed liberal pension laws for the benefit of those who imperilled their lives to save

[100] Department of West Virginia, Grand Army of the Republic, *Proceedings of the Fifteenth Annual Encampment 1897* (Palatine, W. Va., 1897), pp. 32–33.

[101] Grand Army of the Republic, *Journal of the Thirty-first National Encampment 1897* (Lincoln, Neb., 1897), pp. 309–310, 63.

[102] Society of the Army of the Cumberland, *Twenty-seventh Reunion 1897* (Cincinnati, 1898), p. 73.

the Union, these laws should be interpreted by those in authority in the same liberal spirit which prompted a grateful nation to place them upon its statute book." It therefore demanded that "the Union veteran should be given the benefit of every reasonable doubt in the interpretation of the law. We protest against the rejection or delay of claims upon trivial technicalities, and insist that our disabled comrades should be treated with greater liberality." [103]

As the veterans grew increasingly indignant with the administration of the Pension Office, their condemnation of Evans became more outspoken. They denied that a pension commissioner "is appointed to save money for the Government at the expense of the men who saved the Government." [104] The veterans' papers inaugurated virulent campaigns against him, and several encampments demanded either his unconditional removal or at least an investigation to determine whether he should be allowed to continue in office. Though some elements in the Grand Army, especially in his home state of Tennessee, and independent Mugwump journals like the *Nation* defended the commissioner, the rank and file of membership became bitterly hostile. When the order held its national encampment in September 1899, many favored an outright demand for Evans' dismissal. Officially, however, the convention merely asked McKinley to alter the obnoxious rules. In 1900 Congress made the desired modifications, but Evans remained in office until in 1902 Theodore Roosevelt acceded to G.A.R. protests by giving Evans a post in the consular service.

When the members of the Union Army paraded through Washington in a Grand Review at the close of the war in April 1865, the grateful capital had erected over their path a banner which proclaimed, "The Only National Debt We Can Never Pay Is the Debt We Owe to the Victorious Union Soldiers." [105] Even if the emotionalism of the moment possibly produced an overly rhetorical expression of this feeling, in many ways the statement was quite justified. Refusing to accept the slogan literally, the veterans proved entirely

---

[103] Department of Massachusetts, Grand Army of the Republic, *Journal of the Thirty-Third Annual Encampment 1899* (Boston, 1899), pp. 175–176.

[104] Department of Kansas, Grand Army of the Republic, *Journal of the Eighteenth Annual Encampment 1899* (Topeka, 1899), p. 116.

[105] Dixon Wecter, *When Johnny Comes Marching Home* (Cambridge, Mass., 1944), p. 127.

willing to attempt to reduce the impossible to a partial actuality. Despite an occasional rebuff, they had done pretty well at this task by the end of the century. The number of pensioners had increased from 126,000 to 993,000, while, contrasted with the total of $90,000,-000 that all military pensions had cost the government for the entire period from the Revolution to 1861, the annual amount paid out had mounted from $15,000,000 to $138,000,000.[106] In the words of one observer, the record was "both heartening and depressing," [107] heartening as a demonstration of the nation's generosity to soldiers all of whose lives had been affected to one degree or another, depressing in the fashion in which this ideal had been exploited for mercenary and partisan reasons. While the original impetus came largely from the pension attorneys, the veterans themselves had quickly learned how to turn their organizations into effective pressure groups in their own behalf. In a period when industrialization and agrarian unrest were posing new problems of economic security, pensions constituted a primitive form of social insurance that perhaps had a certain rough justice to it. At the same time this persistent and skillful campaigning for legislative favors also inevitably involved the veterans deeply in the political intrigues and battles of the day.

[106] Glasson, *Federal Military Pensions,* p. 273.
[107] David Kinley, "Editor's Preface," in Glasson, *Federal Military Pensions,* p. vii.

IX

The Veterans in Politics

FOR nearly half a century the Grand Army of the Republic and the Republican Party had a public liaison which was about as secret as the relations between Lord Nelson and Lady Hamilton and just as understandable. The existence of hundreds of thousands of individuals who had had a common experience that lent itself readily to emotional exploitation, who were soon developing an insatiable appetite for governmental favors, who through the suffrage had an effective means for achieving their desires, and who were well organized into societies for convenient manipulation scarcely eluded the attention of politicians of the post-Civil War era. At first the Grand Army was merely a device of the Radical Republicans to maintain themselves in power. The position of the Republican Party was far from secure after the war. For continued control of the federal government, disfranchising the Southern whites and directing the Southern Negroes, though essential, were not enough; it was also necessary to garner a substantial Northern bloc. An obvious group was the veterans, whose wartime emotions might be played upon so as to support the Republicans as the party of Union and loyalty. Later the situation was reversed as the G.A.R. became a powerful pressure group often using the party for its own purposes as much as the party used it. Soon the Mexican War veterans attempted to be just as active politically, though the logic of their situation allied them with the Democrats.

The Grand Army itself naturally denied that it was political and insisted that it had always been merely a philanthropic enterprise to advance the veterans' "rights," but, as was indicated earlier in the account of the society's founding, Mrs. Mary R. Dearing has proved practically beyond question that from the moment of its origin the Grand Army was a device of Radical Republican leaders in Illinois like Richard J. Oglesby and John A. Logan to advance their political fortunes. Not only Stephenson but practically all his close associates in the early days of the order had close affiliations with Governor Oglesby, and it seems likely that the funds required for spreading the organization came from these political sources rather than from the pockets of the never very prosperous doctor. Certainly nearly all newspaper stories and correspondence between public figures at the time assumed that the G.A.R.'s primary purpose was partisan. Likewise, the society's expansion beyond the borders of Illinois was equally linked with Radical activities. Governor Oliver Morton of neighboring Indiana deliberately imported it there to bolster the Republican Party, and elsewhere in the Northwest its appearance was the result of active encouragement from Radical governors.[1] Even one of the association's leaders conceded only a few years later, "if not originally conceived in partisan politics, it became the wish of many politicians to make it a great political machine to subserve selfish purpose." [2]

There were good reasons for such a development. Apparently after they emerged from the service many veterans of the white-collar group decided against returning to their previous occupations, and of these, it is claimed, the largest number turned to politics as livelihood.[3] These men might well expect to become the leaders of any association of ex-soldiers, and it was only natural to hope that with the proper emotional trumpet calls they might rally their former comrades to their support once more, this time on the battlefield of politics. Certainly any analysis of the first officials of the order on either the state or national level shows that they were nearly all Radical Republicans. Practically the entire slate elected at the first national encampment in 1866, from Commander-in-Chief Stephen A. Hurlbut of Illinois down, fell into that category. Equally partisan were the men honored in 1868. The new chief was one of the prominent Republican politicians of the day, John A. Logan of Illinois,

[1] Mary R. Dearing, *Veterans in Politics* (Baton Rouge, 1952), pp. 81–95. This is a thorough and invaluable account of all phases of the political activities of Civil War veterans in the late nineteenth century. For an excellent examination of the G.A.R.'s influence within one state, see Frank H. Heck, *The Civil War Veteran in Minnesota Life and Politics* (Oxford, Ohio, 1941).

[2] Department of Pennsylvania, Grand Army of the Republic, *Proceedings of the Encampments of 1867 to 1872* (Pottsville, 1872), p. 45.

[3] Dixon Wecter, *When Johnny Comes Marching Home* (Cambridge, Mass., 1944), p. 197.

who, according to one of his opponents, "worked the machine admirably for his own benefit." [4] All of the subsequent commanders-in-chief up until William Earnshaw, elected in 1879, were active Republicans, and an endless list could be made of lesser officials. On the other hand, only rarely did a Democrat gain office in the order, and so curious an event usually occasioned widespread comment.

Consequently the Grand Army was prominently involved in most of the campaigns of the period, though perhaps never was its participation so flagrant as at the beginning of its career in 1866. Throughout the fall of that year the new order figured in numerous political demonstrations in Illinois and Indiana. In Wisconsin only one member of the first state encampment was not a Radical Republican. Further proof of the society's sympathies came with the Soldiers' and Sailors' National Convention at Pittsburgh in September, a gigantic Republican rally. Not only did G.A.R. leaders in the Middle West issue the calls for the meeting and become delegates themselves, but also a number of posts, especially in Indiana, were officially represented. Since it was through this gathering that the order was introduced into the East, that meant that all the original leaders in that section were active Radicals who converted existing political clubs of veterans into posts.

The Grand Army's partisanship was not only overt but during these tense years of Reconstruction possibly even conspiratorial to an extent that had far more basis than earlier suspicions of the Cincinnati on this score. The present generation can hardly realize the turbulence of the "Tragic Era" and the "Age of Hate," when many feared that the United States had perhaps become accustomed to the forceful settlement of disputes and especially of elections. As the tug of war between President Andrew Johnson and the Radical Congress became more acute, rumors of the G.A.R.'s activities caused Johnson to send out an investigator, one James O'Beirne, who soon began to pepper the executive with lurid tales of the order's "power, danger and devilishness." Not only did he confirm its essentially political nature but he also reported that in Indiana and Illinois the members were secretly arming so as to march on Washington to back Congress in case of a showdown with the

---

[4] Thomas J. McCormack, ed., *The Memoirs of Gustave Koerner 1809–1896* (Cedar Rapids, Iowa, 1909), II, 521.

President. The master-mind behind this plot supposedly was Governor Oliver Morton of Indiana. So alarmed did the spy become that he assured his chief, "I for one shall prepare for fighting when I get home." [5]

Just how exaggerated O'Beirne's fears were it is hard to say. The distribution of arms among Grand Army members seems fairly well-established, but the exact intention of this is more uncertain. Throughout the period between 1866 and 1868 there were constant rumors that actual armed conflict between the President and Congress might lead to a second Civil War and the indications were that various Grand Army leaders were making pledges of support to Congressional leaders.[6] During the crisis at the time of Johnson's impeachment there came further signs that officials were willing to use the order for a military coup. When Secretary of War Stanton's refusal to yield his office precipitated matters, from all over the country Commander-in-Chief Logan received assurances that the Grand Army of the Republic, 100,000 strong, was ready to advance on the capital if Johnson sent troops to eject Stanton.

With this encouragement Logan secretly formed the members in Washington into battalions and gave them arms. Sentinels were on duty constantly day and night, especially near the White House and the War Department building. Countersigns and signals were devised to summon the veterans to the latter spot upon any attempt to oust the Secretary. Logan himself, though continuing to serve in the House of Representatives during the day, at night occupied a cot next to Stanton. One of the society's leaders later declared that, had Johnson used force, "the members of our Posts, without exception, at that time would have rallied to Mr. Stanton's support and would have laid down their lives in his defence." [7]

As the presidential campaign of 1868 approached, the G.A.R. members advocated the nomination of their wartime commander, Ulysses S. Grant. As one veteran wrote from Iowa, "We are organizing a Post of the Grand Army of the Republic here, which will be

[5] James O'Beirne to Andrew Johnson, Oct. 12, 1866, Andrew Johnson Papers, Library of Congress.

[6] William A. Russ, "Was There Danger of a Second Civil War During Reconstruction?" *Mississippi Valley Historical Review*, XXV (June 1938), 44.

[7] Quoted by Robert B. Beath, *History of the Grand Army of the Republic* (New York, 1889), pp. 93–94.

virtually a Grant Club." [8] Both local and state meetings endorsed his candidacy. Conflict developed, however, as to whether the national encampment at Philadelphia in January 1868 should vote formal approval. Although conservative elements checked any official statement, the "unqualifiedly radical" speeches of the retiring commander-in-chief, General Hurlbut, and of the newly elected commander for New York, Daniel Sickles, at an open meeting seemed to express the convention's sentiments.

Just before the Republican National Convention at Philadelphia in May a Soldiers' and Sailors' Convention denounced the Johnson administration and called for Grant's nomination. Technically it had no connection with the G.A.R., but the head of its resolutions committee was Commander-in-Chief Logan. On the very next day after this gathering the order's junior vice-commander-in-chief, Governor Hawley of Connecticut, presided over the Republican session and Logan placed Grant's name before it.

During the ensuing canvass the Grand Army was less obviously political than it had been in 1866. This was chiefly because the Republicans wheeled the veterans into line so well through Boys in Blue clubs and soldiers' conventions that they scarcely needed to use the Grand Army as such. Even so, in many localities the society labored for Grant's success. While the national organization was more circumspect, in a letter to the Republican National Executive Committee marked "Private" and "Strictly Confidential" Logan revealed, "The organization of the G.A.R. *has been and is being run in the interest* of the Republican Party. . . ." [9]

But by this time the Grand Army had gained a notorious political reputation which contributed substantially to its collapse in the early seventies. As it declined in numbers, it played a less conspicuous part in political affairs. Consequently the next few years saw many officials and meetings making pious declarations of nonpartisanship and in 1869 the national encampment officially banned partisan activity. In an effort to prove its good faith and thereby perhaps bolster up its emaciated rolls, in the seventies the order endeavored

[8] Charles P. Brown to Elihu Washburne, Jan. 17, 1868, Elihu Washburne Papers, Library of Congress.

[9] John A. Logan to the Republican National Executive Committee, Sept. 19, 1868, William E. Chandler Papers, Library of Congress.

with some success to attract Democratic veterans, somewhat like a college fraternity rounding up a couple of Jews or Negroes to show that it is not discriminatory. Yet though the national officers were now careful not to commit it publicly, the society still managed to indicate its sympathies. The 1876 encampment displayed significant enthusiasm for Hayes and the next year's meeting saw the new President and nearly all his cabinet turn up at a clambake; it is difficult to imagine Samuel J. Tilden and a coterie of Democratic chieftains ever sharing seafood with the veterans. Nevertheless, when in the midst of the excitement of the disputed election, rumor had the association once more arming itself, this time to install Hayes by force, the order publicly pledged itself to abide by the legal decision.

After each election the leaders now customarily congratulated the membership for not having involved the society. With a straight face the *National Tribune* proclaimed, "There is no great organization of men in the country which is so thoroughly non-partisan as the G.A.R." [10] Actually, however, the association's support of the Republicans had become different in objective and more subtle in form, but not necessarily less potent. Originally Republican politicians had used the organization to win elections but then had abandoned it without giving anything in return. But as the order revived in strength, like Miss Loos's young lady who discovered that a kiss on the hand is very nice but a diamond bracelet lasts forever, it increasingly demanded a *quid pro quo,* ordinarily in the form of pensions, as a more durable memento of its favor on election day.

Typical of the shrewd intermediaries who supervised this extra-legal domestic arrangement was James Tanner, who devoted his talents so energetically to both the G.A.R. and the Republican party that it is difficult to tell whether he was organizing the veterans to benefit his party or to force concessions from it (probably he sincerely believed that the relationship was mutually advantageous). Bluntly he pointed out to the 1887 national encampment, for example, that the members of the next session of Congress were bound to be well-disposed, for "looking at us as the representatives of 375,000 men, with an election pending next year on which the fate of parties depends, they won't be so apt to slap us in the face, and

[10] *National Tribune* (Washington, D.C.), Dec. 1, 1887.

we can get considerable." [11] On the other hand, when the veterans became aroused that same year over the actions of Grover Cleveland, Tanner privately informed Lucius Fairchild, "We are political fools if we do not take advantage of this patriotic revival." [12]

Abetted by the soldiers' papers, the veterans soon devised the strategy of rewarding their friends and punishing their enemies; whenever their allies seemed ungrateful, a threatened realignment of their well-disciplined forces usually proved effective. "When a man of any party offers himself for our suffrages," declared Indiana's commander, "let us investigate his record and his sentiments upon the subject of pension legislation, and if we find he is not sound, whether he be Republican, Democrat, Prohibition, or what not, erase his name from our ticket." [13] The result was that by 1890 past Commander-in-Chief Paul Van Der Voort could boast to the Iowa Grand Army, "We know there is no congressman west of the Mississippi that dare vote against a reasonable pension bill. They do what we tell them, and they don't act without telling us what is just and right." [14]

Soon the politicians themselves, quick to sense a popular issue, were volunteering their support in the hope of capturing the veteran vote. Representative James Johnson told the national encampment of 1887 how he and two other candidates in Indiana held "a council of war" and decided that advocacy of a service pension would overturn usually hostile majorities. "Our opponents were foolish enough to fall into the trap and oppose it," he proudly disclosed. "Hovey carried his district by fourteen hundred majority, and I carried mine by eleven hundred and fifty." [15] Hurriedly leaping on the band wagon, no fewer than four Congressmen begged the Indiana session the following year to endorse so vote-winning a measure. Thus, while the society maintained a technical neutrality on the national level, numerous warnings and reprimands from its officials revealed

[11] Grand Army of the Republic, *Journal of the Twenty-first Annual Session of the National Encampment 1887* (Milwaukee, 1887), p. 227.

[12] James Tanner to Lucius Fairchild, August 15, 1887, Lucius Fairchild Papers, Wisconsin State Historical Society.

[13] Department of Indiana, Grand Army of the Republic, *Journal of the Eleventh Annual Session 1890* (Indianapolis, 1890), p. 81.

[14] Department of Iowa, Grand Army of the Republic, *Journal of Proceedings of the Sixteenth Annual Encampment 1890* (Burlington, Iowa, 1890), p. 74.

[15] G.A.R., *Journal 1887*, p. 232.

that it was having less success doing this in state and local affairs. The presence of post quartets or bands and the wearing of Grand Army uniforms or badges continued to be familiar features of party rallies, while the neighborhood politicians faithfully attended meetings, corresponded on G.A.R. stationery, and in general turned to good account their fraternal contacts. Sometimes they even succeeded in winning the endorsement of these local branches, despite the vigilance of higher officials who on occasion suspended post charters for too overt interference in nominations.

When the G.A.R. claimed that it had become nonpartisan, therefore, it did not mean that it had eschewed all political activity but only that it made no official commitments to any particular party. Actually, as was apparent to any observer, all its bonds were with the Republicans. Practically its entire membership voted that ticket. The commanders-in-chief were nearly always active in Republican politics. William Warner, for example, a delegate to almost every Republican convention between 1872 and 1904, was reëlected to Congress the year he became head of the G.A.R., and later served as United States Senator, while Russell Alger's term came between his occupancy of the Michigan governorship and his elevation first to McKinley's cabinet and later to the Senate. A steady procession of Republican leaders was conspicuous at all national encampments. Among the members of the Ohio delegation in 1886 were both a past and a future President of the United States, Rutherford B. Hayes and William McKinley, and it has already been mentioned how five governors (none of them Democrats) turned up on Mrs. J. B. Foraker's doorstep in 1888.

As long as the Republicans remained sound on the pension question, the veterans showed no disposition to join the Independents or Mugwumps who often bolted the party in these years. "I have no sympathy with so-called reformers who go to the democratic party to get reform," Commander-in-Chief Lucius Fairchild once wrote his brother. "Its worse than going to hell to obtain morality." [16] Ordinarily they detested these mavericks who as civil service reformers opposed veterans' preference and as advocates of clean, effi-

---

[16] Lucius Fairchild to Charles Fairchild, June 29, 1884, Fairchild Papers.

cient, economical government questioned pension expenditures. "But I don't believe there is a comrade in the Grand Army in Ohio who is a mugwump. Is there?" a member of that state's encampment once asked. "If there is, I want to look at you." [17] Presumably no one rose to accept the label. James Tanner suggested that only those veterans in a state of semi-idiocy would cast a Mugwump vote. From a materialistic viewpoint he was right. Through the pension system, the Republicans had devised for the benefit of the ex-soldiers a sort of early limited W.P.A. which, when combined with gifts of home-steads to Western pioneers, land grants to railroads, and tariff bene-fits to industrialists, was a striking demonstration of how the lavish spending of federal funds could long maintain a political party in power. In turn, no more than future generations were the veterans disposed to shoot Santa Claus, then clothed in the garments of Republican respectability.

This working alliance did not become fully apparent until the mid-eighties. Barely emerging from its period of decline and facing two presidential candidates with distinguished war records, the Grand Army exerted little influence in the campaign of 1880. But four years later the order had acquired considerable strength and the rise of the pension issue made it more concerned over the out-come of the election. The *National Tribune,* though not particularly enthusiastic about the vulnerable Republican standard-bearer, James G. Blaine, nevertheless denounced the Democrats for their hostility to pensions and their failure to name a veteran. It was so pleased with the Republican vice-presidential candidate, the former G.A.R. commander-in-chief John A. Logan, even publishing a campaign biography of him, that its columns scarcely indicated that heading the ticket was a plumed knight without military experience.

Though the order's leaders carefully checked the more obvious displays of partisanship, the unofficial understanding was now in full force. "I am doing my level best for the whole ticket and have personally secured pledges from a number of comrades who have always voted the straight democratic ticket," a post commander informed Lucius Fairchild. "I am satisfied they will vote for Blaine

---

[17] Department of Ohio, Grand Army of the Republic, *Proceedings of the Thirty-Second Annual Encampment 1898* (Dayton, 1898), p. 103.

for many of them are under personal obligations to me for labor in securing their pensions without expense to them—and they understand now if they vote against the democratic ticket, they vote against pensions." [18] From the Democratic camp Horatio C. King wailed in disgust, "The G.A.R. is working the Soldier racket for all it is worth." [19]

The various army societies also contributed to the Republican cause. General William T. Sherman, president of the Society of the Army of the Tennessee, asked his brother, Senator John Sherman, to speak at the annual meeting in August 1884. "Of course our Banquet is non-political," he observed, "still you can put in some points to satisfy soldiers that the Republican Party did not use us for their own selfish purpose, and cast us off when done with us, as many feel and believe." [20] When the meeting took place, some delegates opposed a move to admit only ex-army officers to its sessions because it would exclude Blaine. To the inquiry, "Suppose Cleveland should be elected, what would become of him?" Sherman replied amidst laughter, "He would not be there, I promise you that." [21]

Nevertheless, Cleveland was elected, and the unhappy relations that developed between him and the Grand Army further highlighted the order's political sympathies. Grover Cleveland had little to commend him to the veterans. He was the leader of a party popularly associated first with rebellion and then with hostility to pensions. He himself had not served in the war, but had sent a substitute. As President he vetoed numerous private pension bills of a dubious nature, arousing the wrath of the chief soldiers' paper, the *National Tribune*. Early in 1887 his disapproval of the Dependent Pension Bill set loose an avalanche of G.A.R. protests. His acceptance of an invitation, originally sponsored by the commander of a St. Louis post, to attend the national encampment there in the fall of 1887 started an increasingly acrimonious controversy.

At once the *National Tribune* launched a campaign against the

[18] George F. Rowell to Fairchild, Sept. 16, 1884, Fairchild Papers.

[19] Horatio C. King to George B. McClellan, Oct. 18, 1884, George B. McClellan Papers, Library of Congress.

[20] William T. Sherman to John Sherman, June 21, 1884, William T. Sherman Papers, Library of Congress.

[21] Society of the Army of the Tennessee, *Report of the Proceedings 1884-1887* (Cincinnati, 1893), p. 95.

President's attendance on the ground that his pension vetoes made him unwelcome and his presence would occasion political demonstrations. Soon hundreds of posts were threatening to cancel their reservations if the President went. The intemperate remarks of the voluble commander of the Iowa department, General J. M. Tuttle, especially won country-wide attention. Should Cleveland visit the meeting, he announced, "it will be at his own risk. If he gets mixed up in that parade I'll bet it will be the last parade he'll want to review." He didn't anticipate actual violence, "but unpleasant things said and done. But if they want fighting we can give 'em some of that. We've done it before and I guess we can do it again." [22]

More responsible elements in the G.A.R., shocked at the idea of insulting the President, rallied to his support and, at the behest of the local committee in St. Louis, General Sherman wrote a public letter offering to stand at Cleveland's side during the parade. Even the ranks of the veterans' papers broke on this issue. The *Grand Army Record* criticized the *National Tribune*'s attitude and declared, "We are men and as men we should say to the President of the United States, 'Come and Welcome!' " [23] By this time the conflict had attracted editorial comment throughout the nation. Democratic and independent journals united in defending Cleveland and in condemning Tuttle, the *National Tribune,* and various G.A.R. resolutions and called upon the order to repudiate them. Even some Republican papers, voicing confidence that the veterans would receive the President with the courtesy due his office, rebuked Tuttle's extremism and praised Sherman's letter. But more often the Republican press argued that Cleveland had given the veterans good cause to oppose his presence and criticized his acceptance of the invitation.

The situation was already tense enough when on June 15 Cleveland's "rebel flag order," returning captured battle flags to the Southern states, provoked another emotional eruption, the G.A.R.'s commander-in-chief, Lucius Fairchild, even invoking divine punishment. The *National Tribune* now devoted an entire page of one issue to letters from veterans concerning the proposed visit. The opposition filled five columns, while half a column sufficed for the President's supporters. The paper claimed it had published nearly

[22] *New York Tribune,* June 4, 1887.
[23] "He Will Go," *Grand Army Record,* II (June 1887), 4.

all the favorable comments but only one-tenth of the criticisms. Such intense ill-feeling caused Cleveland to reconsider his decision. Toward the end of June the Democratic mayor of St. Louis reported that the local Grand Army men were eager for his attendance, but also feared that it would keep many posts away. In his reply, perhaps unwittingly dated the Fourth of July, the chief executive pointed out that while personally he could endure insults during his visit, "I should bear with me there the people's highest office, the dignity of which I must protect." Though he did not believe that either the G.A.R. as an organization or a majority of its members as individuals would countenance any attack upon that office, yet if there were a few, "as certainly seems to be the case, determined to denounce me and my official acts at the national encampment, I believe they should be permitted to do so unrestrained by my presence. . . ." He therefore withdrew his acceptance.[24]

In addition to the usual support of Democratic and independent newspapers, many G.A.R. members, for the most part Democrats to be sure, wrote the President commending his action and assuring him that not all the order's adherents upheld Tuttle and Fairchild. Some of the veterans' papers, possibly motivated by their dislike for the *National Tribune*, also backed Cleveland, the *Grand Army Record* even calling his letter "one of the noblest and most courtly documents that ever came from the pen of a President of the United States." [25]

But nothing that Grover Cleveland did could please die-hard Republicans. The partisan press made it one more occasion for an attack upon the entire Cleveland administration. Stung by the tone of the letter, the *National Tribune* argued that a gentleman would have merely written a brief note of declination and demanded, "Can anyone imagine Andrew Jackson, Abraham Lincoln or U. S. Grant writing in this whining, self-pitying way?" [26] General Sherman, recovering from his moment of nonpartisan weakness, now felt that the President "be he the Devil himself should go wherever the flag flies— the greater the danger the greater the necessity for his presence. No act of Mr. Cleveland has shocked me more than this of declin-

[24] Grover Cleveland to David R. Francis, July 4, 1887, Allan Nevins, ed., *Letters of Grover Cleveland* (Boston and New York, 1933), p. 145.
[25] "The President's Letter," *Grand Army Record*, II (July 1887), 4.
[26] *National Tribune*, July 14, 1887.

ing to be at St. Louis coincident with the Grand Encampment." [27]

Fresh fuel for the controversy came at the end of August, when a meeting of several thousand veterans at Wheeling, West Virginia, discovered a picture of the President strung across the line of march. As one old soldier later confessed to Cleveland, "when we came to walk under your *Picture* the Captian from Pittsburgh stoped & said to us Pa Soldiers 'How is this for high'—are we agoing to walk under this thing? No, No! was the reply. Not after G.C. vetoing our pension *Bills!* he is no friend of ours!" [28] The column therefore made an elaborate detour to avoid passing under the banner.

More than any previous incident this episode shocked a considerable segment of Grand Army opinion. An officer of the New York branch called the insult "outrageous. It savors of mutiny." [29] Sober second thought made even some of the participants penitent. "O how foolish & simple we acted under the impulse of the moment! as a great meney of us said to each other after wards at the dinner table," the same veteran who had described the event to Cleveland wrote in his letter of apology. "Why we were no better than the *Rebles!*" [30]

Speculation now mounted as to what would happen at St. Louis. Many feared an episode similar to the one at Wheeling, and there was talk of shifting the meeting place. Fairchild became more and more apprehensive. Far from wanting to keep feelings aroused, he was genuinely anxious to avoid any unpleasantness. In his concern he queried various associates as to how to handle the situation; the consensus of their advice was to ignore the unfortunate happenings of the past year as much as possible. Fairchild's brother, though he criticized Cleveland's "silly letter" of declination, expressed satisfaction that the commander-in-chief "had nothing to do with or any sympathy with the Tuttle talk." He suggested that Fairchild announce that the G.A.R. would always welcome the President of the United States, regardless of who he might be.[31] If this was scarcely gracious in its implications, it at least fell more within the bounds of propriety than that favored by the radicals.

[27] William T. Sherman to John Sherman, July 23, 1887, W. T. Sherman Papers.

[28] Josiah Lightner to Cleveland, Sept. 5, 1887, Grover Cleveland Papers, Library of Congress.

[29] "The G.A.R. and the President," *Grand Army Review,* III (Oct. 1887), 574.

[30] Lightner to Cleveland, Sept. 5, 1887, Cleveland Papers.

[31] Charles Fairchild to Lucius Fairchild, Sept. 12, 1887, Fairchild Papers.

Thousands of veterans had congregated in St. Louis by the time the encampment opened on September 28. "To a man they all declare there is no politics in the Grand Army," the New York *Herald* reported, "and to a man they are all expecting a political outburst that they cannot afford to miss." [32] Tuttle, with his "tall commanding form and a bluff and hearty manner," held court at the Iowa headquarters. His supporters argued that any attempt to rebuke him for his attacks on the President would constitute introducing politics into the order, an idea they professed to abhor.

But Fairchild and his colleagues in the inner circle of the national organization were determined to soft-pedal all incendiary issues. In his official address Fairchild ignored most of the controversies of the previous year. He denied that the pension question was a partisan matter. Of the dependent pension veto he merely observed that it had caused "disappointment and regret." [33] This moderation did not satisfy all members. Former Commander-in-Chief Paul Van Der Voort introduced a resolution condemning Cleveland's vetoes. "It is milder than I believe in," he announced, "but, in order to accommodate the wishes of those who are sentimental upon this question, it has been modified until it expresses just the least possible censure upon the President of the United States." He advised that if the veterans wanted President Cleveland "to sign a bill which will go through the next Congress, tell him what you think of the bills he has vetoed in behalf of the Union soldiers. You will gain nothing by being mealy mouthed and timid upon this question." The counsels of more conservative members, anxious to avoid the appearance of political activity, succeeded in defeating the motion. [34]

No sooner had this hurdle been cleared than the selection of a new commander-in-chief posed another problem. The events of 1887 had so irritated the Democratic members that many had resigned and some even contemplated starting a rival organization. Those who remained within the society thought the moment had come for the order to prove its neutrality by honoring a Democrat for the first time. Their candidate was General Henry W. Slocum. But this was too much of a concession. Other G.A.R. leaders, fearing that

[32] *New York Herald*, Sept. 30, 1887.
[33] G.A.R., *Journal 1887*, pp. 40–41.
[34] *Ibid.*, pp. 210–216.

this choice would redound to Cleveland's advantage, were determined to block it, though one past head denied he had ever said that "there never was a democratic Commander-in-Chief of the Grand Army of the Republic, and by the eternal God there never will be." [35] To Democrats the convention's selection of John P. Rea of Minnesota was one more demonstration of the order's partisanship; Republicans contended that the meeting proved its innocence by rejecting a candidate presented on a political basis. Slocum, who had been unacceptable to some on other grounds anyway, was to find his chief claim to remembrance in the association of his name with a tragic steamboat disaster some years later.

As the hectic year 1887 drew to a close, the last word was with President Cleveland. Shortly after the national encampment a post in Pennsylvania asked him for a donation. In reply he issued a dignified rebuke to the extremist elements in the society. Pointing out that "the Grand Army of the Republic has been played upon by demagogues for partisan purposes, and has yielded to insidious blandishments to such an extent that it is regarded by many . . . as an organization which has wandered a long way from its original design," he suggested that such suspicions "will grow and spread unless within that organization something is done to prove that its objects are not partisan, unjust, and selfish." [36]

This series of events inevitably had considerable bearing upon the election of 1888. "There is no disguising the fact that prominent comrades of the Grand Army of the Republic are endeavoring to mould the organization into a huge republican club for the presidential campaign of 1888," the *Grand Army Record* asserted in the fall of 1887.[37] Certainly many Republicans saw the advantages of the pension situation. "I am no prophet," declared the venerable Hannibal Hamlin, who had been vice-president in Lincoln's first term, "but I would predict that a President who will again veto a Disability Pension Bill can never be re-elected President of the United States." [38] Others frankly hoped that the service pension

[35] *Ibid.*, p. 207.
[36] Cleveland to E. W. Fosnot, Oct. 24, 1887, quoted by Allan Nevins, *Grover Cleveland* (New York, 1932), pp. 338–339.
[37] *Grand Army Record*, II (Sept. 1887), 4.
[38] G.A.R., *Journal 1887*, p. 231.

issue would ruin Cleveland. "What I want to see in this country before we come into the campaign of 1888," a delegate informed the Ohio encampment in April 1888, "is Cleveland butting the service pension bill, and that it strikes me, will cement every Union soldier." [39]

The Grand Army veterans proved an important factor in the election. The Republicans condemned Cleveland's vetoes, endorsed pensions, and nominated a "comrade," Benjamin Harrison. They also thoughtfully distributed two hundred tickets to their convention among G.A.R. members.[40] George Lemon, who apparently contributed heavily to the Republican campaign fund, used the columns of the *National Tribune* to keep the Democrats' pension record fresh in the veterans' minds. "Every one of the thousands of veterans who are to-day in the poor-houses of the country," the *Tribune* railed, "is a separate accusation against Grover Cleveland." [41] After the election it exulted in the defeat of the soldiers' "cold, malignant enemy." [42]

The national encampment at Columbus in September was virtually a Republican rally. For its parade a local businessman had the ingenious idea of distributing palm-leaf fans with his business address on one side and Harrison's picture on the other among the paraders as they passed his place. "There were Democrats among the marchers, of course," a witness observed, "but as column after column marched past the reviewing-stand the effect was of just one fluttering picture of Benjamin Harrison after another." The Democratic candidate for vice-president, Senator Allen G. Thurman, who must have been feeling like an outsider anyway, was not amused. "I supposed that I was asked here to review a non-political gathering," he said stiffly, "but I find it's nothing but a damned Republican mass meeting." With that he departed. That evening one of the most popular G.A.R. orators in Ohio, General William H. Gibson, warned the organization against introducing politics into the order and apologized for the fan episode. "But my comrades," he added,

[39] Department of Ohio, Grand Army of the Republic, *Proceedings of the Twenty-First Annual Encampment 1887* (Akron, n.d.), p. 150.

[40] Donald L. McMurry, "The Soldier Vote in Iowa in the Election of 1888," *Iowa Journal of History and Politics*, XVIII (July 1920), 350.

[41] *National Tribune*, Nov. 1, 1888.

[42] *Ibid.*, Nov. 15, 1888.

"if on such an occasion you *should* happen so far as to forget your-
selves as to 'holler' for anybody, be sure that you 'holler' for Harrison." The audience roared.[43]

G.A.R. leaders entered actively into the campaign, though usually
acting outside the organization. Such Grand Army support for
Harrison was most conspicuous in the Middle West. Particularly
effective was Corporal James Tanner, Republican and Grand Army
spellbinder and member of the order's pension committee, who later
confessed that he had "plastered" Indiana with promises of a generous policy if Harrison were elected. Many gave the veterans credit
for the Republican victory, especially in doubtful states like New
York and Indiana. By now Democratic members were so convinced
of the order's partisanship that shortly after the election General
John M. Palmer, an erstwhile Civil War Republican who had long
since returned to the Democratic fold, announced his resignation
and there was another abortive movement to found a rival society.
The election had demonstrated, however, that the combination of
waving the bloody shirt and promising pensions could keep most of
the G.A.R.'s members solidly in the Republican camp, and to this
very day at least one elderly Maine Republican attributes his party
allegiance to what Grover Cleveland did to his father's pension
during his childhood in the 1880's.

With the appointment of Tanner as pension commissioner and
the passage of the Disability Pension Bill the Harrison administration paid its obligations to the veterans. In striking contrast to Cleveland's relations with the national encampment, President Harrison
and his cabinet reviewed the organization's parade at Boston in 1890.
Two years later the order's decision to gather at the national capital
in September 1892, in the midst of the presidential campaign, greatly
distressed the Democrats. "The coming National Encampment of
the Grand Army of the Republic in Washington will be utilized by
the Republicans so far as possible to start a soldier sentiment," a
maverick veteran warned Cleveland. Since it was generally recognized that the pension issue might swing the old soldier vote solidly
to Harrison, he felt that to offset the effect of the assembly the
Democrats should issue pamphlets defending Cleveland's attitude

[43] Julia B. Foraker, *I Would Live It Again* (New York and London, 1932),
pp. 118–119.

toward the veterans.[44] For a brief moment there was a flurry of sentiment, which even received the support of James Tanner, to invite the former President to the meeting, but the secretary of the Democratic Congressional Committee finally informed Cleveland that "after quite a lengthy discussion it was decided to issue invitations only to officials, thereby ending a matter that would, without doubt, have been unpleasant to all concerned." [45]

After the meeting, opinions varied as to its political significance. The *Vedette* hoped that "no similar *jamboree* for political party purposes will ever be repeated in this part of the country." [46] But there was serious doubt whether it really had redounded greatly to the Republicans' advantage. Rutherford B. Hayes lamented that Mrs. Harrison's illness had prevented her husband from appearing at the reunion, as otherwise he might have made a number of short speeches at various meetings. Such an opportunity "would, if improved, as it would have been, have sent thousands home brimful of enthusiasm for him. All lost," he mourned. "It may be the difference between victory and defeat." [47] Others noted the same situation but with more elation. "If I ever had any doubts of your election in November next I doubt no longer," a Democrat wrote Cleveland. "I have been amazed during the past week at the vast number of G.A.R. here attending the Encampment who were for you." [48] The press reported that peddlers who had laid in large supplies of Harrison and Reid badges were astonished to discover a great demand for Cleveland and Stevenson ones and for pictures of such Democratic veterans as McClellan and Hancock. Meanwhile, Joseph W. Kay, head of the Veterans' Rights Union, campaigned energetically for Cleveland, and the Democrats distributed a shrewd circular claiming that Harrison's appointments of veterans had gone to the ex-officers rather than the ordinary enlisted men.[49]

In short, despite its substantial gestures toward the veterans' wel-

---

[44] I. S. Catlin to Cleveland, Sept. 13, 1892, Cleveland Papers.

[45] Lawrence Gardiner to Cleveland, Sept. 6, 1892, *ibid*.

[46] *Vedette* (Washington, D.C.), Dec. 1892.

[47] Rutherford B. Hayes to Col. H. C. Corbin, Oct. 2, 1892, Charles Richard Williams, ed., *Diary and Letters of Rutherford Birchard Hayes* (Columbus, Ohio, 1922–1926), V, 110.

[48] H. B. Bell to Cleveland, Sept. 22, 1892, Cleveland Papers.

[49] Paul Joseph Woods, "The G.A.R. and Civil Service," Ph.D. dissertation, University of Illinois (1941), p. 177.

fare, it was clear that the administration faced hard sledding even among the group all had supposed to be its most faithful supporters. The veterans' papers did their best to keep the soldier vote in line, giving the bloody shirt several vigorous waves, citing Cleveland's pension record and charging that the Democrats consisted largely of ex-rebels in the South and former Copperheads, such as Adlai E. Stevenson, their vice-presidential candidate, in the North. "Every man that proved a traitor to this Government, between 1861 and 1865, *was a Democrat*," warned the *American Tribune*. "Every comrade must decide for himself whether the Rebels shall be permitted to gain by ballots what they failed to gain by bullets!" [50] The *National Tribune* printed full-page cartoons showing Harrison charging into battle while Cleveland hired a substitute or vetoed pension bills or returned the rebel flags. But in 1892 it took more than the dubious warmth of Comrade Harrison's personality or the emotional appeals of these scarcely disinterested sheets to carry the day for the Republicans. Other considerations were obviously beginning to have equal weight with many veterans. But confronted with the verdict of election day, the *American Tribune* could only attribute it to restriction of the suffrage in the South and corrupt voting in Northern slums. A scene at Cleveland's inauguration briefly mellowed its attitude; no man who kissed his mother's Bible after taking the oath of office, it felt, could really have evil in his heart.

But the pension policy of the new administration apparently showed that he could, and certainly converted few veterans to the Democratic party. Within a year the Nebraska G.A.R. declared "the appointment of Hoke Smith as secretary of the interior an insult to the Union soldier and a direct slap in the face of every soldier who fought for the Union." (Smith was from Georgia and as Secretary of the Interior pensions came under his jurisdiction.) The order censured "those who voted for Grover Cleveland and made it possible that such a fellow as Hoke Smith could be appointed to adjudicate upon the pension claims of Union veterans." [51] About the same time the commander of the Kansas branch reminded the members of "the mistake made a year ago in the state and nation, by

[50] *American Tribune* (Indianapolis), Aug. 18, 1892.

[51] Department of Nebraska, Grand Army of the Republic, *Journal of the Seventeenth Annual Session 1894* (Lincoln, 1894), p. 110.

which our friends were defeated and our enemies were victorious, the soldiers of the last conflict humiliated, slandered and robbed. . . ." Insisting that there was still "time to win another victory" in 1894 and 1896, he urged the veterans to "fall in; dress to the right; touch elbows, and make one more charge for our honor, our homes, our comrades and the widows and orphans of those who loved justice, right and the nation more than life itself." [52]

Throughout the summer and fall of 1894 both the *National Tribune* and the *American Tribune* appealed to the veterans to support candidates who favored liberal pension legislation and then pointed out that this meant supporting their only true friends, the Republicans. During the campaign the ex-soldiers repeated an incident of 1887 when in Braddock, Pennsylvania, they again refused to march under a picture of Cleveland and even tore down the likeness. After the election the *American Tribune* attributed the Democratic defeats to the party's pension attitude and boasted that the veterans still held the political balance of power in every Northern state.

The veterans soon girded themselves for 1896. Long before the political conventions the *American Tribune* urged the nomination of William McKinley. Not to be outdone, the *National Tribune,* which as early as 1893 had advised the Ohio veterans to make their comrade governor, was soon selling for only five cents a life of McKinley by its editor, John McElroy. The paper described his prospective nomination as a great uprising of the people similar to that for Lincoln and Grant. The Republicans meanwhile donated to the G.A.R. five hundred tickets for their St. Louis convention.

After the party conclaves the veterans' papers again entered the fray with zest. The *National Tribune* hailed the Republican platform as "simply great" and characterized the Democratic gathering as "an array of malignants, charlatans and noisy, notorious incompetents." It represented free silver as a plot of pension-haters to cut the value of pensions in half. In its view, the Democratic party consisted of former rebels like Ben Tillman and radicals like Altgeld and Bryan, the latter "a cheap, noisy young man" who preached "Sectionalism, Anarchy and Class Hatred." It warned the veterans that Bryan's assault on "industry, sobriety and thrift" would take

---

[52] Department of Kansas, Grand Army of the Republic, *Journal of the Thirteenth Annual Encampment 1894* (Topeka, n.d.), p. 12.

away "their accumulations for the benefit of the lazy and thrift-
less." [53]

The *American Tribune* began its efforts by printing a front-page
picture of the Republican candidate with the caption, "William
McKinley, the Advance Agent of Prosperity and Next President of
the United States." It waved the bloody shirt less than the *National
Tribune* and concentrated on economic arguments. "The democracy
now stands as the promoter of financial revolution," it solemnly
intoned after Bryan's nomination, "which, if effectuated, will overthrow our monetary system and war against the national honor,
industrial safety and prosperity and throw the whole country into
confusion while the readjustment of values on a degraded basis
goes on." In a series of succinct and portentous slogans it indicated
the consequences of the Commoner's success: "Vote for Bryan and
starvation," "A vote for Bryan is a vote for a panic" and "A vote
for Bryan is a vote for anarchy." [54]

Many veterans responded as hoped to these appeals. "We will
never cease to be citizens, never cease to have an interest in the
honour of our country," declared General Smith Atkins to the Society of the Army of the Cumberland, "and we will stand by it, and
stand by our religion and our patriotism, and vote for COMRADE
MCKINLEY." [55] The Union Veteran Legion's meeting in October
even apologized to any political party that might be offended by
partisan remarks made during the convention, and it is doubtful
that this was intended for the Republicans. Yet the nature of the
papers' appeals suggests that, while the veterans perhaps voted for
McKinley, they may have done so for reasons other than that they
were veterans.

The soldiers' journals, of course, rejoiced at their comrade's entrance into the White House. "Happily for the country the reign of
Cleveland ends to-day," wrote the *American Tribune* on March 4,
1897. "As Cleveland steps down and out, to-day, he leaves behind
him the blackest page in our administrative history—a 'damnable
spot' that will not out." [56] "To be quite frank with you," the

[53] *National Tribune,* June 25–Oct. 29, 1896.
[54] *American Tribune,* June 25–Oct. 29, 1896.
[55] Society of the Army of the Cumberland, *Twenty-Sixth Reunion 1896* (Cincinnati, 1897), p. 139.
[56] *American Tribune,* March 4, 1897.

National Tribune declared in its farewell to Cleveland, "not since Buchanan's time have we been so desperately anxious to get rid of a President and his following as we have been to be relieved of you and yours." [57] McKinley's triumph, on the other hand, assured "the ascendancy of the clear-cut, lofty ideals of our forefathers, and the rebuke at the ballot-box of all un-American ideas." [58]

Aside from conflict over the conduct of the Pension Bureau, the Grand Army was quickly on good terms with the new president. With several members of his cabinet McKinley visited the national encampment at Buffalo in 1897, first heading the parade and then reviewing it. Two years later, at Philadelphia, the procession passed before him again. The *American Tribune* meanwhile tried to keep the veteran element in line by urging the formation of Republican Camps of Veterans and Sons, partly to secure or retain government jobs and partly to carry Indiana for the Republicans in 1898. The paper still reminded the old soldiers of the records of both the Democrats and Republicans on the pension issue. "Comment is unnecessary," it concluded, "to enable the old soldier to decide which party is most inclined to deal justly and liberally with them." [59]

At the end of the century the *National Tribune* pointed out that in 1900 there would still be about a million survivors of the war alive who could also influence their sons and sons-in-law. "In brief, then, the veterans are still the strongest political element in the country," it insisted, "and if they stand together upon matters affecting their interest, they can control the elections of Representatives in Congress and even of the President of the United States." [60] Early in 1900 it hinted that if the issue of Commissioner of Pensions Evans was not settled satisfactorily, the veterans might not vote for McKinley's reëlection or for Republican members of Congress. In the fall, however, it fell into line once more, though not with quite the intensity of previous campaigns. Moreover, its support of McKinley was based largely on his foreign policy and advocacy of the protective tariff rather than on matters strictly pertaining to the veterans. The *Grand Army Record* maintained the older tradition in its accusations that

[57] *National Tribune,* March 4, 1897.
[58] Department of Illinois, Grand Army of the Republic, *Proceedings of the Thirty-first Annual Encampment 1897* (Chicago, n.d.), pp. 108–109.
[59] *American Tribune,* Oct. 14, 1897.
[60] *National Tribune,* Nov. 16, 1899.

the ex-Confederate states would all vote for Bryan and that his running mate, Adlai E. Stevenson, was a former Copperhead. "Who
would vote for Benedict Arnold," it asked, "if he were now alive,
and was the Democratic candidate for Vice President of the United
States?" [61]

In October 1900, Commander-in-Chief Robert Dyrenforth of the
Union Veterans' Union issued a circular declaring that "in the
election of Mr. Bryan to the Presidency, we have nothing to gain
and everything to lose" and urging, "Let us all vote for the reëlection
of the President, our Comrade William McKinley, in whose hands
our interests are safer than in any other." He later reported that
when a branch in New York whose members had always voted
Democratic received this, its leader wrote him "that every man of
the regiment would fall into line and vote, as advised, for Comrade
McKinley." [62]

But though even in the early 1900's so skittish a politician as Theodore Roosevelt was still extremely sensitive to pressure from the
Civil War veterans, by 1900 it was clear that their influence was at
an end. That year saw the last election of a member of the Union
Army to the presidency of the United States. Within a few years
the old soldiers were to play a negligible part in both national and
state campaigns.[63] A new generation had arisen, and with it new
issues. The Republicans could no longer triumph merely by reviving
memories of the Civil War or promising pensions to its participants.

Almost unnoticed throughout this same period was the fact that
the Mexican War veterans were equally partisan for the same reasons, though with less success and in the opposite direction. Their
spokesman, the *Vedette*, warned Congressmen that it watched carefully their attitude toward the Mexican Pension Bill. It published
a blacklist of the measure's opponents and insisted that they "should
be bounced by every means fair in politics." [64] Its readers encouraged
this vigilance and promised appropriate action. "Watch things close,
and keep us posted, faithful old sentinel, in regard to the work of

<hr />

[61] "Some Reminiscences," *Grand Army Record*, XIV (Sept. 1900), 8.

[62] Union Veterans' Union, *Proceedings of the National Encampment Sixteenth
Annual Session 1901* (Washington, 1902), pp. 19–20.

[63] Dearing, *Veterans in Politics*, pp. 496–497; Heck, *Civil War Veteran*, pp. 197–
198.

[64] *Vedette*, May 15, 1880.

our enemies in both Houses," a Texas veteran wrote its editor, Alexander Kenaday, "and at any time our votes are needed in our congressional districts we will try and guide our children and friends to vote for men who sympathize with the soldier in his old age and infirmity." [65] At their meetings the veterans announced their intention to support no man for Congress who was opposed to their pension bill.

Certain unfriendly politicians especially aroused the ire of the *Vedette,* which let no considerations of good taste emasculate the vigor of its invective. In an extravaganza of personal denunciation it once called for the defeat of Representative Harry White of Pennsylvania, "whose comical appearance reminded one of a toy 'Jack-in-the-box,' suddenly sprung to startle the children in holiday times; his head resembling a sore pimple or perhaps a toad-stool on a blasted tree trunk. . . ." In this same vein it also paid tribute to his eyeballs, "sunk in their sockets, looking for all the world as if two faded soldier-buttons had been utilized by his Creator in a spirit of economy, as a substitute for the usual peepers allotted to mankind." [66]

The chief victim of its vitriol was Senator George F. Hoar, whom it pictured as the representative of the high-tariff manufacturing interests. "This doughty champion of every political measure tending to make the rich richer and the poor poorer," it asserted, "has always appeared to THE VEDETTE's unglamered visions as one of the identical witches prophetically drawn by Shakespeare for modern delectation and study." [67] As an example of the Senator's Yankee trickery it related how some years previously he had learned of a scheme to name a fashionable hotel being built in Boston for whatever person became its leading stockholder. Though Brahmin society bought shares lavishly, Hoar outdid them and then insisted that the hostelry bear his name. The blue bloods of Beacon Hill and Back Bay, horrified at the prospect of cries of "All aboard for the Hoar House," promptly bought out his stock at a handsome profit to the shrewd young New Englander. [68]

---

[65] R. S. Morris to Alexander Kenaday, Dec. 8, 1881, *ibid.,* Jan. 15, 1882.

[66] *Ibid.,* April 15, 1880.

[67] *Ibid.,* May 15, 1882.

[68] Harvard men, of course, will quickly recognize this as an earlier version of the contemporary legend that only one of the university's first presidents has failed to have a Harvard house named after him.

Though these attacks had a nonpartisan ring, all the politicians thus singled out were Republicans, who had little desire to help the considerable number of Southerners who had participated in the Mexican War. The paper frequently reminded its readers how consistently the Democrats backed pension legislation in their behalf and how the Republicans opposed it. During presidential campaigns it therefore offered stanch support to the heirs of Jefferson and Jackson.

Before the political conventions of 1880 the *Vedette* tried to start a boom for General James Denver, head of the Mexican War Veterans, as the Democratic choice for the presidency. After the nominations it warmly supported General Winfield Hancock's candidacy on the Democratic ticket, declaring that "the Mexican veterans have not outgrown their disposition to resent the insults heaped upon them by the Republican party." [69] During the canvass it printed many letters from former soldiers announcing their intention to back the Democrats. "I have always been a Republican and voted for Mr. Lincoln twice and General Grant twice," wrote a New York veteran, "but I am quits with the party now for good. . . ." Though "not possessed of much influence, because I am poor," he claimed he had "added three of my friends besides my own vote to the Democratic party, and will keep on doing all I can to foil our deadly enemies in Congress." [70] Another lifelong Republican, this time from Akron, hoped to "be nibbled to death by Mexican fleas if I support a man who worked as Garfield did against the bill of the veterans of the Mexican war." [71] Meanwhile, some branches of the Mexican Veterans followed an official recommendation from Kenaday and Denver in Washington to form campaign clubs for Hancock. Though this was not enough to turn the Republican tide, the veterans claimed to have exerted decisive influence in some Congressional elections.

In 1884 the *Vedette* pursued the same course. It first tried in vain to push Denver's cause with the Democrats and then attacked Blaine's candidacy on the ground that the paper's civic duty to the people was "to expose the character and vicious antecedents in public life of individuals claiming their votes for positions that should only

[69] *Ibid.*, July 15, 1880.
[70] *Ibid.*, Sept. 15, 1880.
[71] *Ibid.*

be filled with men possessed of the highest quality of manhood."
Again it printed letters from veterans such as the statement of John
Dawson of Bedford, Iowa, that he, three sons, and a son-in-law
would no longer vote Republican because of the party's opposition
to Mexican War pensions.[72] In 1888 it similarly reviewed the Republicans' record and submitted that the Democrats "have stood by the
old veterans from purely patriotic motives, because 'we do not
amount to a hill of beans' from a political standpoint." [73]

This partisanship did not pass entirely unchallenged, for there
was an undercurrent of Republican sentiment among the Mexican
War veterans. At the meeting of the Illinois association the Republican members, though "very few" in number, opposed endorsing
the *Vedette* because of its open support of Hancock. Kenaday's
Democratic proclivities also produced an abortive effort to prevent
his reëlection as secretary of the National Association in 1881. When,
after the passage of the Mexican War service pension, he complained
that he was receiving very little business as a claims agent, one of the
organization's leaders in Indiana informed him that around Logans-
port, at least, the veterans were mainly Republicans and so resented
his flagrant political maneuvering that only the few Democrats in
that area were giving him their patronage. Despite these occasional
criticisms, right up until its demise in 1893 the *Vedette* continued to
emphasize Republican hostility and Democratic friendship.

In either case, whether with the survivors of the Mexican War or
of the Civil War, it was disheartening how easily veterans, claiming
special privileges because of patriotic service, confused patriotism
with self-interest or partisan advantage. But then, after all, just what
was patriotism anyway? It was a question of vital importance for
self-styled patriotic societies, but the answer was not always simple.

[72] *Ibid.*, March 17–Oct. 1884.
[73] *Ibid.*, Oct. 1888.

X

Patriotism in Practice

I believe it to be every citizen's duty to give some part of each day to patriotic work," wrote the founder of the Sons of the American Revolution to its second president-general in 1889.[1] The writer, William O. McDowell, exemplified what extreme forms such idealism could take. When he first left his country home before he was thirteen, he recalled on another occasion, he "determined to give a part of each day to 'altruistic' work on patriotic lines, and I think I can conscientiously say that since that time there has not a day passed over my head without some part of it being given to the fulfillment of the self pledge that I had made." [2]

McDowell's attitude, of course, was that of the fanatic, and the difficulties he ran into with his colleagues suggest that they were not all quite as ardent as he. But the numerous new hereditary organizations of the nineties of which he was an extreme representative nearly always proclaimed themselves patriotic societies and specifically included among their objectives the encouragement of national fervor and love of country. In these same years the veterans' groups for the first time assumed the same mantle. They now added "Patriotic Instructors" to their lists of officers and began to agitate for "patriotic teaching." The *Boston Herald* was struck by the "consciousness of our National existence" and "abounding demonstration of our patriotic feeling" that pervaded the Grand Army encampment of 1890.[3]

What was happening was that an industrialized urbanized society was dissolving the standards, mores, and bonds of a simpler rural

---

[1] William O. McDowell to W. Seward Webb, Nov. 21, 1889, William O. McDowell Letterbooks, New York Public Library.

[2] McDowell to Luther Tarbell, Dec. 19, 1889, *ibid.*

[3] *Boston Herald*, Aug. 17, 1890, quoted in "The Grand Army of the Republic—Pensions and Other Matters," *Public Opinion*, IX (Aug. 23, 1890), 451.

order and instead was producing a land more and more diversified in national origin, religion, and cultural inheritance, with no national church or royal family or other cohesive traditions and symbols, perhaps in the near future not even a common language, some feared. Consequently many turned to patriotism as a sort of secular religion to unite the American republic. Some individuals made the analogy almost explicit. Though admitting some human errors, McDowell became convinced that his patriotic work was "so clearly from a controlling Power more than human, and the dividing line, where the Divine directing control ended and the human part came in, to me has been so indeterminable that I am slow to use the word 'mistake' for fear I might be judging that which no human mind can judge." [4]

To be sure, there was a great deal of talk about patriotism without much precise definition of the term. A few attempts were made, but they are not especially helpful. At first to the veterans it had merely the negative meaning of opposition to secession or rebellion. Later the Pennsylvania G.A.R. offered another version, complete with split infinitive, but otherwise not very specific: "Patriotism is the love of one's country with the disposition to jealously support and defend it." [5] The *Grand Army Record* stressed the importance of popular government with the suggestion that a patriot had "to believe in and uphold the free institutions of the United States" as well as to insist "that no official trustee of the PEOPLE can lawfully exercise any power or authority which he cannot trace by a clear chain of title from grants by the PEOPLE." [6] Finally, the *American Tribune* came close to the concept of organic nationalism then coming into vogue when it emphasized the nationalistic aspects and the subordination of the individual to group welfare: "Patriotism is that love for country in the hearts of the people which shall make that country strong to resist foreign opposition and domestic intrigue—which impresses each and every individual with a sense of the inalienable rights of others and restrains him from building too greedily for self alone." [7]

[4] McDowell to Henry Baldwin, July 28, 1903, McDowell Letterbooks.
[5] Department of Pennsylvania, Grand Army of the Republic, *Proceedings of the 59th Encampment 1897* (n.p., 1897), p. 193.
[6] "What Is Patriotism," *Grand Army Record*, IX (Sept. 1894), 65.
[7] *American Tribune* (Indianapolis), March 7, 1890.

If the theology of patriotism was a little vague, this was perhaps essential to establish the widest possible appeal among a heterogeneous people in a continental domain. It may be easier to explore the ramifications of patriotism through a consideration of the symbols and rituals which rapidly acquired almost religious significance.[8] There was a stress upon various anniversaries, which became as sacrosanct as any holy days. This really began with the G.A.R.'s introduction of Memorial Day services into the North. On a trip to Richmond during the spring of 1868 Commander-in-Chief and Mrs. John A. Logan discovered the Southern practice of decorating Confederate graves. When Mrs. Logan commented on how much the idea touched her, her husband called upon the Grand Army's members to mark Union graves on May 30. Soon they were dominating annual community observances throughout the country.

Next the Grand Army brought pressure upon state legislatures to have the day declared a legal holiday. Whenever they achieved this, however, the veterans were dismayed that the populace spent the anniversary at fairs, picnics, excursions, dances, ball games, horse and bicycle races, and other public amusements. Across the nation Grand Army encampments protested such desecration of a day supposedly dedicated to the solemn memory of the Union dead and sometimes even urged legislation to suppress these secular activities, thus becoming almost as censorious as any sect demanding strict Sabbath observance. In Pennsylvania, for example, the G.A.R. sought the closing of all saloons on the day. Sometimes this led to attacks upon what otherwise seemed the most respectable of organizations. In Colorado the order persuaded both the state university and school of mines to abandon their scheduled baseball and tennis matches and condemned the refusal of the Associated Cycling Clubs of Denver to give up a road race as "un-American and disloyal." [9] Even the highly Sabbatarian Methodists ran afoul of this definition of sacrilege when the California branch asked their churches in San Francisco to cease holding picnics on Memorial Day and the Oregon branch criticized that denomination's Sunday Schools in

[8] This entire discussion of the quasi-religious significance of patriotic symbolism obviously owes a great deal to the ideas of Crane Brinton and Ralph H. Gabriel.

[9] Department of Colorado and Wyoming, Grand Army of the Republic, *Journal of the Seventeenth Annual Encampment 1896* (Denver, n.d.), p. 36.

Portland for advertising an excursion on the same day. Occasionally the G.A.R. also sought to have Lincoln's birthday made a legal holiday, the equivalent of a martyred saint's day, as it were.

The hereditary societies laid great stress on the anniversaries of historic events, especially of the Revolutionary period. Interest in their proper observance had led to the founding of some of these groups, which usually met at such times. In Massachusetts the S.A.R. induced the legislature to declare April 19 a legal holiday and as a result Patriots' Day had its first celebration in 1894. But particularly these organizations devoted their attention to the Fourth of July. The S.A.R., D.A.R., and C.A.R. all called for a more sober contemplation of its significance and began the movement for a "Safe and Sane Fourth," though this agitation did not gain its real momentum until the early 1900's.

The most extensive patriotic ritualism centered about the cult of the flag. This emerged in the late eighties and gained strength throughout the nineties. The banner became worshiped as the symbol of everything that was worthy of reverence in the American tradition. "It is the emblem of unity, of loyalty to home and to kindred, and to all that is sacred in life," declared the president of the Massachusetts W.R.C. [10] The societies therefore sought to honor and protect it in every way imaginable. One of the first moves was to add another patriotic anniversary, Flag Day. As early as 1890 the Connecticut S.A.R. proposed that June 14, the date that the Continental Congress adopted the Stars and Stripes, should be observed by widespread display of the flag. Around 1895 other branches of the S.A.R. joined the Sons of the Revolution, the Daughters of the Revolution, and the Colonial Dames in taking up the movement.

The Civil War associations were slower to favor this idea. Though in 1892 the Iowa Grand Army began to have the schools observe February 22 as Flag Day and subsequently the Woman's Relief Corps endorsed the American Flag Association's efforts to make June 14 a national holiday, at least twice the G.A.R.'s national encampment refused to lend support. Its reason was that the date was too close to Memorial Day and the Fourth of July and might therefore detract from their observance.

[10] Department of Massachusetts, Woman's Relief Corps, *Journal of the Eighteenth Annual Convention 1897* (Boston, 1897), p. 65.

But ordinarily veneration of the flag was one of the few patriotic ventures uniting both the veterans' and the hereditary organizations. They all agreed in a curious faith in the beneficial effect that the mere physical presence of the banner had upon youth. "Let them learn to add and subtract and multiply under that flag," one Grand Army member declared, "and they will do it a good deal better." [11] In February 1889, the New York department proposed a state law requiring flags on all schools, and in August of the same year the national encampment voted that posts should present the emblem to every public school that did not have one. Commander-in-Chief William Warner predicted that somehow this would teach children the story of liberty as personified by Washington, Lincoln, and Grant. "Let the 8,000,000 boys and girls in our elementary schools be thus imbued with a reverence for the flag and all it represents," he pleaded. "Then the future of the Republic is assured, and that flag shall forever wave." [12]

During the nineties one state encampment after another in twenty-six states and territories from Maine to California insisted that the banner fly over all public schoolhouses. Sometimes the order provided the flags, but more often it demanded that this be done at government expense. Other societies joining the G.A.R. in the campaign were the Woman's Relief Corps, the S.A.R., the Sons of the Revolution, the D.A.R., and the C.A.R. As proof that it had produced "decided results for good," one enthusiastic W.R.C. member in 1892 quoted comments from various states which also supplied interesting clues as to the motives behind the drive: "It is easier to govern the children since the flag was raised," "It has been a grand step toward making brave, manly boys and womanly girls" and, she added, "from the far West, where from seventy-five or eighty per cent, are either foreign born or the children of foreign-born parents, the effect of the presence of the flag has been to make them enthusiastic Americans." [13]

Not content with introducing the emblem into the schools, the

[11] Department of Minnesota, Grand Army of the Republic, *Proceedings of the Twelfth Annual Encampment 1892* (St. Paul, 1892), p. 279.

[12] Grand Army of the Republic, *Journal of the Twenty-Second Annual Session of the National Encampment 1889* (Minneapolis, 1889), p. 41.

[13] Department of Ohio, Grand Army of the Republic, *Proceedings of the Twenty-Sixth Annual Encampment 1892* (Cincinnati, 1892), p. 127.

organized patriots next argued that daily ceremonies in its honor would automatically produce greater love of country. "When our children in their schools are giving the flag salute, I have no doubt their little hearts often swell with feelings they cannot explain, but fills them with love for the flag," declared the president of the Minnesota W.R.C. "And is this not putting more beautiful feathers in the American Eagle, and will he not then soar higher and more proudly than ever before and our flag ever wave for generations to come by the united efforts of our children?" [14] The feminine organizations such as the Woman's Relief Corps and the D.A.R. proved particularly interested in this cause, but the G.A.R. also backed their efforts.

Only an occasional voice like that of the *Grand Army Record* questioned whether "these mysterious flag gesticulations" served any useful purpose.[15] Sometimes these demands led to questionable insistence upon conformity. The president of the Southern California S.A.R., who was also a member of a local board of education, secured a regulation that all pupils had to salute the flag, while any teacher or principal not enforcing the rule "shall be deemed disloyal and shall be at once dismissed. . . ." A recalcitrant child could be readmitted only after the parent had given a written pledge of obedience. "Such pupil shall also first deliver to his or her teacher a written apology for such disloyalty," the dictum concluded, "and a pledge to thereafter comply with this rule." [16] Thus the religious zeal for the flag produced its definition of heresy and an inquisition to combat it.

With this reverence for the flag there also developed a corresponding hostility to its desecration. This counterpart of sacrilege in the religion of patriotism included both commercialization of the emblem and any form of disrespect, conscious or unconscious. As early as 1889 the New York Grand Army urged a federal law prohibiting the use of the banner in advertising or its defacement by any signs, but a year later the Colorado branch still refused to protest the use of the flag as a business sign on saloons and gambling places on the

---

[14] Department of Minnesota, Woman's Relief Corps, *Journal of the Thirteenth Annual Convention 1897* (St. Paul, n.d.), pp. 22–23.

[15] " 'Flag Salute,' " *Grand Army Record*, X (Nov. 1895), 86.

[16] "The United States Flag," *Spirit of '76*, III (Aug. 1897), 599.

ground that "the use and display of the United States flag is the right of every citizen." [17] The real impetus came largely from the efforts of Captain Philip Reade, head of the Illinois Society of Colonial Wars. In 1895 he appointed a committee which attempted to record the name and address of every corporation or organization using the national flag or coat of arms for private gain by public display. It also prepared a pamphlet on the misuse of the flag which was sent to all Congressmen, governors, mayors and postmasters of large cities, presidents and librarians of colleges, prominent clergymen, editors of leading daily newspapers, public libraries, principal social clubs, historical societies, G.A.R. posts, and the heads of patriotic and hereditary societies.

Reade proved highly successful in interesting other patriotic organizations in his work. By addressing meetings and writing leaders he soon secured the support of various branches of the Society of Colonial Wars, S.A.R., Sons of the Revolution, D.A.R., and G.A.R. During 1897 the Grand Army, Loyal Legion, S.A.R., and D.A.R. all appointed committees to work against flag desecration. Finally, in 1898 the American Flag Association coördinated the efforts of the S.A.R., D.A.R., Order of Founders and Patriots, Society of the War of 1812, Loyal Legion, Naval Veterans, and Society of the Army of the Potomac. Its head was Ralph E. Prime, who represented both the S.A.R. and the Society of the Army of the Potomac.

The original objective was a federal law protecting the flag against disrespectful practices. The Society of Colonial Wars, S.A.R., Sons of the Revolution, D.A.R., Grand Army, Loyal Legion, Naval Veterans, and Sons of Veterans, frequently at Reade's instigation, passed resolutions or sent petitions to Congress favoring such a measure. The first chairman of the D.A.R. committee was Mrs. Walter Kempster of Milwaukee, where the local chapter had long agitated for this legislation. Her group sent out some 2700 circulars to all state and chapter regents asking their endorsement as well as personal letters to presumably influential persons. The chairman of the S.A.R. flag committee even visited Washington to interview a number of Congressional leaders, including the Speaker of the House, Senator Henry Cabot Lodge (a member of the Sons' committee), and Sena-

[17] Department of Colorado and Wyoming, Grand Army of the Republic, *Journal of the Eleventh Annual Session 1890* (n.p., n.d.), pp. 40, 43.

tor Hoar, chairman of the Senate Judiciary Committee, but the various bills never made much headway. When this movement showed so little progress, the American Flag Association urged its followers, such as the S.A.R., D.A.R., and Loyal Legion, to turn to state legislation modeled on a law that had been secured in New York. In this narrower field both veterans' and hereditary societies were far more successful.

Especially responsive to patriotic fetishism was William O. McDowell, who so frequently typified the extremes that all these movements could take. Between 1890 and 1893 he agitated for the erection of a large Liberty Flagpole at the Navesink Highlands in New Jersey so that the first thing an ocean vessel approaching New York would see would be the American banner. Among the leaders of patriotic societies whose support he won were Josiah Pumpelly of the S.A.R., Mary Desha and Mrs. Adlai E. Stevenson of the D.A.R., and Mrs. Roger Pryor of the Colonial Dames. Another backer was a founder of the Society of Mayflower Descendants, Mrs. Russell Sage, who decided to utilize the movement to train both her niece and young Helen Gould, daughter of Jay Gould, "in the lines of Christian philanthropy and patriotism." [18] Finally, in April 1893, Mrs. Schuyler Hamilton, honorary state regent of the New York D.A.R., raised the flag. McDowell was unsuccessful in subsequent efforts to have S.A.R. leaders finance the erection of similar Liberty Poles in foreign countries.

McDowell's next enterprise involved another famous patriotic symbol, the Liberty Bell. Toward the end of 1892 he conceived the idea of making a replica, a Columbian Liberty Bell, which would go first to the Chicago Fair and then travel all over the country proclaiming liberty and peace. In the spring of 1893 his chief ally, Mary Desha, as "Vice Chairman of the Columbian Liberty Bell Committee, Representing the National Society of the Daughters of the American Revolution," appealed to members of the D.A.R., S.A.R., Sons of the Revolution, and Society of the Cincinnati for cash contributions and for Revolutionary relics to be used in making the replica. Eventually the two secured as members of the Liberty Bell Committee not only such D.A.R. leaders as Mrs. L. Bradford

---

[18] Mrs. Russell Sage to McDowell, Oct. 24, 1892, William O. McDowell Scrapbooks, LXI, New York Public Library.

Prince of New Mexico, Mrs. Loulie Gordon of Georgia, Mrs. Schuyler Hamilton of New York, Mrs. Julia Hogg of Pennsylvania, and Mrs. Caleb Churchman of Delaware, but also Josiah Pumpelly, Julia Ward Howe, John Clark Ridpath, and Frances Willard. In return for the Daughters' backing, McDowell proposed that in honor of the society's third anniversary in October 1893, the bell be struck three times and then once for every chapter organized up to that time; by counting the strokes, each member would be able to recognize the knell for her chapter and thus know for whom the bell tolled. The president-general, Mrs. Stevenson, was to strike the first note.

The appeal for relics proved highly successful. From Hawaii the wife of the president of the fledgling republic sent some metal. Mrs. Stevenson and her two sisters donated silver spoons. Other contributions included the silver shoe buckle of a participant in the Boston Tea Party, a knob from a clock that had belonged to Jefferson, a silver spoon of Henry W. Grady, and silver eyeglass frames made from a spoon cast in Arlington, New Hampshire at the same time that bullets were being made for the Battle of Bennington. Before the middle of May 1893, the press reported that the top floor of McDowell's house in Newark "is assuming the appearance of an old curiosity shop." [19] The procedure aroused some criticism. If these mementos had any real value, complained the *New York Sun*, should they not be sent to some museum instead of being destroyed? "We wonder why some gentle enthusiast doesn't propose that Independence Hall and Faneuil and Mount Vernon be torn down and made into a composite shed and turret for the Columbian Liberty Bell." [20]

Mrs. Grover Cleveland was originally scheduled to press the button that would start casting the mold. Early in June 1893, a committee of persons active in the scheme traveled to the foundry at Troy to witness the event, but on the day before the appointed time the mold fell into a hole and all work was delayed for two weeks. The delegation nevertheless had a pleasant visit, including an entertainment at Mrs. Ellen Hardin Walworth's home in Saratoga.

At the end of August the bell was finally shipped down the Hud-

[19] *Newark Evening News,* May 10, 1893.
[20] *New York Sun,* May 14, 1893.

son. Seven feet high, seven feet four inches in diameter, it required forty men to move it from the boat to the pier, where throngs of curious persons inspected it. The bell was taken about the city on a large decorated truck drawn by six horses, and then the Pennsylvania Railroad shipped it free of charge to Chicago. "We have the position of honor at the fair," McDowell reported after its arrival, "and it is one constant ovation." [21] On September 20 a representative of each faith in the world sounded the bell "in the name of peace, unity and liberty of all religions and at the same time repeated a silent prayer of their respective divinities, asking blessings on the bell." [22]

For twenty dollars a week one George S. Knapp agreed to become the bell's custodian. Plans now included a tour around the world, beginning with a visit to the Atlanta Exposition of 1895. On September 12 of that year a ceremony at the Chicago City Hall marked a resumption of its travels. Thirteen horses, representing the thirteen original states, then pulled it to the station. Just as it was about to be loaded onto a special car, it was attached for three hundred dollars to complete payment for the car. Knapp paid the sum and started for Georgia with only fifteen dollars in his pocket. For four months he and his son lived in a boxcar on the exposition grounds, with only a single blanket under them and the Stars and Stripes over them. By this time the *New York Daily Tribune* called the bell "a poor imitation gotten up for showman's purpose and trundled about the country here and there, on a par as a spectacle with the learned pig and the wild man of Borneo." [23]

Meanwhile, the bell had become the cause of the most involved financial entanglements. In January 1894, the committee admitted that there was still $2600 due to the firm that had done the casting. "We have paid the Meneely Bell Co. and are out of their debt," McDowell reported a few days later. *"Thank God."* [24] But he had accomplished this through even more complicated dealings. The committee had intended McDowell to borrow the necessary amount and then transfer title to the lender. Instead, he sold the bell outright to the Henry McShane Manufacturing Company and then

[21] McDowell to Mary Desha, Sept. 11, 1893, Mary Desha Papers, in the Breckenridge Family Papers, Library of Congress.

[22] *New York Daily Tribune,* Sept. 21, 1893.

[23] *Ibid.,* Oct. 2, 1895.

[24] McDowell to Miss Desha, Jan. 26, 1894, Desha Papers.

made a contract for them to manufacture souvenir liberty bells. These he intended to sell at fifteen dollars apiece to make up any deficits; he expected the D.A.R. and the schools to prove the best customers.

By the spring of 1896 the committee became suspicious of Mc-Dowell's financial insouciance. In April charges appeared in a Philadelphia newspaper that led to McDowell's resigning his position as chairman and allowing two auditors, Josiah Pumpelly and J. Howard Foote, to go over his accounts. "You can form no idea of the recklessness with which he has handled the funds," Foote soon informed Miss Desha, "and when we get to the bottom of this most extraordinary scheme, it will be a story more like fiction than like fact." [25] Foote, who asserted that the auditors had to "entangle the most intricate mass of so-called accounts that ever existed," [26] soon found the affair too much for him. Falling ill, he "raved incessantly against this fellow McDowell, and every now and then rained down imprecations upon him in his delirium. He died, finally, in a straight [*sic*] jacket; struggling with his enemy whom he thot to be upon him." [27]

The committee at first hoped to keep this financial debacle a secret, but one of the firms to whom McDowell was indebted brought the matter into the open. In sending out an appeal to rescue the bell from debt he had incurred a further obligation of six hundred dollars for the printing, and the company now demanded an accounting of the money he had received in reply. The auditing committee testified in court that McDowell had collected about $31,000 in all for both the original bell and the proposed souvenirs, but that some $10,000 remained unaccounted for. Various persons active in the D.A.R. now complained to Miss Desha that they had paid for the souvenirs but never received them and, following the newspaper publicity, began to disassociate themselves from the project.

Yet McDowell never lost faith in his patriotic mission. "I cannot bring myself to believe that Providence means the Worlds Liberty Bell to fail," he informed Miss Desha. "Believing as I do the Story of Christ I can understand that suffering may be the lot of those

[25] J. Howard Foote to Miss Desha, April 27, 1896, *ibid.*
[26] Foote to Miss Desha, April 18, 1896, *ibid.*
[27] Edward Summer to Miss Desha, May 22, 1896, *ibid.*

who dare to give themselves to a great cause." [28] As for the bell itself, it remained in the possession of George Knapp, who claimed $5,000 was due him for its care, and when last heard of was resting in his Chicago home. The enterprise admittedly had quickly acquired fantastic proportions that made it scarcely typical of the interests of sober patriotic societies (though it wasn't much different from the more recent idea of a Freedom Train), but that so many reputable figures in hereditary organizations had given their support testified to the significance such symbolism had acquired.

In addition to reverence for the flag as the symbol of the American way of life, the nurture of a common tradition through emphasis upon the "usable past" was another method of promoting patriotism. A favorite device was the erection of monuments, reminders of past tribulations and glories which became the images and icons of the new faith. Fairly soon after the Civil War the army societies began littering the country with statues of generals perpetually about to charge into space. Usually they raised part of the necessary funds and then automatically turned to the government for substantial sums to complete the task. The Indiana G.A.R. spent many years seeking money and securing legislative appropriations for the soldiers' and sailors' monument that still so conspicuously adorns the center of Indianapolis; the Naval Veterans wanted Congress to commemorate John and Ulric Dahlgren; the Society of the Army of the Tennessee won a $50,000 Congressional grant for a memorial to General Sherman; while the United Confederate Veterans intended to honor Jefferson Davis in the same way but had to let the U.D.C. take over the work.

The new hereditary societies quickly joined in this activity. In 1884 an American Committee raising money to complete the pedestal for the Statue of Liberty was about to suspend construction when the Sons of the Revolution appointed a committee to help secure funds. One of its members was William O. McDowell, whose flair for publicity soon won the matter widespread attention. The committee issued an appeal for one-dollar contributions and induced President Chester A. Arthur to head the list. Next McDowell persuaded all steamboats to salute the island when they passed it as a reminder of the uncompleted base. Finally, he had a procession, headed by a

[28] McDowell to Miss Desha, Dec. 21, 1896, *ibid.*

G.A.R. post's fife and drum corps, march from the Battery through the downtown financial district to Union Square; en route it collected six hundred dollars.

These tactics at least rescued the statue from obscurity. The *New York Commercial Advertiser,* though taken aback by the use of steam whistles and brass bands, nevertheless decided that an unfinished pedestal was worse: "The methods adopted by the Sons of the Revolution, therefore, to open the purses of the people of New York are in the circumstances to be commended." [29] The American Committee of the Statue of Liberty, headed by William M. Evarts, was less pleased. It felt that the Sons were infringing on its work and was particularly incensed by McDowell's writing Evarts that, unless the American Committee completed the base, his group would take over the entire project. After a meeting of the two committees in November 1884, the Sons withdrew. In December, however, the society appointed another committee to ask Congress to contribute to the pedestal, and McDowell was instrumental in causing the *World* to start its successful popular subscription campaign. When the statue finally was unveiled, the Sons participated in the official parade.

Meanwhile, in 1886 the society began raising funds for a monument to Nathan Hale. Nearly all the members contributed. One of them, George Parsons Lathrop, dedicated his poem, "Gettysburgh; A Battle Ode," to the fund, and three hundred copies were sold for its benefit. In 1889 the society accepted Frederick MacMonnies' design, and his statue of the patriotic martyr is now a prominent feature of New York's City Hall Park. Similarly the D.A.R. worked for a memorial to Mary Washington; the Daughters of the Revolution and the C.A.R. sought funds to perpetuate the memory of the prison ship martyrs; and the Society of Colonial Wars unveiled a monument at the ruins of Louisbourg. Such an enterprise involved the Tacoma, Washington D.A.R. in a curious episode. The order presented a public drinking fountain to the city in commemoration of the massacre of Narcissa Whitman. "At the dedication of this memorial the Indian band of twenty members from the state school for Indians took part in the exercises," the chapter reported solemnly. "They were descendants of those who perpetrated the massacre. This feature was unique and more than usually impressive." [30]

The different groups also endeavored to mark and preserve historic spots. The Mount Vernon Ladies' Association quietly continued its work of guarding the old mansion and keeping the grounds in good condition. Each state branch made a room in the building its particular concern to which it contributed furniture and historical relics. Campaigns were occasionally conducted among school children; in this way Kansas raised $1000 for the care of the shrine.

The Civil War associations were anxious that the battlefields of that conflict be preserved. Many G.A.R. state encampments urged Congress to establish a National Military Park at Vicksburg and in 1899 secured this measure. The Grand Army also agitated, though less universally, for a similar national park at Gettysburg, and the Society of the Army of the Tennessee wanted them at Chickamauga-Chattanooga and Shiloh. The Woman's Relief Corps maintained the wartime prison grounds at Andersonville, Georgia, while the Alabama U.D.C. worked to purchase the First White House of the Confederacy at Montgomery. The Daughters of the Republic of Texas contributed their influence to have the state preserve the San Jacinto battleground.

The societies based on the American Revolution, like the D.A.R., S.A.R., and C.A.R., were particularly active in locating and marking the graves of its soldiers. The hereditary groups also busily labeled historic sites and preserved famous landmarks. Thus the Massachusetts Sons of the Revolution identified an old powder house at Somerville, Griffin's Wharf, the site of the Green Dragon Tavern, and the homes of Sam Adams and General Joseph Warren. The Colonial Dames indicated where Roger Williams first landed in Rhode Island, where Anne Hutchinson was killed, and where the Georgia Sons of Liberty met in Savannah. They also took charge of the Van Cortlandt Mansion in New York. Since this activity preceded the modern interest of state historical commissions by many years, patriotic organizations have never received sufficient credit for this voluntary work for the public benefit which undoubtedly rescued many spots from oblivion.

[30] Daughters of the American Revolution, *Third Report 1898–1900* (Washington, 1901), p. 268.

Many groups also included among their objectives the collection and preservation of manuscripts and records. The D.A.R., S.A.R., and Sons of the Revolution particularly urged that the federal government classify, index, and publish all documents on the American Revolution in its possession. The G.A.R. acted similarly to secure legislative appropriations for gathering and printing Civil War material, especially the records of military service.

The organizations did not do much publishing of historical material themselves. The Loyal Legion frequently issued collections of "War Papers," which had usually been read before their meetings. They usually came under the heading of personal reminiscences, though they often included detailed military studies of some value to the historian of the war itself. Of the hereditary societies the most active was the Society of Colonial Wars. The Massachusetts branch, for example, printed diaries, letters, and records concerning the various expeditions of the French and Indian Wars, while the New York Society issued the journal of a chaplain at the siege of Havana in 1762. The other associations contributed occasional items. The D.A.R. chapter in New Haven assembled forgotten songs and ballads of the Revolution, the Maine S.A.R. published histories of the regiments from that region, and the Ohio Sons of the Revolution printed lists of Revolutionary soldiers who later moved to that state. Though well intentioned, nearly all these attempts were in an antiquarian or genealogical rather than scholarly vein.

As another method of spreading knowledge of American history, the hereditary societies frequently sponsored lectures. The Daughters of the Revolution was fortunate in having as regent of its Brooklyn chapter the distinguished social historian, Mrs. Alice Morse Earle, who used to talk on colonial marriage customs or the deeds of women in the Revolution. More often the organizations had to go outside their ranks. Edward Eggleston, George Sidney Fisher, S. Weir Mitchell, J. Franklin Jameson, Edwin E. Sparks, and John Bach McMaster were among those who addressed the D.A.R. and Colonial Dames. The most popular of these speakers was probably John Fiske, who himself noted that his talk on the Boston tea party before the New York S.A.R. "was received with deafening applause." [31] Fiske exerted a wide historical influence among these

[31] Ethel F. Fisk, ed., *The Letters of John Fiske* (New York, 1940), p. 626.

groups because in addition to hearing his speeches the members also read widely in his books.

At least two associations, the D.A.R. and U.C.V., urged the establishment of chairs of American history in colleges. The D.A.R. endeavored to have professorships established at Barnard and Elmira Colleges, the Peabody State Normal School in Tennessee, and the College for Women at Cleveland. Similarly the United Confederate Veterans' committee on history repeatedly recommended that all Southern legislatures provide for such posts in state institutions. The committee wanted their occupants not only to teach but to have time for historical research and writing. It also felt that every public and private school throughout the South should offer at least a one-year course in American history. In Tennessee its desires coincided with those of the D.A.R., and the two societies coöperated with educational groups like the State Teachers' Association, the Public School Officers' Association, and county teachers' organizations to secure a legislative grant for the chair at Peabody College. The U.C.V. committee then deplored that other states did not follow this example.

Though encouraging a greater interest in American history, the societies had their own ideas as to its correct interpretation. In formulating their gloss upon the sacred canon the hereditary bodies tended toward stereotyped accounts of the colonial and Revolutionary periods which found little fault with the past conduct of the nation or its heroes. There were, however, occasional indications of a more critical approach. One speaker at a D.A.R. meeting heretically pointed out that some historians questioned the traditional view that deliberate English oppression had produced the Revolution and suggested that, if some measures had seemed tyrannical in effect, they had not been so framed deliberately. This came, however, at the very close of the nineties when a more mellow attitude toward England was developing. Similarly, the East Orange, New Jersey branch of the Daughters of the Revolution did not deem it unduly cynical to debate whether French aid in the Revolution "was prompted by hostility to England rather than by love of liberty." To be sure, the ladies voted for the more idealistic negative side, but only by a small majority.[32]

[32] "Meeting and Debate," *Magazine of Daughters of the Revolution*, II (July 1894), 14–27.

Even the character of George Washington occasionally received mature treatment. "We have chiselled him, as it were, in faultless marble, and have placed him on a pedestal in magnificent loneliness," complained the state historian of the New Jersey Daughters of the Revolution. "Or perhaps on the other hand we have overlaid him with tradition, we have made him the model of filial piety, probity, heroism and statesmanship; we have wound him about and about with every conceivable virtue, swathing him in fables until he presents as little human aspect as does the mummified form of Rameses II." [33] From there on, however, her picture of the great patriot leader was scarcely a precursor of Rupert Hughes's debunking technique. But the Connecticut S.A.R. heard with apparent equanimity that "nothing has been so detrimental to the character of Washington as the widespread though somewhat apocryphal story of the cherry tree and the hatchet." Contending that the anecdote produced "a disagreeable impression," the speaker daringly concluded, "From the point of view from which misguided moralists have hammered it into the youth of the land it has been and is exceedingly damaging." [34]

Ordinarily the hereditary societies were more filiopietistic in their attitudes. The Society of the Colonial Wars defended the Puritans against charges of intolerance that began to appear at the end of the century. A Presbyterian minister treated the S.A.R. of New Jersey to a divine rather than an economic or social interpretation of the Revolution which attributed nearly every bit of American good fortune to direct supernatural intervention, usually in the form of manipulation of the weather: "It was God who sent the tempest that drove the British ships from Dorchester Heights and gave Washington possession of Boston. It was God who spread the dense fog over the Long Island shores for Washington's safe retreat in that critical hour," right down to the arrival of De Grasse under heavenly auspices.[35] Both the S.A.R. and D.A.R. criticized British-born Goldwin Smith's account of the Revolution as pro-English.

The most aggressive champion of respectful traditional history was

[33] "New Jersey Celebration," *ibid.*, III (May 1895), 91.

[34] Connecticut Society, Sons of the American Revolution, *Year Book for 1895 and 1896* (New Haven, 1896), p. 92.

[35] New Jersey Society, Sons of the American Revolution, *Proceedings From Its Foundation in 1889 to 1893* (Morristown, N.J., 1893), pp. 225–226.

Jonathan Trumbull, president of the Connecticut S.A.R. In addresses before the S.A.R. and D.A.R. and in articles in the Hartford press he stanchly upheld the Revolutionary heroes against calumny. Summoning the Sons "to join hands with me in defending the good name of some of our revolutionary patriots against base insinuations, false charges and even libels which are appearing in the current literature of our day," he denied that Israel Putnam had been cowardly or treacherous or that his Trumbull ancestors had been involved in the Conway Cabal. He also deplored accounts too kindly disposed toward the Loyalists and critical of the lawlessness of the Boston Tea Party. "Let us hope, however, that notwithstanding the views and statements emanating from members of the faculties of Trinity, Harvard and Yale," he observed to the Hartford D.A.R., "we may still number a few friends of the patriots among those who have charge of the training of our young men, even in these institutions; and especially let us hope that such of these young men as are descendants of patriots of the revolution may not learn at these institutions to deride or utterly despise their ancestors." [36] It was not clear whether those not so descended were to be allowed to learn another version, but certainly his words suggested that future revisionists of our early history might find the hereditary societies determined guardians of a more reverent outlook.

The Civil War presented even more possibilities for controversy. As was natural for the defeated side, the Confederate organizations were extremely sensitive as to how the conflict should be interpreted. In 1892 the U.C.V. established a committee on history whose original function was to collect historical data and prepare an impartial history of the war. As an indication of the objectivity expected, the same meeting recommended Jefferson Davis' *History of the Confederate States* as the account that should be in every Southern home. The committee's report in 1897 made explicit its conception of history

as a form of literature, treating of past events, akin to science, in that it endeavors to express with accuracy and system the results of knowledge, but also akin to poetry, in that it endeavors to reproduce the former thoughts and motives of men, and to represent the noble and great

[36] Conn. S.A.R., *Year Book 1895–1896*, pp. 135, 184.

in a way which appeals to the imagination as well as instructs the judgment.[37]

The purpose of the discipline was to stimulate the patriotic emotions of students and to encourage them to emulate great deeds.

With this approach the committee consequently failed to view the great internecine struggle with cool detachment.

It is not to be expected that those who fought on the Southern side will admit that they were wrong simply because they were beaten, or that the highest and noblest purposes of their lives are worthy of execration of mankind [it declared]. The nation cannot afford to have the people of the South lose their self-respect, or the future citizens of that large and most promising section of the country brought up without that pride in their ancestors which leads to moral and patriotic action.[38]

Other Confederate veterans took every opportunity to proclaim the rectitude of their course. At times this led to an almost incredibly idealistic picture, as when a speaker before the Confederate Survivors' Association of Augusta, Georgia announced, "Nothing sordid mingled with our motives. No vulgar ambition stained our high resolve. No selfishness tainted our lofty aspirations." [39] The old soldiers particularly attacked the theory that they had fought to preserve slavery. Instead, they argued that secession had resulted from a difference in constitutional principles and therefore had been neither treasonable nor illegal. Some drew attention to New England's separatist sympathies in the early years of the republic. In justifying the South's record, others tried to prove that ever since the founding of the colonies Dixie had outstripped the North in patriotic services.

Though the organizations of victorious Northern veterans were inclined to feel somewhat smugly that might had meant right and that argument was therefore unnecessary, some members rose to the Southern bait. They denied that secession was legal or that the Southerners had any just grievances and insisted that slavery had caused the war. Hence they could conclude that

[37] United Confederate Veterans, *Minutes of the Seventh Annual Meeting 1897* (New Orleans, 1898), pp. 49–50.

[38] *Ibid.,* p. 48.

[39] F. Edgeworth Eve, *Address Delivered Before the Confederate Survivors' Association 1895* (Augusta, Ga., 1895), p. 16.

it is not true that the leading conspirators who fomented the Rebellion thought that they were right. They knew that they were wholly in the wrong, both legally and morally. But they were recklessly hell-bent on destroying the Government of the United States solely and only because Abraham Lincoln . . . had been lawfully elected President of the United States.[40]

With fanatics on both side taking attitudes that often made little sense logically but carried a strong emotional appeal, it was almost impossible for a neutral pen to give satisfaction. So staid a chronicle as the *Encyclopaedia Britannica* suffered attacks from both directions. But even greater difficulties faced the authors of school histories. In the period between the Civil War and the close of the century one expression of the nationalist spirit of the times was the passage of numerous state laws requiring the teaching of United States history in public schools. In turn this naturally led to the appearance of a number of histories intended as textbooks which in their attempts to offend no one antagonized both the North and the South.[41]

Feeling secure enough by the early nineties to organize, the Confederate veterans decided that they also dared to insist that the schools embrace their interpretations. At its 1892 meeting the U.C.V. instructed its first historical committee to condemn all untrue books and to select a proper United States history for Southern public and private schools. Throughout the remainder of the decade this group, headed by General Stephen Lee of Mississippi, protested that nearly all Northern-written histories did not do justice to the Confederacy and urged their exclusion from schools. It endorsed several volumes by Southern writers like Mrs. Susan P. Lee and J. L. M. Curry and recommended a number of books on the Civil War as suitable for libraries and schools, including Jefferson Davis' *Rise and Fall of the Confederate States of America,* Alexander H. Stephens' *War Between the States,* several lives of Robert E. Lee, and such dispassionate works as *The Southern Side of the Prison Question* and *A Confederate View of the Treatment of Prisoners.* On the whole Stephen Lee exercised a moderating influence. In 1897 he announced

---

[40] "Comments," *Grand Army Record,* XII (Nov. 1897), 87.

[41] The best summary of this agitation is Bessie Louise Pierce, *Public Opinion and the Teaching of History in the United States* (New York, 1926), pp. 12–23, 146–171.

that the committee would no longer "endorse historical works as true, or recommend them as containing the real history of the greatest events of our history's past. . . . Apart from the danger of error, to embark on such a course would be to make discrimination between deserving works." [42]

To implement the reports of the historical committee, in 1895 the U.C.V. petitioned all Southern legislatures and boards of education to discard partisan histories in favor of the ones recommended by the committee. Four years later Lee, while denying that the Confederate veterans intended "to exercise any system of censorship over the histories used in the schools," urged that a subcommittee of three in every state examine school histories and then endeavor, through "friendly correspondence," to have the authors and publishers rectify any omissions or biased statements.[43]

Some of the local branches did press the matter. In Virginia, for example, the state history committee, insisting that the children must be taught that secession was legal and that their fathers had been neither rebels nor traitors, induced the state board of education to drop Barnes' *A Brief History of the United States* and to add works by Mrs. Lee and J. William Jones, a leader of the U.C.V. Next John Fiske's history came under scrutiny. The objections were only to his account of the Civil War period, and especially to his version of Preston Brooks's attack upon Charles Sumner, but that was enough. When the veterans held their state reunion in October 1898, they denied a representative of Houghton, Mifflin, who had appeared to defend Fiske, permission to speak. The committee's report set off an excited debate. Those who opposed a denunciation of Northern histories found themselves branded as hirelings of the publishing houses. Finally, the meeting condemned both Fiske and another volume while formally endorsing the works of Mrs. Lee and Jones.

In this drive the old soldiers received the backing of their allied societies. The United Sons of Confederate Veterans joined in censuring partisan histories; groups in Richmond and Charleston were especially active. Even stronger support came from the United Daughters of the Confederacy. In North and South Carolina, Geor-

[42] U.C.V., *Minutes 1897*, p. 48.
[43] United Confederate Veterans, *Minutes of the Ninth Annual Meeting 1899* (New Orleans, 1900), pp. 151–152.

gia, Florida, Alabama, Mississippi, and Texas the women attacked
Northern texts and often secured the substitution of more acceptable
books. In 1897 the central organization appointed a committee on
histories. Its report the following year asked state legislatures and
boards of education to remove certain texts such as that of Barnes
in favor of works like those of Mrs. Lee and Jones.

At the turn of the century the U.C.V. avowed its satisfaction. "A
decided improvement may be noted in the tone of the school histories which have been written or revised since the publication of
the report of your committee," General Lee announced in 1899. "The
style of historical authors has become less sectional and controversial,
and much more liberal and patriotic." [44] The mere fact of the committee's existence, he felt, prevented the introduction of books likely
to offend the veterans' sensibilities. Eventually Northern publishers,
primarily interested in keeping valuable markets, yielded to the
clamor by preparing special textbooks for Southern consumption.

But at the very time that the ex-Confederates found these volumes
not sufficiently pro-Southern, the G.A.R. thought that they were
entirely too much so. As early as 1888 a committee of the Wisconsin
department reported that textbooks' "efforts to be impartial and
non-sectional have gone beyond the bounds of reason," but that even
so Southern schools would not use them. It then titillated the
encampment with extensive quotations from several Southern school
histories, most of which had been written shortly after the war and
were not, it is true, exactly the highest products of impartial scholarship. The report concluded that these volumes "proclaim the righteousness of their cause, vindicate state sovereignty, and school history
that teaches anything different finds little encouragement in that
section." The meeting frequently interrupted the reading of this
document to express its approval and then voted to distribute it in
pamphlet form to the national encampment, all departments and
various teachers' associations. [45] Declaring that Southern histories
were "teaching a thoroughly studied, rank, partisan system of sectional education," former Commander-in-Chief Fairchild presented
the report to the national encampment of 1888. Calling it "a most

[44] *Ibid.,* p. 151.
[45] Department of Wisconsin, Grand Army of the Republic, *School Histories Report
and Resolutions Adopted by the Department Encampment 1888* (Milwaukee, 1888),
pp. 8–9.

valuable document" which "presents some truths which are shameful," the G.A.R.'s head drew the attention of the entire order to it in an official circular.[46] Several other states endorsed its findings and in some cases undertook similar investigations.

Although the Grand Army and the soldiers' papers long criticized these texts, especially the one by Mrs. Lee so highly praised by Southern organizations, there was, after all, little that they could do about instruction south of the Mason and Dixon line. But in the nineties, partly in reaction to the U.C.V.'s spirited drive in the South, they began to cock a critical eye at the more vulnerable books by Northerners intended for both sections. In March 1894, the protest of a Pennsylvania post concerning the histories used in that state caused the department to appoint a committee which studied the situation and sent its criticisms to the 1894 national convention. Commander-in-Chief Thomas Lawler then distributed the statement to all the posts, asking that it be read in their meetings and also published in the newspapers. About the same time the *Grand Army Record* launched a virulent campaign, perhaps hoping to build up circulation through sensationalism. One writer in the paper exhorted the veterans "to aid in dashing down the cup of moral poison that our school histories are holding to your youth." They should no more hesitate "than if these books taught obscenity or other immorality." [47]

In 1897 a national committee reported that none of the books in general use "merits the unqualified endorsement of this organization." It criticized them for calling the conflict a war between sections of the country instead of a rebellion against the national authority, for giving inadequate space to certain battles, for not discussing Union generals at sufficient length, and for overpraising the Confederate leaders. The convention voted to issue the critique in pamphlet form to all posts, auxiliary organizations, and school boards.[48] Beginning in 1898, the inspector general asked all departments to report how their schools taught the Civil War. During the

[46] Grand Army of the Republic, *Journal of the Twenty-Second Annual Session of the National Encampment 1888* (Minneapolis, 1888), pp. 210–211.

[47] Frank E. Farnham, "The Text Book Question," *Grand Army Record*, IX (Nov. 1894), 87.

[48] Grand Army of the Republic, *Journal of the Thirty-first National Encampment 1897* (Lincoln, Neb., 1897), pp. 234–235, 259.

middle and late nineties a number of branches from Massachusetts to Oregon named committees of investigation which nearly always discovered that school histories were pro-Southern in tone and inadequate or erroneous on the war's military history. Though the Grand Army took the lead in this attack, representatives of the Woman's Relief Corps and the Sons of Veterans worked in close coöperation.

The volumes that aroused the most controversy were D. H. Montgomery's *Leading Facts of American History* and *Beginners' American History*. The *Grand Army Record* bitterly denounced this author for wasting time on trivial matters like Coxey's Army, for not describing fully the horrors of Southern prisons, for treating Lee and Davis too mildly, for stating that many prominent men had believed that the states had a right to secede, and for terming the Confederates belligerents rather than rebels. An especially sore point was an anecdote about an old lady in the North who gave her son an umbrella as he marched off to war; this seemed to ridicule the Union Army. When Professor Albert Bushnell Hart of Harvard penned a defense for the *Boston Journal,* the reply came: "If he had been the paid attorney of Montgomery and his publishers, in a professional way, he would have defended Montgomery in precisely the way that he has elected to defend him." [49] The paper printed a list of Massachusetts towns using the book as a "roll of dishonor" and spread its attacks widely among Grand Army leaders and school superintendents, urging them all to be on the alert. When the effects of the *Record*'s campaign became apparent, Montgomery's publishers, Ginn and Company, asserted that rival firms were behind this turmoil, but the periodical virtuously denied this.

School committees were at first evasive in answering the *Record*'s queries about what action they would take. In the first few months of 1896 the journal induced the G.A.R. to conduct considerable agitation in the Boston area. Its editor, John M. Perkins, personally led the fight in Arlington and Brockton, while the Grand Army member who instigated a similar assault in Wakefield fortified himself with several hundred copies of the *Record*. The paper was also largely responsible for the Grand Army's assailing the book in Chelsea, Lowell, Woburn, Waltham, and Stoneham.

[49] "Montgomery Sustained," *Grand Army Record,* XI (Jan. 1896), p. 7.

The matter finally reached the state encampment in February 1896, when a resolution demanding that Montgomery be banished from all schools was referred to the incoming council of administration. In August a committee reported that the author and publishers had made some fifty changes—such as calling the Civil War the War of the Rebellion and omitting the umbrella story—to the extent of endangering Southern sales. The committee now felt that the history "may be profitably used by the children of the public schools of this Commonwealth without injury to their patriotism." The 1897 encampment therefore refused to attack the volume further.[50]

The *Record,* however, declared itself still unsatisfied and denounced the department leaders. The paper intransigently maintained that "the publishers of Montgomery's school history either wrote or inspired the white-washing report in its favor." [51] Its influence, meanwhile, had spread even beyond metropolitan Boston. In Delhi, New York, a G.A.R. member was shocked to discover his daughter was using the very volume whose faults the *Grand Army Record* was exposing. "I consider it almost notorious that a work so falsifying history should become a text book in our schools," he wrote the editor. "I will have a talk with the Principal of the Academy on this subject when the first opportunity presents itself." [52]

In other areas the Grand Army attacked Montgomery apparently quite independently of the *Record*'s campaign. In the summer of 1895 the Indiana department's committee on school histories presented a detailed critique to the state board of education. Though Ginn and Company sent out representatives fortified with a seventeen-page defense and the board twice compelled substantial revisions to meet the veterans' objections, the G.A.R. remained critical. Insisting on an explicit statement of which side had been right, its 1897 meeting again condemned the book. Eventually concessions were made that satisfied the organization. The volume also received the castigation of Grand Army committees on school histories in New York and Ohio as well as of the president of the Ladies of the G.A.R. Yet at the same time the committees of the New Jersey Grand

[50] Department of Massachusetts, Grand Army of the Republic, *Journal of the Thirty-First Annual Encampment 1897* (Boston, 1897), pp. 160, 183–184.

[51] "History at the Boston State House," *Grand Army Record,* XII (Nov. 1897), 84.

[52] "Montgomery's 'Confederate' School Histories in Southern New York," *ibid.,* XII (April 1897), 27.

Army and the New York W.R.C. found Montgomery the most acceptable of the texts!

Montgomery was only one of several histories that attracted the hostile attention of the G.A.R., the W.R.C., and the Ladies of the G.A.R. These organizations frequently demanded their expulsion from the schools and sometimes succeeded in forcing revisions. Barnes' *A Brief History of the United States,* which had pained Southern sensibilities, irritated the New York Grand Army's committee, for example, because it called Lincoln ungainly and unrefined, did not mention the terms "treason," "traitor," or "patriotism," and used the word "flag" only once. Even John Fiske, so admired by the hereditary societies and so distrusted by the U.C.V., fell under the *Grand Army Record*'s ban because he left out the middle initial in the names of William H. Seward and Edwin M. Stanton and used expressions like the "Civil War" instead of the "Pro-Slavery Rebellion." He also seemed too favorable to Lee and offended his readers by saying Sumner's speech on Senator Butler which provoked Preston Brooks's attack had not been in good taste, the very passage that to the Confederate societies breathed Northern sympathies.

Though chiefly the veterans assailed books already in use, they also made some effort to substitute approved works. The *Grand Army Record* endorsed a "lost school history" by William H. Seavey of Boston, which proved its patriotism by strong condemnation of Robert E. Lee. True, the work went only as far as 1880, but "It could easily be brought down to 1896 by the addition of 15 or 20 pages." [53] There was also sentiment in the G.A.R. to sponsor the writing of a satisfactory account of the Civil War for schools. For a few months in 1897 the possibility that a text being prepared by John Bach McMaster might appear under G.A.R. auspices aroused considerable discussion both pro and con.[54] The University of Pennsylvania history professor, who was as conservative and nationalistic as the most belligerent super-patriot could desire, had made the first move, asking A. C. Marsh, chairman of its school history committee, what kind of a history the Grand Army would like. Marsh wrote back in considerable detail, indicating that so far John Fiske's work

[53] " 'The Lost Cause' in Boston," *ibid.,* XII (Jan. 1892), 2.

[54] Eric F. Goldman, *John Bach McMaster* (Philadelphia, 1943), pp. 80–88, tells the story of this curious episode.

seemed the most satisfactory to the committee but that none could really be endorsed, so that "the time is right for a real patriotic loyal history of the rebellion, written in a philosophical spirit, with a desire to present facts and at the same time in sympathy with the cause that triumphed because it was right." [55]

In the spring of 1897 McMaster even took his manuscript to Chicago to show Marsh and another member of the committee, a Presbyterian minister from Manhattan, Kansas named Duncan Milner. Next John Perkins, editor of the *Grand Army Record,* got into the act with a request to see the proofs of the work, but by now unfavorable publicity had made McMaster wary and he fended off the Bostonian. He did have his publisher send the proofs to Marsh just before the 1897 encampment, but the committee failed to make any specific mention of the work and on the eve of the publication of his *School History* in September 1897 McMaster issued a denial that he was writing an official G.A.R. text. By 1900 Marsh's successor, Milner, though still distressed by several Southern works, felt able to report "great improvement. Several publishers gladly accepted suggested amendments, and it can now be said that the general character of these histories is satisfactory." [56]

This emphasis upon school histories reflected the importance the societies attached to the educational system in disseminating patriotism. As part of their civic responsibilities they encouraged its extension and watched its operation. Especially they felt that it was the schools' function to instill love of country in the future citizens. In the nineties the Grand Army of the Republic, the Woman's Relief Corps, and the D.A.R. increasingly emphasized the need for patriotic instruction. "Whatever can be done to create in the minds of the young an enthusiastic devotion to their country will contribute much to the well-being of the republic," declared a committee of the New York G.A.R. "We believe that the cultivation of this spirit should form a necessary part of every system of education." [57] Such teaching was imperative, its proponents usually argued, to counteract the immense foreign immigration which knew little of the obligations of Amer-

[55] Quoted *ibid.,* p. 82.

[56] Grand Army of the Republic, *Journal of the Thirty-fourth National Encampment 1900* (Philadelphia, 1900), p. 143.

[57] Department of New York, Grand Army of the Republic, *Proceedings of the Thirty-Second Annual Encampment 1898* (New York and Albany, 1898), pp. 65–66.

ican citizenship and might otherwise become the source of various forms of radicalism, particularly anarchism.

At the instigation of Duncan Milner, the 1891 national encampment of the G.A.R. named a committee "to devise plans to insure the successful inauguration of some systematic plan of teaching the lessons of loyalty to our one country and one flag." [58] In the next few years a great many departments set up similar groups on patriotic education. Soon following suit, in 1897 the Woman's Relief Corps established the positions of national and department patriotic instructors to encourage such training. Through the W.R.C. the idea spread to other women's organizations. As early as 1894 its representative to the National Council of Women, Mrs. Kate Sherwood, persuaded that body to endorse the teaching of patriotism in all schools and became chairman of a committee on the subject. During the decade several states made this a legal requirement.

The approval of such instruction was by no means the same as its accomplishment. Even though the veterans had a dismaying tendency to accept the word for the deed, they were not unaware of the obstacles. "Such a feeling cannot be taught in the ordinary meaning of the word," admitted the Pennsylvania G.A.R.'s committee. "There can, therefore, be no distinctive teaching of patriotism. But it may be instilled into the mind and heart by appropriate appeals to reason and sentiment." [59] The societies therefore advanced various methods of inducing the proper reactions.

A common device of the Grand Army was to have the veterans visit the schools, usually the Friday before Memorial Day, to talk to the students. Originating in the Middle West, the practice soon spread throughout the rest of the country. A closely related proposal was that the schools hold regular patriotic exercises. The national encampment of 1892 voted that one school day during the year should be set aside for this purpose. In the next few years both the Grand Army and the D.A.R. were active securing legislation or directions from school boards for such ceremonies.

These observances took different forms. William Morey, chairman of a committee of the New York G.A.R., felt that if the children

---

[58] Grand Army of the Republic, *Journal of the Twenty-Fifth National Encampment 1891* (Rutland, Vt., 1891), p. 275.

[59] Penn. G.A.R., *Proceedings 1897*, p. 193.

learned about the lives of national heroes, "they would receive an inspiration which could be derived from no other source." He also recommended reading patriotic literature. "The burning words which have kindled the love of country in times that are past will continue to warm the heart in years that are to come," he predicted. "American literature is rich with the poems of patriotism, and with these every boy and girl should be familiar." [60] Strong emphasis also developed for the learning and singing of patriotic songs. The G.A.R.'s Committee on a Systematic Plan of Teaching the Lessons of Loyalty to Our Country and One Flag contended, somewhat ambiguously, "The impression made by such songs on the minds of the youth will be life-long in their effect." [61]

The W.R.C.'s Committee on Patriotic Teaching stressed the introduction into schools of a "Patriotic Primer for the Little Citizen" and a "Declaration of Independence Chart," donated in large numbers by local branches of the order. By 1900 the national patriotic instructor reported that 2446 schools were displaying the chart. The D.A.R. voted to petition state legislatures to require the reading of the Declaration and the Constitution at least once each term in all public schools. In the late nineties the W.R.C. began to include within the scope of patriotic work humane education which would "inspire in the lives of the rising generation gentle thoughts and just and loving deeds." [62]

With an almost mystic trust in postnatal influence, the women's hereditary societies felt they could foster patriotism among school children by furnishing appropriate pictures, especially of George Washington. But the chief educational activity of the ancestral leagues was their frequent awarding of prizes and medals for essays, nearly always on historical topics, particularly from the Revolutionary period.

In these efforts to compel additions to the school curriculum the societies met with varied responses. Sometimes they recognized the need to proceed cautiously. The usual method was to interview school officials and to visit state, county, and township gatherings

[60] N.Y. G.A.R., *Proceedings 1898*, p. 71.

[61] Grand Army of the Republic, *Journal of the Twenty-Sixth National Encampment 1892* (Albany, 1892), p. 82.

[62] Department of Oregon, Woman's Relief Corps, *Journal of the Thirteenth Annual Convention 1897* (Oregon City, Ore., n.d.), p. 54.

of teachers to tell them about the work. "Be careful in your inquiries not to give the impression to teachers and superintendents in schools, that you are demanding these things to be done, or that you hold a rod of correction if they are omitted," the New York W.R.C. warned, "but be sure you have them understand that the W.R.C. is deeply interested in the good work of teaching the children patriotism and reverence for our flag and stand ready to furnish flags, charts, and patriotic primers to help them." [63] In some cases the officials proved very coöperative. In New York the State Superintendent of Public Instruction was so impressed by the G.A.R. committee's report that he had 40,000 copies printed for circulation among the state's teachers. But other educators were rather cool, feeling that students already had enough to keep them occupied.

(The Grand Army had to move with particular circumspection in the South. One delegate told his comrades at the 1892 national encampment that they could succeed there only if they utilized anniversaries unconnected with the Civil War and employed "guarded language." In Georgia the G.A.R. decided not to push the subject at all, "believing that the time was not quite ripe in this Department for active measures, upon which the sentiment of the southern people is growing more healthful and progressive every year." [64])

(Though the organizations usually regarded students in elementary and secondary schools as the most promising subjects for patriotic propaganda, they did not ignore entirely those on the college level. With a higher proportion of their membership college graduates, the hereditary societies were more interested in higher education than the veterans' groups. The D.A.R., Daughters of the Revolution, Colonial Dames, and Sons of the Revolution offered awards for essays, chiefly of a historical nature, in such institutions as Radcliffe, Barnard, Bryn Mawr, Vassar, Brown, the University of Michigan, and the University of Pennsylvania. In 1896 the winner of the S.A.R.'s silver medal for a paper on "The Principles Fought For in the War of the American Revolution" was young John Calvin Cool-

---

[63] Department of New York, Woman's Relief Corps, *Journal of the Seventeenth Annual Convention 1900* (n.p., n.d.), p. 86.

[64] Department of Georgia, Grand Army of the Republic, *Journal of the Seventeenth Annual Session 1895* (Atlanta, 1895), p. 17.

idge of Amherst College. Occasionally these groups also sponsored scholarships, and in Rhode Island the veterans joined in with a $10,000 gift to Brown University to establish a Grand Army of the Republic fellowship.)

Many members of hereditary societies became greatly interested in the movement to establish a National University at Washington, partly because it was identified as a desire of the country's first president. Within the D.A.R. its first proponents, Mrs. Mary D. Putnam, the Iowa state regent, and Mrs. R. Ogden Doremus, regent of the New York City Chapter, began their agitation in 1893. The president-general, Mrs. Stevenson, then named a committee to work for Congressional support. Throughout the last part of the decade its chairman was one of the society's founders, Mrs. Walworth, who stirred up considerable enthusiasm among the Daughters. To her mind the proposed university was a patriotic enterprise because it would divert American graduate students from European schools "who would thus be instructed in special and advanced work while breathing the spirit of American institutions, inspired by a truer and broader Americanism." [65] Another women's group, the W.R.C., also endorsed the movement.

The intrigues of an even more energetic campaigner for the National University, William O. McDowell, probably harmed the cause more than they aided it. His chief ally was a credulous Connecticut Yankee, Henry Baldwin of New Haven, member of hereditary societies, author of a manuscript history of the S.A.R., but primarily a leader in nativist movements. At a meeting of the "National Executive Committee of the National Council of Patriotic Organizations" (representing secret and nativist rather than veterans' and hereditary societies) in Chicago in February 1891, McDowell bestowed on Baldwin the title of "Custodian of American History." His modest task was "to verify all the facts of American History, and to collect a Library Americana," which was to be the nucleus of the National University's library.[66] Among those who agreed to be trustees of the Library Americana were Baldwin, Mc-

---

[65] "Proceedings of Fifth Continental Congress," *American Monthly Magazine,* VIII (April 1896), 514.

[66] Form letter issued by McDowell, Sept. 1898, Henry Baldwin Scrapbooks, New York Public Library.

Dowell, the historian John Clark Ridpath, and Mrs. Loulie M. Gordon of Atlanta, the Georgia D.A.R. regent. The group announced its intention "to maintain American institutions" and "to spread American liberty over the entire continent." [67]

To secure funds for the proposed school, in the late nineties McDowell induced Baldwin to invest $20,000 in a machine which he and one Erastus E. Ford had invented as a means of beating the stock market. McDowell informed Baldwin that "when you and your son had investigated and you brought your twenty thousand dollars to New York with you, it seemed to me that God in his own way, was through you and Mr. Ford starting the ball rolling that would bring into existence what Washington had wanted, just right." [68] But the investment did not prove a happy one. "I am more and more impressed with the fact that Mr. Ford is a great genius," McDowell confided to Baldwin a few months later, "but not in every particular a good business man." [69] By the turn of the century Baldwin's money was lost, and he and McDowell were debating whether to prefer criminal charges against Ford.

McDowell's advocacy of the National University did little to spur enthusiasm for it among his erstwhile colleagues in the S.A.R. When Josiah Pumpelly asked the national meeting of 1898 to endorse a Congressional bill, the president of the New Jersey Society, John Whitehead, at once announced, "If there be the slightest suspicion that this man McDowell has anything to do with this resolution, I move that it be laid upon the table." He emphasized his remarks by stamping his feet upon the floor, and the motion was abandoned.[70]

The veterans made intermittent but not particularly successful efforts to support colleges dedicated primarily to training their offspring in the ideals for which they had fought. The U. S. Grant University, at Athens, Tennessee, secured only fifty dollars toward its building fund from the state G.A.R., and though the Woman's Relief Corps endorsed the Grand Army of the Republic Memorial

---

[67] Circular issued by Baldwin, April 1, 1894, Henry Baldwin Papers, New York Public Library.

[68] McDowell to Baldwin, July 1, 1898, Baldwin Scrapbooks.

[69] McDowell to Baldwin, Feb. 27, 1899, *ibid.*

[70] Sons of the American Revolution, *National Year Book 1898* (New York, n.d.), p. 76.

College in Oberlin, Kansas, the veterans of that state and Colorado proved unwilling to do much for it. Undiscouraged by the fate of these schools, the Iowa Sons of Veterans urged its national organization to found a military college as a memorial to the Civil War soldiers. A survey of all the camps showed the vast majority in favor of the idea and the Iowa legislature suggested that the institution be located in that state. In 1899 the order voted to attempt the experiment and appointed a committee to receive bids for its location and to circulate pledges for its support. But the story of the vicissitudes and eventual collapse of the Sons of Veterans' Memorial University at Mason City, Iowa belongs to the new century.

On the whole, however, the veterans were suspicious of too much learning. Not highly educated themselves (in one Ohio post, it turned out in the 1890's, only five of the twenty-three members could even write),[71] they resented the academic standards established by civil service commissions for government jobs. Particularly the old soldiers disliked Harvard University. They recalled that many of the school's alumni were prominent Independents and Mugwumps who advocated civil service legislation, tariff reduction, and economy in government and voted for Grover Cleveland, the foe of liberal pension legislation. They remembered how John Fiske and Albert Bushnell Hart had dared to interpret the Civil War in independent fashion and how President Eliot had castigated their lobbying for federal funds. Since class prejudice also molded their views, they pictured Harvard students as a group of rich, snobbish Anglophile loafers with no sympathy for the common soldiers who had saved the Union. The new developments in college life, moreover, lacked the sturdy virtue of the manual labor in which so many veterans engaged. "There was a time within the memory of living man," sneered the *Grand Army Record,* "when 'college education' did not mean playing ball, boating, and general debauchery and lawlessness." [72]

Finally, under a broad interpretation of one of its objects, the diffusion of knowledge, the D.A.R. encouraged another form of adult education, the spread of libraries. In many communities they

---

[71] Elmer Edward Noyes, "A History of the Grand Army of the Republic in Ohio from 1866 to 1900," Ph.D. dissertation, Ohio State University (1945), p. 64.

[72] "College Education," *Grand Army Record,* IX (April 1891), 25.

gave entertainments to raise funds to establish free public libraries, whose first rooms were often in the Daughters' chapter houses; in some cases the members themselves served as librarians in the early years. In towns that already had such institutions, the D.A.R. often endeavored to build up the American history collection.)

(These, then, were the ways that the organizations hoped to spread patriotism. In preserving the landmarks of the American past and in enlarging the facilities for education, patriotic societies performed services for which they have received too little credit, but their efforts to dictate the precise contents of an expanded curriculum, their reliance upon outward symbols and ritualism, and their insistence that the interpretation of the past conform to their prejudices obscured and perhaps negated their other contributions. Whether all this fuss and bother actually resulted in any greater amount of patriotism than would have been otherwise the case seems doubtful but is, of course, impossible of scientific proof. It all depends on whether one believes that a person who salutes the flag every day thereby grows more patriotic, and such a conviction is an act of faith like belief in any other religious observance.)

XI

Division and Reunion

WHEN patriotic societies faced their patriotic duties in the late nineteenth century, particularly challenging was the correct attitude to take toward the former Confederacy. Was the proper role to proclaim loyalty to the United States by denouncing treason and rebellion, thereby perpetuating sectional antagonism at the expense of national solidarity, or was the better part to foster reconciliation between once warring regions so as to produce a really united country? The Civil War associations, both Northern and Southern, answered this first one way and then another; the Mexican War Veterans took a quite different tack from the G.A.R.; and the hereditary societies, appearing late on the scene, proved the most conciliatory, yet also the most truly nationalist minded, of them all.[1]

In the late sixties and the seventies, with the veterans fresh from the battlefield, flushed with victory and closely allied with the Radical Republicans, the influence of the Civil War associations in the North was little directed toward appeasement of the recent foe. It is perhaps surprising that the addresses at their meetings expressed as much moderation as they did. Speech after speech followed the same pattern: insistence upon the South's criminal responsibility and warnings not to lose the fruits of victory quickly followed nearly every profession of friendship; offers of forgiveness depended upon the South's admission of how grievously it had sinned. General Phil Sheridan, who felt that "we should not pay so much attention to this matter of 'forgetting our differences,'" probably represented the

---

[1] The most perceptive and succinct appraisal of the role of the Civil War soldiers is the chapter, "The Veteran Mind," in Paul H. Buck, *The Road to Reunion* (Boston, 1937), pp. 236–262, which, however, does not consider the influence toward reconciliation of either the Mexican War veterans or the hereditary societies.

prevailing sentiment. "Laughter and applause" was the Society of the Army of the Potomac's response to his tart comment, "I am willing to shake hands with any Southern man that I meet, but I am not willing to make any particular display about it." [2] Memorial Day exercises became a source of friction. In the spirit of reconciliation a few posts decorated the graves of Confederate as well as Union dead, but most members of the Grand Army denounced this practice as honoring disloyalty.

A few veterans pointed the way toward future understanding by emphasizing forgetting, rather than forgiving. Some even substituted for unqualified condemnation of the Southern cause an effort to understand it. The willingness to explain Confederate psychology in terms of such environmental factors as education, political philosophy, and the whole structure of Southern society was an important step toward sectional harmony. The approach of the Centennial celebrations of 1876 produced hopes that emphasis upon the common heritage of the Revolution would hasten reconciliation. But those who displayed a readiness to meet with their former enemies and to reminisce without bitterness usually found the G.A.R. unresponsive.

If the seventies on the whole contributed little toward reunion, on the other hand by the nineties a strong case can be made that the Civil War veterans' associations had become an important force in that direction. The eighties, however, constituted a more complex period of curious ambivalence. At different times the same societies, periodicals, or individuals made assurances of friendship as well as generous gestures to implement their good intentions and then would almost immediately qualify their remarks or in the excitement of some delicate episode reveal how strong the wartime heritage still was. The difficulty was that the decade was the watershed between two opposing sentiments, the old rancor and the new good feeling.

The signs of increasing friendliness among the Northern Civil War societies were widely evident. "It was easy to forgive—it was hard to forget," General Horace Porter observed shrewdly to the Society of the Army of the Potomac, "but the soldier element on both sides was the first to forget the rancor, the partizan bitterness

---

[2] Society of the Army of the Potomac, *Record of Proceedings at the Sixth Annual Re-Union 1874 and the Annual Business Meeting 1875* (New York, 1876), p. 32.

of the struggle." [3] The first step toward reconciliation was a growing recognition of the bravery of the former foe. Gradually there also came the realization that the Southerners had not madly committed a deliberate crime but had believed that their course was right. G.A.R. leaders began to deny that their organization tended to preserve sectional animosities. In 1883 Lucius Fairchild announced that he was unable to find within the Grand Army "any apparent hatred of the people of the once rebellious states. There is now, and has been always, only the kindest feeling manifested toward them. No word of abuse of them is ever heard in a post." [4]

Though a paper like the *National Tribune* seldom yielded to the rising tide of reunion, at times some of its rivals expressed the new spirit. The *Grand Army Record* conceded that instances of Southern intransigence were exceptional and represented the views of only a few extremists. Remnants of Northern Radicalism it viewed as merely the professional stock in trade of a few demagogues. It looked forward to the "glorious day when these sectional bickerings between a common people cease, and the world has learned to look upon us, not as Southerners and Northerners, Yankees or Rebels, but as Americans." [5] The *Grand Army Review* announced from the very beginning that in its pages "a prominent feature will be an endeavor to promote the 'era of good feeling' between the Blue and the Gray, and we trust we shall have many a lively yarn spun by ex-Confederates." [6]

In 1886 an earthquake at Charleston produced widespread Grand Army sympathy. Accompanied by the adjutant-general of the order, Command-in-Chief Lucius Fairchild hastened to the spot, assuring its inhabitants that he had no thought of sectional differences or harsh memories of Fort Sumter, "but only a feeling that these were our people, loyal to the same flag as I, and in distress." He insisted that the survivors of both sides "have no bitter animosities. I have none in my breast I know, and today if I should meet the soldier whose aim made this armless sleeve, I would grasp his hand by the

---

[3] Society of the Army of the Potomac, *Report of the Fifteenth Annual Re-Union 1884* (New York, 1884), p. 36.

[4] Society of the Army of the Tennessee, *Report of the Proceedings at the Sixteenth Meeting 1883* (n.p., n.d.), p. 517.

[5] "The War Is Over," *Grand Army Record*, III (Nov. 1887), 4.

[6] "General Salute," *Grand Army Review*, I (May 1885), 3.

only hand he left me, and have no hard feelings towards him. I believe all the Grand Army men feel as I do." [7] Declaring that conditions required "an immediate and extraordinary effort" and "confident that every comrade is anxious to do what he can for the comfort and happiness of this stricken people," on September 14 he asked every G.A.R. post to collect funds to repair the city's homes. More than $7000 had been raised before the mayor wired Fairchild in the middle of October that no further subscriptions were necessary, and the commander-in-chief was certain that $100,000 could have been secured if necessary.[8]

This episode had a pleasant effect. From Charleston Fairchild reported to his wife, "The people I have met seem profoundly impressed with this move of the G.A.R." [9] The Palmetto Guard of the city, composed of Confederate veterans, made him an honorary member and placed on its minutes an extract of the speech he made to the citizens. Shortly thereafter he wrote from Washington, "The southern people I meet almost shed tears when they speak of my action in going to Charleston, & I see that the northern papers approve." [10]

Other helpful contacts between the veterans of both sides multiplied throughout the decade. Though the Grand Army never met in the former Confederacy in these years, the national encampment at Baltimore in 1882 witnessed demonstrations of good feeling. Cheers and applause greeted a former Southern soldier who was a speaker. Soon the commander of the New Mexico branch declared that "to-day there is scarcely a gathering of the members, or celebration of the order, that is not participated in by ex-Confederate officers and soldiers, who have manfully accepted the situation, and vie with us in devotion to the stars and stripes." [11] After making trips into the South other members reported cordial receptions by their former foes.

[7] Quoted by the Palmetto Guard of Charleston to Lucius Fairchild, Sept. 28, 1886, Lucius Fairchild Papers, Wisconsin State Historical Society.

[8] Grand Army of the Republic, *Journal of the Twenty-first Annual Session of the National Encampment 1887* (Milwaukee, 1887), pp. 36–37, 268–270.

[9] Fairchild to Mrs. Fairchild, Sept. 14, 1886, Fairchild Papers.

[10] Fairchild to Mrs. Fairchild, Sept. 17, 1886, *ibid.*

[11] Department of New Mexico, Grand Army of the Republic, *Organization and Minutes of Encampments 1883–1885* (Las Vegas, N.M., 1885), p. 14.

The army societies were more active than the G.A.R. in welcoming Confederate visitors or meeting jointly with Southern groups. When the Robert E. Lee Camp of Confederate Veterans from Richmond attended the Society of the Army of the Potomac's session at Baltimore in 1885, bands played "Dixie," "The Star Spangled Banner," "The Bonnie Blue Flag," and "Marching Through Georgia" amidst applause and cheering. The Society of the Army of the Cumberland ventured even farther south of the Mason and Dixon line for some of its meetings. Its gathering in 1889 featured a Blue and Gray reunion on Chickamauga Battlefield, with addresses by survivors of both sides and the smoking of peace pipes made of local wood.

At the same time the Confederate veterans, though not yet fully organized, often expressed their loyalty to the nation, either through representatives at meetings of Northern soldiers or at their own gatherings. One of the R. E. Lee Camp's delegates to the Baltimore assembly of the Society of the Army of the Potomac asserted that were Lee alive, he would be there fraternizing, while another proclaimed that "The Star Spangled Banner" now thrilled him the way that "Dixie" and "Maryland, My Maryland" had twenty years before. The assassination of Garfield evoked many testimonials of grief for this national calamity. As the president of the Confederate Survivors' Association of Augusta, Georgia expressed it, the members were anxious to prove that "the Northern hand which smote, so far from finding countenance for the hellish deed from Southern hearts, encounters naught but abhorrence, condemnation, and utter detestation." [12] This same group, "remembering him now as the generous victor," also extended its official sympathies to Grant when he fell ill. [13]

Despite these evidences of improved feeling, at other times the societies of Civil War veterans served to keep alive unpleasant memories. A condescending attitude frequently marred the best of intentions. One member of the Society of the Army of the Cumberland did not display great tact when he publicly proclaimed that the ex-Confederates "are beginning to see that it was a mighty good

[12] Col. Charles C. Jones, Jr., *An Address Delivered Before the Confederate Survivors' Association 1882* (Augusta, Ga., 1882), p. 3.

[13] Col. Charles C. Jones, Jr., *An Address Delivered Before the Confederate Survivors' Association 1885* (Augusta, Ga., 1885), p. 8.

thing for them, as well as for the civilization of all the ages, that they got the terrible whipping we gave them." [14] Others were endeavoring to be friendly when they declared that the war had been beneficial to the South because it abolished the economic burden of slavery, but General Sherman did not express the idea very happily when he thanked God that removal of the institution at last enabled Southern men "to earn an honest living." [15]

The emphasis of many veterans upon the South's criminal responsibility for the war likewise did not improve relations. "Comrades, remember that forgiveness simply relieves the offender of the penalty," a commander of the Oregon G.A.R. warned, "it does not relieve him of the crime." [16] Strong suspicion lingered as to the sincerity of Southern loyalty. In the words of a head of the Sons of Veterans, "the treasonable sentiments that come to us occasionally from the South" made him unwilling "to beat my sword into a plow share and lay aside the habiliments of war and teach 'Peace on earth and good will to men.'" [17] The veterans' papers, whose existence to a large extent depended upon a vivid memory of war days, often contributed to this feeling.

Even when willing to forgive the average Southern soldier, the veterans still vented their emotions upon the leaders of the Confederacy, especially Jefferson Davis. Not even his death softened this hostility. "At last Jeff Davis is dead," the *Grand Army Record* reported. "Well, we are finding no fault with the Lord on that account." [18] Several departments of the G.A.R. congratulated Secretary of War Redfield Proctor for not making any recognition of his predecessor's death. On the pages of the veterans' journals, at least, Robert E. Lee fared no better. To the *Grand Army Sentinel* he "was a breeder of human cattle, and was ready like other East Virginians, to shed human blood, if necessary, for the 'liberty' of human

[14] Society of the Army of the Cumberland, *Fifteenth Reunion 1883* (Cincinnati, 1884), p. 102.

[15] Society of the Army of the Tennessee, *Report of the Proceedings at the Fifteenth Annual Meeting 1882* (n.p., n.d.), p. 369.

[16] Department of Oregon, Grand Army of the Republic, *Proceedings of the Sixth Annual Encampment 1887* (Portland, 1887), p. 43.

[17] Sons of Veterans, U.S.A., *Proceedings of the Fifth National Encampment 1886* (n.p., n.d.), p. 3.

[18] *Grand Army Record*, V (Dec. 1889), 4.

slavery." [19] Other periodicals, recalling that "he was a traitor to his flag and country," protested the movement in the Southern states to make his birthday a public holiday.[20]

The veterans' reactions to certain specific incidents often revealed a strong undercurrent of suspicion and hostility, though the fact that they so often took the form of protests against excessive fraternalism suggests that they were increasingly representing a minority opinion. Not all Union soldiers welcomed the tendency for association with former enemies. "Short of abject apology and admission that the defence of the Union was a crime," the *Grand Army Review* observed bitterly of such joint reunions, "nothing has been left unsaid by our gushing comrades at these pleasant gatherings to express our sorrow at having been compelled to use the bullet and bayonet." [21]

Die-hard elements consistently blocked proposals that the Grand Army hold its national encampment in the former Confederacy. For four successive years, beginning in 1883, Nashville failed in its efforts to become the meeting place. Subsequent bids by Chattanooga, Dallas, and Atlanta were equally unsuccessful. The discussions revealed that many veterans disliked excessive sentimentality toward Southerners. A Massachusetts delegate protested that "there are some of us yet, who don't like our blue and grey too thoroughly mixed in these Grand Army Encampments; and we feel that when we meet together here, we don't want to have somebody come on to the platform and tell us that we are forgiven for what we did." [22] The following year another member won applause when he deplored the "touching allusions to the Confederate soldiers as have been made here to-day." He called upon the meeting to remember "that the fifty thousand graves we are asked to visit in Tennessee were caused by those men who are now asking us to visit them." [23]

The existence of conflicting emotions among Grand Army mem-

[19] "A War Incident Recalled—the Lees," *Grand Army Sentinel,* II (May 20, 1886), 324.

[20] *Grand Army Record,* IV (Sept. 1889), 4; *National Tribune* (Washington, D.C.), Sept. 19, 1889.

[21] "A Tortured Phrase," *Grand Army Review,* III (Sept. 1887), 555.

[22] Grand Army of the Republic, *Journal of the Eighteenth Annual Session of the National Encampment 1884* (Philadelphia, 1884), p. 218.

[23] Grand Army of the Republic, *Journal of the Nineteenth Annual Session of the National Encampment 1885* (Toledo, 1885), p. 144.

bers became even more apparent in 1884, when the Robert E. Lee Camp of Confederate Veterans at Richmond asked the order's aid in raising funds for a Confederate home. Perplexed as to whether he should give his endorsement, the commander-in-chief sought the advice of the heads of state branches. The response was a varied one. Some agreed with Indiana's chief "that the victors should heed the cry that comes from the vanquished," [24] but others felt that posts as such should make no contributions. Colorado's commander replied indignantly that the Grand Army "does not fraternize with those who attempted to destroy the Union. It extends charity to comrades, not to enemies. . . . It also encourages *justice* to all men and there is not much said in the rules and regulations about mercy." He therefore declared that the proper reply to the appeal "is to consign it to the flames." [25] Two years later, when some G.A.R. men proposed that the federal government establish homes for Confederates, the District of Columbia's head opposed placing "a premium upon disloyalty and rebellion." [26]

The irreconcilables also disliked the growing custom of some of their comrades, especially in the South, of participating in the unveiling of Confederate monuments. The commander of the Colorado Grand Army wished "to see no monuments over the grave of a dead Confederacy. Let it lie in the grave where we laid it 'unwept, unhonored and unsung.' It should be the mission of the Grand Army to encourage a sentiment which will make men anxious to conceal the fact that they fought in the rebel army." [27] In 1887 the national encampment voted that no G.A.R. post or department should encourage or countenance "the erection of monuments in honor of men who distinguished themselves by their services in the cause of treason and rebellion." [28]

These elements still protested, though less frequently than in earlier years, the decoration of Confederate graves on Memorial Day.

[24] Department of Indiana, Grand Army of the Republic, *Journal of the Fifth Annual Session 1884* (Indianapolis, 1884), p. 246.

[25] Department of Colorado, Grand Army of the Republic, *Journal of the 6th Annual Session 1885* (Longmont, Colo., 1885), p. 14.

[26] Department of the Potomac, Grand Army of the Republic, *Proceedings of the Eighteenth Annual Encampment 1886* (Washington, 1886), pp. 18–19.

[27] Colo. G.A.R., *Journal 1885,* pp. 14–15.

[28] Grand Army of the Republic, *Journal of the Twenty-third Annual Session of the National Encampment 1889* (St. Louis, 1889), p. 169.

"Let no mawkish sentiment, no false feeling of chivalry," implored a commander of the Minnesota branch, "induce us to step aside on that day to cast a flower upon the grave of one who fought for the disruption of the Union." [29] When a similar statement by the California commander in 1887 produced considerable controversy, nearly all the department's posts upheld him. Others objected to the appointment of ex-Confederates to federal offices after the return of the Democrats to power in 1885 and especially denounced Cleveland's naming L. Q. C. Lamar to the Supreme Court in 1887.[30]

The incident which did the most to stir up all the smoldering embers of sectionalism was Grover Cleveland's attempt in June 1887 to return the captured Confederate battle flags to the Southern states. During the evening of June 15 word of this order reached a "brilliantly lighted" hall at Fourth Avenue and 129th Street in the Harlem district of New York City, where shortly before Commander-in-Chief Fairchild had arrived in "full uniform and empty coat sleeve" for a reception tendered him by two hundred members of a local post. The verbal explosion that followed can only be understood in terms of the terrific emotional shock that the news gave a group of veterans gathered to commemorate the war. Fairchild later informed his wife that he had "never seen a body of men more excited than were the old soldiers there. They, many of them, stood with their eyes full of tears." As for Fairchild himself, "Hardly ever in my life have I been so wrought up. . . . I fairly trembled with excitement—& when called upon to say something my heart was so full that my lips gave utterance to the most bitter sentence that ever came from them." [31] In his emotion the man who had rushed to aid the sufferers at Charleston the year before uttered a malediction that rang across the country: "May God palsy the hand that wrote the order! May God palsy the brain that conceived, and may God palsy the tongue that dictated it!" His fervor infected the audience: "There was a moment's silence. A wild hurrah, like the old battle cry went up. For a moment nothing could be done. Men cheered

---

[29] Department of Minnesota, Grand Army of the Republic, *Journal of the Annual Sessions of the Department Encampment 1881–1885* (Minneapolis, 1885), p. 90.

[30] Elmer Edward Noyes, "A History of the Grand Army of the Republic in Ohio from 1866 to 1900," Ph.D. dissertation, Ohio State University (1945), pp. 217–218.

[31] Fairchild to Mrs. Fairchild, June 19, 1887, Fairchild Papers.

and hurrahed, wild with the old spirit so thoroughly aroused." [32]

Fairchild's extremism certainly stemmed largely from the contagion of being with the very element among the ex-soldiers whose active participation in a veterans' organization suggests particular susceptibility to such emotions. But though he later conceded, "I did not know what I was saying until the words were out and gone," even on second thought he did not regret his choice of language, "for the very extravagance of the denunciations sent them at once to the farthest corner of our country & called attention to the outrage contemplated." [33] In fact, he eventually concluded that "the good Lord" had put the expressions into his mouth.

Whether or not his phraseology had divine inspiration, instinctively he had been an accurate spokesman for the Grand Army members. Regardless of the platitudes they had previously uttered about the spirit of reunion, this crisis stirred up half-forgotten emotions among nearly all veterans at a time when they were still smarting from Cleveland's numerous and pungent vetoes of private pension bills and his recent rebuff to the Dependent Pension Bill. Old soldiers descended by the score upon the Fifth Avenue Hotel, where the commander-in-chief was staying, to shake his hand and congratulate him. Typical comments in New York City were "Hurrah for Fairchild! " "Good for the old Boy! " "Three cheers for our commander! " and "No surrender of the flags that belong to the nation." [34] "You have made a *personal* friend of the 15,000 comrades in New York and Brooklyn—every one," a member of the Harlem post assured Fairchild, adding, with what would seem considerable understatement, "The comrades of Post 182 will never forget your visit." [35]

Outside of New York the members likewise backed their chief. As Fairchild continued his travels, he found that "the 'boys' every where overwhelm me with their thanks, & hundreds of others too—they nearly shake my arm off." [36] Other Grand Army men hastened to pen their approval, though among them was a high proportion

[32] *New York Herald,* June 16, 1887.
[33] Fairchild to Mrs. Fairchild, June 19, 1887, Fairchild Papers.
[34] *New York Herald,* June 17, 1887.
[35] William C. Reddy to Fairchild, June 17, 1887, Fairchild Papers.
[36] Fairchild to Mrs. Fairchild, June 28, 1887, *ibid.*

of persons already known as opponents of the Democratic party. Alonzo Williams of Providence reported that at a recent meeting, "The boys from Conn. Maine, Mass. and R. I. who filled the hall responded to every sentiment and cheered to the echo, especially every allusion to your name." [37] One of the order's adherents in Washington, who also happened to be a not entirely disinterested claims agent, informed Fairchild that he "had organized a movement to seize the first package of flags and prevent their shipment from the City. Had plenty of volunteers, but the 'back down' saved us trouble." [38]

Not only did the governors of Ohio and Iowa forward the protests of the Grand Army of their states to Cleveland (who, incidentally, revoked the order almost immediately), and a number of department commanders endorse Fairchild's stand, but the leaders of affiliated organizations added their outcries. The founder of the Ladies of the G.A.R. wrote Cleveland that she believed him "untrue to the cause of freedom, country and God," while the commander-in-chief of the Sons of Veterans, after warning the entire membership in a "general order" that "The incidents of the last few days show that there is a volcano under our Capitol which might make a fatal eruption and again bring war upon us as a Nation," rejoiced that "we have true men, positive men, loyal, not only to their country, but to God, who spoke with the lightning of the telegraph and subdued the fire while it was yet a spark." [39] Once again this identification of their viewpoint with that of the deity shows how sharply the President's order had struck at his critics' basic emotional values.

Perhaps the most startling demonstration of the powerful prejudices aroused was that on this particular matter Cleveland alienated even the Democratic veterans who in other conflicts between him and the Grand Army had usually come to his support. Though one wrote, "I notice that comrad Fairchild wants God to paralyze you. Dont be allairmed I am allmost as wicked as he is probably—and my prayer is just the opposite of his," [40] such outstanding Demo-

[37] Alonzo Williams to Fairchild, July 6, 1887, *ibid.*

[38] E. W. Whitaker to Fairchild, June 18, 1887, *ibid.*

[39] Mrs. Edward Roby to Grover Cleveland, July 12, 1894, Grover Cleveland Papers, Library of Congress; Sons of Veterans, U.S.A., *Proceedings of the Sixth National Encampment 1887* (n.p., n.d.), p. 24.

[40] Charles G. Lewis to Cleveland, July 8, 1887, Cleveland Papers.

cratic ex-soldiers as Generals Horatio C. King and Daniel E. Sickles expressed indignant dismay, while almost approaching Fairchild's bitterness was the comment of Joseph W. Kay of the Veterans' Rights Union: "If it should be so, if he has issued such an order, and that order is to be executed, then let him go to the hell he has made for himself." [41] A veteran's son in Bellaire, Ohio, who claimed never to have "voted other than the Democratic ticket," now charged that "Cleveland would insult his *Mother* to show his hatred of the Union soldier." [42] Clearly there was an upsurge of emotion that affected most veterans regardless of party. Fairchild merely expressed it more violently and then received more publicity because of his position as the head of an organization claiming a near-monopoly on patriotism.

Yet Fairchild's subsequent conduct soon indicated his outburst had been a temporary aberration. At the national encampment in September he went out of his way to assure a public gathering of St. Louis citizens that the veterans had no use for "waving the bloody shirt." In his official report he reverted to his words of four years earlier with his insistence that within the Grand Army there was no "bitter feeling of hate for those of our fellow-citizens who, once in arms against us, but now being loyal, have long ago taken their old-time place in our hearts, never, we devoutly hope, to be removed therefrom." [43] Two years later he labored in vain to have the national encampment approve his proposal that Congress mark Confederate as well as Union positions at Gettysburg "and thus show to the world that our brave boys met and repulsed a 'foe worthy of their steel.'" [44] Such was the schizophrenia of the decade, or, more accurately, its sentimentality, which could be excited to contradictory positions with equal facility.

Meanwhile the many Southern members among the Mexican War Veterans made that group more of a force for sectional reunion than

[41] "Most Righteous Wrath," *Grand Army Review*, III (July 1887), 494.
[42] J. E. Peterson to Fairchild, June 18, 1887, Fairchild Papers.
[43] G.A.R., *Journal 1887*, p. 50.
[44] G.A.R., *Journal 1889*, p. 169. Therefore it hardly seems fair to classify Fairchild among the "insincere demagogues" who took political advantage of this situation, as Allan Nevins appears to do in *Grover Cleveland* (New York, 1932), p. 333. For a full treatment of this issue, see Wallace E. Davies, "Was Lucius Fairchild a Demagogue?" *Wisconsin Magazine of History*, XXXI (June 1948), 418–428.

were the Civil War associations. Since it was truly a national society, delegates from both North and South attended its annual sessions held on both sides of the Mason and Dixon line, in Norfolk, Nashville, and Fort Worth as well as in Columbus, Indianapolis, and Des Moines. To its assembly in 1881 it invited not only Grant, Garfield, and John A. Logan but also Jefferson Davis, General Pierre G. T. Beauregard, and Governor Alfred H. Colquitt of Georgia, none of whom seems to have accepted. In 1887 the *Vedette* hoped that Davis would attend the forthcoming convention at Fort Worth. "No member of the National Association will be more cordially greeted by his old comrades from all sections of the country," it promised, "than the gallant leader of the Mississippi rifles at Monterey and Buena Vista." [45]

During these meetings bands played "Dixie" and speakers predicted that the association would contribute heavily to the spirit of unity that should prevail among all Americans. In 1877 the Michigan survivors debated not whether to endorse President Rutherford B. Hayes's withdrawal of federal troops from the South but how eulogistic the resolution should be. The only consideration dampening their enthusiasm was that too pro-Southern an utterance might damage their chances for pension legislation. A few years later the president of the Mexican War veterans in the Norfolk-Portsmouth area of Virginia urged that the 1881 national convention be held in Washington so that the veterans could join in Garfield's inaugural as a step toward "killing fanatic bigotry and sectionalism." [46]

But sometimes the association's large Southern following impelled the *Vedette* to criticize any measures directed against the region of the former Confederacy with a vigor which may have injured the cause of reunion as much as it forwarded it. Proposals for a federal force bill to supervise elections especially aroused its wrath. "A true soldier considers it a glory to risk his life under the flag of his country against a foreign foe," it announced, "but to be detailed as a constable to shoot down his fellow-citizens, from whom he derives his pay and rations, for exercising his right to vote as he pleases, is an insult to his manhood and vocation." [47]

[45] *Vedette* (Washington, D.C.), Oct. 1887.
[46] *Ibid.*, Dec. 15, 1880.
[47] *Ibid.*, April 15, 1880.

When a Vermont Congressman opposed a Mexican War pension bill because it would aid many former Confederates, the paper resorted to typical vituperation. Declaring that the state had always been given to "Innate hatred of the whole southern people," it argued that "level-headed Christians usually listen, with a feeling akin to pity, to the inane gabble about their 'loy'lty' to the Government, and opposition to 'traitors and rebels,' because those played out terms of opprobrium so illy conceal the mental infirmity which so largely prevails in the people around the Green Mountains." It suggested that the state be traded to Canada "in payment of some ancient fish indemnity" and then "be put on exhibition, as a fossil annex, at some future World's Fair, if well fenced in and properly guarded." [48] Meanwhile, the as yet poorly organized Confederate veterans did not constitute a force for sectional bitterness, but they scarcely needed to do so through their own leagues when they could express their views so freely through a bona fide patriotic association of the veterans of an earlier war.

If the record of the ex-soldiers' groups in the eighties is therefore a confusing and contradictory one, the nineties presents quite a different picture. The organizations professedly devoted to the nation's welfare then decided that patriotism required harmonizing sectional differences rather than preserving wartime bitterness. Though the veterans retained many remnants of the old animosity, they increasingly responded to the rising nationalist spirit of the day. Meanwhile, the new hereditary societies consciously tried to bridge the gulf between the North and the South.

Not surprisingly, fanatics who still waved the bloody shirt found their last haven within the Civil War associations. In various statements former Union soldiers showed a lingering suspicion of the South's loyalty and insisted upon recognition of the righteousness of their cause. Rutherford B. Hayes noted in regard to the Ohio Grand Army encampment of 1891, "The only thing to disturb was the disposition to scold the South—to discuss irritating topics in an ill-tempered way." [49] The very existence of such an organization

---

[48] *Ibid.*, Jan. 1880.
[49] Charles Richard Williams, ed., *Diary and Letters of Rutherford Birchard Hayes* (Columbus, Ohio, 1922–1926), IV, 1.

as the Ex-Prisoners of War Association tended to keep unpleasant memories fresh. The badge of the Massachusetts branch, according to the *Grand Army Record,* represented a supine Union soldier, the "only son of a widow, who is herself, at that moment, tilling the farm in the Old Bay State," who had escaped over the stockade but who has been tracked down and whose "scanty and poor red blood" is about to be sucked "with bloodhound avidity into the maw of this symbol of Rebel Christianity and mercy—a bloodhound to devour a starved, emaciated and helpless Union Soldier." [50] Certainly such reminders did little to promote good feeling. But it was to the advantage of such groups to exploit these recollections if they were to attract a following and secure their legislative demands; their sentiments were not necessarily representative of the veterans at large.

Although the old soldiers frequently insisted that they had forgiven the South, an attitude whose implications were sometimes more irritating than soothing, several specific issues always aroused the ire of extremists. To begin with, there was often a complete failure to comprehend the psychology of the Lost Cause. "I am unable to understand," complained one of the G.A.R. commanders-in-chief, "why so many who, like the prodigal son, wandered from their father's house, will persist in living upon husks, cherishing love for a cause that is forever lost, and refuse to return and eat the bread of loyalty under the Stars and Stripes." [51] This inability to see how loyalty to the Confederate past could exist together with loyalty to the American present led the chairman of the New York W.R.C.'s committee on school histories to seek the expulsion of songs like "Maryland, My Maryland" and "The Bonnie Blue Flag" from public schools.

Particularly strong opposition developed toward the erection of monuments to Confederate leaders or the Southern dead. In the words of the *Grand Army Record,* the practice "makes treason and loyalty equally commendable." [52] Concerning a proposed joint

[50] *Grand Army Record,* VI (Oct. 1891), 1.
[51] Grand Army of the Republic, *Journal of the Twenty-Eighth National Encampment 1894* (Boston, 1894), p. 58.
[52] "Rebel Monuments," *Grand Army Record,* VI (Aug. 1891), 5.

memorial to the two great military chieftains of the war, the same paper insisted that "no Grand Army man in good standing can honorably lend his name to any movement which shall dignify to posterity the name of the traitor Robert E. Lee, or shall make him the equal of the loyal, victorious Grant." [53]

Great excitement arose in 1895 after the unveiling of a Confederate monument in Chicago on what seemed to many Grand Army men the most inappropriate of dates, Memorial Day. "Comrades, the blood of our martyred Lincoln, of our noble Grant and of all the men who struggled for freedom's cause," declared the commander of the Massachusetts G.A.R., "cries out in protest against this blasphemy." [54] Other proposals which aroused irritation were the government's allowing the Confederates to mark their positions and honor their heroes in military parks such as Chickamauga and the suggestion of a Confederate Day at the Chicago World's Fair.

The growing number of Blue and Gray reunions, though proof of the rising tide of reconciliation, also produced a certain amount of criticism. The *American Tribune* attacked such gatherings as "sickly and spurious sentimentality and an insult to the memory of the Union dead and to the living veterans," while the *National Tribune* asked how could the Northern veterans "fraternize with organizations of the very men who did all in their power to destroy the Government, and whose only bond of union is comradeship in that terrible disloyalty?" [55] The matter came to a head in 1895 when Charles A. Dana proposed to Commander-in-Chief Ivan Walker that the Grand Army join in a parade and reunion of all Civil War veterans of both sides in New York. Walker replied that it was "the unalterable conviction of the Grand Army of the Republic" that the North had been right and the South wrong and that "no sentimental nor commercial efforts to efface these radical distinctions should be encouraged by any true patriot," and the project was abandoned.[56]

[53] *Ibid.,* V (June 1890), 4.

[54] Department of Massachusetts, Grand Army of the Republic, *Journal of the Thirtieth Annual Encampment 1896* (Boston, 1896), p. 270.

[55] *American Tribune* (Indianapolis), Oct. 16, 1891; *National Tribune,* Sept. 24, 1891.

[56] Grand Army of the Republic, *Journal of the Thirtieth National Encampment 1896* (Indianapolis, 1896), p. 58.

But the practice which perhaps aroused the warmest emotions among the more excitable veterans was the public display of the Stars and Bars. The 1890 national encampment of the Grand Army declared that it "is an affront to patriotism, encourages disloyalty, and lessens respect for our government and the stars and stripes" and should be forbidden by federal law.[57] In November 1891, Commander-in-Chief John Palmer issued an official mandate against members in uniform participating in any public affair at which the Confederate banner was carried. Again a misunderstanding of the Southern mind led him to suspect that "there still lurks in the hearts of a few a desire, by the display of that flag, to fire the hearts of the young generation of the south to rebellion." [58] This ruling, known as Order No. 4, attracted so much attention that in the next few months Palmer explained his action to a number of state encampments, many of which then endorsed his position. The national encampment of 1892 also upheld him.

Actually, however, the most determined wavers of the bloody shirt were the veterans' papers, which possibly hoped that extremism would attract more subscribers. The *American Tribune* kept alive the canard that the South had sent clothing infected with yellow fever to the North during the war and insisted, "The ex-Rebels are still disloyal at heart and would engage in another rebellion as they did in 1861 were the conditions favorable." [59] As its contribution to sectional bitterness, the *National Tribune* ran articles on the atrocities of Andersonville Prison and finally reprinted a book its editor, McElroy, had written on the subject twenty years earlier. The *Grand Army Record* objected to "saintly slopping over Robert E. Lee" and wanted a wider dispersal of a picture of Andersonville among young people. *"Why is this educational picture never seen elsewhere than in the Post room of the G.A.R?"* it asked plaintively.[60]

The Confederate associations were still not yet strongly enough established to contribute much toward sectional animosity. They

[57] Grand Army of the Republic, *Journal of the Twenty-fourth Annual Session of the National Encampment 1890* (Detroit, 1890), pp. 210, 212.

[58] Grand Army of the Republic, *Journal of the Twenty-Sixth National Encampment 1892* (Albany, 1892), p. 312.

[59] *American Tribune*, June 23, 1892.

[60] "Andersonville," *Grand Army Record*, VI (Dec. 1891), 4.

had hesitated to organize until this decade and perhaps were cautiously testing public reaction to their very existence. Actually, in the long run the bitterest sentiments were to come not from the veterans but, as might have been expected, from the United Daughters of the Confederacy. The Southerners nevertheless made it clear that they had no apologies to make. Especially they protested the term "War of the Rebellion." As a substitute the U.C.V. suggested "The Civil War Between the States," while the *Confederate Veteran* favored "The Confederate War." But the U.D.C. turned to a volume by the Confederacy's vice-president, Alexander H. Stephens, and championed "The War Between the States" as the proper expression for loyal Southerners to employ and even induced the D.A.R.'s Continental Congress to endorse it.

These groups expressed their devotion to the Lost Cause by their reverence for its leaders and especially for the family of Jefferson Davis. The U.D.C. labored to have Southern states declare the birthdays of Davis and Lee legal holidays. The U.C.V. always made a great fuss over Winnie Davis, whose annual appearances set off pandemonium and whose death in 1898 produced widespread expressions of grief among Confederate organizations. The *Confederate Veteran* then started a movement to dub Davis' only surviving child, Mrs. Margaret Hayes, the "Daughter of the South." At the U.D.C. reunion in 1899 Mrs. Hayes and her son, Jefferson Hayes Davis (who had had his name legally twisted about), received considerable homage, and every state division was urged to name Mrs. Davis honorary life president and Mrs. Hayes honorary life member.

All of this, of course, indicates that a considerable residue of divisive influences was still at work well into the nineties. Another potentially explosive issue, the racial question, may serve as a touchstone of shifting sentiment that was leading to greater harmony between the dominant white populations of the two sections. In this decade the Southern states enacted their constitutional restrictions upon Negro suffrage, the capstone in their system of economic, social, and political subordination for the ex-slaves. The United Confederate Veterans viewed the tendency favorably, and at the close of the century one speaker suggested that the difficulties which the United States was having with a different race in the Philippines might cause "our Northern brethren to meet us hereafter rather in a spirit of inquiry than of rebuke." [61]

Already there were indications that such was becoming the case. The tradition of supporting Negro rights did not vanish entirely from the hearts of Northern veterans. At its 1899 meeting the Union Veterans' Union condemned the disfranchising movement in the South and the Grand Army occasionally insisted upon equal rights for Negroes and attacked lynchings. Nevertheless, there were signs that the veterans were growing more sympathetic to the Southern white viewpoint. At least two G.A.R. encampments thought it unwise to adopt resolutions against lynchings in Georgia in 1899, and even the *American Tribune* admitted that for regions where the Negroes were ignorant and yet outnumbered the whites it did not know the solution. "In some districts in the South," it asserted, "the condition is one of absolute menace to the whites." [62]

This was indeed a far cry from the crusading Radicalism of the Reconstruction days, but even more revealing was the order's embarrassed reaction to the efforts of its Southern branches to bar colored members.[63] By the early nineties there were more than three hundred G.A.R. posts throughout the former Confederacy which had enrolled nearly eleven thousand veterans. Their response to Negro applications dramatically illustrated the swift accommodation of Northern immigrants to Southern mores. In their anxiety to build up the society among the whites and at the same time to win acceptance in their new homes, the local leaders quickly decided to introduce the color line.

In Louisiana, where the issue first became acute, the white members most clearly revealed the economic and social compulsions for conforming to the racial arrangements which they found below the Mason and Dixon line. In 1883 survivors of the Union Army formed the state's first post in New Orleans "at a time when it was a disgrace to be seen with an army button, or the badge of the Grand

---

[61] United Confederate Veterans, *Minutes of the Ninth Annual Meeting 1899* (New Orleans, 1900), pp. 26–27.

[62] *American Tribune*, Aug. 1, 1890.

[63] For a more thorough account of this episode, see Wallace E. Davies, "The Problem of Race Segregation in the Grand Army of the Republic," *Journal of Southern History*, XIII (Aug. 1947), 354–372.

Army of the Republic." Organization of a Department of Louisiana and Mississippi followed the next year, and gradually, the members later reported, "we made ourselves respected individually, and made the Grand Army an honorable organization, so recognized amongst the strongest and worst confederates of Louisiana." [64] Since they thought that this cordiality depended on their remaining solely a white association, they were almost unanimous in their refusal to admit Negroes.

The matter came out into the open in 1891, when the state commander, apparently more out of pique than principle, authorized the formation of several colored posts. The white members' immediate protests disclosed how sensitive they had become to their new environment. The department's senior vice-commander frankly pointed out that the Southern veterans lived in a region of "peculiar social conditions . . . which they are powerless to change." If a white man mingled equally with Negroes, he was "barred from all association with people of the white race and practically excluded from the privilege of earning a living," while his wife and children had to face "the finger of scorn and derision." [65] Others revealed that they had no objections to this attitude. One member in New Orleans asked why Southerners who had been coöperating in Memorial Day observances should continue to do so "when they are compelled by virtue of their friendship to us to march with those whom neither they nor the majority of us consider their social equals?" [66] About the same time developments in Alabama and Georgia indicated that this expressed the sentiments of Grand Army men elsewhere in the Deep South. At no point was there any question of whites and blacks belonging to the same posts; the issue was whether there could even be segregated posts within the same state organization.

Louisiana's delegation arrived at the 1891 national encampment in Detroit threatening that within a year there would not be a white member left in the Grand Army south of the Potomac if it was not allowed to form a separate white Department of the Gulf. "Those

---

[64] Grand Army of the Republic, *Journal of the Twenty-fifth National Encampment 1891* (Rutland, Vt., 1891), p. 259.

[65] Department of Louisiana and Mississippi, Grand Army of the Republic, *Proceedings of the Eighth Annual Encampment 1891* (New Orleans, 1891), p. 16.

[66] *Springfield* (Mass.) *Republican,* Jan. 11, 1890, quoted in "Certain Sectional Matters," *Public Opinion,* VIII (Jan. 18, 1890), 354.

of you who have never lived any length of time in the South, can have no conception of the state of society there," one of them announced flatly in words that echoed one of the oldest Southern racial arguments, ". . . we live in a country that we have chosen as our homes. We have made up our minds to live there. Our children are growing up there. They marry. It is right that we should conform to the social laws and rules that surround us." [67]

Such unvarnished endorsements of racial discrimination within the Grand Army of the Republic seemed so incongruous that they received national publicity and occasioned widespread discussion. A few leaders and scattered meetings in Massachusetts, Illinois, Oregon, and even the border state of Maryland denounced efforts to bar veterans because of color, and the *Grand Army Record* remained true to Boston's abolitionist tradition. The cautious attitude of the order's national officials, however, suggested that others had begun to shift ground. Indeed, the Louisiana members claimed that at the 1889 national encampment the newly elected commander-in-chief, Russell A. Alger, had privately advised them against forming colored posts. Certainly his public pronouncements at Boston the following year had reflected a politician's evasiveness: "It is the same question that today is disturbing many localities in the southern part of this country," he observed noncommittally, "and which will require patience and concessions from all parties to settle." [68] There was clearly a growing sentiment among Northerners for separate Negro departments in the South. Even the most prominent of the veterans' papers, the *National Tribune,* whose publication in Washington perhaps gave it a perspective different from the Boston of the *Grand Army Record,* felt that to insist upon equality would be to "cram an obnoxious arrangement upon people without any advantage whatever." [69]

At the time of the crucial session of 1891 the commander-in-chief was Wheelock Veazey, who came from Miss Ophelia's home state of Vermont and revealed much of the same sense of bafflement in coping with the Southern racial problem as had Mrs. Stowe's fictional character. Under the impression that it was agreeable to the

[67] G.A.R., *Journal 1891,* pp. 259–260.
[68] G.A.R., *Journal 1890,* p. 6.
[69] *National Tribune,* Dec. 6, 1890.

Negroes involved, he recommended a separate department as the solution. To his surprised dismay, this proposal merely produced another storm. The practice at each Grand Army convention was to refer the commander-in-chief's address to a committee to report its approval or disapproval. At Detroit all but one member of this group, which included three former commanders-in-chief, condemned Veazey's suggestion as furthering the color barrier. The lone dissenter, W. S. Decker of Denver, insisted that the issue could never be settled except "according to the condition of affairs as we find them in Louisiana, Mississippi, South Carolina and the southern States. You must not judge the condition of affairs down there to be such as you see in the State of Michigan and other northern States." [70] Such an outburst of hisses greeted this statement that the presiding officer had to threaten to clear the galleries. After a considerable display of oratory, the meeting finally voted down the idea of a separate department.

Early in the nineties, in other words, the order was unwilling to make a formal abandonment of the principle of racial equality, but enforcement was another matter. In Louisiana the upshot was that several white posts surrendered their charters and all but one declined in size, and it became predominantly a Negro department. No sooner had the question been resolved in Louisiana, largely by the withdrawal of the white members, than it arose in Texas and Alabama. But as the decade wore on it was apparent that the organization had learned to be more wary in handling the problem. Its leaders now accepted the bland assurances of local officials that the subterfuge of barring Negroes through various technicalities did not constitute racial discrimination, and this formula made it unnecessary to probe into an increasingly awkward situation. About all that the national organization could really accomplish, as it fully realized by the turn of the century, was to make such gestures of appeasement to its colored members as electing Charles H. Shute, a Louisiana Negro, junior commander-in-chief in 1894.

The problem of admitting Negroes without losing its white supporters was equally perplexing to the Woman's Relief Corps. In 1897 the Kentucky and Maryland branches asked the national convention for separate departments on the ground that white women would

[70] G.A.R., *Journal 1891*, p. 253.

not join an organization that included Negroes. Once again, many of the society's leaders in the North showed a willingness to recognize and accept this situation. A former national secretary, Mrs. Harriette Reed, confident that "as a Massachusetts woman, no one will accuse me of drawing the color line," reminded the meeting that the Maryland branch had started out with "the very best women in the city of Baltimore," but was steadily losing them because of the "peculiar conditions" there. In the same vein as her male colleagues she insisted, "it is this *condition* and not a *theory* that we are now discussing . . . it is not Ohio, it is not Massachusetts, it is not Maine that we are considering. The conditions of life are entirely different than with us. . . ." Her verdict was that "there can never be in our day a Department of white and colored Corps working together harmoniously." [71] But like the G.A.R., the women were reluctant to repudiate the Negroes officially and, listening to the pleas of Mrs. Annie Wittenmyer and a prominent Negro member, Mrs. Julia Layton (a former slave), they tabled the petition.

But, once again like the Grand Army, the unwillingness of the national organization to sanction the color line did nothing to alter the determination of the Southern whites to avoid social association with the Negroes. Though denied a formal separation, in practice Maryland's white members carefully seated the Negroes in one corner of convention halls and at different tables for luncheons. When Kentucky and Maryland appealed again for a division of white and colored units in 1900, more Northerners now agreed with a past national president from Indianapolis that "We cannot wipe out this prejudice of the Southern States" and granted the request.[72]

These episodes within both the G.A.R. and W.R.C. revealed that by the nineties there was no unanimous belief that in joining patriotic societies commemorating the ideals of the Civil War their adherents had incurred any obligation to defend Negro rights against the dominant Southern social arrangements. While some members in the North did deprecate racial discrimination, many others, from

[71] Woman's Relief Corps, Auxiliary to the Grand Army of the Republic, *Journal of the Fifteenth National Convention 1897* (Boston, 1897), pp. 322–323.
[72] Woman's Relief Corps, Auxiliary to the Grand Army of the Republic, *Journal of the Eighteenth National Convention 1900* (Boston, 1900), pp. 294–297.

above the Mason and Dixon line as well as below, obviously felt that the time had come to accept segregation. As long as one ignored its implications for the future of the Negroes, such harmonizing of views among the whites of both sections marked an important step on the road to reunion.

This significant shift in attitude was one reflection of the predominant theme of these years, a growing spirit of reconciliation. The veterans' meetings now produced many more statements tending toward reunion than toward continuing sectionalism. "Is there a thought of bitterness within us towards those who fought against us?" a speaker asked the Society of the Army of the Tennessee in 1896 and then answered his own question. "Not one . . . the war is over and we cherish no ill towards any American citizen. We cherish only love and affection for all American citizens and for everything American." [73]

An increasing number of Grand Army leaders reported cordial welcomes from ex-Confederates on trips to the South. "My receptions there will ever be a warm spot in my memory," declared Commander-in-Chief T. S. Clarkson in 1897. "I met no warmer grasps, no heartier Godspeeds in patriotic work than from our once enemies, now friends." [74] Another sign of the times was the growing number of Confederate veterans who addressed meetings of the G.A.R. and of the army societies, usually deploring continued sectional bitterness and asserting their love for the flag and the national government. A typical occasion was the Society of the Army of the Tennessee's banquet at Chicago in 1891, where Henry Watterson replied to the toast, "The War Is Over—Let Us Have Peace." When a statue to General John A. Logan was to be unveiled at Chicago, the Grand Army's commander-in-chief invited the head of the U.C.V., General Gordon, to ride with him "that all the world might see that the war was over." [75]

A further indication of a new spirit was the changed reaction to proposals that the Grand Army meet below the Mason and Dixon line. Early in 1894 Louisville started an intensive campaign to bring

[73] Society of the Army of the Tennessee, *Report of the Proceedings at the Thirty-eighth Meeting 1896* (Cincinnati, 1897), p. 142.

[74] Grand Army of the Republic, *Journal of the Thirty-first National Encampment 1897* (Lincoln, Neb., 1897), p. 55.

[75] *Ibid.,* p. 57.

the 1895 national encampment there. In its invitation the city's general council predicted that "such a meeting would lead to a better understanding and a higher appreciation between the people of the various sections of our united country . . .," while in its seconding resolution the Kentucky House of Representatives declared that a warm reception to the Grand Army "will drive away forever the fading shadows of the great fraternal strife." [76] These invitations went out to numerous state encampments of the G.A.R. in the hope that their delegations to the 1894 convention would support the city's bid.

When the order met at Pittsburgh in September 1894, Henry Watterson appeared to urge Louisville's cause. He stressed the loyalty of the Southern people and their devotion to "the flag of a reunited people and a glorious republic." The decision involved a lengthy discussion. While some still questioned how cordially the South would actually welcome the Northern veterans, the majority approved the proposal as a means of demonstrating how sectional lines had vanished. One member predicted that the meeting "will do more to make this a united Republic than any one act that has been done since the surrender at Appomattox." [77]

When the veterans finally assembled at Louisville a year later, the official report of the meeting declared that "never before have the 'blue and gray' joined in giving to the world such exhibition of genuine fraternal feeling and unquestionable loyalty to the Union. . . ." [78] In a sentimental vein perhaps influenced by the type of romantic novels which had come into vogue, past Commander-in-Chief William Warner foresaw the time "when, hanging over many a mantel in far New England and glorifying many a cottage in the Sunny South, bound together in bonds of everlasting love and honor, shall be seen two crossed swords, carried in battle respectively by the one grandfather on one side who wore the blue, and the grandfather on the other side who wore the gray." [79] The nation's newspapers hailed "this glorious love feast" both as proof of the decline of sec-

---

[76] Department of Kentucky, Grand Army of the Republic, *Proceedings of the Twelfth Annual Encampment 1894* (Covington, 1894), pp. 73–74.

[77] G.A.R., *Journal 1894*, pp. 15, 262.

[78] Grand Army of the Republic, *Journal of the Twenty-ninth National Encampment 1895* (Rockford, Ill., n.d.), p. 430.

[79] *Ibid.*, pp. 10–11.

tional feeling and as a step toward its final obliteration. Certainly
the delegates returned to their homes throughout the country with
this conviction. The commander of the District of Columbia branch
felt that the assembly had "done more to heal old differences and
to bridge the bloody chasm than anything else perhaps in the last
quarter of a century." [80]

Meetings of the Society of the Army of the Cumberland at Chickamauga in 1892 and at Chattanooga in 1895 produced further testimonials of amity. The same was true of the Sons of Veterans' convention at Knoxville in 1895. The organization's adjutant-general
declared that its reception there proved "that Mason and Dixon's
line had been blotted out forever, and that the soldiers and civilians
of the South took a hand in its obliteration." [81]

Various types of closer coöperation between Union and Confederate organizations were also developing. More and more frequently
the Grand Army invited Confederate veterans to join its parades, to
attend its meetings, and to share in such projects as the erection
of monuments and the establishment of military parks. Associations
of the veterans of both armies appeared, such as the United American Veterans in Texas. The growth of Blue and Gray reunions,
according to a former G.A.R. head, Lucius Fairchild, "can only be
productive of good results." [82]

Gradually the Grand Army began to reverse its stand on questions which previously had produced considerable bitterness. The
organization now was far more willing to support efforts to establish
homes for Confederate veterans. There was even a good deal of
sentiment to have the national government provide such an institution, as well as to return the Confederate flags, though these ideas
proved too extreme for official G.A.R. sanction. Meanwhile, speakers
at meetings of the United Confederate Veterans and the pages of
the *Confederate Veteran* were also expressing their desire for reunion, their loyalty to flag and country, and an increasing willingness to have Union men at their meetings and to coöperate with
Northern groups.

[80] Department of the Potomac, Grand Army of the Republic, *Report of the Twenty-
Eighth Annual Encampment 1896* (n.p., n.d.), p. 32. Cf. Buck, *Road to Reunion*, pp.
239–240.
[81] Sons of Veterans, U.S.A., *Journal of Proceedings at the Fourteenth Annual
Encampment 1895* (Des Moines, 1895), pp. 177–178.
[82] Fairchild to Eugene A. Guilbert, Feb. 19, 1890, Fairchild Papers.

This feeling of reconciliation came to a climax at the time of the Spanish-American War. At the 1897 reunion of the U.C.V. one veteran had predicted that, if the government should call for volunteers in any future war, the ex-Confederates would "offer more men than could be accepted." [83] After the outbreak of the conflict the U.C.V. pledged "the hearty support of our organization, standing ready at all times, with men and money, irrespective of political affiliation, to support the President of the United States as Commander-in-Chief of our Army and Navy, until an honorable peace is conquered from the enemy." [84]

President McKinley expressed Northern sentiment when he replied to this offer, "The present war has certainly served one very useful purpose in completely obliterating the sectional lines drawn in the last one." [85] Throughout the country G.A.R. leaders and encampments stated their pleasure at seeing the Blue and the Gray fight side by side and confidently proclaimed that the sectional chasm had been bridged forever. They were particularly touched by the services of Joe Wheeler and Fitzhugh Lee. The commander-in-chief of the Sons of Veterans related how one old veteran had described his feelings toward "Fighting Joe": " 'Jones, thirty-five years ago I tried to shoot that man,' and the tears trickled down his face and he said, 'I am glad I didn't shoot him, I am glad I didn't get the opportunity; I think he is a grand man; he loves the old flag now as you and I loved it then, and I love him for that love.' " [86]

Actually the war did not eliminate all traces of sectional feeling as immediately as McKinley had hoped. The proposal of some enthusiasts that a reunited nation should now pension Confederate as well as Union survivors still struck some G.A.R. members as rewarding treason. The *Confederate Veteran,* in turn, disliked seeing Southerners wearing the blue uniform and wished the color had been changed to brown. "By and by the fraternity may be complete between the North and the South," it declared, "but it will not occur

[83] United Confederate Veterans, *Minutes of the Seventh Annual Meeting 1897* (New Orleans, 1898), p. 23.

[84] United Confederate Veterans, *Minutes of the Eighth Annual Meeting 1898* (New Orleans, 1899), p. 55.

[85] *Ibid.,* p. 56.

[86] Sons of Veterans, U.S.A., *Journal of Proceedings of the Eighteenth Annual Encampment 1899* (Boston, 1900), p. 140.

through anything that is humiliating to the people of the latter section. Personal honor is above country." [87] The magazine felt that the North was a little too pleased at how the war had proved the South's loyalty. Unless it still had some suspicions, it would have taken Dixie's patriotism for granted.

As a conciliatory gesture President McKinley next suggested that the care of Confederate graves become a national duty. His proposal provoked a long debate at the U.C.V.'s reunion in 1899. General Stephen Lee moved that the organization endorse the idea, but this merely opened up an excited discussion as to whether the President's remarks constituted an official offer from the government or had been made merely for political effect. The meeting finally adopted a substitute resolution thanking McKinley for his sentiments, welcoming such action for their comrades buried in the North but declaring that within the former Confederacy the care should be left in the hands of Southern women. On the other hand, the reaction of the G.A.R., which in previous years had steadily frowned upon any such activity, was milder than ever before. By 1900 it was clear that the victors finally felt that they could afford to be large-minded. The Confederates, never able to express themselves as freely as the Northerners until much later and as the defeated side always much more on the defensive, understandably clung more tenaciously to their traditions, but properly interpreted this constituted no real barrier to national patriotism.

In previous decades the Mexican War veterans had been a minor force for minimizing sectional animosity, though chiefly in the sense of being pro-Southern. Never important, by the nineties this group had lost whatever influence it once possessed. Its role as a harmonizing agent was now assumed more successfully by the new hereditary societies. The founders of the S.A.R. and D.A.R. in particular consciously sought to minimize sectionalism by emphasizing the common heritage of the American Revolution. Yorktown's location in Virginia always seemed especially felicitous for this purpose. The regent of the Daughters' first chapter in St. Louis predicted that the formation of these two groups "will be the silken cord which will unite the North and South once more, and which will wipe out of

[87] *Confederate Veteran*, VI (July 1898), 304.

the memory all the unpleasant associations of the late deplorable war." [88]

The originator of the S.A.R., William O. McDowell, clearly conceived that the new association "has a special field in doing its part to wipe out sectionalism in this country." Since the Southern man was just as eligible as the Northerner, the organization "gives him the chance to assert his patriotism, and confidentially you would be surprised how enthusiastic they are, and hungry for the opportunity." [89] As the son of a Union veteran and the son-in-law of a Confederate soldier, he had a greater understanding of both sides than did many Northerners. When the founder of the Sons of Veterans protested against the S.A.R.'s admitting all Revolutionary descendants regardless of whether intervening forebears had ever fought against the United States, McDowell in reply expounded the favorite Southern argument that each region had fought sincerely for different constitutional principles and concluded, "The men of the Confederacy, the men of the Gray, are as patriotic to-day and as devoted to the old flag as the men of the North." [90] If this interpretation had its historical weaknesses, it was at least more conducive to reconciliation than older explanations. He therefore deliberately took care that the South had an equal share in the offices of the national society. The original vice-presidents for different states included such prominent ex-Confederates as Simon Buckner in Kentucky, Wade Hampton in South Carolina, and Fitzhugh Lee in Virginia.

The society's first national congress shared McDowell's outlook. In his report as acting president-general Lucius Deming declared that the Sons aimed "to harmonize sectional jealousies" and the secretary-general hailed the cordial attitude displayed by the survivors of both armies who were present. "They all showed the warmest feeling of fellowship," the *Newark Daily Advertiser* reported of the delegates, "and the fact of being descended from Revolutionary ancestors brought the people of the North and South

[88] "Chapter in St. Louis," *Adams' Magazine of General Literature,* I (July 1891), 24.
[89] William O. McDowell to William E. Bundy, July 3, 1889, William O. McDowell Letterbooks, New York Public Library.
[90] McDowell to Major A. P. Davis, June 18, 1889, *ibid.*

together upon a foundation, the sentiments of which was of a time prior to any States' rights or slavery idea." [91]

The state branches expressed the same views. Again and again speakers responding to toasts like "Unity of Feeling Between the South and North" or "The Sons of the American Revolution Have Obliterated the Mason and Dixon's Line," stated the need for sectional harmony and praised the Sons' part in bringing it about. In border states, such as Kentucky, it constituted an association in which Union and Confederate veterans mingled without rancor. Though the ever conservative Sons of the Revolution seemed less conscious of this mission, the chaplain of its Pennsylvania society asserted its aim also was "to obliterate sectionalism and to bind together in an indissoluble bond of national patriotism the Sons of the Revolution, whether they wore the blue or the gray in the great Civil War." [92]

The D.A.R. was as aware of this obligation as were the men. With her New Hampshire rearing and Louisiana marriage Flora Adams Darling had both Northern and Southern ties like McDowell and was equally clear as to her purpose. "As founder of this Society I admit I have an ambition to see the women of the North and South unite in social bonds," she told the New York chapter. "I have had my dream of victory, and have heard the song of triumph, No North, no South, no East, no West, but union forever." [93] As scrupulous as McDowell in her choice of the first officers that Dixie be well represented, she wanted the society to be "broad and comprehensive willing to embrace all patriots who are eligible regardless of former condition." [94] Later when organizing the Daughters of 1812 she included both Mrs. U. S. Grant and Mrs. Jefferson Davis among the honorary vice-presidents.

The other original leaders of the D.A.R. were equally well-suited

---

[91] Henry Hall, *Year Book of the Societies Composed of Descendants of the Men of the Revolution* (New York, 1891), pp. 28, 34; *Newark* (N.J.) *Daily Advertiser,* May 8, 1890.

[92] Pennsylvania Society, Sons of the Revolution, *Eighth Annual Report 1895–96* (Philadelphia, 1896), p. 38.

[93] Flora Adams Darling, *Founding and Organization of the Daughters of the American Revolution and Daughters of the Revolution* (Philadelphia, 1901), p. 92.

[94] Flora Adams Darling to William O. McDowell, Oct. 7, 1890, William O. McDowell Scrapbooks, XXXVIII, New York Public Library.

to heal the sectional breach. They lived in Washington, the meeting place of North and South. Of the three original founders, Miss Washington, though a native of the former Confederacy, was descended from the family that had supplied the first President of the United States, Miss Desha was from a border state that had been Southern in sympathies but Unionist in decision and Mrs. Walworth reversed Mrs. Darling's career by being a woman of Southern birth who had married a Northern man. Symbolically enough, all these women had become employees of the national government. Similarly, Mrs. Cabell, the first presiding officer, was the daughter of a Union soldier from Virginia but had married a Confederate veteran.

The early members and friends of the society firmly believed that it contributed much toward reuniting the sections. "No organization of men or women, it is safe to say," confidently asserted the *Spirit of '76* in 1895, "has done more, if as much, towards promoting the national feeling and doing away with sectional differences, besides stimulating patriotic ardor, than the DAUGHTERS OF THE AMERICAN REVOLUTION." [95] The experience of Mrs. H. V. Boynton, a prominent national official whose husband had been a Civil War officer later active in army societies as well as an important behind the scenes intermediary in the Compromise of 1877, may be cited. "With Northern birth, education and sympathies," an account of her work with the D.A.R. disclosed, "she has learned through its influence not only to forgive the Southern sisters against whom her prejudice was strong in her youth, but to believe in and love them as American women who share with her the feeling of devotion to America." [96] As further proof of her conversion she later joined with her Virginia-born colleague, Miss Washington, to initiate the Daughters of Founders and Patriots.

The Continental Congresses of the D.A.R. provided opportunities for women from all parts of the country to mingle. "It is safe to assert that no such community of feeling had ever been aroused among the women of the country," declared the official report of the first assembly in February 1892. "The sense of a common heritage in the flag, of a common concern in the welfare of the land, for which

[95] "A Progressive Society," *Spirit of '76,* I (May 1895), 191.
[96] M.G.H., "Mrs. H. V. Boynton," *American Monthly Magazine,* I (Nov. 1892), 422.

the fathers fought side by side, made this meeting more memorable than was realized at the time." [97] To the applause of her associates a Georgia delegate proclaimed that the "unwritten work" of the Daughters was "the reuniting of Georgia and Massachusetts in the same bond of love that found them in the days of Valley Forge and Yorktown." [98]

The comments supposedly exchanged among some delegates at another congress illustrate the effects of these contacts. "I can easily guess you are from the South; a certain grace and sweetness of manner proclaims it," said one across the table in a hotel dining room, to which sally came back the prompt response, "And you . . . are from the North. An entire absence of conceit and elegant ease in style is evidence of it." Northern women even apologized for eavesdropping in the lobby of the Willard with, "It is your pretty voices we wish to hear, your soft Southern accents are so musical and sweet; do let us hear you talk," while the Southerners replied, perhaps a shade too sweetly, "you Northern ladies converse with so much intelligence, let us listen to you, that we may learn something from your advanced ideas." [99] This all seems a bit too much for the modern ear, but perhaps D.A.R.'s did talk that way to each other in the 1890's. In any case, the mere fact that the members thought their intermingling was having this influence itself was significant. By the time of the Spanish-American War the state regent for California was certain that the unison of sentiment throughout the country was all due to the D.A.R.

While the establishment of national rather than sectional societies doubtless did much to bind the country closer together, the movement may have been as much the result of better feeling as the cause. The concern of both veterans' and hereditary groups for internal unity in the nineties was another demonstration of the heightened sense of nationalism so characteristic of those years.

[97] Daughters of the American Revolution, *Report 1890 to 1897* (Washington, 1899), p. 40.

[98] "Proceedings of the First Continental Congress," *American Monthly Magazine,* I (Sept. 1892), 242.

[99] *Montgomery* (Ala.) *Advertiser,* quoted in "Among the Societies," *Spirit of '76,* I (April 1895), 165.

XII

Judgments on Public Questions

As sentinels of patriotism both veterans' and hereditary societies
felt themselves entitled to pass pronouncements on a wide variety
of public issues, though their prescriptions lacked the unanimity
that might have been expected. Neither scornful liberals nor complacent conservatives will find the record as simple as they assume.
While the veterans' and hereditary associations often presented a
united front on these questions, signs of divergence between the two
groups also appeared, and the range of opinion within the total
membership covered a wide gamut. Within the soldiers' leagues the
Mexican War Veterans frequently took an unconventional contrary
course, and a few individual leaders in all organizations expounded
a radicalism that was startlingly at variance with majority dogma.

For a long time the veterans paid little attention to matters that
did not concern them directly and it was not until they assumed
the role of patriotic elder statesmen in the eighties and nineties that
they began to offer guidance to a citizenry perplexed as to the proper
course in an increasingly complicated society. Women's associations
like the W.R.C. were even more hesitant to consider anything un-
related to their original purpose of respectable charitable activity
or to advance into more thorny and somehow masculine fields. The
development of a larger concern with social problems evidenced
itself in relations with an organization known as the National Council of Women, founded in 1888 by May Wright Sewall, a feminist
and suffragist who the following year also became the first president
of the General Federation of Women's Clubs. The head of the
Ladies of the G.A.R. was dismayed by the advanced ideas she encountered at its meeting in Washington in 1888, and the W.R.C.
debated at length whether to affiliate. A majority of members, as

well as many Grand Army men, were said to oppose the move. In 1890 the national convention voted that the Woman's Relief Corps existed only to honor dead soldiers and to assist needy veterans, their widows and orphans.

But, as was the case in other women's clubs at the time, during the nineties opinion shifted. "In this, the last decade of the nineteenth century," a W.R.C. committee observed in 1890, "wonderful opportunity is given the wise and thoughtful women, of which there are not a few among us, to educate and raise to a higher plane thousands of America's women whose privileges have been limited."[1] According to Indiana's president shortly thereafter, membership "has opened up new opportunities for social and benevolent work on the part of women . . . thus developing and nursing into power the talents God has given her."[2] The attitude toward the National Council therefore changed. "If we have representation in this National Council of Women," the national president declared in 1893, "it enlarges our sphere; it enables us to lay our aims and plans before representatives of almost every society in the world, and tell them what we are doing and what we hope to accomplish."[3] One of the society's founders, Mrs. Kate Sherwood, argued that so large and important a group should participate in any union of women's associations. Although another prominent leader, Mrs. Annie Wittenmyer, fought the proposal with every parliamentary device she could command, the convention finally voted affiliation.

Throughout the rest of the decade delegates from the W.R.C. appeared regularly at the Council's meetings and took an active part in its programs. The Council described itself as "a confederation of workers committed to the overthrow of all forms of ignorance and injustice and to the application of the Golden Rule to society, custom and law."[4] Among the other organizations represented were the W.C.T.U., the National American Woman Suffrage Association, the National Free Baptist Woman's Missionary Society,

[1] Woman's Relief Corps, Auxiliary to the Grand Army of the Republic, *Journal of the Eighth National Convention 1890* (Boston, 1890), p. 250.

[2] Department of Indiana, Woman's Relief Corps, *Journal of the Eighth Annual Convention 1891* (Noblesville, Ind., 1891), p. 44.

[3] W.R.C., *Journal 1890*, p. 198.

[4] Quoted in Woman's Relief Corps, Auxiliary to the Grand Army of the Republic, *Journal of the Thirteenth Annual Convention 1895* (Boston, 1895), p. 164.

the National Council of Jewish Women, the American Anti-Vivisection Society, Wimodaughsis, the Young Ladies Mutual Improvement Association, the National Association of Women Stenographers, and the Universal Peace Union. Associating with these groups understandably made the W.R.C. aware of many new problems.

The new women's hereditary societies were equally divided as to the proper feminine sphere. Though the very fact of their appearance was an indication of the emancipation of women, they were reluctant to face all its implications. "The country is advancing its claim upon its women and they must be ready to answer the call," declared an officer of the New Jersey Daughters of the Revolution. "They can no longer take their knowledge second hand and their opinions ready framed. . . ."[5] But in the early months of the D.A.R. Mrs. Cabell warned Mrs. Darling "to keep our Sisterhood of Daughters free from entangling alliances with bands of women aiming at any of the fads of the day. . . ."[6]

Among these "fads" she almost certainly included agitation for woman suffrage. Here the women's organizations proved extremely conservative in their apprehension that they might be labeled eccentric suffragist clubs. In highly traditional form the president of the Ladies of the G.A.R. informed the International Council of Women "that woman has a sphere of her own, distinctive and essential—as is man's domain—that *her* power is her influence, and to exert it, the power need be expressed neither visibly or clamorously, but like . . . the attractions of gravitation and cohesion, it can work silently and continuously."[7] Far more disturbing to her was the denial of the vote to the inmates of soldiers' homes. But even she had to admit that strong support for woman suffrage at the Council meeting came from other members of her own society.

"This is in no sense a suffrage movement," the Connecticut D.A.R. similarly emphasized. "A very large proportion, we are sure, of the thinking women of our time are very far from wishing any wider

[5] "New Jersey Celebration," *Magazine of Daughters of the Revolution,* III (Feb. 1895), 26.

[6] M. V. E. Cabell to Flora Adams Darling, Jan. 17, 1891, Flora Adams Darling, *Founding and Organization of the Daughters of the American Revolution and Daughters of the Revolution* (Philadelphia, 1901), p. 175.

[7] Ladies of the G.A.R., *Proceedings of the First and Second National Conventions 1886 and 1888* (n.p., n.d.), p. 14.

range of responsibilities." Like the Ladies of the G.A.R. president, the argument was that "the influence of women in society and in the home, if rightly appreciated, is far greater than any power the right of suffrage could confer upon her." [8] In meetings of the Daughters of the Revolution the controversial subject was apparently taboo. Yet once again this caution did not always prove complete hostility. Susan B. Anthony herself belonged to a D.A.R. chapter in Rochester, New York, and was allowed to speak briefly before at least two Continental Congresses. When Julia Ward Howe, another member who was an outstanding feminist leader, was asked to address the Boston Daughters, she "dreaded the meeting, feeling that I must speak of suffrage in connection with the new womanhood, and anticipating a cold or angry reception." But to her surprise, she found her words "warmly welcomed." Mrs. Howe could not help adding, "Truly the hour is at hand!" [9]

Ordinarily the men's groups ignored this subject, but, whenever they did express an opinion, those in the western states were more apt to be sympathetic. Though the Illinois Grand Army decided that an endorsement of woman suffrage for all township offices was beyond its scope, the sentiment of the gathering was clearly favorable, while in response to a request from Miss Anthony, the South Dakota branch wished the Woman Suffrage Association success. The *Vedette* and the *Grand Army Record* were also friendly. "Personally I am a believer in female suffrage," declared the president of the California Sons of the Revolution, which in the East at least was usually a highly conservative body. His support was largely limited to the "woman of property and intelligence," but with the same logic that had seemed so self-evident at the first women's rights convention half a century before, he pointed out, "In denying her a vote we are false to the principle for which our ancestors fought—no taxation without representation." [10] But ordinarily the men's commemoration of the American Revolution did not lead them to such explicit conclusions.

To many members of hereditary organizations a more pressing

[8] "Chapters," *American Monthly Magazine,* V (Aug. 1894), 193–194.

[9] Laura E. Richards and Maud Howe Elliott, *Julia Ward Howe 1819–1910* (Boston and New York, 1915), II, 179.

[10] Holdridge O. Collins, *Address Delivered at Los Angeles . . . 1897* (n.p., n.d.), p. 5.

problem than the enfranchisement of women seemed to be the shocking corruption of public life. The men who belonged to ancestral societies came from an educated and professional group rather sympathetic to the mild form of political liberalism prevalent among many cultured gentlemen of the late nineteenth century. This pattern involved support of "good government" reform candidates, economy in government, extension of civil service, and very often a reduction in the protective tariff along the lines suggested by the Manchester school of economics. The program was to be found in almost any issue of Godkin's *Nation,* was highly approved by college professors and literary men of New England antecedents, and often led to acquiring the label of Independent or Mugwump. At the meetings of hereditary groups speakers therefore denounced the sale of votes and boss rule and were not in the least restrained by the facts that these evils could be so glibly attributed to those of more recent stock. Their most common solution (aside from the restriction of immigration), a more active participation in government by the best people, lay well within the genteel tradition and indeed intellectually had not wandered too far from Harvard Square or Gramercy Park.

So high-minded an approach to the relations between patriotism and civic problems had little appeal to the veterans. They came from a quite different social and academic background and were frequently party hacks of the very type that the aristocratic Sons so disliked. Certainly their pressure group activities committed them far more to political deals and machine organization and made them scarcely critical of governmental expenditures. Not well educated but extremely anxious for public positions on the mere basis of their war service, they developed strong hostility to "unjust, aristocratic and oppressive" civil service legislation, which one Grand Army member denounced as "probably the greatest political humbug that has ever been presented to a free and intelligent people, not excepting Barnum's 'Wooly Horse' and other of his professed humbugs." [11]

Since few veterans had college degrees or even any formal schooling at all for many years past, they particularly objected to the "textbook standard" of civil service examinations which required aca-

[11] John McClarly Perkins, "Justice to the Veterans," *Grand Army Record,* II (June 1887), 1.

demic knowledge such as "the color of Caesar's hair" and flayed them as mere tests of memory, "which is next to the lowest order of the intellect." In any case, as the *American Tribune* pointed out, "Very few of the great men of history stood at the head of their classes in school." This paper had no high regard for the highly educated "one-idea" civil service "faddists" and preferred "the plain, practical citizens . . . who when it comes to a test of the sturdy manhood that has made this country what it is are their superiors." [12] In like manner the Union Veteran Legion protested that "the honorable discharge certificate of a veteran soldier of the Union should be at least equally potent in securing employment under the Government he assisted in saving from destruction as any college diploma or professional 'sheepskin' presented by other enemies or lukewarm friends of the Union in the day of its direst need. . . ." [13]

The soldier element also disputed the Mugwumps' assumption that a public official should not be an active politician. "It would be more manly, and an added qualification, if, in addition to his examination, he had also done some service for his party," argued the *American Tribune,* "and thus, in a measure, earned the place." [14] Indeed, the party vacillations and foreign origins of some civil service leaders, especially Carl Schurz, led that paper to label their ideas as "un-American." The *National Tribune* attacked the reform for creating a bureaucracy or official aristocracy, directly contrary to the intentions of the founding fathers. The *Grand Army Record* also repeatedly criticized civil service legislation as undemocratic, because it affected the lower paid positions but not the higher salaried ones.

Hence came demands to modify or repeal both federal and state civil service laws. A resolution presented to the Massachusetts Grand Army encampment in 1898 declared that civil service had "proved an absolute failure," that its continuance was "a useless expenditure of the public money and a detriment to the public service," that its originators were an "unpatriotic, unloyal, and a selfish class of men —while in a minority, they seek to control the majority at the

---

[12] *American Tribune* (Indianapolis), April 15, 1897, and Jan. 6, 1898.
[13] Union Veteran Legion, *Proceedings of the Fourteenth National Encampment 1899* (Philadelphia, n.d.), p. 72.
[14] *American Tribune,* Dec. 2, 1897.

expense of the State government under the cloak of Civil Service reform" and that the members should bring pressure on legislators for its abolition in state and nation. The decision of the committee on resolutions that this problem did not fall within the G.A.R.'s jurisdiction evoked numerous testimonials as to the civil service commission's hostility to veterans, who by that time were also facing age difficulties. Though the meeting eventually upheld the committee, the motion and debate had revealed the feelings of many veterans.[15] Similarly, when the chief examiner for the New York Civil Service Commission criticized laws giving preference to veterans not entitled to it by merit, the New York encampment declared that these views "stamp him not only as being unfitted to hold a position requiring the exercise of discretion and judgment, but also as being unpatriotic. . . ." [16] Sometimes the veterans endeavored to circumvent such situations by demanding representation on state civil service commissions.

On the other hand, veterans' papers like the *Vedette,* the *National Tribune,* and the *American Tribune* were more advanced than the hereditary groups in advocating the direct election of United States senators, a measure which then seemed quite radical and was not to gain its popularity until the early twentieth century, but this was partly because they thought that elected officials would be more susceptible to their lobbying for pensions.

The pension question also caused many veterans to view the protective tariff more favorably than did the liberals of the day. Knowing that the fortunes of the Civil War soldiers were closely identified with those of the Republican party and fearing that any reduction might affect the funds available for pension expenditures, their papers defended protection, attacked the free trade movement and urged their readers to thwart any downward changes.[17] Since "the nurture and development of all our industries is the highest patriotism . . . a duty of the same exalted nature as that of entering the army to suppress the rebellion," the *National Tribune* praised

[15] Department of Massachusetts, Grand Army of the Republic, *Journal of the Thirty-Second Annual Encampment 1898* (Boston, 1898), pp. 270–271.

[16] Department of New York, Grand Army of the Republic, *Proceedings of the Thirty-Second Annual Encampment 1898* (New York and Albany, 1898), p. 328.

[17] See Donald L. McMurry, "The Political Significance of the Pension Question, 1885–1895," *Mississippi Valley Historical Review,* IX (June 1922), 19–36.

the tariff for preserving America's economic prosperity and for benefiting farmers and laborers as well as manufacturers. The proposed lowering of rates in the Mills Bill of 1888, it predicted, would mean flooding the country with cheap foreign goods, falling prices, the closing of factories, and the loss of farmers' markets. These journals naturally were ardent defenders of the McKinley Act of 1890, and during the 1892 campaign the *American Tribune* tried to win the soldier vote for the Republicans on the high tariff issue. "A vote for Harrison and Reid," it declared, "is a vote for the United States of America and a vote against John Bull, the pauper labor of Europe and in favor of protection to American labor and American industries." [18]

After the electorate was so unperceptive of the benefits of the McKinley Act as to return Cleveland and the Democrats to office, the papers violently opposed the Wilson Bill for lowering the tariff. The *American Tribune*'s chief argument was that its defeat would help overcome the current depression, while the *National Tribune* stirred up the ashes of sectional feeling with the comment that the veterans would be unable to "find any men who once fought for or sympathized with the Confederacy in opposition to the bill." [19] With the advent of a Republican administration in 1897, the journals urged the passage of a protective measure that would restore prosperity and, incidentally, provide money for pensions. The Dingley Act was therefore greatly to their satisfaction. How far these considerations actually influenced Grand Army men is not entirely clear; probably most of them were Republicans and already believed in high tariffs as a matter of party faith. On the other hand, the *Vedette*'s support of the Democratic party, the only group strongly sympathetic to a Mexican War pension bill, led it to oppose "the protection of wealthy manufacturers at the expense of consumers" and to argue that reduction would benefit the working people.[20]

As time went on, the members of patriotic societies became concerned over more fundamental social and economic problems which accompanied the growth of an industrial civilization. Like many

---

[18] *American Tribune,* Oct. 13, 1892.

[19] *National Tribune* (Washington, D.C.), May 17, 1894.

[20] *Vedette* (Washington, D.C.), Oct. 1888.

Americans the veterans first became aware of these difficulties with the outbreak of capital-labor violence in 1877, and they shared the highly conservative reaction of most middle-class people. Commander-in-Chief John Robinson of the Grand Army assured President Hayes that the order could "furnish thousands of volunteers for the restoration and preservation of order." [21] Throughout the country various posts and departments made similar offers, and in some parts of New York the members were called upon. This episode doubtless influenced the opposition of the Central Labor Union of New York in 1883 to a bill to furnish G.A.R. posts with arms on the ground that the railroads intended the veterans eventually to use the weapons to shoot down strikers. Meanwhile these disturbances made many leaders of veterans' societies hostile to labor and fearful of the republic's future. Soon they were raising the specter of anarchism and predicting the destruction of property rights. Only an occasional speaker felt that capital shared the blame for the growing unrest or attacked the wealth and power of corporations.

The numerous industrial conflicts between 1884 and 1886, climaxed by the Haymarket Affair, revived these apprehensions and produced widespread denunciations of all leftist doctrines such as nihilism, anarchism, socialism, and communism. Several Grand Army posts offered their services to Governor J. M. Rusk of Wisconsin to combat labor riots in Wisconsin. In a letter which also described the purchase of a house on Bellevue Avenue in Newport as well as the activities of his two sons at Princeton, past Commander-in-Chief George Merrill hailed Wisconsin's firm attitude as contrasted with "the appalling apathy or cowardice displayed by officials and by citizens in many other localities." [22] In 1889 Commander-in-Chief William Warner announced, "The membership of the Grand Army of the Republic constitutes the great conservative element of the Nation. . . ." [23]

The increased rather than diminished tensions of the nineties

[21] Grand Army of the Republic, *Proceedings of the Twelfth Annual Meeting of the National Encampment 1878* (New York, n.d.), p. 522.

[22] George Merrill to Lucius Fairchild, June 13, 1886, Lucius Fairchild Papers, Wisconsin State Historical Society.

[23] Grand Army of the Republic, *Journal of the Twenty-third Annual Session of the National Encampment 1889* (St. Louis, 1889), p. 34.

caused further condemnations of radicalism in which the new ancestral groups now joined their voices. Patriotism clearly demanded opposition to these foreign importations so contrary to the free institutions established by the founding fathers. Anarchism in particular, because it defied the execution of laws, was treason, and therefore patriotic veterans had to help its suppression. "The anarchist, the disturber of the public peace, the demagogue that would insidiously assail the conservative forces of society and social order," declared the commander of the Missouri department, "will find no place in the ranks of the Grand Army of the Republic." [24] At the S.A.R.'s national meeting in 1893 the Oregon-Washington branch wanted to add to the organization's objects a pledge "to oppose by moral means the spread of anarchical ideas and lawlessness." A determined champion of the motion was Bishop Charles E. Cheney of Chicago; other members doubted its wisdom. "This society has no more business trying to put down anarchy," snorted General J. C. Breckinridge of Washington, "than it has to put down hell." According to press reports, "The General ripped out the exclamation with a force that made the good Bishop start." [25] Though the amendment finally met defeat, the societies usually had no such qualms about their obligation to destroy this menace.

Along with the hostility to anarchism there developed a distrust of too literal democracy. A speaker before the Sons of the Revolution so far forgot his audience's ancestry as to deny the right of revolution even if a majority favored it and declared that the Sons' object should be "an education, out of all these crass and crazy notions of popular rights, . . . into a true understanding of American liberty as handed down by our Fathers." [26] From the chaplain of the New York branch came a rather disturbing "man on horseback" solution to these disorders: "If, for instance, at some future day, a great number of soured and discontented men, their brains clouded by envy and passion, should, by the use of the implement of universal suffrage, attempt to upset the state and derange the order of society,

[24] Department of Missouri, Grand Army of the Republic, *Proceedings of the Sixteenth Annual Encampment 1897* (St. Louis, 1897), p. 22.

[25] *Cincinnati Commercial Gazette*, June 17, 1893.

[26] Missouri Society, Sons of the Revolution, *Addresses Delivered Before the Society* (Kansas City, Mo., 1895), p. 5.

some strong man will come on the stage able to throttle the public enemy and drive him back." [27]

The underlying conservatism of the societies became explicit during the decade's bitter labor disturbances. This was not quite so apparent at the time of the Homestead strike in 1892, which produced scant but divided opinion. At first the *National Tribune* suggested that both the workers and employers were partly at fault, though it later concluded that the strikers were more responsible for disorder than management and that despite the reductions in their wages the workers were still highly paid and therefore undeserving of sympathy. Feeling that women's role should be the urging of "compromise" and "forebearance," the D.A.R.'s magazine advocated "law and order," the use of ballots rather than firearms. "If the laws are unjust, change them," it declared. "This is in the power of the majority. Let us not mar the records of a free country with violence and bloodshed and set an example of lawlessness to the ignorant and the stranger." [28]

The Pullman Strike of 1894 and the resultant paralysis of the railroads produced far greater alarm. Most members of both veterans' and hereditary societies agreed with the commander of the Michigan Grand Army that the episode was "a rebellious attempt to overthrow constitutional government, to destroy the avenues of interstate commerce and to suppress individual liberty. . . ." [29] The *National Tribune* accused Eugene Debs of acting like an autocrat and treating the American people with contempt. His methods seemed "violently and flagrantly un-American." "All that the wage earners have to do," it suggested, "is to make their grievances known, invite public judgment upon them, pass the necessary laws, and elect the proper men to enforce them." [30] The *American Tribune* viewed the sympathetic strike which had crippled the railroad network as "incipient anarchy." "The man who stands idly by and sees without protesting the forces of the State or Country or Nation attacked by mobs, commits treason," Lucius Fairchild informed the

---

[27] New York Society, Sons of the Revolution, *Supplement to Year Book of 1899* (New York, 1903), p. 277.

[28] "Editor's Note Book," *American Monthly Magazine,* I (Aug. 1892), 188–189.

[29] Department of Michigan, Grand Army of the Republic, *Journal of the Seventeenth Annual Encampment 1895* (Muskegon, Mich., 1895), p. 18.

[30] *National Tribune,* July 19 and July 12, 1894.

Society of the Army of the Potomac. "Between 1861 and 1865 we all declared with one voice that the men who stood in the pathway against the armed forces of the United States should be shot. It is a good rule now." [31] Here at last, it also developed, was an issue on which Confederate veterans found themselves allied with their former foes.

In the ensuing controversy between President Cleveland and Governor Altgeld of Illinois concerning the propriety of federal intervention, the organizations backed the chief executive. A D.A.R. leader in Evanston, for example, denounced Altgeld as "a crying disgrace to every citizen, . . . a man devoid of principles of patriotism, a foreigner and a demagogue of the worst type." [32] That hereditary groups, largely composed of people of property, should pass resolutions endorsing Cleveland's conduct was perhaps not surprising. More striking was the fact that for the first time the veterans' associations agreed with the head of the Democratic party whom they had so often reviled in the past. The founder and president of the Ladies of the G.A.R., Mrs. Edward Roby, wrote Cleveland that "we are proud of our Commander-in-Chief. We can sleep nights assured that the pilot is true to his trust, and that you, and not our anarchist governor, are shaping and guiding our ship of state." [33] In Ohio, Michigan, Indiana, Illinois, and Missouri a number of G.A.R. posts promptly sent Cleveland resolutions of support and made their services available either to him or their state executives. The commander of the Illinois Grand Army assured the governor "that the Department of Illinois can, and WILL turn out 10,000 able-bodied men inside of forty-eight hours, if he needs them to restore law and order." [34] Commander-in-Chief John Adams later disclosed that "my ear was to the ground and my eye along the horizon." Such vigilance meant that "Had the men on duty been unable to restore order, I should have called on the Grand Army of the

---

[31] Society of the Army of the Potomac, *Report of the Twenty-fifth Annual Reunion 1894* (New York, 1894), p. 40.

[32] Cornelia Gray Lunt, "Address to Fort Dearborn Chapter," *American Monthly Magazine*, V (Sept. 1894), 239.

[33] Mrs. Edward Roby to Grover Cleveland, July 12, 1894, Grover Cleveland Papers, Library of Congress.

[34] Department of Illinois, Grand Army of the Republic, *Proceedings of the Twenty-ninth Annual Encampment 1895* (Chicago, n.d.), p. 115.

Republic, and am confident that every comrade able to bear arms would have responded." [35]

The turbulent events of 1894 reinforced the determination of many members of both veterans' and hereditary societies to suppress any similar outburst in the future. In the words of the head of the Ohio G.A.R., "As an organization the Grand Army keeps its ear to the 'phone and its thumb on the button, with forty rounds ready, to defend any legal administration against anarchists or others who violate the law." [36] The commander of the Indiana branch felt that the Sons of Veterans "ought to be made our most reliable and available safeguard against the encroachment of the anarchistic and socialistic tendencies so prevalent among us." [37] Leaders of the S.A.R. and S.R. voiced similar sentiments.

Accompanying this mounting apprehension over economic unrest was a noticeable shift in attitude toward immigration. In the early eighties the veterans' papers welcomed the influx of newcomers from the British Isles and Continental Europe. "Let us give them all a hearty greeting—all seeking homes under a flag which recognizes the brotherhood of humanity," declared the *National Tribune* in 1880. "We can absorb the teeming population of the old world and like Oliver Twist cry for 'more.'" It had great confidence in the assimilative effects of education: "A smart country school teacher will make a good American out of a green Norwegian in six months, and the same boy in twenty years may ably represent his district in Congress. The school house does the work." [38] With a similar conviction that there was "plenty of room here in our opinion for all," the *Vedette* denied that immigration constituted any threat to American labor if the government would aid in the development of strong labor unions.

But, as is well known, during the eighties the nature of immigration into the United States shifted radically. Until that time it had been largely Teutonic and Celtic, from northern and western Eu-

[35] Grand Army of the Republic, *Journal of the Twenty-Eighth National Encampment 1894* (Boston, 1894), p. 63.

[36] Department of Ohio, Grand Army of the Republic, *Proceedings of the Twenty-ninth Annual Encampment 1895* (Sidney, Ohio, 1895), p. 46.

[37] Department of Indiana, Grand Army of the Republic, *Journal of Sixteenth Annual Session 1895* (Indianapolis, 1895), p. 113.

[38] *National Tribune*, Sept. 1880.

rope. The *National Tribune*'s original concept of an immigrant, it should be noticed, had been a strapping Scandinavian, almost overflowing with blonde virtue and vigor. But now came the phenomenon of the tremendous "New Immigration" from southern and eastern Europe; this influx was predominantly Latin, Slavic, and Jewish. By 1888 the *National Tribune* had altered its views. America had gladly been an asylum for earlier settlers who loved liberty, understood democratic institutions, and themselves contributed much to the United States. But the hordes of Italians, Bohemians, and Poles, "the driftwood and sediment of centuries of brigandage, piracy and tyrannical government," did not come to build homes but merely to make enough money to return to Europe.[39]

Ordinarily, however, the members of patriotic groups feared that these immigrants were all too permanent settlers who preserved foreign customs and ideas and failed to understand American institutions and ideals, which might soon be submerged. "What good results either to ourselves or themselves can be referred to by the presence of our foreign born rotten banana sellers, thieving rag dealers, Italian organ grinders, Chinese washmen and Bohemian coal miners, whose aspirations would make a dog vomit?" asked the *American Tribune*.[40] At the D.A.R.'s first national meeting the chaplain-general, picturing "the millions of poor and ignorant pouring into our commonwealth," trembled for the future. "Can we absorb such a heterogeneous mass of humanity," she queried, "give them power to vote, and still keep the purity of our institutions?"[41]

This matter of the political power of ignorant and illiterate foreigners particularly alarmed the hereditary groups, more apt to be concerned about good government. The regent of the Michigan D.A.R. protested that the newcomers viewed "this new country as a great grab-bag, the prizes of political preferment, fat offices and electioneering jobs as their rightful possessions."[42] Josiah Pumpelly warned the New Jersey S.A.R. that in eighteen states men could vote merely upon giving intention of naturalization and "that in

[39] *Ibid.*, Aug. 2, 1888.
[40] *American Tribune*, July 1, 1890.
[41] "Proceedings of the First Continental Congress," *American Monthly Magazine*, I (July 1892), 51.
[42] "Proceedings of Fifth Continental Congress," *American Monthly Magazine*, VIII (May 1896), 678.

fifteen States, a man who has only signified his intention of becoming a citizen and who may possibly never be naturalized, can vote at a National election, and thus it might happen that the vote of the country might be determined by men who were still aliens, on American soil." [43] The veterans' papers were disturbed by the more practical consideration that the immigrants usually supported the political party traditionally opposed to further pension legislation.

Others thought of immigrants as turbulent, lawless individuals who committed most of the crimes in the country. The president of the California Sons of the Revolution was convinced that the first instance of violent rioting in the United States had occurred when some aliens fired into a group of Americans in 1844. Closely allied to the fear of the immigrants' criminality was a dislike of their poverty. The members of hereditary and officers' groups, who were apt to bear the brunt of taxation, feared the strain upon the poor relief structure. General A. L. Chetlain, before the Society of the Army of the Tennessee in 1886, charged that European countries had "poured in upon us the scum and refuse of their population to fill our almshouses, our bridewells, and our penitentiaries." [44]

The veterans were more concerned about the economic competition that this created. The *National Tribune* attacked the newcomers' low standard of living in cities like New York and Philadelphia. The result, it felt, was that immigrant labor displaced the native working class and "reduces it to the abject poverty and pauperism of the labor of Europe." [45] Finally, members of both hereditary and veterans' organizations associated foreigners with radicalism and particularly held them responsible for the bugbear of the nineties, anarchism. This mounting distrust of the large foreign element was a prominent reason for the founding of so many hereditary societies from the late eighties on and also explained the simultaneous interest which the G.A.R. and W.R.C. developed for patriotic teaching, reverence for the flag, and military instruction.

As a solution for the foreign invasion, the members of both veter-

[43] New Jersey Society, Sons of the American Revolution, *Proceedings From Its Foundation in 1889 to 1893* (Morristown, N.J., 1893), p. 173.

[44] Society of the Army of the Tennessee, *Report of the Proceedings 1884–1887* (Cincinnati, 1893), p. 359.

[45] Department of Massachusetts, Grand Army of the Republic, *Journal of the Thirtieth Annual Encampment 1896* (Boston, 1896), p. 222.

ans' and hereditary associations increasingly favored the restriction of immigration. By the mid-nineties only an occasional figure still voiced the old American welcome to all comers. The president of the Daughters of the Revolution felt if exclusion were adopted, "then let the statue of Liberty put out her light." Asking the older stock, "Has it occurred to you that our ancestors were immigrants?" she argued that "with countless acres untilled and unexplored there should be welcome for millions more coming in with the same right with which came the forefathers to Plymouth." [46] But most of her associates in patriotic organizations now qualified this greeting. While the Grand Army's Committee on a Systematic Plan of Teaching Lessons of Loyalty to Our Country maintained that it "would place no pebble of obstruction in the way of any class with the purpose and ability to add to the strength of America's toilers," it also called for limits to "that portion of the tide of immigration sweeping upon our shores which represents only the poverty and crime of other lands." [47] Grand Army encampments and leaders of the D.A.R., D.R., S.A.R., S.R., and Society of Colonial Wars echoed these sentiments and called for restrictive legislation.

Despite their hostility to immigrants the societies usually avoided explicit entanglements with the more outspoken nativist movements, but there were some signs of such feeling among the hereditary groups. Presiding at the first national convention of the S.A.R., General Alexander Webb, president of the College of the City of New York, asked the delegates whether it was not time "that you who are thinking men began to exert your personal influence at your own homes to obtain a recognition of the rights of Americans, as better than the rights of ignorant foreigners? If you don't feel it as severely as we in New York do, then you can say, 'Thank God, you are not in such circumstances as they in New York.' " [48] His brother, W. Seward Webb, president-general of the society, told the second congress that "it behooves all good Americans to awake to the fact that we must take a more active part in the administration

---

[46] "Proceedings of the Sixth Continental Congress," *American Monthly Magazine,* X (April 1897), 360–361.

[47] Grand Army of the Republic, *Journal of the Twenty-Sixth National Encampment 1892* (Albany, 1892), p. 82.

[48] Quoted in *The Republic,* May 7, 1890, in William O. McDowell Scrapbooks, XXXVII, New York Public Library.

of our affairs, and not leave it, as in the past, to the foreign element." [49] At the third congress an Oregon delegate proposed that the president of the United States select higher officials from native Americans, and a speaker at the first banquet of the Utah S.A.R. demanded that "none but native-born Americans should be permitted to teach American children Americanism." [50]

The only important link between the new hereditary societies and organized nativism, however, lay in the person of Henry Baldwin. A resident of New Haven and Atlantic City, he belonged to both the S.A.R. and the Order of Founders and Patriots. He was the author of such works as *Americans for America, America for Americans* and was closely connected with the newly formed American Protective Association, serving on its New Jersey committee.[51] In the spring of 1889 Baldwin summoned a meeting in New York to combat dangers to American institutions which attracted groups like the Patriotic Order of Sons of America, the Patriotic Order of True America, and the Loyal Orange Institution. This gathering, known as the Morton House Conference, was directed primarily against Catholics and did not involve any of the hereditary associations. Late in 1889 Baldwin organized the American Patriotic League, whose program included the restriction of immigration, a longer period for naturalization, an educational qualification for all voters, a prohibition of the use of public funds or property for sectarian purposes, and the reservation of American lands for American settlers.

Soon thereafter Baldwin became friendly with William O. McDowell, sending him information on this work and contributing to McDowell's various projects. On the ground that "The country is now ripe for action upon distinctly American lines, for the protection and preservation of American institutions," in December 1890 Baldwin called a Conference of Patriotic Orders of the United States to meet in Chicago the following February.[52] This time he invited not only nativist and anti-Catholic organizations such as the Order of Native Americans and the Ladies Loyal Orange Associa-

[49] Clipping from unidentified Hartford newspaper, *ibid.*, XLIV.
[50] "What We Are Doing," *American Monthly Magazine*, VII (Sept. 1895), 262.
[51] For Baldwin's nativist connections, see John Higham, "The Mind of a Nativist: Henry F. Bowers and the A. P. A.," *American Quarterly*, IV (Spring, 1952), 21 n.
[52] Circular, Dec. 4, 1890, McDowell Scrapbooks, XL.

tion but also several hereditary groups, including the D.A.R., Colonial Dames, and Huguenot Society. Presumably this was the meeting at which McDowell appointed Baldwin "Custodian of American History." But there is no indication that the ancestral bodies responded in any degree to Baldwin's activities. While he himself continued his membership in them as well as his connection with McDowell, he could not persuade them to endorse his outright nativist program. The Daughters of the Revolution even attacked "any such special and selfish motto as 'America for Americans!'" and declared that people were now ashamed of the title of "Know Nothing." [53] The veterans were even less responsive. Though the District of Columbia G.A.R. protested the appointment of aliens to government positions, this was chiefly because they wanted the jobs to go to the ex-soldiers. Their organizations had too many Germans and Irish on their rolls to be very nativist-minded, and the *American Tribune* denounced the leaders of the A.P.A. as "un-American and unscrupulous." [54]

Instead of the more radical discriminatory nativist program, the hereditary societies wanted their members to teach the duties of American citizenship to the foreign-born and, as it were, assume "the white man's burden" at home. Around Chicago the D.A.R. worked extensively among Bohemian and German immigrants, concentrating on the children. Ordinarily, however, the Daughters did not compete with the patriotic education in schools being carried on by the G.A.R. and W.R.C. but turned their attention to the adults. In the East the most active chapter was in Buffalo, where lived 75,000 Poles and 25,000 Italians. Members of the society wrote a series of six lectures covering the history of the country from the period of discoveries through Reconstruction. Translated into Italian and Polish, these were then delivered with stereopticon slides. The Polish ones were the more successful, at times attracting audiences up to six hundred people. Through the chapter's reports at state conferences the idea spread to other cities.

Meanwhile, Mrs. Daniel Lothrop urged the Children of the American Revolution not to neglect those so underprivileged as to be

---

[53] Rev. George R. Van De Water, "Our Country," *Magazine of Daughters of the Revolution*, I (Jan. 1893), 29.

[54] *American Tribune*, June 20, 1895.

ineligible for membership. Pointing out with a guarded optimism that verged on heresy that such children "are perhaps just as patriotic as if their ancestry included the colonists and the Revolutionary soldier," she argued that the local societies should exert an influence upon them by inviting them to all public meetings. Mrs. Lothrop concluded, with an accuracy possibly not entirely intentional, "No estimate of the good achieved in this direction can be made." [55]

This record of apprehension over anarchism, hostility to unlimited immigration, and distrust of organized labor, all of which were closely interrelated in the eyes of patriotic societies, sounds quite familiar to modern ears, and its occasionally antiquated language can be quickly brought up to date by substituting "communism" for "anarchism." For both veterans' and hereditary groups to dislike any fundamental changes in the nation's political and economic structure and for the ancestral leagues to put their hopes for continued stability in the older stock seems scarcely surprising. But to view these organizations as forming a united force for conservatism would be a serious misconception. By the nineties the concentration of wealth, the rise of monopolies, and the growth of conflicts between capital and labor had aroused the attention of more thoughtful members who, though perplexed as to remedies, often expressed a realization that there existed problems which blind reaction would not solve.

When a Southern veteran observed bitterly in the critical year of 1894, "If the Confederate soldier had triumphed, there would not be in this country a system of finance which puts the people in a wine press, as it were, and grinds them to a pulp for the benefit of multimillionaires," it was not as startling as it first sounds. There had been a strong ante-bellum distaste for Northern capitalism and his solution was a genuinely reactionary one of a return to the "principles of strict construction of the Constitution, of a close limitation of government power, and a rigid economic administration. . . ." [56] More significant was the way in which the papers for Northern veterans, always aware that their constituency was of low economic

---

[55] Daughters of the American Revolution, *Report 1890 to 1897* (Washington, 1899), p. 43 and *Third Report 1898–1900* (Washington, 1901), p. 49.

[56] Confederate Survivors' Association of Augusta, Ga., *Memorial Resolution . . . at the Sixteenth Annual Reunion 1894* (Augusta, Ga., 1894), p. 11.

status, adjusted their tone in recognition of the unrest of the day. From the eighties on they often displayed a sympathy for the working class and hostility to big business which they must have thought would appeal to their readers. Their pages therefore perhaps told more about the feelings of the rank and file than did the utterances of leaders who came of more prosperous and conservative background and were often trying to keep the organizations in line.

The *Grand Army Review* was friendly toward T. V. Powderly and the Knights of Labor's demands as to hours and pay. The *National Tribune* recognized labor's right to strike, though the resulting wage losses made such action seem unwise, and criticized management's use of Pinkerton detectives. In its early days it showed a surprising cordiality toward the nihilist movement, even predicting that the future would hail the Czar's assassination in 1881 as "the work of liberty-loving enthusiasts." [57] More subdued by the next decade and inclined to argue that trusts were inevitable and should not be prevented as they cheapened production and thereby benefited the community, it nevertheless conceded that they should be rigorously controlled. It became a strong backer of a bill to establish postal savings banks, but was suspicious of an income tax because it was often proposed as a specific source of pension payments. The paper attacked this as "pure demagoguery," intended to turn opinion against the whole pension system. The *American Tribune* hailed the spread of labor unions and, fearing that men thrown out of work by the rise of industrial combinations would vote Democratic, spurred the Republicans to antitrust activity. In 1896 it endorsed the entire reform program of Governor-elect Hazen Pingree of Michigan: the suppression of trusts and monopolies, popular votes on granting street car and similar franchises, a direct primary law, taxation of railroads, and legislation against undue influence of banks and railroads in elections. Finally, the *Grand Army Record,* though admitting that big business had supported McKinley's candidacy in 1896, optimistically denied that the new President would be "the supporter of trusts, monopolies, huge corporations, and of organizations whose life blood is made up by laying oppressive burdens on the laboring classes of the country." For him to become so, the paper reasoned, "would be suicide, politically and morally." [58]

[57] *National Tribune,* April 1881.
[58] *Grand Army Record,* XI (Nov. 1896), 88.

Since farmers as well as laborers constituted a large element in the membership of Civil War organizations, these journals were also responsive to the agrarian unrest which was so pronounced during the nineties. For about a year the *American Tribune* ardently supported the Farmers' Alliance movement. In the summer of 1890 the paper announced that the farmers and the Union veterans were natural allies. Both favored the expansion of the currency, and many branches of the Alliance were endorsing a service pension as one way to achieve it. The journal therefore became sympathetic to the farmers' difficulties, attacked the Wall Street money power which was constricting the currency, swung over to the free silver panacea, and eventually so far forgot the veterans' Republican tradition as to favor the formation of a third party. In the spring of 1891, however, it suddenly discontinued its interest in the Alliance movement and confined itself strictly to veterans' affairs. Behind this shift was dismay over the increasing Southern membership of the Alliance, which opposed a service pension and favored aiding only indigent veterans, with payment in subtreasury notes at that, clearly a "wild and dangerous scheme." [59] Thereafter the paper became a strong opponent of free silver.

In the early nineties the *National Tribune* also decided that the platform of the Ohio Farmers' Alliance was "an unusually able, practical document, and urges genuine reforms, all of which are practicable and much needed." [60] It found free silver more of a poser, especially as Grand Army sentiment seemed to be divided geographically. As late as 1898 Utah's commander was denouncing the "concentration of the money into the hands of the money power, an oligarchy which is sapping the life blood out of the nation and making slaves of the people." [61] But the organization avoided committing itself on so controversial a matter, the New York encampment tabling a resolution favoring sound money and the Oklahoma branch doing the same to a cheap money motion. Fearful of antagonizing any Western subscribers, yet largely committed to orthodox Republican doctrine, the *National Tribune* finally lit on the expedient of urging its readers to insist on receiving all payments for

[59] *American Tribune,* Nov. 27, 1891.

[60] *National Tribune,* April 30, 1891.

[61] Department of Utah, Grand Army of the Republic, *Proceedings of the Sixteenth Annual Encampment 1898* (n.p., n.d.), p. 6.

wages or crops in silver, thus reviving it as a circulating medium. But this concession was so lukewarm that nevertheless the paper found itself attacked as being "under the thumb of the London and Wall Street brokers," [62] and when it came to the Bryan campaign of 1896, both the *American Tribune* and the *National Tribune* were right back pitching for the old Republican ball team. Moreover, their opposition to the Democratic party was based as much on its economic radicalism as for its attitude on matters more specifically affecting the ex-soldiers.

By all odds the most radical of these papers was the organ of the Mexican War Veterans, the *Vedette*. This was due to its publisher's antecedents, which were somewhat unusual for a leader of a veterans' society. Alexander Kenaday had been one of the pioneers of the early labor movement in California. Before leaving the west coast he headed a typographical union in San Francisco, served as secretary and later as president of the first union of all trades in that city, established the first labor paper on the Pacific seaboard, the *Journal of Trades and Workingmen,* led the first agitation for an eight-hour law there, and acted as vice-president as well as state organizer for the National Labor Union. This background makes less surprising the paper's announcement toward the close of 1882, "THE VEDETTE has also espoused with some degree of enthusiastic ardor THE CAUSE OF OPPRESSED LABOR. . . ." [63] For several months it actually subordinated the interests of the Mexican War veterans to this issue and even received the official endorsement of the Brotherhood of Carpenters and Joiners, No. 1 of the District of Columbia. The paper sympathized with various strikes and at the time of the Homestead disorders in 1892 declared that newspaper criticisms of the employees were the natural expressions "of the capitalistic press, who derive their sustenance from the corporations." [64]

Convinced that an "irrepressible conflict" loomed between the money power and the proletariat, the paper favored the mobilization of labor and particularly urged women wage earners to form unions. It recommended that the workers throughout the country organize on a military basis into companies, regiments, and divisions and

---

[62] *National Tribune,* Aug. 8, 1895.
[63] *Vedette,* Dec. 15, 1882.
[64] *Ibid.,* July 1892.

then send delegates to Washington to combat the lobbying of the capitalists. Next it publicized the efforts of Kenaday, who had meanwhile become president of the District of Columbia Federation of Labor Unions, to create a National Federation of Labor that would act as such a pressure group and, when that failed, urged closer relations with the Knights of Labor. Finally, there came the bizarre proposal that all workers join the Catholic Church, convert it into a vast universal labor union, and then vote to use the church's wealth to establish coöperative enterprises. The ordained priests were to become clerks, arbitrators, teachers and advisers, while the toilers could "dispense with the useless mummery performed in the churches and cathedrals and turn them into lodges for mixed assemblies of the industrial population." [65]

As a result of this identification with labor, the *Vedette* assailed all its enemies, whether in the form of monopolies, railroad corporations, Wall Street, or Jay Gould, endorsed an income tax, looked favorably at the prospect of complete governmental control of railroads, and suggested repudiation of the public debt on the ground that the interest paid to "bonded aristocrats" was a burden on the laboring classes. These sympathies reinforced the paper's political prejudices. It denounced the Republicans, already in its bad graces because of the pension issue, as the foe of the workers and hailed the Democrats as the true friends of the proletariat. But losing confidence in that party's radicalism and fearing that the big corporations might dominate both political conventions in 1888, it next suggested a general strike until the government be reorganized in the interests of the people. To achieve this goal it urged a labor party, to be led by such persons as Samuel Gompers, T. V. Powderly, Henry George, and Father McGlynn.

At other times the paper flirted with even more extreme doctrines. It endorsed the views of Henry George, asked workingmen to buy *Progress and Poverty,* and praised his candidacy for mayor of New York in 1886. More startling was its sympathy with Johann Most, the anarchist. Moreover, the journal indicated that if published in Russia it would support the nihilists, and the assassination of Alexander II produced only kind words for "the brave revolutionary patriots who have devoted their lives to the cause of downtrodden

[65] *Ibid.,* June 15, 1882, July 15, 1883, and June 1886.

humanity." [66] From this dalliance with the most chaotic of political philosophies it turned to recommending that the Knights of Labor and other unions join forces with the German Socialists.

To be sure, this amazing series of pronouncements tells more about the lively and eclectic mind of Alexander Kenaday and even possibly about the radicalism of the early California labor movement than it does about the considered opinions of the rank and file of Mexican War veterans, some of whom were considerably taken aback by these excursions into leftist ideologies. "I liked to read the VEDETTE when it was filled with letters from the veterans of the army of Mexico," wrote one member, a Missouri carpenter, as he canceled his subscription, "but when you slip into the advocation of labor strikes, unions and societies, I do not want anything more to do with it." [67] Nevertheless, the paper's record does refute the theory that the influence of ex-soldiers' groups has always been to bolster the conservative elements in American society.

Though on the whole the members of hereditary societies represented a segment of the population less disposed towards radicalism, an occasional leader was almost as outspoken as Kenaday. Josiah Pumpelly, a founder of the S.A.R., read the *Arena* and admired the writings of Edward Bellamy. As was true of many of his middle-class contemporaries, a strong religious note infused his social consciousness. In his view, " 'The Brotherhood of humanity' and 'Let thy will be done on Earth' is what we are working for." He reported that Leo XIII's *Rerum Novarum* "has worked me up tremendously." "That part of the pronunciamento as to 'Right of a minimum wage,' " he declared, "should be carved in letters of gold over every shop & factory in the world." [68]

As a member of the Knights of Labor, William O. McDowell served so successfully as one of Powderly's intermediaries with Jay Gould during the great railroad strike of 1886 that in some circles he became known as "Powderly's nigger." Achieving a momentary prominence when he testified before a House committee investigating labor disturbances, he was discussed as a possible member of the

[66] *Ibid.*, April 15, 1881.
[67] *Ibid.*, Oct. 1883.
[68] Josiah Pumpelly to William O. McDowell, July 9 and July 10, 1891, McDowell Scrapbooks, XLVI.

first Interstate Commerce Commission and as a labor candidate for
Congress. Active in labor politics in Newark, he supported Henry
George's campaign in New York in 1886. Early in 1890 he outlined
to Powderly his solution for industrial conflict. He questioned the
remedies advanced by Bellamy and George. Favoring coöperative
enterprise rather than government ownership, he wanted the workers in factories and railroads to buy up the stock of their companies
and run them themselves. At various times in the early nineties he
sought publication of these ideas in organs ranging from the *Boston
Transcript* to the *Journal of the Knights of Labor*. When nearly
everyone else was denouncing the Pullman strikers in 1894, the
president of the Universal Peace Union, Alfred H. Love, one of the
few to put the blame on management, proposed to President Cleveland that McDowell be a member of a committee to investigate the
troubles at Chicago.

Though McDowell's interests were by no means typical of the
average S.A.R. member, others revealed the same concern, if perhaps
in lesser degree. A leader of the S.A.R. informed the D.A.R. that
modern trusts and corporations had little that was "just, honest,
truthful or patriotic" in them. One of his colleagues, himself a
prominent manufacturer, deplored the growth of millionaires since
the Civil War. "The glamour of this inordinate wealth blinds us
to the manner in which it may have been obtained," he warned.
"The passion to be rich makes it unimportant by what method the
coveted riches may be gained." Not surprisingly, however, another
member at once protested, "when he says Jay Gould did wrong in
'making or stealing sixty millions,' I beg to differ with him if he
merely *made* the millions and did not *steal* them. Why shouldn't
he make 'sixty millions,' if he could—fairly and honestly?" [69]

Not only great wealth but excessive poverty distressed the con-
sciences of some Sons. A member of the Kentucky branch painted a
graphic picture of "progress and poverty" as he described how "We
have multiplied our millionaires, but we have also multiplied our
paupers." [70] According to a New Jersey Son, no one could read
General William Booth of the Salvation Army's *In Darkest Eng-*

[69] N.J., S.A.R., *Proceedings 1889–1893*, pp. 241, 248.
[70] Kentucky Society, Sons of the American Revolution, *Year Book 1894* (New
York, 1894), p. 43.

land, "especially as he thinks of the conditions of our great cities," without feeling "that he is, according to his position, and is bound to be in proportion to his power, his brother's keeper." The demand of labor for better social and economic conditions "is one which ought not to be stifled, but listened to in patience and anxious desire for justice." [71] The Daughters of the Revolution's official magazine endorsed the *Arena,* praising its "unceasing fight against corruption and oppression" and "honest work . . . in trying to uplift the poor and degraded. . . ." [72] Finally, the same S.A.R. member in New Jersey concluded that "in view of the social changes going on about us, the old doctrine that the State is governed best which is governed least, is not true at this day, or of this country, but that having already made great and safe strides in the direction of a true State socialism, we must soon be prepared to make more, and must strive to make them wisely." [73] Such an echoing of Sir Wiliam Harcourt's "We are all Socialists now" again proved that there are important qualifications to any hasty generalization as to the reactionary tendency of hereditary societies.

In their discussions of current problems the societies ordinarily stayed clear of religious and moral questions more apt to divide than unite their followings. Some members, indeed, tried without success to make the G.A.R. completely unsectarian by removing a reference to Jesus Christ from its ritual. When a clerical member of the Sons of the Revolution lamented, "What of the scepticism, the irreverence or indifference of the age, the attempt to enforce ethical morality instead of the teaching the Son of God, . . . the neglect of public worship, the desecration of Sunday, the decay of family prayer, the unopened Bibles, oh, what of these?" [74] on only one of these points was there even a feeble response. A few devout Grand Army men protested the holding of campfires on Sunday and Mrs. Daniel Lothrop, founder and head of the Children of the American Revolution, appealed "for the preservation of the Amer-

[71] N.J., S.A.R., *Proceedings 1889–1893,* pp. 121, 123.
[72] "Book Reviews," *Magazine of Daughters of the Revolution,* IV (Aug. 1896), 156.
[73] N.J., S.A.R., *Proceedings 1889–1893,* p. 123.
[74] Pennsylvania Society, Sons of the Revolution, *Register of Members, Annual Report of the Board of Managers 1896–97* (Philadelphia, 1897), p. 100.

ican Sabbath, that glorious institution that . . . should be kept as part of our heritage left us by our ancestors." [75] But the G.A.R.'s 1892 encampment took no action on a resolution that the World's Fair be open on Sunday because the order proved as divided on this point as were the American people.

On only one religious issue did the forces of patriotism and piety seem to be in alliance. The Mormons proved a recurrent source of revulsion and alarm to both veterans' and hereditary societies. The *National Tribune* led the way with exposé articles on the order of "Horrors of Polygamy," while in the enemy's strongholds of Utah and Idaho the G.A.R. became strong opponents of the Latter Day Saints. Both the paper and the order further stimulated this agitation by endorsing Kate Field's anti-Mormon lectures.

There were two peaks of excitement on this point. The first came around 1886. At the Utah department's request the national encampment of that year condemned Mormonism and asked Congress to break up the sect's control of the territory. The following year another resolution declared that admitting Utah to statehood "would be rewarding treason for continued insult to the flag and nullification of wholesome laws." James Tanner reported to the assembly that on a visit to Salt Lake City he had heard the United States flag hissed. But other delegates hesitated to involve the Grand Army in religious and political controversies and the meeting finally tabled the motion unanimously.[76]

The matter appeared in other organizations. The Society of the Army of the Potomac heard a former governor of Utah attack Mormonism and applauded Tanner's plea to wipe out "from the face of the earth that foul institution that is an insult to our country." [77] But at the Woman's Relief Corps' national convention in 1886 a resolution condemning "the vile practice and the continued disloyalty of Mormonism" ran afoul of the order's timidity of political or sectarian questions. Instead, the ladies confined themselves to

[75] "Young People's Department," *American Monthly Magazine*, X (June 1897), 1101.

[76] Grand Army of the Republic, *Journal of the Twenty-first Annual Session of the National Encampment 1887* (Milwaukee, 1887), pp. 199–203.

[77] Society of the Army of the Potomac, *Report of the Seventeenth Annual Re-Union 1886* (New York, 1886), pp. 72, 75.

opposing "the further importation of Chinese women, for purposes of prostitution." [78]

The second outbreak of hostility came over the seating of Representative Brigham Roberts in Congress in 1899. Both the Grand Army of the Republic and the Daughters of the American Revolution protested any recognition of an alleged polygamist. The D.A.R. chapter in Salt Lake City publicized the issue throughout the nation and eventually secured the support of the Continental Congress.

Closely allied to religious sentiment in its moral basis, the temperance crusade sometimes intruded itself into the organizations' councils. In 1887 the chaplain of the New Mexico G.A.R. reported "that so far as we can judge the most of our comrades, to say the least, are moral, and many of them religious. We are sorry to say that profanity and intemperance are far too prevalent with a few of them." [79] The *National Tribune,* warning against the dangers of intoxication, urged the national encampment to ban liquor in post rooms and the *Grand Army Record,* though "aware that some of our patrons believe in whiskey while we do not," insisted that it would "always oppose drunkenness and rum rule." [80]

But although an occasional leader publicly aligned himself against "the demon drink habit," on the whole the men's organizations were not responsive to prohibition sentiment. The G.A.R. in beer-loving Wisconsin first spurned a motion against posts' serving beer or liquor at public meetings and later rebuffed a local unit's suggestion that no person selling intoxicating beverages be eligible for post commander. When "the beautiful and loving women" of the W.C.T.U. asked the 1891 national encampment to cease giving intoxicants to old veterans at public banquets, the meeting tabled the resolution by a vote of 166–72. Similarly, the Sons of Veterans defeated a proposal to exclude from meetings and to court martial all members under the influence of alcohol. The *Vedette,* rejecting the W.C.T.U.'s request to endorse a federal prohibition amendment, proposed instead the establishment of hospitals for the cure of alcoholism.

As might have been expected, the temperance advocates found

---

[78] Woman's Relief Corps, Auxiliary to the Grand Army of the Republic, *Proceedings of the Fourth National Convention 1886* (Boston, 1886), pp. 153–154, 131.

[79] Department of New Mexico, Grand Army of the Republic, *Minutes of the Department Encampments 1886 and 1887* (Albuquerque, N.M., 1887), p. 49.

[80] "Louisville," *Grand Army Record,* X (Aug. 1895), 60.

more sympathy within the affiliated women's organizations. In 1893 the Indiana W.C.T.U. asked the Ladies of the G.A.R. "to give the influence of your great society by public protest and local effort to the suppression of intemperance and the extermination of its chief source—the licensed saloon." The order's national convention expressed its appreciation of these efforts and pledged "our individual co-operation." [81] Four years later the Ohio W.R.C. requested a law closing all saloons on Memorial Day, a form of desecration which the New York G.A.R. had refused earlier to decry.

On one vexatious question, the sale of liquor in army canteens, there was a complete divergence of opinion within the societies. Although some members of both the Grand Army and the W.R.C. favored a prohibition of this practice, the organizations refused to take a public stand. Speaking from her observations as the wife of an army officer, one D.A.R. perhaps startled a chapter in St. Paul when she argued that the canteen prevented drunkenness by selling beer in moderation.

In conclusion, the interest that patriotic societies showed in the past and their reverence for American institutions tended to make them resist alterations in the framework of society, but at the same time humanitarian and idealistic impulses also present in the American heritage made more equalitarian-minded members criticize the rise of trusts and sympathize with the demands of labor. In nearly all cases, however, they condemned violent efforts at change and by the mid-nineties their growing hysteria over the bogey of anarchism seriously undermined much of the sentimental liberalism which had previously existed.

[81] Ladies of the G.A.R., *Proceedings of the Seventh National Convention 1893* (Pittsburgh, n.d.), pp. 71–72.

XIII

Nationalism vs. Internationalism

W HEN the veterans' and hereditary societies considered what attitudes the United States should adopt toward the rest of the world, they displayed a combination of cocky nationalism and idealistic internationalism. Their conscious patriotic zeal bred a dislike of other countries as well as a jingoistic spirit which welcomed the Spanish-American War and the imperialist adventures at the turn of the century, but there also long lingered traces of America's mission of spreading democratic institutions and aiding the oppressed. There existed a sturdily militaristic outlook that favored stronger national defense and military instruction in the schools at the same time that there was a growing interest in peace and arbitration. The societies showed, in short, the same dichotomy that has already been observed in their views on sectionalism and domestic social problems.

The pronounced nationalistic fervor of the nineties confidently assumed the supremacy of the United States over all other lands. To a large extent this pride rose from the country's physical magnitude and resources.

No American boy [declared the New York Grand Army's committee on teaching history], can contemplate the wide extent of our country, the variety of its climate, its magnificent river systems, the superb and imposing grandeur of its mountain ranges, the vastness of its mineral resources, the fertility of its soil and the bountifulness of its agricultural products, the extent and variety of its manufactures, the industrial enterprise, the inventive genius and superior plane of living of the American people, without feeling proud that he was born on American soil.[1]

[1] Department of New York, Grand Army of the Republic, *Proceedings of the Thirty-Second Annual Encampment 1898* (New York and Albany, 1898), p. 67.

The judge advocate of the Kansas G.A.R. told the State Teachers' Association to "teach the children of this land that this is the grandest country on earth . . . that our mountains are the grandest, our fields and valleys the most beautiful, our rivers the most majestic." [2] From this awareness of the material greatness of the United States stemmed the belief that "our nation is the grandest under the sun, socially, religiously, intellectually and financially," as well as "the most enlightened, the most powerful, the most humane and the most generous of all governments ever established among men." [3]

A corollary of these nationalistic claims to superiority was a disdain of other countries, especially evidenced by the traditional hostility toward Great Britain. Whenever the veterans' papers wanted to discredit the Boston Brahmin and Harvard College group which contained so many civil service and tariff reformers, they denounced its "Anglomania." England's record as our old ruler against whose tyranny we had revolted, as the enemy in a second conflict in 1812 and as an unfriendly power during the Civil War made these journals strongly Anglophobe. The *Vedette* disclosed that it had "always entertained a suspicion that the ravenous British lion, crouched on our northern border, has been awaiting a favorable opportunity to recapture the American States and establish a Viceroy of the Guelph family in the White House in Washington." [4] The history of Britain's dealings not only with the United States but with such regions as India, Ireland, and the Transvaal was recalled. "England has never failed to take advantage of America in a diplomatic contest, whenever she could; as indeed, she has of all countries," the *American Tribune* pointed out, "until at last, the term—'Perfidious Albion,' is universally applied to her." The paper described her "familiar weapons" in both war and diplomacy as "bribery, coalition and coercion." [5] "Her course toward this and other countries has been so mercenary in the numerous acts of injustice and aggression," asserted the *Spirit of '76,* "that Americans feel a degree of contempt

[2] Department of Kansas, Grand Army of the Republic, *Journal of the Fifteenth Annual Encampment 1896* (Topeka, n.d.), p. 61.

[3] Department of Arkansas, Grand Army of the Republic, *Proceedings of the 16th and 17th Annual Encampments 1898–1899* (n.p., n.d.), p. 34; Society of the Army of the Tennessee, *Report of the Proceedings 1898* (Cincinnati, 1899), p. 101.

[4] *Vedette* (Washington, D.C.), Aug. 1888.

[5] *American Tribune* (Indianapolis), Jan. 28, 1897.

for a great power which so often condescends to the ignoble occupation of picking international pockets." [6]

The argument that the two countries had similar institutions little impressed these papers. Instead, they emphasized Britain's "aristocratic government whose chief feature is to rob the laboring man of the fruits of his labor that a class of useless loafers may live without work." [7] At the time of Queen Victoria's golden jubilee celebration in 1887 the *Vedette*'s strong republican and labor sympathies caused it to sneer at the "bloated aristocrats" who "with brazen assurance exhibited themselves to the honest toilers on the sidewalks in all their ill-gotten jewels and display of wealth wrung from the patient slaves of labor" and "graciously condescended to exhibit their manly forms and breathe the common atmosphere with the common people on this golden wedding of Mrs. Guelph to the crown." [8] "It has long been painfully apparent that English noblemen possessed the smallest brains in the world," observed the *American Tribune* when word came that a British peer owned the smallest book in the world, "and it is a hopeful sign that one, at least, is endeavoring to have his library conform in size to his brain." [9] Those who opposed certain privileges of past G.A.R. officials considered the expression "House of Lords" the most effective disparagement. The *National Tribune* printed parody Mother Goose rhymes satirizing the amount England spent supporting the royal family and particularly criticized the Prince of Wales for not performing any useful functions. The revelation of the heir apparent's gambling debts caused the *Grand Army Record* to recall the visit to Washington of "this same 'royal' dead beat (who never did an honest day's work in his life). . . . He was the same blackleg then that he is now. Although a married man, he was notoriously the associate of French prostitutes and dancing girls." [10]

The papers also played upon apprehensions of economic rivalry. "The main trouble is that England has a grasping policy," stated the *National Tribune*. "She wants to dominate other countries for business and commercial reasons, and is particularly anxious to have a

---

[6] "The United States Will Not Object," *Spirit of '76,* II (Jan. 1896), 118.

[7] "What Is Patriotism," *Grand Army Record,* IX (Sept. 1894), 65.

[8] *Vedette,* June 1887.

[9] *American Tribune,* May 31, 1894.

[10] *Grand Army Record,* VI (June 1891), 5.

controlling interest in ours." [11] It viewed the free trade movement in
the United States as a British plot to ruin American manufactures.
"English money has been sent, and is being sent here without stint,"
it warned, "for use in influencing public opinion against the veterans
and the tariff system." [12] The *Grand Army Record* protested the
participation of English constructors in building American naval
vessels. "What with English capitalists controlling millions of acres
of American soil and English noblemen designing war vessels for
the American navy," it mourned, "it is enough to make our glorious
flag droop with sorrow, and the proud bird of freedom howl with
rage." [13] Consequently, whenever the United States and the British
government had a diplomatic dispute, such as over fisheries, the
veterans' papers became strongly jingoistic and urged prompt warfare if England did not yield.

But while these papers were whipping up dislike for England, in
the nineties came signs that the new hereditary societies might form
the nucleus for a "hands across the sea" spirit. Although many of
them commemorated former conflicts with Great Britain, they were
equally conscious of the English stock that distinguished them from
more recent immigrants. "We nurse too carefully old prejudices, we
remember too long ancient injuries," lamented the historian James
K. Hosmer in a speech before the Missouri S.A.R. in 1891. Did not
the Revolutionary descendants realize "that possibly half of England
were, in the Revolution, really on our side, regarding our cause as
their own,—and that the descendants of the great masses who felt
with us, prayed with us, and rejoiced in our success, now hold England in their own hands?" He favored an informal Anglo-Saxon
union. "For some such clasping of hands, the world is certainly
ripe." [14] Another speaker hoped that the Society of Colonial Wars
would spread to Canada and England and thus "unite the mother
with the greater offspring in closer bonds of intercourse and friendship." [15]

[11] *National Tribune* (Washington, D.C.), Sept. 22, 1892.
[12] *Ibid.*, Oct. 3, 1889.
[13] "Our English Navy," *Grand Army Record,* II (Jan. 1886), 4.
[14] James K. Hosmer, *Address . . . of Historian of the Missouri Society of Sons of
the American Revolution* (St. Louis, 1891), p. 21.
[15] Society of Colonial Wars, *Constitution and By-Laws Membership* (New York,
1893), p. 52.

The Venezuela crisis with Great Britain in 1895 tested which viewpoint had become the more representative. The patriotic journals at once assumed an aggressive tone. So ingrained was its nationalistic and anti-British feeling that for once the *National Tribune* strongly backed Cleveland and insisted that the question must not be arbitrated. The *Spirit of '76* found the American willingness to fight if necessary "a source of solemn satisfaction to those who had feared that this country had lost much of its virile manhood in the growth of its material prosperity." The *American Tribune* boasted that "Grover has handed a Christmas gift to Johnny Bull on the point of a bayonet, in the name of all the American people who are worthy of the name," though later it hoped that, instead of war, the two nations might find "an honorable and amicable settlement of their disputes." [16]

The Civil War veterans shared this truculent attitude. At the annual encampment of New York's Grand Army James Tanner reminded England "that while the eagle soars over the United States, what his wings shadow, his beak and talons can protect and defend, so help us God." [17] Surely the American people supported the Monroe Doctrine and "mean to fight for it if necessary. I know the Naval Veterans do," proclaimed a speaker at that organization's national convention. "The sentiment of old glorious Commodore Decatur is a good one to remember at this time: 'My country,—may she always be right, but right or wrong, my Country.'" [18] Further support came from some of the men's hereditary societies. The president of the California Sons of the Revolution declared that Cleveland voiced "the unanimous sentiment of this land." [19] The New Jersey and District of Columbia S.A.R. also commended the President's action, while on the west coast the Washington branch warned "Johnny Bull to keep hands off every foot of the Territory of Alaska." [20]

But American patriotic societies did not present a united front

[16] "A Lesson from the Venezuela Incident," *Spirit of '76*, II (Feb. 1896), 144; *American Tribune*, Dec. 26, 1895, and Jan. 2, 1896.

[17] Department of New York, Grand Army of the Republic, *Proceedings of the Thirtieth Annual Encampment 1896* (Albany and New York, 1896), p. 103.

[18] William Simmons, *History of the National Association of Naval Veterans* (Philadelphia, 1895), p. 108.

[19] California Society, Sons of the Revolution, *First Report of the Historian* (Los Angeles, 1896), p. 22.

[20] "Among the Societies," *Spirit of '76*, II (Dec. 1895), 94.

during the dispute. The commander of the Rhode Island G.A.R. expressed "disapproval of invoking the dread arbitrament of war, until so far as is consistent with honor, every resource of diplomacy has been exhausted. The spectacle of a great nation carrying a chip upon its shoulder and indulging in either bluster or idle threats is both reprehensible and highly mischievous."[21] Though among the hereditary associations the men's groups tended to be more bellicose than the women's, the Minnesota S.A.R. refused to endorse Cleveland's policy. The Massachusetts Society of Colonial Wars voted unanimously "that it deprecates that extreme position which drives to war men of kindred blood of two of the foremost nations in Christendom, and that it believes that the sentiment which should animate the American people at this time is 'Peace on earth, good will towards men.'"[22] When the Daughters of 1812 met in New York in January 1896, Mrs. Edward Roby, who was president of both the Illinois branch and of the Ladies of the G.A.R., proposed that the women ask Queen Victoria to use her influence for peace between the English-speaking nations. They appointed Flora Adams Darling to frame such resolutions and Mrs. Roby to request Secretary of State Olney to transmit them.

To a large extent the shock of the Venezuela episode proved a turning point in the attitude toward England. While the *Spirit of '76* still insisted "that the Englishman wants the greater part of the earth" and a Grand Army member informed the citizenry of Lowell, Massachusetts, "that the ruling classes of England are intensely and savagely hostile to us as a nation" and "that nothing save our vast numerical strength and almost unlimited resources as a nation have prevented Great Britain from waging open warfare against us and despoiling us of our possessions,"[23] even the tone of the veterans' papers thereafter became less harsh. On Queen Victoria's diamond jubilee in 1897 the *American Tribune* once more cited the record of England's "ruthless invasion of the rights of others," but this time followed it up with the significant concession "that civilization has

[21] Department of Rhode Island, Grand Army of the Republic, *Journal of the Twenty-ninth Annual Encampment 1896* (Providence, 1896), p. 25.

[22] "Celebrations and Proceedings," *American Historical Register* (Feb. 1896), p. 690.

[23] *Spirit of '76*, IV (June 1898), 310; William H. Osborne, "Oration," *Grand Army Record*, XI (June 1896), 46.

followed in the wake of the British flag, and that, wherever it floats, better conditions prevail than before." As for the Queen herself, "only good can be said. Her reign is not only the longest, but it is also the greatest in the world's history." [24]

At the close of the century the conviction that England had shown herself the friend of the United States during the Spanish-American War produced a great outburst of pro-British sentiment. Especially members of the hereditary societies welcomed friendlier relations between the two English-speaking nations and declared that their common ideals and aims made an informal alliance both natural and desirable. In the words of one Son of the Revolution, "The drawing together of England and America will be recognized as the normal and irresistible advance of those principles with which the Saxon races have been entrusted for the good of the world." [25] "Let us make an alliance of hearts if not of hands with our kinsmen over the sea," proposed Mrs. Mary S. Lockwood in the D.A.R.'s magazine. "The God of their battles has been the God of our battles, their prophecies have been our prophecies. We are of one tongue, one blood, one purpose—the uplifting of humanity." [26] By 1901 William O. McDowell was proclaiming that "one of the most important steps that can be taken at this time in the world's history, is to bring about a postal union of Great Britain and the United States, as a forerunner of political union around the principles of the Great Charter, and the Declaration." [27]

Several minor episodes reflected this change of attitude. While in the early years of this period the Prince of Wales was held up to scorn, in later years reverence for the aged Queen at Windsor was emphasized. Upon her eightieth birthday the D.A.R. journal declared that, although King George III had lost the thirteen colonies, "Queen Victoria's sympathy and good will have won back their love, their respect, and has again re-united the Anglo-Saxon race in sentiment, if not in political bonds." Instead of recalling England's hos-

---

[24] *American Tribune,* June 24, 1897.

[25] New York Society, Sons of the Revolution, *Supplement to Year Book of 1899* (New York, 1903), p. 150.

[26] Mary S. Lockwood, "Parallels in History," *American Monthly Magazine,* XIII (Oct. 1898), 329.

[27] William O. McDowell to Theron McCampbell (?), Dec. 29, 1901, William O. McDowell Letterbooks, New York Public Library.

tility in the Civil War, it gave the Queen credit for the peaceful out-come of the *Trent* affair. "We shall still pay homage to the Queen of our Mother Country," it concluded, "and nowhere in any country will there be deeper affection shown to-day than in the United States for the woman who has rounded four score years in a reign crowded with glorious memories." [28]

Another sign of collaboration was the encampment of the Vermont Grand Army in Montreal in June 1899, the first gathering of veterans outside the United States. The meeting hailed the develop-ment of Anglo-Saxon friendship and hoped "that nothing may arise to interrupt the present good fellowship of these two people nor the progress of Anglo-Saxon civilization on the world." [29] But perhaps the most startling demonstration of an altered spirit was the favor-able reaction to a proposal that a monument be erected to the British soldiers who fell at Bunker Hill. Even the *Spirit of '76*, which previously had been so hostile to the British, felt that "The growing friendly relations between England and this country, would find most appropriate expression in an act of this kind." [30]

If the hereditary bodies based on the American Revolution agreed to overlook England's role in that conflict, they felt that America had too quickly forgotten France's part. Speakers at S.A.R. gather-ings frequently recalled French assistance. "One of the most amazing things in our history," declared the *Spirit of '76*, "is the tardiness with which this fact is recognized. No adequate expression of this gratitude has yet been made. The debt has not been paid." [31] Feeling that some return should be made for the Statue of Liberty, the Sons' first congress in 1890 endorsed the suggestion of the *Detroit Journal* that one-dollar contributions be collected for a testimonial to France. Among the prominent members serving on the fund-raising com-mittee were President-General W. Seward Webb, McDowell, Lucius Deming, Chauncey Depew, and S. B. Buckner. After one of the early presidents-general, Horace Porter, became minister to France, a branch was established there in 1897 whose announced purpose was "to cultivate friendship between France and America, create

[28] "Current History," *American Monthly Magazine*, XIV (June 1899), 1256.
[29] Department of Vermont, Grand Army of the Republic, *Proceedings of the Thirty-Second Annual Encampment 1899* (Lyndonville, Vt., 1899), p. 36.
[30] *Spirit of '76*, V (Aug. 1899), 260.
[31] "America's Obligation to France," *Spirit of '76*, I (Dec. 1894), 70.

a liberal interchange of literature, professors and students, and finally provoke an increase of commercial and political relations between the sister republics of France and America." [32]

The D.A.R. shared this good feeling toward France, welcoming a descendant of Lafayette, the Marquise de Chambrun, as a guest of honor at the 1896 Continental Congress. It too wished to show its gratitude by erecting some memorial. Mrs. Donald McLean, leader of the New York Daughters, induced the organization to appoint a Franco-American Committee to present a statue of Washington to France during the Paris Exposition of 1900; the Children of the American Revolution also contributed to this project. The only incident to mar this friendly attitude was the Dreyfus Case. The D.A.R.'s magazine was "horrified" by the verdict and felt that "France, not Dreyfus, is disgraced in the eyes of the world." [33] On the whole, however, one suspects that these societies felt a romantic attachment to a France of the time of Lafayette about whose institutions and development since then they actually knew little. Certainly the reference to the naughty French prostitutes so admired by the Prince of Wales indicated a suspicion, in veterans' circles at least, that an undesirable element had crept into the French character since the days of De Grasse and Rochambeau.

Despite this growing *rapprochement* with Great Britain and historic friendship with France, the general attitude of the patriotic societies toward the rest of the world was highly chauvinistic. "When jingoism has disappeared, the wild beasts will take possession," declared the *American Tribune,* "for we will no longer have the spirit to protect ourselves even from them. We will arbitrate and evacuate." [34] Attacks on excessive nationalism produced in reply this bit of verse at a banquet of the Iowa Sons of the Revolution:[35]

> Well, what's the matter with Jingo?
> Who is going to say
> The Great American Eagle
> Shan't get gay?

[32] Sons of the American Revolution, *National Year Book 1905* (Coshocton, Ohio, n.d.), p. 141.

[33] "Current History," *American Monthly Magazine,* XV (Oct. 1899), 519.

[34] *American Tribune,* July 1, 1897.

[35] Iowa Society, Sons of the Revolution, *Seventh Annual Meeting 1896* (Davenport, Iowa, 1896), p. 31.

What's the matter with Jingo?
Who's a-going to growl
When your Uncle Samuel
Makes Rome howl?
What's the matter with Jingo?
Will anybody cry
Just because Old Glory
Waves on high?
What's the matter with Jingo?
The Red, the White, the Blue
Can beat the whole creation,
P.D.Q.

On the ground that "We should be as proud of the products of our industrial successes just as we glory in the exploits of American heroes," for a while the D.A.R. sponsored a movement to buy only American goods.[36] Yet once again there was not complete unanimity, for a heretical speaker at a Connecticut S.A.R. dinner denied that "this is the only country in the world worth living in. . . . This grand country of ours has a great deal to learn by contact with the older countries of the world before it will take the place it is to be given by common consent. It may be fashionable to sneer at the characteristic social and political conditions that exist elsewhere, but it is not sensible." [37] Such restraint, however, was not the dominant note of the patriotic societies of the day.

This nationalism and jingoism produced both a "tough" or "hard-boiled" school of imperialism (exemplified by the highly practical strategic and economic considerations of Captain Alfred Mahan) and a "tender" or "soft" school (exemplified by the civilizing and missionary impulses of the clergyman Josiah Strong), both of which turned up in the thought of patriotic groups. At its worst the complacent concern for spreading American institutions could easily become a rationalization for annexing much of the Western hemisphere. This became evident for a moment just after the Civil War. At that time a revolt in Cuba stirred up interest that was not entirely

[36] "Proceedings of the Fifth Continental Congress," *American Monthly Magazine*, VIII (May 1896), 704; "What We Are Doing and Chapter Work," *ibid.*, IX (Nov. 1896), 453.
[37] Connecticut Society, Sons of the American Revolution, *Year Book for 1895 and 1896* (New Haven, 1896), p. 84.

unselfish. Though some gatherings of the veterans preferred to avoid the subject as too controversial, more imperialistic-minded members frankly voiced their sympathy and showed a willingness to acquire the island. Even more bellicose was General Joseph Hooker. "I'm ready for the next war! It will be with Canada, and it is bound to come," he told the Society of the Army of the Cumberland in 1870. "We want no British possessions nearer than across the Atlantic ocean. We don't want to buy Canada, we want to *whip* her." [38] But on the whole for many years it seldom occurred to the veterans' societies to consider international questions at all.

In the mid-eighties the *National Tribune* anticipated the expansionist spirit so prevalent a decade later with arguments that would delight a neo-Marxist. The United States, it declared, would have to adopt an aggressive foreign policy to find a market for the goods it produced in excess of the home demand. The competition of England and France, as well as the moral duty of preventing international injustice, required such a program. "We may occasionally have to shell a seaport or land a column of troops, as England and France do, but that is no serious matter," the paper added. "As a rule, their military operations against imperfectly civilized people have been entirely justified and resulted in general good." [39] Asserting that all trade with Latin America rightfully belonged to the United States, it pressed a commercial invasion of Mexico and South America before the Germans should get there. Finally, it proclaimed that the United States should annex Cuba: "We should have the island if for no other reason than to give us command of the Gulf of Mexico, protect our growing commerce with South America, and impregnably shield our southern coast from ravages by hostile fleets. Cuba is necessary to the security of the immense Mississippi Valley." [40] In the next few years the *Tribune* added San Salvador, Costa Rica, Nicaragua, Honduras, and Guatemala to this list. These views, however, were considerably in advance of the official attitudes of the veterans' organizations.

[38] Society of the Army of the Cumberland, *Fourth Re-Union 1870* (Cincinnati, 1870), pp. 13–14.
[39] *National Tribune*, Aug. 14, 1883.
[40] *Ibid.*, Aug. 2, 1888.

By the nineties the other journals for ex-soldiers joined this chorus. "The time is ripe for extending to the Nations of this continent especially, the blessings of democratic institutions," the *Vedette* announced in 1893. After disclosing that the "discovery of this continent by Christopher Columbus four hundred years ago was a part of the Divine plan to unite the nations of the earth under a central authority, to know one God, one Church, and a uniform system of government," it advocated the annexation of Canada, Mexico, Central and South America, and the building of a railroad from Canada to Patagonia. It too argued for this policy on economic grounds: "We would find in these newly opened lands a market for our manufactures and everything they need, and would transport in return their fruits and spices to supply the markets of the whole world." The resultant prosperity would alleviate the condition of the workingmen, which otherwise "will drive them to frenzy." [41]

The veterans' papers particularly pressed the acquisition of Hawaii, because it was essential for naval security and, if we did not take the islands, some other power would; naturally it opposed Cleveland's cautious policy. According to the *American Tribune,* anyone opposing annexation "is an enemy of his country." [42] The organizations themselves, however, hesitated to take a formal stand. The most outspoken group was the Hawaii Society of the Sons of the American Revolution, which in May 1897 issued an address appealing for annexation. It cited Captain Alfred Mahan's opinion as to the islands' strategic importance, warned that otherwise Japan would seize them, and also emphasized their commercial value. The local Grand Army and Sons of Veterans endorsed the statement.

But it would be a mistake to emphasize solely the self-seeking materialistic aspects of expansionism. Just as potent, perhaps more so, in the minds of many patriotic Americans was the more idealistic version of the same spirit which sincerely believed in exporting American principles to the rest of the world, either by mere example or by more positive means. A speaker before the Society of the Army of the Tennessee announced rather smugly that "the place of this nation is at the head of the column of civilization. Not that we would put

---

[41] *Vedette,* Feb. 1893.
[42] *American Tribune,* March 24, 1898.

other nations down. . . . Our idea has always been and is now to point out to other nations the way to come up higher." [43]

The professional patriots therefore hailed the spread of republican principles. The commander of the Michigan Grand Army praised Brazil's overthrow of the empire: "Hereditary monarchy, the determined enemy of human rights, and the liberties of the people, has received a fatal blow." He hoped that free institutions would continue their march "until sometime in the future liberty will be the rule, and despotism the rare exception." [44] Others voiced the same opposition to monarchy and titles of nobility. Devoted as it was to one form of ancestor worship, the *Spirit of '76* reprimanded efforts to trace lineage to the royalty and nobility of Europe whose "principles and morals are, and have been during the existence of European States, detestable." [45] When the D.A.R. made the Infanta Eulalia of Spain an honorary member, its bitter rival, the Daughters of the Revolution, was prompt with the pious comment, "The word 'American' is misplaced in any society that professes to honor the heroism and deeds of those who defended the Country's Liberty, yet bends the sycophantic knee before members of the blood royal of a despotic power. . . ." [46]

In the mind of William O. McDowell the mission of the Sons of the American Revolution was to spread republicanism over the entire globe. He wanted the descendants of Revolutionary soldiers to "reach out our hands to the men throughout the world, not only to those who have secured self-government, but for those who are still 'hoping against fate.'" [47] On June 10, 1889, McDowell issued an address to the S.A.R. "Two paths open to our Society," he announced. "It may collect and treasure relics, trace ancestors, and extol the heroic era of the Nation. It may cultivate knee-buckles, cocked hats, swords, wigs, scarlet vests and stockings, and all those ancient costumes once so picturesque, so brilliant, and so suitable."

[43] Society of the Army of the Tennessee, *Report of the Proceedings 1896* (Cincinnati, 1897), p. 142.

[44] Department of Michigan, Grand Army of the Republic, *Journal of the Twelfth Annual Encampment 1890* (Big Rapids, Mich., 1890), p. 13.

[45] "Editorial," *Spirit of '76*, IV (April 1898), 242.

[46] "A Pertinent Question," *Magazine of Daughters of the Revolution*, I (Oct. 1893), 49.

[47] McDowell to Luther L. Tarbell, June 13, 1889, McDowell Letterbooks.

This would appeal to those who "look behind rather than before for the golden age of our humanity." McDowell, however, felt that the Sons had "a nobler mission than devotion to the antique and esthetical." They should correspond with the descendants of such French friends of the American Revolution as Lafayette and De Grasse. "But why confine ourselves to a single country?" he continued. "On our own continent we have sister republics," he observed in an early declaration of Pan-Americanism. "Let us form with them leagues of fellowship. Our hearts should embrace self-government throughout the world." [48]

Among the S.A.R. leaders signing this statement were the first president-general, Lucius Deming; the vice-president-general, Luther Tarbell of Massachusetts; the national secretary, James Cresap of Maryland; and the president of the Vermont society, E. A. Crittenden. At the time of the first national convention in April 1890, another member, Ethan Allen of New York, praised McDowell for having rekindled the patriotic fires of 1776. "In the struggles for freedom our fathers wanted only the thirteen colonies," he declared, "but their Sons want the Earth. May the great 'Order' this day meeting at Louisville become irrepressible until Monarchy every where goes down in disaster and is entombed beneath Bunker Hill." [49]

Instead, the Louisville gathering sheared McDowell of most of his power in the society. In June 1890, he, Allen, and William H. Arnoux, also prominent in the Sons, "recognizing that there is a natural conflict between the two forms of government that now rule the world, the one based on the theory of the Divine right of Kings and aristocracy, and the other based on the beliefs of the Divine rights of the people as expressed in the Declaration of Independence," met at Fraunces Tavern in New York to form the Order of the American Eagle, which appropriated the S.A.R.'s professed objects and made Allen's statement of April its declaration of principles. It ruled that admission "should be based wholly upon service rendered in extending the area of political freedom formulated in the

[48] Address to the Society of the Sons of the American Revolution, William O. McDowell Scrapbooks, XXVIII, New York Public Library.
[49] Ethan Allen to McDowell, April 30, 1890, Minutes of the Order of the American Eagle, William O. McDowell Papers, New York Public Library.

American Declaration of Independence and carried out in the
American Republic." [50] Among those so recognized in the next
few months were Admiral David D. Porter, James G. Blaine, Presi-
dent Fonseca of Brazil, Louis Kossuth, Edmond Lafayette, Andrew
Carnegie, Yung Wing (a long-time Chinese associate of McDowell),
Emilio Castelar (a Spanish republican leader), and Mrs. Mary S.
Cushing (whose four sons had died in the service of their country).
McDowell even wrote to the Japanese consul in New York asking
what Nipponese would be eligible for having done the most to bring
about constitutional government in Japan.

The Order of the American Eagle never proved to be more than a
paper association of three S.A.R. members in New York, and Mc-
Dowell soon turned to another project for promulgating world-wide
freedom. In a circular letter on June 17, 1890, the same day as the
founding of the American Eagle, he proposed that the S.A.R., Cincinnati, G.A.R., Loyal Legion, Sons of Veterans, D.A.R., Colonial
Dames, U.C.V., Huguenot Society, Odd Fellows, Masons, and
Knights of Labor send representatives to a Pan Republic Congress
in Washington. McDowell, whom a California paper described at
this time as "an amiable gentleman with a fondness for punching
off very wearisome letters on a type-writer," [51] now bombarded
numerous persons, both inside and out of patriotic societies, with
appeals for support.

Several individuals active in hereditary groups quickly gave their
backing. Allen promptly asserted that the plan "must demand the
respect of every creature who has soul enough to feel and mind
enough to appreciate that man is debased wherever found, who is
'subject' to any other man or held by any government in which he
has no voice to make or mar." [52] "I am with you in spirit and may
God bless your efforts . . .," declared William D. Cabell, a Washington member of the S.A.R. who was the husband of the D.A.R.
leader, "the work done by our Fathers *must stand!* and never perish
from the minds and hearts of the Sons of the American Revolution." [53] Other well-known S.A.R. endorsers were Lucius Deming

[50] Minutes of the Order of the American Eagle, *ibid.*
[51] *Alta California* (San Francisco), Oct. 16, 1890.
[52] Allen to McDowell, June 16, 1890, McDowell Scrapbooks, XXXIII.
[53] William D. Cabell to McDowell, Dec. 5, 1890, *ibid.*, XXXVIII.

of Connecticut, Josiah Pumpelly of New Jersey, Walter S. Logan of New York, William Wirt Henry of Virginia, and Champion Chase of Nebraska. From other men's organizations came the support of Persifor Frazer, active in the Sons of the Revolution, and John Cadwalader, president of the General Society of the War of 1812. As a member of the Sons of Veterans, McDowell also sought that order's approval. Its commander-in-chief, Leland J. Webb, assured him that "the sons of the men who saved this nation will ever be found on the side of right and justice, ever working to ameliorate the condition of mankind." [54]

In addition to this wide response within patriotic societies, a number of other distinguished citizens expressed their approval. Rutherford B. Hayes, while feeling unable to contribute much time, declared himself "so well satisfied that America can and ought to be the great peace-maker of the world, and that this movement will tend in that direction, that my wish is to be counted among its earnest friends and advocates." [55] Frances Willard allowed the use of her name, and John P. Altgeld, declaring "the scheme an excellent one," wanted the Congress to be held in Chicago.[56] Contributions came not only from leaders in patriotic groups like Allen, Frazer, Chase, Arnoux, Henry Baldwin, and Russell Alger, but also from Andrew Carnegie, William C. Whitney, Vice-President Levi P. Morton (an S.A.R. member), and Cardinal Gibbons. By the spring of 1891, letterheads carried David Dudley Field's name as honorary chairman and Champion Chase's as chairman. Advertised as committee members were Grover Cleveland, John C. Ridpath, Carl Schurz, Lyman Abbott, Robert Ingersoll, and Cardinal Gibbons. McDowell's inner circle of followers, chiefly associates in the S.A.R., held most of the important positions. Arnoux was chairman of the General Committee of 200, Allen of the Executive Committee, Logan of the Committee on Congressional Action, and Frazer of the Committee on Invitation to Patriotic Societies.

There were a few discordant voices from both the societies and elsewhere. "It is in my opinion a grand idea, but *premature,*" Flora Adams Darling reported. "After the Sons have become a world-wide

---

[54] Leland J. Webb to McDowell, Jan. 2, 1891, *ibid.*
[55] Rutherford B. Hayes to McDowell, May 22, 1891, *ibid.*, XIV.
[56] John P. Altgeld to McDowell, July 2, 1890, *ibid.*, XXXIII.

and admired organization we can embrace the world." [57] The head
of the Connecticut S.A.R., Jonathan Trumbull, felt that for a long
time to come the society could keep sufficiently busy "doing whatever it legitimately can toward making our own Republic a model
one." [58] "Of one thing I am certain that some of the names attached
to the document you sent me as contributors to the expense fund
are not friendly to the interests that I represent," the head of the
Knights of Labor, T. V. Powderly, informed McDowell, "and, furthermore, that they are diametrically opposed to my idea of a democratic form of government, and when such men contribute it seems
to me it is a pretty good idea for me to have nothing to do with." [59]
"Your project is so vast that it confounds me," observed the famous
liberal clergyman, Washington Gladden. "I haven't a word to say.
The weather is too hot. And I am the last man in the world for such
a conglomeration of associations. I shouldn't know what to do in a
crowd like that." [60] James Russell Lowell wrote that he had never
accepted a place on the committee and asked to have his name removed, while Lew Wallace, who in the fall of 1890 had declared his
election "is very agreeable," by the spring of 1891 refused to be chairman of the Committee on the Address to the People of the World,
adding, "In my judgment a more unfitting paper for the purpose
could hardly have been prepared." [61]

The group's first meeting occurred in New York in December
1890. Those present included Arnoux, who presided, Allen, Frazer,
Ridpath, Yung Wing, Charles F. Deems (a minister who had been
associated with McDowell in the Institute of Christian Philosophy),
and President E. Benjamin Andrews of Brown University. McDowell made "a long and rambling report" on the objects of a Pan
Republic Congress, such as uniform coinage, weights and measures,
and a plan of arbitration. The *New York Times* unkindly titled its
account: "Members of the Big Committee Meet, But Accomplish
Little." [62] At another session in Philadelphia in April 1891, the committee decided to form a Human Freedom League which would

---

[57] Flora Adams Darling to McDowell, Sept. 12, 1890, *ibid.,* XXXV.
[58] Jonathan Trumbull to McDowell, Aug. 28, 1890, *ibid.,* XXXVI.
[59] T. V. Powderly to McDowell, Feb. 5, 1891, *ibid.,* XXXVIII.
[60] Washington Gladden to McDowell, June 30, 1890, *ibid.,* XXXIII.
[61] Lew Wallace to McDowell, Nov. 10, 1890, *ibid.,* XLI and March 9, 1891, *ibid.,*
XLIII.
[62] *New York World,* Dec. 7, 1890; *New York Times,* Dec. 7, 1890.

sponsor Pan Republic Congresses every five years in cities of outstanding republics like Rio de Janeiro and Berne.

Meanwhile McDowell became an editor of *Home and Country,* until then exclusively a veterans' journal, and now could publicize his schemes through it. In its pages Pumpelly, Frazer, A. Brown Goode, national registrar of the S.A.R., Charles Edwin Cheney, the chaplain-general, and William H. Jack, president of the Louisiana Sons, asked members of the S.A.R. and S.R. to have their leaders endorse the Pan Republic Congress and the Human Freedom League. Through the magazine McDowell also urged the Grand Army, W.R.C., and Sons of Veterans to send representatives to the next meeting in Philadelphia in October 1891. The head of the G.A.R., John Palmer, did turn up at this affair, over which Ridpath presided this time. McDowell secured the official formation of the Human Freedom League but shortly thereafter became absorbed in the Columbian Liberty Bell project, and the Pan Republic Congress idea faded out of existence. Though the movement accomplished nothing, it revealed how strongly many of the original members of hereditary societies supported the ideal of republicanism to the extent of involvement in so curiously chimerical a scheme.

This sentiment resulted in a feeling of obligation to aid those struggling to achieve their freedom. Applause greeted a past commander of the New Jersey S.A.R. when he announced that "it is our duty as American citizens to lend our sympathy; to extend the cordial hand of fellowship to the people all over the face of this earth who are seeking to break down the bonds of tyrants. . . ." [63] Oppressed minorities in the Ottoman and Russian empires especially attracted attention. Both veterans' and hereditary groups became deeply indignant over reports of Turkish atrocities against the Armenians. Many felt that the United States should take some action. The *Spirit of '76* advocated American intervention to restore order. The Pittsburgh chapter of the D.A.R. wanted the government to help persecuted Christians "to throw off the yoke of their cruel, bigoted and blood-thirsty tyrant," but the national congress tabled the resolution.[64] The commander of the Rhode Island G.A.R. favored sending a fleet which would end the massacres by threatening to bombard

---

[63] Department of New Jersey, Grand Army of the Republic, *Proceedings of the 30th Annual Encampment 1897* (Camden, N.J., 1897), p. 89.

[64] "Proceedings of Fifth Continental Congress," pp. 520–521.

Constantinople. A little later Crete's revolt against Turkey also aroused sympathy. The Minnesota Grand Army announced that "by the brutal, relentless, and remorseless butchery and slaughter of its innocent subjects, the Turkish government has forfeited its right to its existence as a nation and it should be utterly destroyed and blotted out from among the nations of the earth. . . ." [65]

Conditions in Russia attracted less attention. Though the *National Tribune* was convinced that it would require a revolution to effect any permanent improvement there, 117 G.A.R. posts in the spring of 1892 contributed 255 barrels of flour to aid starving Russian peasants. McDowell's Pan Republic Congress scheme brought him into touch with Alfred J. McClure, secretary of the Siberian Exile Association. The meeting of the Pan Republic Congress Committee at Philadelphia in October 1891 commissioned McDowell and Edward Everett Hale, who were to be delegates to an international peace congress in Rome, also to present the Czar with a petition for better treatment of political prisoners. McDowell then suggested that for each signature on the plea a bushel of corn be sent to relieve famine in Russia. McDowell and Hale never made their trip, but six shiploads of food were sent by a group of persons, many of whom were connected with the Pan Republic Congress movement. McDowell was also interested in the cause of Polish liberty, and in the spring of 1893 a group of Polish-Americans presented him with a Polish flag in appreciation of his sympathy.

But these evidences of good will toward downtrodden peoples were insignificant compared with the tremendous enthusiasm for Cuba's efforts to secure her freedom from Spain. Numerous leaders and encampments of the Grand Army from Maine to California protested Spanish atrocities and declared their sympathy with the rebels, often comparing them with the colonists in the American Revolution. Usually they wanted Congress to recognize the Cubans as belligerents. Other Civil War organizations, like the Union Veteran Legion, the Societies of the Army of the Potomac and of the Tennessee, and the Loyal Legion, expressed similar sentiments. Though the veterans' papers advocated annexing Cuba, the organizations themselves did not go so far. But they did object strongly

---

[65] Department of Minnesota, Grand Army of the Republic, *Journal of Proceedings of the Thirty-first Annual Encampment 1897* (St. Paul, 1897), p. 115.

to the attitude of the Cleveland administration. While the Union Veteran Legion declined to condemn "the un-democratic, the un-patriotic and un-American Executive of this nation," [66] the Minnesota G.A.R. attacked "the complacent manner" in which the government had reacted to Spanish indignities to Americans, and the head of the Rhode Island department deplored the United States' policy as "both feeble and vicious. It has been sinister, perverse, deceptive, pusillanimous and impotent, and of a character heretofore unknown in our foreign relations; some one has blundered, and every true man must blush with shame over the cowardly position we have so far occupied." [67] The *American Tribune* suggested that at the end of his term Cleveland might "for a salary, consent to continue as Spain's representative in the United States." [68]

The Sons of the American Revolution and the Sons of the Revolution, even more conscious of the similarity between the Cuban insurrection and the American Revolution, also sympathized with the insurgents. Naturally McDowell reacted promptly to this struggle to throw off monarchical rule. As early as the uprising of 1868 his close friend, Ethan Allen, had organized a Cuban League of the United States. When he revived the organization in 1896, he found willing support from McDowell, who three years earlier had assured Allen that the Columbian Liberty Bell was also intended to ring for Cuban liberty. Allen was president of this group, which had among its officers such S.A.R. leaders as Walter S. Logan and Chauncey M. Depew. McDowell, though interested enough to devote considerable time to its efforts, for once realized the importance of "keeping my name entirely in the background." [69] The association agitated for Congress to declare war on Spain and secure Cuban independence. Allen's endeavors to get the New York G.A.R. to endorse a vast national subscription fund to free Cuba and to appoint a committee to work with his organization did not succeed, as the veterans hesitated to move faster than President McKinley. Later

[66] Union Veteran Legion, *Proceedings of the Eleventh National Encampment 1896* (Wilmington, Del., n.d.), p. 56.

[67] Minn. G.A.R., *Journal 1897*, p. 114; Department of Rhode Island, Grand Army of the Republic, *Journal of the Thirtieth Annual Encampment 1897* (Providence, 1897), p. 24.

[68] *American Tribune*, Feb. 11, 1897.

[69] McDowell to Mary Desha, Dec. 21, 1896, Mary Desha Papers, Library of Congress.

McDowell founded a Cuban-American League, which advocated annexation at the same time that it was selling the bonds of the non-existent "Republic of Cuba."

The veterans at least fully realized the possible consequences of their aggressive attitude. At the Minnesota Grand Army's encampment in February 1897, a quartet sang: [70]

> Oh, what will you do when you have to go to Cuba?
> You know there's trouble in that island of the sea,
> Old Spain is getting hot at us Yankees in America,
> You may be called upon to set those patriots free.

"The United States needs a foreign war, and Spain needs a thrashing," the *American Tribune* announced succinctly. "Both these wants can be supplied in Cuba. Order out the ships." [71] The Oklahoma G.A.R. declared that if American aid should lead to hostilities, "we will hail such a result with delight," while a past commander of the New Jersey department predicted confidently that "a war with Spain could be ended by the tug boats of New York City alone." [72] After the sinking of the *Maine* the soldiers' papers insisted that there be no arbitration but that war be declared at once; they did not conceal their disgust at McKinley's hesitancy. The D.A.R. chapter in Dedham, Massachusetts seems to have been the only group that actually tried to influence Congress to keep peace.

The declaration of war enabled all self-styled patriotic organizations to display their devotion to the country. They had no doubts as to the unselfish character of the conflict. "No other war by any other people since the formation of government," declared the commander of the Iowa G.A.R., "has been waged solely upon the broad principles of Christian humanitarianism," while to the national president of the Daughters of the Revolution it was "a war undertaken in behalf of human liberty and to secure a wider freedom and a larger opportunity for mankind . . . a necessary step in the progress of civilization and the advancement of mankind." [73] Grand

---

[70] Minn. G.A.R., *Journal 1897*, p. 142.

[71] *American Tribune,* June 10, 1897.

[72] Department of Oklahoma, Grand Army of the Republic, *Proceedings of the Seventh Annual Encampment 1897* (Guthrie, Okla., 1897), p. 18; N.J. G.A.R., *Proceedings 1897*, p. 89.

[73] Department of Iowa, Grand Army of the Republic, *Journal of the Twenty-fifth Annual Encampment 1899* (Mason City, Iowa, 1900), p. 37; Daughters of the Revolution, *Proceedings of the Annual Meeting 1898* (New York, 1898), p. 10.

Army members were, for the most part, past the age of active service. But along both the Atlantic and Pacific seaboards they offered themselves for coast defense and in the interior an occasional post proposed that the ex-soldiers contribute part of their pension money for the building of a battleship to be called *The Veteran* or *The G.A.R.* To some extent, however, the veterans were probably a bit jealous of the new crop of combatants who might dispute their honors and whose achievements they contemptuously regarded as child's play.

For the hereditary societies it was their first chance to prove their patriotism in wartime. Mrs. Daniel Lothrop, head of the Children of the American Revolution, urged the youngsters to give up candy and soda water and instead to raise money for the soldiers and sailors through lawn parties and loan exhibits. Heeding her injunction, local societies contributed reading matter, jellies, and bath towels to camps and hospitals. The original organization of Colonial Dames raised over $46,000 for war work. A Relief Association established by its rival, the National Society of Colonial Dames, secured more than $18,000, while from members within the state branches came $28,000 more.

The most active group was the Daughters of the American Revolution. In May the national board of management asked all chapters to aid the needy families of service men and to furnish comforts to the armed forces. It also suggested that a "D.A.R. War Fund" be started for emergency purposes, which eventually obtained over $5000. The society presented the hospital ship *Missouri* with a steam launch, painted in the order's colors with the D.A.R.'s initials on its bow. Meanwhile the local chapters also went into action, often working with the Red Cross or community relief associations. Even in the pacifist-minded chapter in Dedham, "no one held back. . . . Many members spent a large part of every day, all through the summer, in making and collecting garments, supplies and funds for the soldiers," it proudly reported. "Ten thousand volumes of magazines, and barrels of illustrated papers were sent to hospitals and camps to relieve the tedium of convalescence." [74] In Jacksonville, Florida, the members, foreseeing the importance of that region, attended lectures on the care of the sick and wounded and, when the war brought twenty thousand soldiers to the city, deluged the military hospital

[74] Daughters of the American Revolution, *Second Report 1897–1898* (Washington, 1900), pp. 136–137.

with sheets, pillowcases, nightshirts, mosquito netting, soups, jellies, flowers, and books.

The Daughters' most important war project, however, was the establishment of a corps of trained female nurses, an innovation which once more signalized the changing status of women in America. Dr. Anita Newcomb McGee, daughter of the scientist, Simon Newcomb, and herself a physician and vice-president-general of the society, originated the idea, hoping thereby to gain for professional nurses recognition never previously granted by the government. Aided by a committee of prominent D.A.R.'s married to men high in official circles such as Mrs. Russell A. Alger and Mrs. Charles W. Fairbanks, she persuaded the Army and Navy to disregard the prevalent suspicion of women nurses and to turn all their applications for such service over to the society, which organized a D.A.R. Hospital Corps. Whenever nurses were needed, a call was sent to the D.A.R. office.[75] In September 1898, Dr. McGee became Acting Assistant Surgeon in the Army to supervise the 1200 trained nurses thus recruited. As a result of this experience Dr. McGee started her agitation for the establishment of a regular Army Nurse Corps which Congress finally approved in 1901.[76]

When the war was over, members of both veterans' and hereditary associations agreed that there could now be little doubt as to the preeminence of the United States, the virtues of expansion, and the obligation to spread liberty and freedom throughout the world. Commander-in-Chief W. C. Johnson of the Grand Army boasted that "when this country wants to 'expand' she will just simply 'expand,' and the other fellow must keep out of the way; and wherever humanity demands and duty calls, there our flag will go, and, if necessary, she will remain." [77] Usually speakers pointed out that this was a divinely ordained responsibility. Josiah Pumpelly disclosed "that a Divine Providence has appointed the Anglo-Saxon race the peculiarly noble task of providing an honest and humane

[75] Motivating Surgeon General George M. Sternberg of the Army's acceptance of the idea were both his dislike of the American Red Cross, which would have liked to perform this service, and the presence of Mrs. Sternberg on the D.A.R. committee. Foster Rhea Dulles, *The American Red Cross* (New York, 1951), p. 52.

[76] *Evening Bulletin* (Philadelphia), Feb. 2, 1951.

[77] Department of Indiana, Grand Army of the Republic, *Journal of Twentieth Annual Session 1899* (Indianapolis, 1899), p. 188.

government for peoples who alone and unaided are unable to throw off the rule of tyranny and misrule. . . ." [78] "The Anglo-Saxon race, with the bible in one hand and the sword of protection in the other," predicted the commander of the Colorado Grand Army, "will carry the English tongue and the principles of liberty which it teaches throughout the world until all people be free from the oppressor's power." [79] "God sets a pace for nations and men must follow," Senator John Thurston told his fellow Sons of Veterans between bursts of applause, "and having the blessings which we enjoy, if the God of the universe has set upon us the task of bearing liberty and civilization to distant lands, I will be the last man to stand up and kick against God Almighty." [80] Such sentiments were common at gatherings of patriotic organizations throughout 1898 and 1899.

These views meant strong support of the government's policy concerning the Philippines. The Grand Army of the Republic repeatedly endorsed McKinley's program. The arguments that the flag should not be lowered once it had been raised anywhere and that the United States must suppress any rebellion against its authority were particularly persuasive to Civil War veterans. In the words of a member of the Society of the Army of the Tennessee, "whenever the flag is thrown to the breeze, it will never be furled until the American people so order. It must be in our own good time, and not because hostile guns are aimed at it. Rebellion by any tribe or section must be crushed before any other question can be discussed." [81] As for the broader issue of permanent possession of the islands, some advanced hard-headed selfish reasons for their retention. Foreseeing "a very large and profitable market for our products," the *National Tribune* pictured Filipino shop windows filled with American sewing machines, books, shoes, and bicycles.[82]

But the usual attitude toward the new territory combined idealistic with practical considerations. "It furnishes just that outlet which is

[78] J. C. Pumpelly to Sir Thomas Lipton, Sept. 14, 1898, *Spirit of '76,* V (Dec. 1898), 74.

[79] Department of Colorado and Wyoming, Grand Army of the Republic, *Journal of the Twentieth Annual Encampment 1899* (n.p., n.d.), p. 71.

[80] Sons of Veterans, U.S.A., *Journal of Proceedings of the Eighteenth Annual Encampment 1899* (Boston, 1900), p. 112.

[81] Society of the Army of the Tennessee, *Report of the Proceedings at the Thirty-first Meeting 1899* (Cincinnati, 1900), p. 90.

[82] *National Tribune,* May 19 and May 26, 1898.

necessary, first, as a stepping stone to the markets of the far East for the enormous surplus of industry and agriculture which we have," Senator Chauncey M. Depew told the S.A.R.'s national congress, and then added, "and next, for its own development it furnishes an opportunity for our people and for the good of those people." [83] Little satisfaction as it may give to the determinedly Marxist historian, the chief factors forming opinion on the Philippines were genuine humanitarianism and a rather smug sense of divine mission. "Blind must be the man who cannot see that God would not let Dewey sail away from Manila after he had destroyed the Spanish fleet," the chaplain-in-chief, who may or may not have had special sources of information, revealed to the national encampment of the G.A.R. in 1899, "and there never has been an hour since then when McKinley dare look God in the face and order the troops home and have barbarism to bear sway." [84]

Only an occasional voice protested this wave of imperialistic feeling. The eccentric *Grand Army Record,* so frequently in disagreement with official G.A.R. policy, warned against acquiring regions whose people were not ready for self-government or trying "to civilize all the half-civilized and savage people in the world." [85] Among the journals of the hereditary societies, the *Spirit of '76* decried imposing American rule where it was not wanted, while President David Starr Jordan of Stanford tried to rouse the S.A.R. of California against territorial expansion and American occupation of the Philippines. But these objections merely evoked a storm of criticisms.

Though carefully paying lip service to the rights of free speech and free discussion, the G.A.R. bitterly attacked the anti-imperialists. The latters' dismay at the government's forcible suppression of Aguinaldo's rebellion caused the veterans to brand them as traitors giving comfort to the enemy. Recalling the careers of Benedict Arnold and Clement Vallandigham, an officer of the Illinois Grand Army asserted, "Treason has hatched another traitorous brood in

---

[83] Sons of the American Revolution, *National Year Book 1899* (Chicago, n.d.), p. 144.

[84] Grand Army of the Republic, *Journal of the Thirty-third National Encampment 1899* (Philadelphia, 1899), p. 87.

[85] *Grand Army Record,* XIII (July 1898), 51.

the persons of so-called scholars and philanthropists." [86] The California department denounced "the traitorous junta of so-called educators, united with a handful of political demagogues, who are giving substantial aid and comfort to our enemies in time of war, and who are prolonging the war in the Philippines and increasing the daily death roll of our army," [87] while the commander of the New York branch could scarcely express his "scorn and contempt for the treasonable efforts of self-righteous Pharisees to hinder and embarrass the President" and branded them as "directly responsible for the suffering and death of our gallant soldiers." His supporters unanimously proclaimed critics of the war "guilty of treason, not entitled to the protection of the flag they dishonor and unworthy the name of American citizens." [88] Their dislike for this group, of course, was hardly lessened by the fact that so many of the anti-imperialists were the very good government, civil service, and tariff reformers of Mugwump inclinations they had already long detested for opposition to veterans' preference and lavish pensions.

Meanwhile, the combination of the growing spirit of coöperation with England and the emergence of America's own imperialistic difficulties made the societies less sympathetic than formerly to struggles against British rule. Whereas in the eighties the *National Tribune* had backed the Irish against the English and the Iowa Grand Army in 1887 had commended their efforts to secure "the inalienable rights which justly belong to all men," [89] by 1896 the president of the Iowa Sons of the Revolution was criticizing the Irish-Americans, "seeking in a new home and under a new allegiance to embroil this land in the avenging of wrongs we may deplore but can in no sense recognize." [90] Nor did the Boer War produce the same expressions of encouragement for the underdog as had Cuba's struggles against

[86] Department of Illinois, Grand Army of the Republic, *Proceedings of the Thirty-third Annual Encampment 1899* (Chicago, n.d.), p. 196.

[87] Department of California, Grand Army of the Republic, *Proceedings of the Thirty-second Annual Encampment 1899* (San Francisco, 1899), p. 64.

[88] Department of New York, Grand Army of the Republic, *Proceedings of the Thirty-Third Annual Encampment 1899* (New York and Albany, 1899), p. 176, 248, 250.

[89] Department of Iowa, Grand Army of the Republic, *Journal of the Thirteenth Annual Encampment 1887* (Denison, Iowa, 1887), p. 105.

[90] Iowa S.R., *Meeting 1896,* pp. 11–12.

Spain a few years previously. Though the *Spirit of '76* was stanchly pro-Boer and anti-English, the Ohio S.A.R. tabled a resolution of sympathy for the two small South African republics.

Deriving their claims to glory and special privilege from a long bloody conflict in which they had been triumphant, largely identifying patriotism with wartime service, hailing the Spanish-American War and backing an aggressive imperialist policy, the veterans consequently formed an important force for militarism. Their banquets usually included toasts to the army and navy. The members of the Society of the Army of the Potomac were urged to foster "the increase throughout the land of a military spirit and of military organization and discipline." [91] Speakers discovered various justifications for war, and particularly for the struggle in which they themselves had engaged. One assured the Society of the Army of the Potomac that the Civil War had been God's will, "since He ordained that progress should be made through war." [92] Others hailed the valuable effect of the discipline acquired through fighting. The chaplain of the Connecticut Grand Army announced that compulsory military service in Germany had produced "a finer, manlier, nobler race of Germans than we otherwise possibly could have." [93] An orator before the Society of the Army of the Tennessee similarly praised the influence of the Civil War upon the youth who participated in it: "Army life taught him self-reliance, it taught him the necessity of obedience and the value of discipline; it cultivated in him respect for authority, and when he returned home, if he had been a good soldier, he would be a good citizen." Army experience, he concluded, "acts as a crucible. It burns out selfishness and preserves the true metal of the man." [94]

Stanch believers that preparation for war was the surest guarantee of peace, the veterans bolstered the military establishment whenever possible. Commander-in-Chief John Adams of the G.A.R. praised

[91] Society of the Army of the Potomac, *Report of the Twentieth Annual Re-Union 1889* (New York, 1889), p. 47.

[92] Society of the Army of the Potomac, *Report of the Eleventh Annual Re-Union 1880* (New York, 1880), pp. 24–25.

[93] Department of Connecticut, Grand Army of the Republic, *Twenty-Second Annual Encampment 1889* (Hartford, 1889), p. 119.

[94] Society of the Army of the Tennessee, *Reports of the Proceedings 1881–1883* (Cincinnati, 1885), p. 103.

the volunteer militia. "In every possible way should we encourage this spirit," he insisted. "Visit the armories of our National Guards, encourage the best class of young men to join their ranks, invite them to our camp-fires and our Memorial Day services. Assure them that the soldiers that were are in full sympathy with the soldiers that are, and will support them in the discharge of their duties to the fullest extent." [95] The Grand Army, the officers' groups and the soldiers' papers united in urging stronger national defense and particularly a bigger navy. The first resolution adopted by the National Association of Naval Veterans pledged the organization "to use all reasonable and proper means to induce the Government to strengthen and so develop the Navy of the United States that it will be able to protect all American interests. . . ." [96]

Ever conscious of their martial heritage, the Sons of Veterans society was constantly endeavoring to appear more soldierlike. From the first it conferred army titles upon its officials. In the spring of 1887, sentiment appeared for the order to adopt military drill. Ready with its usual stock of arguments, the *National Tribune* contended not only that this would benefit the members physically, but also that the training in the art of organization would greatly aid those entering large-scale industry. Moreover, such an experienced militia would make the country better prepared for the war that occurred in every generation and at the same time it would be "a guarantee of social order." [97] The adjutant-general of the G.A.R., also pointing out that no nation had ever gone more than thirty-two years without a conflict, urged the same policy to the Sons' commander-in-chief. The latter, in addition to the customary reasoning that such experience would enable the members to "cut off the shoot of treason, rebellion or anarchy before it grew to a tree," also felt that "you will nearly always find that a True Soldier is a True *Gentleman*" and therefore recommended in June 1887 that all camps "secure arms and equipments, and acquire as much proficiency as possible in the manual of arms and evolutions of the line. . . ." [98]

[95] Grand Army of the Republic, *Journal of the Twenty-Eighth National Encampment 1894* (Boston, 1894), p. 63.

[96] Simmons, *History*, p. 21.

[97] *National Tribune*, March 24, March 31, and April 14, 1887.

[98] Sons of Veterans, U.S.A., *Proceedings of the Sixth National Encampment 1887* (n.p., n.d.), p. 24.

Two years later, Commander-in-Chief G. B. Abbott of the Sons reported to the Grand Army that it had become a military organization, using military titles for its officers, who discharged their duties in the same fashion as if they were in the regular army. "At no expense to the government," he pointed out, "we form a National Militia, a bulwark of safety which can ever and always be relied upon for faithful services wherever the 'Old Flag' may be attacked either from foe without or within." [99] He hoped that the states would repeal laws which restricted the carrying of arms to the state militia so that the Sons could become a genuinely military society. In 1890 the inspector-general announced that, although in several states social features still predominated, in others the prevailing one was the military. The head of the Ohio division promulgated these rules for its meeting that year: "The Encampment will be conducted under strict military provisions," "U. S. military regulations will be strictly enforced upon the field" and "The officers desire to impress upon the visiting brothers the necessity of obeying orders, of submitting to discipline, of dignified and military deportment." [100]

These martial features provoked debate at nearly all the order's gatherings throughout the nineties. In 1891 the society dropped the military terminology for its officers, a practice that had always irritated the Grand Army men, who had really seen service in the field. The same convention also transferred soldierly activities to a Sons of Veterans Guards. Members of one or more neighboring camps were to form companies for drilling with equipment and uniforms similar to the regular army. By 1895, some 1285 individuals had enrolled in this body, chiefly in Illinois, Ohio, Pennsylvania, and Maine.

During the next few years the members argued as to how close a connection to maintain with the Guards and whether to revive the order's military attributes. Apparently the younger men were anxious to flaunt the titles of colonel and general. "The great majority of the members of this organization have inherited the blood of a soldier," contended a Massachusetts delegate, "and they feel that in the uniform of a soldier they look best, act best, and possibly live up to the

[99] Sons of Veterans, U.S.A., *Proceedings of the Eighth Annual Encampment 1889* (n.p., n.d.), p. 71.

[100] Ohio Division, Sons of Veterans, *Journal of Proceedings of the Eighth Annual Encampment 1890* (Toledo, 1890), p. 112.

requirements of the order best." [101] But the older Sons felt rather foolish with such grandiloquent nomenclature which they had not earned. "I have been called General—and I am known rather extensively in my own State," testified a junior vice-commander-in-chief, "and I never yet have failed to see a look of derision or smile of amusement pass over the face of an old soldier when I was introduced to him as General Bookwalter." [102] While a majority favored restoring the old terminology, the necessary two-thirds could not be obtained. Toward the close of the century the order turned to agitating for a Congressional bill to make it a trained military reserve similar to the militia or national guard.

Too old to engage in such activities themselves, in the nineties the G.A.R. encouraged a warlike spirit by campaigning for military instruction in the public schools. The veterans gave a variety of justifications for such an innovation. First, they declared that it would keep America prepared for any future conflict. The order's Special Aide in Charge of Military Instruction, a retired army captain, warned that tense relations with England, Spain, and Japan and general dislike for American tariff policy "will possibly force complications, which will lead to the arbitrament of arms. This will be all the more likely if they see us neglecting our defensive preparations. Arbitration will not be resorted to with the weak and defenseless." [103]

The labor disturbances of the 1890's reinforced the sentiment for such instruction. Indeed, the movement first gained its real momentum in a year of great unrest, 1894. "In this way," declared the commander of the Idaho Grand Army in May of that year, "the government can be sustained at a much less cost than to keep a large standing army, to prevent these scenes of lawlessness which are being enacted all over our land, and which are a disgrace to the civilization of the age." [104] Though these were the fundamental considerations, others argued that military training would instill

[101] Sons of Veterans, U.S.A., *Journal of Proceedings of the Sixteenth Annual Encampment 1897* (Reading, Pa., 1897), p. 155.

[102] Sons of Veterans, U.S.A., *Journal of Proceedings of the Eleventh Annual Encampment 1892* (Topeka, Kan., 1892), p. 243.

[103] Grand Army of the Republic, *Journal of the Thirty-first National Encampment 1897* (Lincoln, Neb., 1897), p. 214.

[104] Department of Idaho, Grand Army of the Republic, *Journal of the Seventh Annual Encampment 1894* (Boise, 1895), p. 10.

certain virtues in the young: respect for law, obedience to authority, courage, punctuality, and neatness. In addition, it would develop their physique, and the discipline would prove its value in case of fire in schools.

At the suggestion of the Lafayette Post in New York City, the G.A.R. national encampment of 1893 endorsed military instruction in public schools and in January 1894 the commander-in-chief asked all department commanders and local branches to start work to secure it. In October 1894, Commander-in-Chief Thomas Lawler appointed a Special Aide in Charge of Military Instruction with power to designate assistants in each department who were to raise the issue with school boards. At the 1895 meeting the special aide, George M. Wingate, reported that he had distributed 2500 copies of a pamphlet on military instruction as well as other circular letters among the deputies he had named in thirty-five states. By the next year his successor, Henry H. Adams, announced that aides in every state were in turn choosing assistants in the principal cities.

While strong encouragement came from the national organization, the state branches implemented the program. Numerous department commanders and encampments from Massachusetts to California urged state legislatures to authorize the introduction of military instruction. The assistant special aides induced posts to appoint committees to push the work locally. Both the aides and these committees circulated literature and appeared before gatherings of school teachers, principals, superintendents, boards of education, and lawmakers. In Iowa the special aide, S. A. Moore, himself organized the public school boys of his home city, Bloomfield, into a military company. Writing an open letter to the youth of Iowa to follow this example, he distributed a thousand copies among G.A.R. posts, school principals, and superintendents, and the newspapers of the state.

In 1895 the national special aide reported that the Grand Army had been most successful in this work in the large cities of the Eastern and Middle Western states. Particularly effective was the Lafayette Post in New York City, which had originated the movement. In December 1894, representatives of posts throughout the city joined with principals of grammar schools and the Board of Education to form an organization to promote military training, which now began in most of the male grammar schools. The department's special aide, Henry T. Bartlett, also corresponded with 115 posts in 44 cities with over 10,000 inhabitants. In the course of a few months he circulated 550 pamphlets as well as some 200 newspaper clippings. He also addressed numerous meetings on the order of the New York convention of grammar school principals. Whenever he found a board of education unfriendly, he outflanked it by appealing to school principals, teachers, or even pupils. A committee of New York and Brooklyn posts also campaigned for a law to provide arms and equipment for military instruction. The state encampment endorsed this measure, which passed the legislature but received the governor's veto. Nevertheless, within a year the Grand Army could boast that it had secured military training in at least fourteen of the state's prominent cities.

This drive aroused considerable opposition. School officials, themselves unaccustomed to military discipline, were often apathetic or unwilling to introduce another feature into what seemed an already overcrowded curriculum. Greater objections arose from what the G.A.R. rather impatiently called "sentimental" reasons. In Pennsylvania and Delaware Quaker hostility proved effective. The W.C.T.U. declared that the movement would make students bloodthirsty, and Felix Adler, Henry George, and William Dean Howells opposed it as a step toward militarism. One school superintendent replied to a G.A.R. communication "that the men who put guns into the hands of children and train them for a life of warfare are traitors and should receive the contents of the guns if ever ordered to kill human beings." [105] Even a Grand Army post commander in Lockport, New York suggested "that the youth of the country should be educated in something higher and better than the science of murdering their fellow men." [106]

Further resistance developed from both the left and the right. Labor unions suspected that military instruction would "tend to create an army which will threaten the liberties of the masses" and in parts of the Far West the Populists attacked the new trend. On the other hand, jittery conservatives feared that "if the children of the masses . . . are taught the use of arms it will endanger the

[105] Grand Army of the Republic, *Journal of the Twenty-ninth National Encampment 1895* (Rockford, Ill., n.d.), p. 242.
[106] *Ibid.*, p. 233.

property of the country." [107] The movement fared least well in the South. Not only was this region too poor to afford additions to its school program, but the United Confederate Veterans, already annoyed by the G.A.R.'s criticisms of the very textbooks it most approved, resented any fresh attempt of the Union organization to suggest what Southern schools should teach.

Undiscouraged by these obstacles, in the late nineties the Grand Army began to agitate for a federal statute authorizing United States army officers to give military instruction in the public schools. Declaring that recent events "have emphasized the fact that there is a spirit prevailing amongst foreign nations, antagonistic to us" and that "we must be measurably prepared for war if we would avoid having it forced upon us," the 1897 national encampment endorsed such a bill.[108] The G.A.R.'s special aide on military instruction stirred the branches to its support, many department conventions expressed approval and the Sons of Veterans offered their aid, but by 1900 the veterans still had not achieved their wish.

All this support of nationalism, expansionism, and militarism would seem to leave little room for more pacific sympathies. Yet at the same time that the veterans and their sons were becoming so deliberately bellicose, there were also signs of interest in the peace movement among patriotic societies. Organizations of veterans, it is true, seemed to produce few pacifists. When a Universal Peace Convention asked the G.A.R. to add its protest against war, the national encampment of 1871 replied with aggressive rectitude, "The Grand Army of the Republic is determined to have peace, even if it has to fight for it." [109] The commander of the Pennsylvania department probably expressed the limitations in the thinking of most ex-soldiers on the subject: "The comrades of the Grand Army of the Republic having passed through the furnace of war, and known the evils, sufferings, destitution and horrors that are its unavoidable attendants, are for peace, but only when accompanied by honor to our flag and justice to our citizenship." [110]

[107] *Ibid.*

[108] G.A.R., *Journal 1897,* p. 294.

[109] Grand Army of the Republic, *Proceedings of the Fifth Annual Meeting of the National Encampment 1871* (New York, 1871), p. 34.

[110] Department of Pennsylvania, Grand Army of the Republic, *Proceedings of the 32nd Annual Encampment 1898* (n.p., 1898), p. 39.

Though most of the ex-soldiers favored a big army and navy to preserve peace, an occasional speaker deplored large military establishments, seemed sympathetic to disarmament, or shuddered at the prospect of renewed conflict. "Do we seek more war, my comrades? No; no more war," insisted one orator before the Society of the Army of the Potomac. "The world begins to see that great questions can best be solved by cabinets, instead of cannons. War marches with bloody feet, and puts out Joy's lamp in every heart." [111] But such sentiments, infrequent at best, appeared almost exclusively within the army societies, composed mainly of officers, who for some reason seem to have been more disturbed by the implications of modern warfare than were the enlisted men assembled in their organizations.

Except for the G.A.R.'s recommendation in 1881 that the United States ratify the Geneva convention of 1864 for the care of the wounded in war, for many years the veterans showed little interest in any form of international coöperation. After the Venezuela crisis in the mid-nineties, however, the growth of the arbitration movement aroused considerable interest among both veterans' and hereditary societies. Several leaders and encampments of the Grand Army endorsed the idea. When the commander of the Massachusetts department in the spring of 1896 asked the opinion of all his posts about it, he discovered an overwhelming approval, which in his opinion "placed Massachusetts where she belongs as a leader in all great reforms." [112] In the New York encampment of the same year a motion of endorsement produced greater controversy. The commander was favorable, and a member of the committee on resolutions advocated its passage at some length. Another delegate was as strongly opposed. "We are a nation that is in favor of war," he declared. "This country never could have existed nor achieved the place it holds if it had not been for war. The Christian religion could never have attained the place it has before this world but for war." [113] Nevertheless, the motion passed.

Among the hereditary societies the women's groups, more respon-

[111] Society of the Army of the Potomac, *Report of the Seventeenth Annual Reunion 1886* (New York, 1886), p. 33.

[112] Department of Massachusetts, Grand Army of the Republic, *Journal of the Thirty-First Annual Encampment 1897* (Boston, 1897), p. 52.

[113] N.Y. G.A.R., *Proceedings 1896*, p. 325.

sive to anything working for peace, took up the cause. In their meetings and periodicals the D.A.R. and the Daughters of 1812 showed a sympathetic interest in arbitration and the New Jersey Daughters of the Revolution endorsed a permanent Anglo-American court of arbitration to prevent any future wars. The men's organizations took no official stand, but individual members expressed approval. William O. McDowell and his close S.A.R. associates in the Pan Republic Congress project included peace and arbitration in its program. Since "War, and the possibility of war, is now the greatest obstacle on the world's progress," Walter S. Logan hoped that the proposed gathering would lead to "a Congress of Nations with a jurisdiction which shall enable it to provide for the settlement of all international disputes and make possible the disbanding of all armies and navies." [114] He later became a member of the International Arbitration Committee and spoke to D.A.R. chapters in its behalf. "The time is coming when there will be no more war," Lucius Deming similarly predicted, "but when one grand court of arbitration will settle differences between nations either by submission, by agreement, or by some agreed upon process as our courts now settle differences between litigants." [115] In a circular which Josiah Pumpelly sent out to all members of the S.A.R. and S.R., he urged them to work for "the abolition of war as a last resort in case of differences" and for the establishment of an international body on the order of the United States Supreme Court.[116] The hereditary bodies perhaps favored arbitration because it was so often specifically identified with an agreement with England which would contribute further to the good relations they now favored.

McDowell's Human Freedom League, which included arbitration among its objects, appointed him and Edward Everett Hale delegates to a peace conference at Rome in 1891. They were unable to go, but Mrs. Mary Frost Ormsby took a peace flag which they were to have given the meeting. "I have *faithfully* performed the *commission* you gave me to *fulfill*," she reported to McDowell. "I presented the *Flag of Peace* to the Congress on the second day of its session, and it was at once placed in a most *prominent position*,

---

[114] Walter S. Logan to McDowell, Dec. 24, 1890, McDowell Scrapbooks, XXXVIII.
[115] Lucius P. Deming to Josiah Pumpelly, Sept. 26, 1891, *ibid.*, XLIX.
[116] Circular, Aug. 16, 1891, *ibid.*, L.

which, strange to say, without any particular intent, proved to be *the arms* of a *'Dying Gladiator.'* " [117]

When McDowell became editor of *Home and Country* a few years later, he used its columns to advocate an international court to prevent wars. He also rewrote a poem by Paul Cushing, "England's Prayer," which allegedly began:

> Give us war, O Lord
> For England's sake.

McDowell's version ran: [118]

> Give us peace, O Lord
> For woman's sake

and continued:

> Give us the loves and hopes of peace,
> Make our manliness increase
> While our world-wide hates do cease,
> For woman's sake

Meanwhile, McDowell became very friendly with Alfred H. Love of Philadelphia, president of the Universal Peace Union. As a result he spoke at several meetings of peace groups, eventually becoming a vice-president of the Union.

Yet despite these indications that a large number of men and women of good will existed within American patriotic societies, the encouragement of military spirit and nationalistic fervor probably outbalanced their efforts for international conciliation.

[117] Mary Frost Ormsby to McDowell, Nov. 17, 1891, "The Flag of Human Freedom League in Rome," *Home and Country,* VII (Dec. 1891), 1662.

[118] William O. McDowell, "War or Peace?" *ibid.,* VIII (Jan. 1893), 462.

XIV

Conclusion

WE have seen how patriotic societies expressed their interest in a wide range of subjects—veterans' preference, pensions, flag desecration, the teaching of history, sectional animosity, immigration policy, labor disturbances, military instruction in schools, expansionism and arbitration, to name only a few of the more prominent. It remains to indicate how the rest of the nation regarded these organizations which interfered in so many matters of concern to all citizens, and then to make a final evaluation of these activities.

The obvious partisan affiliations of the Grand Army in its early years quickly led to many attacks upon it from the Democratic press, and, as in the case of the Cincinnati a hundred years previously, there were apprehensions that a secret, political-minded military association might overthrow the republic and inaugurate a regime of Caesarism. As the order's decline in the 1870's made it less conspicuous politically, there was a slackening in hostility on this score. But meanwhile those who desired a rapid reconciliation between North and South deplored the influence of veterans' societies. As early as 1867 the *New York Tribune* condemned the G.A.R's tendency "to prowl over the battlefields of the past and to dig up the bodies of the slain" and declared its effect was "to ever keep alive a war with brothers and fellow countrymen, to exult in victories over Americans, to rejoice over the destruction of men in whose blue veins run blood which courses in our own." [1] Right down to the close of the century many felt that the order contributed substantially to the maintenance of sectional bitterness.

The society's secrecy and ritual led certain religious sects like the Catholics, United Brethren, United Presbyterians, and Evangelical

---

[1] *New York Daily Tribune*, July 2, 1867.

Lutherans to frown upon their followers' becoming members. In 1883 a National Christian Convention at Philadelphia condemned the G.A.R. as a dangerous and useless body, and in 1892 the Minnesota-Dakota District of the Evangelical Lutherans decided to expel any of its adherents who joined it. By an explanation of purposes, however, the veterans' leaders usually won the churches' approval of the organization.[2] Peace advocates often objected to the G.A.R.'s militaristic influence.

Not until the eighties did there develop the most frequent criticism of the Grand Army on the score of its pension activities. At first the press, though critical of increased pensions, did not blame the G.A.R. but attributed such measures as the Disability Pension Bill to a Congressional bid for the soldier vote and the anxiety of tariff interests to prevent a revenue reduction. The Democratic journals, however, soon charged that the order had degenerated into a group of organized plunderers of the public purse. The mounting clamor within the society for a universal service pension naturally confirmed this impression. "Make it a point of not taking any united action or passing any resolutions asking for more pensions," Lucius Fairchild's brother warned him just before the 1887 national encampment. "On this point the public are sore." He pressed the commander-in-chief to "make it clear that the G.A.R. is not organized for the purpose of raiding the U. S. Treasury." [3]

His prediction of a strongly hostile reaction proved correct. The *Nation,* for example, expressed the attitude of many Eastern liberals when it described the society as a political party "formed for the express purpose of getting from the Government a definite sum in cash for each member of it." The journal argued that the better class of veterans had little to do with the order after their discovery that it consisted of "almost all the self-seekers, the men who were only tempted into the army by high bounties, and the men who are always trying to trade upon their services in the war." [4] An article in the January 1889 issue of *Forum* entitled "A Raid Upon the

---

[2] Frank H. Heck, *The Civil War Veteran in Minnesota Life and Politics* (Oxford, Ohio, 1941), p. 6.

[3] Charles Fairchild to Lucius Fairchild, Sept. 12, 1887, Lucius Fairchild Papers, Wisconsin State Historical Society.

[4] "A 'Spot-Cash' Party," *Nation,* XLIX (Oct. 10, 1889), 286; "The Grand Army Machine," *ibid.,* XLV (July 14, 1887), 26.

Treasury" expressed an almost identical view that the veterans' associations had "turned into political machines, not for the promotion of public ends, but for the one purpose of public plunder for the personal profit of the members." [5] Since the author was an erratic Congregational minister, L. W. Bacon, noted for his controversial tendencies and slashing style, the *National Tribune* thought the proper rebuttal was to denounce the article's "bristling falsehoods, sophistry and malignity" and to charge the writer "was drunk with his own venom." [6]

Yet he had only stated in extreme form the opinion of the Mugwump-Independent element which found in the G.A.R.'s pension record, not to mention its opposition to civil service and tariff reform, one more reason to support Grover Cleveland and his program. When the 1889 national encampment thanked President Harrison for appointing Tanner commissioner of pensions, it merely intensified such criticism, and the dismissal of the popular veteran hero shortly thereafter seemed almost an official indictment of the Grand Army itself. Distrust of the society's pension policy and suspicion that it had padded the rolls with undeserving names continued unabated through the nineties. Meanwhile, the organization's close alliance with the Republican party on this question inevitably revived all the former accusations of partisanship, which the acrimonious events of 1887 in particular did nothing to diminish.

Despite these substantial evidences of popular distrust, the Grand Army did not lack defenders. The Republican papers nearly always rallied to its support, though their interpretations of its responsibility in the pension question did not always harmonize. One journal, for example, which opposed the Dependent Pension Bill, insisted that the G.A.R. had no share in it, but another, which favored it, praised the organization's request "that deserving ex-soldiers be relieved from the ignominy of pauperism" and solemnly announced that "the ten thousand Grand Army posts scattered throughout the country will zealously guard against the pensioning of unworthy persons under the bill." [7] Doubtless many Americans accepted the G.A.R.

[5] Leonard Woolsey Bacon, "A Raid Upon the Treasury," *Forum*, VI (Jan. 1889), 546.

[6] *National Tribune* (Washington, D.C.), Jan. 3, 1889.

[7] *Boston Journal* quoted in "Pension Legislation," *Public Opinion*, II (Feb. 12, 1887), 369.

at its own assessment of itself as a group of exemplary patriots; the person most likely to do so was probably a Middle Western farmer who voted the straight Republican ticket and had never gone beyond grade school. More favorable publicity came as the nineties drew to a close, when the G.A.R. veterans lost their political significance and assumed the more benevolent role of gray-bearded heroes marching with dignified step in Memorial Day parades or instilling reminiscences of the war and lessons of patriotism into the minds of school children.

The appearance of so many hereditary societies did not pass unnoticed either. The introduction of the S.A.R. into Ohio, Illinois, Wisconsin, and Minnesota, coming almost simultaneously with the formation of the A.P.A., produced widespread newspaper reports that it was a secret nativist organization, and leaders of the society in those states spent the first few months denying such tendencies. This perhaps explains why later they were always careful to avoid any such entanglements officially. Though the fears of a new Know-Nothing movement soon subsided, these groups inherited some of the original feeling against the Cincinnati. Throughout the nineties members had to meet charges that the associations of Sons, Daughters, and Dames were undemocratic and snobbish, fostering an aristocratic spirit through their concern for ancestry and social position.

The publicity given early meetings of the societies accentuated this impression. The press headlined S.A.R. and D.A.R. gatherings under such captions as "Genuine Aristocracy," "Women of Pedigree," "Worthy Sons of Gallant Sires," "Their Grandsires Were Heroes," "Proud of Their Ancestry," "Their Papas Fought," and "Blood Tells Here/Must Have a Record to Get In." When the D.A.R. started its first chapter in New York, one paper reported that "every lady applying for membership must be prepared to make affidavit that she has had at least six grandfathers." [8] The societies' rebuttal was that they were democratic in that wealth alone could not secure membership. "The millionaire, the political leader, or the social autocrat cannot pass the portals of our halls, unless he is descended from a participant . . . in our War for Independence," pointed out the California branch of the Sons of the Revolution, though one feels that it was being a little disingenuous when it

---

[8] *New York Continent*, Feb. 21, 1891, in McDowell Scrapbooks, LXII.

added, "The laborer who earns his bread in the sweat of his daily toil, if qualified, is as welcome to us as he who sits in the Executive Chair, or presides in our Courts of Justice." [9]

Overemphasis on social functions and especially the "elaborate dresses and display of jewels" of the women caused many to suspect that the societies were actually little interested in promoting the cause of patriotism. Others objected that the members were too content to bask in the reflected glory of their ancestors without making any contributions themselves. There "seems to be a tendency to lapse into self-gratification if not self-glorification," observed one critic. "Patriots of old were men and women who sacrificed. Their descendants often do not imitate the sacrifices, but merely praise them." [10] "All honor to the men who achieved American independence," similarly declared a Pennsylvania newspaper, "but this is a practical age, and men of today are taken for what they are, not for what their forefathers did and to bank on the ever-glorious reputation of a past age is not wise, save it be to emulate their example." [11] When William O. McDowell tried to interest his old friend, T. V. Powderly, in the S.A.R., the labor leader replied, "I have no use for anything of the kind, the Sons of the present day have enough work ahead of them and it will take all of their time to do it without digging up a particle of the past." [12] Many within the United States, then and since, shared the opinion of a Canadian paper that the D.A.R. formed "a hard-working mutual admiration society." [13]

McDowell drew down criticism upon the S.A.R., at least among conservative persons more sympathetic to the Sons of the Revolution, because of his high-pressure methods and efforts for rapid expansion of the order. A Philadelphia journal sniffed that he had "started out to boom the society as if he were selling lots in Oklahoma Territory." [14] His unfortunate public misspelling of the names of Revolu-

---

[9] California Society, Sons of the Revolution, *Year Book* (Los Angeles, 1895), p. 14.

[10] Edward L. Underwood, "Patriotism and the Patriotic Societies," *New England Magazine*, XXXIV (New Series; March 1906), 104.

[11] *Pottstown* (Penn.) *Ledger*, April 18, 1890.

[12] T. V. Powderly to William O. McDowell, June 18, 1889, William O. McDowell Scrapbooks, XXVIII.

[13] *Toronto Mail and Express*, quoted in "Current Topics," *American Monthly Magazine*, XIII (Dec. 1898), 620.

[14] *Philadelphia Inquirer*, May 5, 1892.

tionary heroes like Greene and Mühlenberg produced considerable ridicule. The rivalries between groups with similar names and purposes struck outsiders as a "Tournament of Pedigrees." A New York newspaper reported that the Revolutionary descendants were "splitting up in the most distracting fashion into all sorts of little societies of Sons, which go dashing and threshing about in comet-like fashion and seem likely to injure each other." With so many accusations and counteraccusations, "the puzzled outsider can only look aghast and murmur, 'What is Truth?' " [15] The multiplicity of patriotic societies led to a feeling that a fad was being overdone. When the mania for these associations led to organizing tots into Children of the American Revolution, matters definitely seemed to have gone too far.

The controversies and quarrels within the D.A.R. allowed the press to portray the ladies in amusing fashion. Accounts of the 1894 congress appeared under such headings as "Warring Daughters" and "Storm of Confusion/Ladies of the Continental Congress Hold a Gusty Session." Two years later articles in the *Washington Post* greatly annoyed the delegates. When the reporter tried to defend his stories, matters were not helped by shouts from the assembled ladies of "Shame! Shame!" "Bad Man!" and "Put him out!" [16] After the culprit explained that the exclusion of journalists would only lead to even more distorted accounts, the congress decided to appoint a press committee to conduct publicity relations. But ridicule of the squabbling Daughters continued for some time, as novels like "Octave Thanet" 's *The Lion's Share* testified.

In spite of these varied and widespread criticisms, there were many who approved the emergence of numerous groups devoted to a respect for ancestry, an interest in the American past, and the stimulation of patriotism. The *Cleveland Leader* contended that the S.A.R., D.A.R., and the like were "to be encouraged by all good citizens. They make for morality, loyalty to the nation, and for the personal virtues of manhood and womanhood." [17] A Philadelphia journal similarly argued that the attempts of the Sons of the Revolution "to arouse the republic's old, patriotic spirit, to show men that

[15] *New York Journal,* Feb. 24, 1890.
[16] "Proceedings of the Fifth Continental Congress," *American Monthly Magazine,* VIII (May 1896), 669, 761–762.
[17] *Cleveland Leader,* April 9, 1893.

country means more than gold, and that liberty must be prized, if it is to be retained, can only do good." [18] The influence of hereditary societies toward a stronger nationalism and the ending of sectional feelings especially won approbation. This division of opinion on their merits has continued to the present day.

Especially striking, however, is the fact that except for organized labor's natural suspicion of the Grand Army's readiness to rush to arms at times of industrial violence to "restore law and order," before 1900 there was surprisingly little criticism of either veterans' or hereditary societies for a super-nationalism that was later to breed an isolationism of the *Chicago Tribune* variety. This conservative, not to say reactionary, definition of Americanism was based largely on a *Saturday Evening Post* and N.A.M. type of business philosophy, a censorship of textbooks and interference with freedom of teaching in the direction of intellectual conformity, a dubious record on racial prejudice, and a hostility to immigrants that has extended even to the tragic D.P.'s of our day. Such attacks came only when the societies intensified their activities along these lines in the twentieth century.

But certainly, whether for good or evil, by 1900 both veterans' and hereditary societies had established themselves as permanent fixtures in American life. According to the reader's temperament, their history may shock, please, amuse, or merely inform him. Despite the excitement caused by the Cincinnati at the close of the Revolution, such organizations were of no importance until after the Civil War. Compared to later orders, the Cincinnati was a poorly organized and ineffective affair. Collecting at its height a few hundred officers, it had no local units, its state societies were largely autonomous, its general meetings attended by a handful of delegates every few years, and the only bond was an informal system of correspondence. In short, its influence upon American life was negligible.

The turning point came in the second half of the nineteenth century after the tremendous conflict of 1861–1865 furnished hundreds of thousands of potential members for veterans' groups and their affiliates. At the same time the nation's economic development made possible large-scale associational activity of all sorts. The growth of cities encouraged strong local chapters, while the expanding rail-

[18] *Philadelphia News*, April 21, 1890.

road network allowed hordes of veterans and their families to flock annually to both state and national encampments. Between sessions, improvements in communication enabled the Grand Army of the Republic to exert strict military discipline over its thousands of posts and thereby wield the order into a powerful pressure group.

The second great wave of new organizations came in the 1890's, when several factors produced an epidemic of Sons, Daughters, and Dames. Among the causes were alarm at the flood of foreign immigrants, the older stock's resultant avid efforts to establish its genealogical superiority, a concern over the social problems of an industrialized society that turned to the stabilizing influence of patriotism, and a heightened sense of nationalism which endeavored to eradicate the remnants of sectionalism. These forces all combined to produce that curious anomaly in a democratic, republican country, the hereditary society. But perhaps the distinguishing feature of this busy decade was the mounting number of women's groups. The founders and first members of such leagues as the Daughters of the American Revolution were very proud of their role in enlarging the sphere of women's activities. In large measure, therefore, the rise of the D.A.R. and Colonial Dames should be viewed as a phase of the women's club movement which the economic revolution, urbanization, and increased leisure bestowed as a social by-product.

By 1900, when this story halts, most of the present hereditary organizations were in existence, though they were just beginning to develop the wide range of interests that prevailed a few years later. While the Civil War veterans were ceasing to be a potent factor in American life, first the Spanish-American War soldiers and later the World Wars I and II survivors were to continue the precedents they had established. With the possible exception of the A.V.C., there have been no important changes in the pattern devised before the turn of the century. The Veterans of Foreign Wars and the American Legion proved to have learned well the lesson of the G.A.R.

In many respects the two categories of societies, the veterans' and the hereditary, displayed so many more differences than similarities that it is almost impossible to discuss them under one rubric. The ex-soldiers' associations usually endeavored to be as large as possible so as to exert the maximum pressure upon legislatures. The Grand Army thus achieved a following of over four hundred thousand, a

354 PATRIOTISM ON PARADE

size which alone makes it worthy of consideration. But the hereditary bodies, anxious to preserve their snob value, consciously sought limitations on membership. Except for the D.A.R., which therefore alone among them achieved any considerable importance, most hereditary groups numbered only a few hundred or thousand adherents. Though their mere existence reflected certain tendencies in American society, they exerted little direct influence.

One result of this basic divergence was that the two classes of societies appealed to quite different economic levels. The records of hereditary associations radiate a comfortable prosperity and assurance with little disquieting suggestion of the depressions which have periodically blighted American economic life, but the archives of veterans' societies record numerous scars from recurrent hard times. In the 1890's many a tramp won a meal or railroad fare by pretending to be a Grand Army man (and often he was), but no hobo thought that a claim to S.A.R. membership would seem creditable. Large numbers of humble folk found excitement, glamor, and a sense of importance in the ritual and impressive nomenclature of the Grand Army and the Woman's Relief Corps, but the Colonial Dames and Sons of the Revolution catered in far more sophisticated fashion to a well-to-do, educated and leisured, if also beribboned, class that patronized Delmonico's and Sherry's in New York (which, together with Philadelphia and Washington, constituted the backbone of such orders), or, in the case of the D.A.R. and S.A.R., formed the socially ambitious local gentry in many an American small town. The American passion for joining became so great that in each category many organizations duplicated members and officers, but few were the persons whose fervor for associationalism led to affiliation with both types.

This division extended beyond time of founding, size, and personnel to the very nature of their programs. The veterans had all contributed important personal services to the state; indeed, the Civil War survivors thought that they had acquired a first mortgage upon the country. Their orders existed primarily to secure some immediate personal rewards from the government, such as pensions, veterans' preference laws, or the establishment of homes. But the hereditary societies consisted of descendants who could make no such claims; there was no taint of the mercenary in their concept of patriotic action. Instead, their lineage led to self-appointed roles of the guardians of the American past and interpreters of its ideals. They busied themselves with the preservation of historic spots, the diffusion of knowledge of American history, and the education of foreigners in what they regarded as traditional American principles.

On some matters, particularly in the nexus of activities that stemmed from the cult of the flag, the two groups did pool their energies. Moreover, in their whole approach toward patriotism both types displayed a curious emphasis upon form rather than substance. They were too often satisfied once they had achieved such proofs of outward conformity as the flag salute. The singing of patriotic songs or the presence of the flag over a schoolhouse seemed sufficient demonstration of the successful inculcation of love of country. Finally, a very important common attribute was the predominance of the social element. While both groups talked often and loudly about their patriotic mission, their members prized chiefly the opportunities for good fellowship and social display. The delegates who thronged convention cities usually ignored formal business sessions in favor of the more entertaining extracurricular features. Hence the statements of noble purpose often appeared merely unusually lofty rationalizations for trips into town or junkets to Washington. Sometimes one wonders if these societies, the hereditary ones particularly, appealed to those who have what one school of modern psychology would describe as the "viscerotonic" temperament which stems from the "endomorphic" physique. They are the plump gregarious souls, highly conscious of position and social distinctions, who love to "dangle their badges and pendants." This might also explain why they so easily became "emotional slobs" on the subject of patriotism but then placed their greatest emphasis on ritualistic ceremonies and outward observances. This must remain a hypothesis, however, for scientific confirmation would require the "somatotyping," or taking pictures in the nude, of all D.A.R.'s, which seems an unlikely possibility.

Thus, while differing fundamentally in many respects, as examples of associationalism the two classes generally conformed to the same pattern. The origins of many orders were shrouded in mystery and became the source of bitter, drawn-out battles among contenders for pioneering honors. This was true of the G.A.R., U.D.C., and

D.A.R. Frequently the founders were fascinating but decidedly eccentric individuals whose fanaticism lifted to initial success organizations which later discarded them as too unconventional. Such figures as William O. McDowell, Flora Adams Darling, and Alexander Kenaday, while admittedly on the periphery of American history, are amazing demonstrations of the curious forms that professional patriotism can take. Since the societies attracted an intense and emotional following (who else would have taken such leaders seriously in the first place?), they often found themselves more engaged in bickering than in the promulgation of patriotism. Much of this dissension stemmed from the rivalries of individuals who saw in these associations possibilities for social advancement and personal power. The ambitions of Mrs. Donald McLean, for example, for years kept the D.A.R. in an uproar that had nothing to do with spreading love of country.

The result of these quarrels was a multiplicity of rival and splinter groups which duplicated the same program. There was no philosophical difference between the Daughters of the American Revolution, the Daughters of the Revolution, and the Dames of the Revolution; the Sons of the American Revolution advocated no different brand of patriotism from that of the Sons of the Revolution; it took a trained observer and a pretty clear day to distinguish between the Colonial Dames of America and the National Society of the Colonial Dames of America. Yet how much time of the Grand Army was spent adjudicating (or more often diplomatically avoiding) the rival claims of the Woman's Relief Corps and the Ladies of the G.A.R.! This preoccupation with the trivial again suggests that these bodies should not be taken too seriously as patriotic societies.

But it would be equally incorrect to suggest that these organizations made no impress upon the American nation. The veterans' groups in particular left their mark upon the statute books. The most conspicuous example was the drive for pensions, but they were even more successful within the states, winning veterans' preference laws, the erection of monuments, the establishment and maintenance of soldiers' and orphans' homes, and appropriations for the G.A.R.'s expenses. These activities inevitably drew the old soldiers into politics until they constituted an important, though probably not decisive, element in the Republican party. In fact, the lure of pensions probably confirmed more veterans in their Republicanism than it converted.

Recognizing that the success of patriotic propaganda depended largely upon reaching impressionable youth, both veterans' and hereditary societies had considerable influence upon the schools. They censored history textbooks and introduced such features into the curriculum as the flag salute, military training, and other "patriotic" exercises. Of a more constructive nature, perhaps, was their insistence upon the teaching of American history (though professional historians may wince at the efforts to impose certain interpretations) and the frequent awarding of prizes and medals for historical essays. The hereditary societies did a particularly good piece of work in their marking of historic sites and preserving historic places. A nation only now becoming proud of its heritage may well be thankful that for half a century there have been private organizations preserving these physical survivals.

As to the broader question of whether these societies on the whole exercised a conservative or reactionary influence on American society, it is difficult to form a valid generalization. Certainly there is no evidence that the "vested interests" engaged in any sinister financing of the best known organizations. There were many instances of extreme conservatism, especially among the veterans during labor disturbances. This was partly because they identified any resistance to government authority with secession and immediately began to suppress the rebellion all over again. Yet at other times certain societies or individual members expressed the most liberal sentiments. Which attitude should be taken as typical? Some members, it is true, seemed interested primarily in the protection of property rights, but others contended that a genuine application of American ideals involved a concern for social justice.

The same variety of opinion was evident on international affairs. To many, Americanism demanded a militaristic and imperialistic outlook, but at times a sizable minority showed a great interest in the cause of peace. Often the founders interpreted patriotic ideals in a more radical fashion than did later members; perhaps another way of expressing this is that the originators took the organizations' professed ideals more literally. William O. McDowell and Alexander Kenaday flirted with many of the liberal and radical movements of the late nineteenth century; while in each case these men had a coterie of followers, they probably did not speak for most Sons of the American Revolution or Mexican War Veterans. On the other hand, the equally fanatical conservative leaders of recent years are perhaps no more representative of the rank and file of membership.

A case could be made out that up until the First World War the veterans' and hereditary societies merely reflected, though perhaps in exaggerated or distorted form, the dominant trends of the day. The essential dilemma of the 1890's is seen in these bodies' awkward vacillation between exuberant nationalism and social conscience. In women's organizations the growing awareness of larger problems is in line with the entire history of the club movement. During the fifteen years following 1900 the associations, particularly the D.A.R., were amazingly responsive to many liberal ideas, proving how deep rooted the progressive spirit really was in those years of hope. Even their World War I emphasis upon, first, preparedness, and then "Americanism," with its hostility to any alien innovation that smacked of "Bolshevism," was merely an intensification of wartime hysteria among people who felt that their membership required taking patriotic formulas a bit more seriously than the rest of the country. It is true that the nation at large recovered both more swiftly and to a greater extent than did the vociferous self-styled patriots. In fact, during the past thirty years the leadership of these organizations has become increasingly reactionary, but it could be argued that in the 1920's this was only one aspect of the smugness and conservatism that produced the Harding, Coolidge, and Hoover administrations. With the advent of the New Deal the societies' definition of "Americanism" probably varied more sharply from the dominant social ideals of the day, but the trumpet calls and fervent backing of martial enterprises in recent years, not to mention the alarm over any taint of communism, suggests considerable reconciliation is at hand.

Were one to tell the story of one society, or to trace only a single activity, it would be easier to form generalizations about those orders. But the more groups one studies, the more thoroughly one investigates all their interests, the more complex the picture becomes. In their total effect patriotic societies represent the variety—call it confusion or richness—that is America.

Bibliographical Essay

Primary Sources

THE basic material for this study comes from the innumerable proceedings and reports which military and ancestral orders have obligingly issued. The General Society of the Cincinnati has printed its *Proceedings 1784–1929* (3 v., Baltimore, 1925–1930) and there also exist published records of the state societies in Connecticut, Georgia, Maryland, Massachusetts, New Hampshire, New Jersey, New York, Pennsylvania, and Virginia. Of the utmost importance are the far more detailed *Proceedings of the Annual Meetings of the National Encampments* of the Grand Army of the Republic for the years 1866 to 1900, and in addition the annual proceedings in forty-four states and the District of Columbia have been examined for the same period. Other Northern Civil War organizations whose annual reports have been similarly studied are the Military Order of the Loyal Legion of the United States for 1885–1900, the Society of the Army of the Cumberland for 1865–1900, the Society of the Army of the Potomac for 1869–1900, the Society of the Army of the Tennessee for 1866–1900, the Union Veteran Legion of the United States for 1892–1900, and the Union Veterans' Union for 1895 and 1898–1900. Information on the auxiliary and affiliated Civil War organizations comes from the *Journals of Proceedings* of the Sons of Veterans, U. S. A., for 1884–1899, the *Journals of the National Conventions* of the Woman's Relief Corps, Auxiliary to the Grand Army of the Republic, for 1883 to 1900, as well as scattered *Journals* for seventeen state departments, and the *Proceedings of the National Conventions* of the Ladies of the G.A.R. for 1886–1888, 1893–1894, and 1896–1897. For the Confederate societies there have been available the *Minutes of the Annual Meetings and Reunions* of the United Confederate

Veterans for 1889–1900 and the *Minutes of the Annual Meetings* of the United Daughters of the Confederacy for 1894–1900.

Proceedings, reports, or year books for the decade of the 1890's, in many cases of state branches as well as of the national organization, have been examined for the following hereditary societies: the Baronial Order of Runnemede, the Colonial Dames of America, the Colonial Order of the Acorn, the Dames of the Revolution, the Daughters of the American Revolution, the Daughters of the Cincinnati, the Daughters of Founders and Patriots of America, the Daughters of Holland Dames, the Daughters of the Republic of Texas, the Daughters of the Revolution, the General Society of the War of 1812, the Holland Society, the Huguenot Society, the Military Order of Foreign Wars of the United States, the Military Society of the War of 1812, the National Society of Colonial Dames of America, the Order of Founders and Patriots of America, the Society of American Wars of the United States, the Society of Colonial Daughters of the Seventeenth Century, the Society of Colonial Wars, the Society of Mayflower Descendants, the Sons of the American Revolution, the Sons of the Revolution, and the United States Daughters of 1812. The best collection of the reports of all these groups, both veterans' and hereditary, is in the Library of Congress, though the New York Public Library also has a large number.

Next in importance come the specialized magazines and newspapers, some put out by the societies themselves as official organs, others published as private ventures hoping to win the patronage of the members of these groups. Into the first category fall the *Vedette* (Washington, 1879–1893), practically the only source for the activities of the Mexican War Veterans, the *Illustrated Mount Vernon Record* (Philadelphia, 1859–1860), important for the early years of the Mount Vernon Ladies' Association of the Union, and the *American Monthly Magazine* (Washington, 1892–1900), indispensable for the D.A.R. since it included the proceedings of the "Continental Congress," the minutes of the National Board of Management and accounts of state conferences and chapter work, as well as a "Young People's Department" for the Children of the American Revolution. The most valuable example of the second type for the Northern Civil War organizations is the *National Tribune* (Washington, 1877–1900), but also useful are the *American Tribune* (Indianapolis, 1890–1900), the *Grand Army Journal* (Washington, 1871–1872), the *Grand Army Record* (Boston, 1885–1901), the *Grand Army Review* (New York, 1885–1888), the *Grand Army Sentinel* (Nashville, Tenn., 1885–1886), the *Great Republic* (Washington, 1866–1867), *Home and Country* (New York, 1889–1895), the *Soldier's Friend* (New York, 1864–1869), the *Soldier's Record* (Madison, Wis., 1867–1871), and the *Veteran* (Columbus, Ohio, 1881–1883). The *Confederate Veteran* (Nashville, Tenn., 1894–1900) is one of the most important sources for all the Confederate societies, while the *American Historical Register* (Philadelphia, 1894–1897) and the *Spirit of '76* (New York, 1894–1900) catered to the following of hereditary groups. Again, the Library of Congress is rich in its collection of these periodicals, though the New York Public Library's excellent genealogical department has the files of the outstanding journals for the ancestral-minded.

On the whole, manuscript collections are less helpful. The papers of the many prominent figures who were original members of the Cincinnati, especially those of Henry Knox and Timothy Pickering in the Massachusetts Historical Society and of Horatio Gates, Allen McLane, and Baron Friedrich Wilhelm von Steuben in The New York Historical Society, have material on the early tribulations of the society. In the period after the Civil War the papers of various military and political leaders in the Library of Congress, such as Benjamin Butler, William E. Chandler, Andrew Johnson, George B. McClellan, William T. Sherman, Lyman Trumbull, and Elihu B. Washburne, afford considerable insight into the G.A.R.'s activities. The most valuable collections are those of Lucius Fairchild, commander-in-chief of the Grand Army during one of its most tempestuous years, in the Wisconsin State Historical Society, and of Grover Cleveland, whose correspondence, also in the Library of Congress, bears ample testimony to his difficult relations with the veterans. For my knowledge of this manuscript material on the G.A.R. I am deeply indebted to Marie L. Rulkotter's Ph.D. dissertation, "The Civil War Veterans in Politics" (University of Wisconsin, 1938).

Of overwhelming importance for the early history of the S.A.R. and D.A.R. is the immense William O. McDowell collection in the

New York Public Library. In addition to various letterbooks and sundry papers in the manuscripts division, there are seventy scrapbooks covering the period 1875–1895, unfortunately not arranged chronologically. The papers of Ethan Allen and Henry Baldwin, two of McDowell's close associates, are also in the New York Public Library. In the Library of Congress the papers of Mary Desha (in the Breckenridge Family Papers), a founder and early official of the D.A.R., are helpful, especially on the Columbian Liberty bell episode, but those of Mrs. Daniel Manning and of Horace Porter, who served as heads of the D.A.R. and S.A.R. respectively, are disappointing. The published works, correspondence, or memoirs of such individuals as John Adams, Samuel Adams, Benjamin Franklin, Thomas Jefferson, Rufus King, William Maclay, Arthur St. Clair, James Warren, and George Washington also contain a good deal of material on the Cincinnati, while those of Julia Foraker, Rutherford B. Hayes, Mrs. John A. Logan, and Mrs. Roger Pryor have a little on the veterans' and hereditary groups.

Among government documents the debates in the *Congressional Record* often supply information on the political role of the G.A.R., especially during the controversies of 1887, and *House Report,* 48 Cong., 2 sess., no. 2683 (1885) has a great deal on the relationships between the claims agents, the Grand Army, and pension legislation. Newspapers, of course, constitute a constant source of information on the doings of the various groups. Much of the material on the excitement over the Society of the Cincinnati comes from the papers of 1783–1784, such as the *Connecticut Courant* (Hartford), the *Connecticut Journal* (New Haven), the *Freeman's Journal* (Philadelphia), the *Gazette of the State of South Carolina* (Charleston), the *Independent Chronicle and the Universal Advertiser* (Boston), the *Maryland Gazette* (Baltimore), the *New York Packet,* the *Pennsylvania Packet* (Philadelphia) the *Providence Gazette and Country Journal,* the *South Carolina Gazette and General Advertiser* (Charleston), *Thomas' The Massachusetts Spy* (Worcester), and the *Virginia Gazette* (Richmond). For subsequent developments the newspaper coverage has been less thorough. For press accounts of the G.A.R.'s early years I again relied heavily on Miss Rulkotter's thesis. At the height of the order's pension and political activities the pages of *Public Opinion* supply numerous newspaper comments. The innumerable clippings in the McDowell Scrapbooks furnish press references from all over the country on the early career of the D.A.R. and S.A.R.

Secondary Literature

The best introduction to the subject of American patriotism is Merle Curti, *The Roots of American Loyalty* (New York, 1946), which puts greater emphasis on the period before the Civil War. The same author's earlier article, "Wanted: A History of American Patriotism," Middle States Association of History and Social Science Teachers, *Proceedings,* XXXVI (1938), 15–24, is a stimulating essay. Arthur M. Schlesinger gives an authoritative sketch of "joining" in America in "Biography of a Nation of Joiners," *American Historical Review,* L (Oct. 1944), 1–25. Charles W. Ferguson supplies a longer, more jaunty but still useful, popular account of a wide variety of voluntary associations in *Fifty Million Brothers* (New York, 1937), which includes a chapter on the D.A.R. and another on several other hereditary and Civil War societies. Helpful lists of patriotic societies can be found in Jennings Hood and Charles J. Young, *American Orders & Societies and Their Decorations* (Philadelphia, 1917); Sydney A. Phillips, *Patriotic Societies of the United States* (New York, 1914); Frederick Adams Virkus, *The Handbook of American Genealogy* (4 v., Chicago, 1932–1943); and Eugene Zieber, *Ancestry* (Philadelphia, 1895).

William S. Thomas, *The Society of the Cincinnati 1783–1935* (New York and London, 1935), brings a lot of useful information together in one volume, such as lists of all the general and state officials since the order's founding, but its historical sketch is too slight to be very valuable. Far more outstanding are a number of articles by Edgar Erskine Hume, though as a member he sometimes becomes overzealous in defense of the organization against accusations. The nearest to a general survey of the society's early years is his "Early Opposition to the Cincinnati," *Americana,* XXX (Oct. 1936), 597–638. Wallace E. Davies covers "The Society of the Cincinnati in New England 1783–1800" in the *William and Mary Quarterly,* Third Series, V (Jan. 1948), 3–25.

For a comprehensive account of veterans in general, with some attention to their organizations, Dixon Wecter, *When Johnny Comes Marching Home* (Cambridge, Mass., 1944), is excellent, though limited to the survivors of the Revolutionary, Civil, and First World Wars. Wallace E. Davies has written the story of "The Mexican War Veterans as an Organized Group" in the *Mississippi Valley Historical Review,* XXV (Sept. 1948), 221–238. As for the Civil War's participants, the few pages on "The Veteran Mind" in Paul H. Buck, *The Road to Reunion* (Boston, 1937), are unsurpassed for succinctness and insight. Robert B. Beath, *History of the Grand Army of the Republic* (New York, 1889), was long the standard reference simply because it was the only major effort at a history of the organization in print. Actually it comes closer to being an original source, since Beath was an early member and subsequent commander-in-chief of the G.A.R. Therefore his book is extremely useful for his revelations of the order's political activities, his sketches of the first officials, and his accounts of the founding of related Civil War organizations, but the very factors that give his book such value keep it from being an objective history.

Recently, however, there has appeared an excellent scholarly study, Mary R. Dearing, *Veterans in Politics* (Baton Rouge, 1952). This is a careful revision of her Ph.D. dissertation, "Civil War Veterans in Politics" (written under the name of Marie L. Rulkotter, University of Wisconsin, 1938), which was especially noteworthy for its coverage of manuscript and newspaper material. The book is subtitled "The Story of the G.A.R.," but is actually both more and less than that. On the one hand, it surveys all the activities of the veterans between 1865 and 1900 instead of merely the one organization, but on the other it actually concentrates on the veterans as a political force and on the G.A.R. as a pressure group rather than as example of associationalism. The dissertation reflected something of the liberal 1930's dislike of all veterans' organizations, but the published version has toned this down and is certainly the most important single work on the G.A.R. Limited in area but in many respects more comprehensive in treatment is Frank H. Heck, *The Civil War Veteran in Minnesota Life and Politics* (Oxford, Ohio, 1941), a model scholarly account of the social as well as political significance of the G.A.R. and related organizations in one state. Elmer Edward Noyes, "A History of the Grand Army of the Republic in Ohio from 1866 to 1900" (Ph.D. dissertation, Ohio State University, 1945), is a good analysis of the functioning of the society as an organization, based upon the unpublished official records of the department as well as the printed proceedings.

More specialized aspects of the veterans' activities have received detailed treatment. For the background of the G.A.R.'s role during Reconstruction, see W. A. Russ, Jr., "Was There Danger of a Second Civil War During Reconstruction?" *Mississippi Valley Historical Review,* XXV (June 1938), 39–58. The real impetus behind the veterans' drive for land grants appears in James B. Hedges, "The Colonization Work of the Northern Pacific Railroad," *Mississippi Valley Historical Review,* XIII (Dec. 1926), 311–342. For the pension issue, John W. Oliver, *History of the Civil War Military Pensions 1861–1885* (Madison, Wis., 1917), covers the origins of the G.A.R.'s activities, and William H. Glasson, *Federal Military Pensions in the United States* (New York, 1918), also lays considerable stress on the role of the order. Norma Adams Dooley, "The G.A.R. in American Politics" (M. A. thesis, Clark University, 1936), is actually confined almost entirely to the pension question; it is an adequate but superficial account. The best studies of the relationships between the G.A.R., the Republican Party, pension legislation, and tariff appear in the various articles by Donald L. McMurry: "The Soldier Vote in Iowa in the Election of 1888," *Iowa Journal of History and Politics,* XVIII (July 1920), 335–356; "The Political Significance of the Pension Question, 1885–1895," *Mississippi Valley Historical Review,* IX (June 1922), 19–36; and "The Bureau of Pensions During the Administration of President Harrison," *Mississippi Valley Historical Review,* XIII (Dec. 1926), 343–346. Wallace E. Davies tells the story of the G.A.R.'s relations with Grover Cleveland, with particular attention to the episode of the rebel flag order, in "Was Lucius Fairchild a Demagogue?" *Wisconsin Magazine of History,* XXXI (June 1948), 418–428.

Paul Joseph Woods, "The G.A.R. and Civil Service" (Ph.D. dissertation, University of Illinois, 1941), is a fairly brief but helpful survey of the efforts for federal veterans' preference legislation which unfortunately omits the more successful efforts on the state level.

Bessie Louise Pierce, *Public Opinion and the Teaching of History in the United States* (New York, 1926), is an important pioneer study of the efforts of patriotic organizations to censor school histories; it devotes considerable space to the activities of both the G.A.R. and the U.C.V. in the 1890's. Wallace E. Davies examines "The Problem of Race Segregation in the Grand Army of the Republic" as well as in the Woman's Relief Corps in the *Journal of Southern History,* XIII (Aug. 1947), 354–372. Very little scholarly attention has been paid to the Confederate groups, though Mary B. Poppenheim and others, *The History of the United Daughters of the Confederacy* (Richmond, 1938), is a handsomely gotten out and useful survey of that society's work.

For the social and intellectual background of the rise of hereditary societies in the 1890's Arthur M. Schlesinger, *The Rise of the City 1878–1898* (Arthur M. Schlesinger and Dixon Ryan Fox, eds., *A History of American Life,* X; New York, 1933); Ralph H. Gabriel, *The Course of American Democratic Thought* (New York, 1940); and Harvey Wish, *Society and Thought in Modern America* (New York, 1952), all have valuable suggestions. But compared with the veterans' groups, very little detailed scholarly work has been done on these organizations. While there are several accounts of the D.A.R., they are mostly pieces of special pleading for recognition of the author's importance in founding the society. Perhaps the most colorful but the least reliable of these is Flora Adams Darling, *Founding and Organization of the Daughters of the American Revolution and Daughters of the Revolution* (Philadelphia, 1901). Somewhat more trustworthy are the versions by two other founders: Mary Desha, *The True Story of the Origin of the National Society of the Daughters of the American Revolution* (n.p., n.d.), and Mary S. Lockwood and Emily Lee Sherwood, *Story of the Records* (Washington, 1906). But the usual history of a hereditary society is by some well-intentioned member who writes in sufficiently pietistic tone to win official endorsement but lacks the training to fit the organization into the general pattern of American social and intellectual history. There is, however, one unpublished study of the D.A.R. : Lucile La Ganke, "The National Society of the Daughters of the American Revolution—Its History,

Policies and Influence 1890–1949" (Ph.D. dissertation, Western Reserve University, 1951).

A more complete bibliography may be found in the author's "A History of American Veterans' and Hereditary Patriotic Societies 1783–1900" (Ph.D. dissertation, Harvard University, 1946), available in the Widener Library.

Index

Harvard Historical Studies

(Early titles now out of print are omitted.)

4. *Frederick William Dallinger.* Nominations for Elective Office in the United States. 1903.
15. *Everett Kimball.* The Public Life of Joseph Dudley: A Study of the Colonial Policy of the Stuarts in New England, 1660–1715. 1911.
16. *Robert Matteson Johnston.* Mémoire de Marie Caroline, Reine de Naples, Intitulé, De la Révolution du Royaume de Sicile, par un Témoin Oculaire, Publié pour la première fois, avec Introduction, Notes critiques, et deux Facsimiles. 1912.
17. *Edward Channing.* The Barrington-Bernard Correspondence. 1912.
20. *Morley de Wolf Hemmeon.* Burgage Tenure in Mediaeval England. 1914.
21. *Charles Howard McIlwain.* Wraxall's Abridgment of the New York Indian Records, 1678–1751. 1915.
23. *Robert Howard Lord.* The Second Partition of Poland: A Study in Diplomatic History. 1915.
25. *Charles Wendell David.* Robert Curthose, Duke of Normandy. 1920.
26. *Charles Homer Haskins.* Studies in the History of Mediaeval Science. Second edition, 1927.
29. *Dexter Perkins.* The Monroe Doctrine, 1823–1826. 1927.
30. *William Leonard Langer.* The Franco-Russian Alliance, 1890–1894. 1929.

31. *Frederick Merk.* Fur Trade and Empire: George Simpson's Journal, 1824–1825, together with Accompanying Documents. 1932.
32. *Lawrence D. Steefel.* The Schleswig-Holstein Question. 1932.
33. *Lewis George Vander Velde.* The Presbyterian Churches and the Federal Union, 1861–1869. 1932.
34. *Howard Levi Gray.* The Influence of the Commons on Early Legislation. 1932.
35. *Donald Cope McKay.* The National Workshops: A Study in the French Revolution of 1848. 1933.
36. *Chester Wells Clark.* Franz Joseph and Bismarck: The Diplomacy of Austria before the War of 1866. 1934.
37. *Roland Dennis Hussey.* The Caracas Company, 1728–1784: A Study in the History of Spanish Monopolistic Trade. 1934.
38. *Dwight Erwin Lee.* Great Britain and the Cyprus Convention Policy of 1878. 1934.
39. *Paul Rice Doolin.* The Fronde. 1935.
40. *Arthur McCandless Wilson.* French Foreign Policy during the Administration of Cardinal Fleury, 1726–1743. 1936.
41. *Harold Charles Deutsch.* The Genesis of Napoleonic Imperialism. 1938.
42. *Ernst Christian Helmreich.* The Diplomacy of the Balkan Wars, 1912–1913. 1938.
43. *Albert Henry Imlah.* Lord Ellen-